AN ENVIRONMENTAL COURT IN ACTION

Over its 40-year existence, the New South Wales Land and Environment Court has become world-famous for its multi-faceted contributions to environmental law. And yet much of what the Court does remains underexamined. This edited collection is the first international collection on the Court. It brings together leading lawyers and academics to examine and evaluate the work of the Court from different scholarly perspectives. It explores the functions, doctrines and processes of the Court and its contributions to both Australian environmental law and environmental law worldwide. This book is a must-read for anyone who wants to understand the Court as well as the nature and possibilities of environmental courts more generally.

An Environmental Court in Action

Function, Doctrine and Process

Edited by
Elizabeth Fisher
and
Brian Preston

•HART•
OXFORD • LONDON • NEW YORK • NEW DELHI • SYDNEY

HART PUBLISHING

Bloomsbury Publishing Plc

Kemp House, Chawley Park, Cumnor Hill, Oxford, OX2 9PH, UK

1385 Broadway, New York, NY 10018, USA

29 Earlsfort Terrace, Dublin 2, Ireland

First published in Great Britain 2022

A catalogue record for this book is available from the British Library.

A catalogue record for this book is available from the Library of Congress.

Library of Congress Control Number: 2022934762

ISBN: HB: 978-1-50994-103-2
ePDF: 978-1-50994-105-6
ePub: 978-1-50994-104-9

Typeset by Compuscript Ltd, Shannon

To the Land and Environment Court of New South Wales and the lawyers and law that make it flourish

FOREWORD

LORD CARNWATH

I am pleased to welcome this in-depth study of perhaps the most interesting and versatile specialist court that I have come across in my career as practitioner and judge. The Land and Environment Court of New South Wales was established by statute as long ago as September 1980. As the website tells us: 'There was a desire to create a specialised "one stop shop" for environmental, planning and land matters', to replace the range of different tribunals and courts which had previously dealt with such matters, noting that at that time 'there was no environmental law as it is now known'. What emerged was a hybrid legal institution: at one level, a superior court of record exercising traditional judicial functions, such as judicial review of administrative decisions, and enforcement of laws; and at another an administrative tribunal exercising merits review of administrative decisions, notably in the planning field. It combines the skills of both legally qualified 'judges', and expert 'commissioners' with specialist experience in relevant disciplines.

When I first visited the Court more than thirty years ago, as a barrister specialising in planning and property law, I was particularly interested to see how the Court was able to adapt its judicial role to deal with matters which in my own country were seen as the province of planning inquiries before ministry-appointed 'planning inspectors'. It seemed then a very successful model, and that view has been more than confirmed by its subsequent history, as now authoritatively recorded and analysed in this book.

In particular, the Court has been able to adapt to the increasing demands and sophistication of issues arising in environmental law, and most recently climate change, while giving full weight to the three pillars of access to justice: access to information, public participation and access to the Court. Unlike many courts operating in this field, it is not constrained by the ordinary boundaries of judicial review, but can relate the narrow legal issues to their full social and scientific context. This has given many of its judgments an importance and authority extending well beyond its own jurisdiction. (The *Gloucester Resources* case, examined in detail by Jacqueline Peel in her chapter, is a prime example.) Over recent years, as Brian Preston points out, the Court has placed greater emphasis on adjudication as a form of 'expository justice', going beyond simple dispute resolution. He cites the Court's exposition of the principles of ecologically sustainable development (ESD), climate law, and restorative and reparative justice in criminal law.

I commend this study, not just to environmental lawyers, but to all who are concerned with the role of the courts and the adjudicative process. The experience of the Land and Environment Court, and its remarkable evolution over the 40 years of its existence, have important lessons for us all.

Robert Carnwath
24 December 2021

PREFACE

Courts are of fundamental importance to the architecture of environmental law. As institutions they fulfil a variety of roles including, but not limited to, dispute resolution, enforcement, providing expository justice and maintaining legal stability. In doing all these things they contribute to a process of legitimate governing. With that said, in relation to environmental law, generalist courts have been perceived to be limited due to their lack of expertise in dealing with environmental problems and the specific challenges of this area of law. To address these limitations, many jurisdictions have created environmental courts and tribunals – over 1,200 are now said to exist.

This collection is a study of an environmental court in action. It focuses on the oldest of these courts – the Land and Environment Court of New South Wales, which turned forty in 2020. This collection brings together authors to provide an in-depth account of the Court's work from different perspectives. As explained in Chapter 1, this collection of essays not only illuminates the work of the Court but also provides a structured approach to interrogating the role of courts in environmental law more generally.

This intellectual project began life in early 2020 just before the global pandemic hit. We want to thank everyone who has been involved. They have stuck with it during extraordinary times. The thought and commitment that authors have shown in developing their chapters has given us great editorial joy. Daniel Leyva and Elizabeth Orr provided excellent research and administrative assistance. Sinead Moloney and Sasha Jawed from Hart Publishing have been inspirational in their practical and intellectual support. A final thank you goes to our families who have sustained us in this collective intellectual endeavour.

Elizabeth Fisher (Oxford) and Brian Preston (Sydney)
11 November 2021

TABLE OF CONTENTS

PART II
DOCTRINE

PART III
PROCESS

CONCLUSION

LIST OF CONTRIBUTORS

Paul Adam is an Honorary Associate Professor in the School of Biological, Earth and Environmental Science at the University of New South Wales, where he has had a long academic career since 1978. He has interests in plant ecology and conservation biology, across saltmarshes, coastal heathland, rainforests and urban bushland. He was the inaugural deputy chair of the Scientific Committee established by the Threatened Species Conservation Act. He has been an Acting Commissioner in the Land and Environment Court of New South Wales since 2007.

Ben Boer was Professor in Environmental Law between 1992 and 2008 and is now Emeritus Professor at Sydney Law School. He served as Co-Director of the IUCN Academy of Environmental Law between 2006 and 2008. In 2011 he was appointed as Distinguished Professor in the Research Institute of Environmental Law, Wuhan University, China. He was Deputy Chair of the IUCN World Commission on Environmental Law between 2012 and 2016. He is the co-founder of the *Chinese Journal of Environmental Law.*

Tim Bonyhady is Emeritus Professor at the Australian National University College of Law. He is one of Australia's foremost environmental lawyers, cultural historians and curators. His many books include *The Colonial Earth, Good Living Street: The Fortunes of My Viennese Family, The National Picture: The Art of Tasmania's Black War* and *The Enchantment of the Long-haired Rat: A Rodent History of Australia.* His latest book is *Two Afternoons in the Kabul Stadium: A History of Afghanistan through Clothes, Carpets and the Camera.*

Megan Davis is the Balnaves Chair in Constitutional Law, Pro Vice-Chancellor, Indigenous UNSW, Professor of Law and Director, Indigenous Law Centre, and UNSW Law and Justice Chair. She serves as an expert for the United Nations Expert Mechanism on the Rights of Indigenous Peoples, Geneva and is an Acting Commissioner of the Land and Environment Court of New South Wales.

Douglas Fisher is Emeritus Professor of Law at the Queensland University of Technology in Australia. After some fifty years practising, teaching, researching and writing in the area of environmental law, he formally retired in 2014.

Elizabeth Fisher is Professor of Environmental Law, Faculty of Law and Corpus Christi College, University of Oxford.

Gitanjali Nain Gill is Professor of Environmental Law at Northumbria Law School, Northumbria University, UK. Her research interests include access to justice through environmental courts and tribunals, SDGs, and climate change in India. Currently, her projects include a monograph on the interrelationship between just sustainabilities and a transformative Indian judiciary (Routledge, 2022) and a British Academy grant (2020–24) involving India-based empirical research on rehabilitation and resettlement due to compulsory land acquisition, involuntary displacement, and disregard of human rights.

Sue Higginson is an environmental lawyer who runs her own legal practice in Australia. She specialises in public interest environmental law and criminal law, as it relates to environmental protest.

Jacqueline Peel is Director of Melbourne Climate Futures and a Professor of Law at the University of Melbourne.

The Honourable Justice Brian J Preston FRSN SC FAAL is the current Chief Judge of the Land and Environment Court of New South Wales, having practised as a solicitor, barrister and senior counsel. He has lectured in postgraduate environmental law for over thirty years. He is an Adjunct Professor at the University of Sydney, Western Sydney University and Southern Cross University. He has published extensively on environmental law, including Australia's first book on environmental litigation and over 140 articles, chapters and reviews. He was conferred an honorary Doctor of Letters by Macquarie University in 2018.

Eloise Scotford is Professor of Environmental Law, Faculty of Laws, UCL. At the core of her research is an exploration of the richness, variety and openness of legal institutions, doctrines, and cultures in responding to and accommodating environmental problems.

Jeff Smith is a solicitor in NSW Australia, who has practised as a public interest environmental lawyer for the past twenty years and is a member of the Australian centre for Climate and Environmental Law.

Leslie Stein is an Adjunct Professor of Urban Planning Law at the Department of Architecture, Design and Planning at the University of Sydney. Professor Stein is the author of nine books including *Principles of Planning Law*, *Comparative Urban Land Use Planning: Best Practice* and *Urban Legal Problems*.

Mary Walker OAM, is a barrister, arbitrator, leading mediator, ADR specialist and Co-Chair of the International Bar Association Mediation Committee. At the forefront of ADR in Australia for the last thirty years she was awarded the Inaugural Australian Mediator of the Year Award in 2016 by the Australian Disputes Centre, again awarded Mediator of the Year in 2017 and 2018 and was also awarded International Mediator of the Year in 2018 and 2019. Mary was inducted into the Australian ADR Awards Hall of Fame as its Inaugural member in 2019.

Ceri Warnock is a Professor of Law at the University of Otago in New Zealand, where she teaches and researches environmental and public law.

Rob White is Distinguished Professor of Criminology at the University of Tasmania. He has written widely in the areas of criminology, youth studies and eco-justice. Among his recent books are *Theorising Green Criminology* (Routledge, 2021) and *The Extinction Curve: Growth and Globalisation in the Climate Endgame* (with John van der Velden, Emerald, 2021).

LIST OF ABBREVIATIONS

ADR	alternative dispute resolution
ALRA	Aboriginal Land Rights Act 1983 (NSW)
ALRC	Australian Law Reform Commission
ANTSO	Australian Nuclear Science and Technology Organisation
BCA	Biodiversity Conservation Act 2016 (NSW)
CBD	Convention on Biological Diversity
CPA	Civil Procedure Act, 2005 (NSW)
ECTs	environmental court and tribunals
eDNA	environmental DNA
EDO	Environmental Defenders Office
EEC	endangered ecological community
EF(IP)A	Endangered Fauna (Interim Protection) Act 1991 (NSW)
EIA	environmental impact assessment
EIS	environmental impact statement
EMRIP	United Nations Expert Mechanism on the Rights of Indigenous Peoples
EPA Act	Environmental Planning and Assessment Act 1979 (NSW)
EPA Regulation	Environmental Planning and Assessment Regulation 2000 (NSW)
EPBC Act	Environment Protection and Biodiversity Conservation Act 1999 (Cth)
EROL	environmental rule of law
ESD	ecologically sustainable development
ESPA	Endangered Species Protection Act 1992 (NSW)
FCRAG	Fullerton Cove Residents Action Group
GHG	greenhouse gas
GRL	Gloucester Resources Ltd
GSC	Greater Sydney Commission
GSRP	Greater Sydney Region Plan

IBA	International Bar Association
IDO	Interim Development Order
IGAE	Intergovernmental Agreement on the Environment
IPC	Independent Planning Commission
IPCC	Intergovernmental Panel on Climate Change
IUCN	International Union for Conservation of Nature and Natural Resources
LEC Act	Land and Environment Court Act 1979
LEP	Local Environment Plan
LSPS	Local Strategic Planning Statement
MSA	market substitution assumption
NADRAC	National Alternative Dispute Resolution Advisory Council
NDC	Nationally Determined Contribution
NGOs	non-governmental organisations
NGT	National Green Tribunal of India
NPM	new public management
NPWA	National Parks and Wildlife Act 1974
NPWA	National Parks and Wildlife Act 1974 (NSW)
NSW	New South Wales
NSWLEC	Land and Environment Court of New South Wales
NVA	Native Vegetation Act 2003 (NSW)
PAN	Proposed Acquisition Notice
PIL	public interest litigation
POEA Act	Protection of the Environment Administration Act 1991 (NSW)
SEPP	State Environmental Planning Policy
SIS	Species Impact Statement
SSD	State Significant Development
SSI	State Significant Infrastructure
SSSG	Shoalhaven Sand Soil and Gravel
TSCA	Threatened Species Conservation Act 1995 (NSW)
UCPR	Uniform Civil Procedure Rules 2005 (NSW)
UNDRIP	United Nations Declaration on the Rights of Indigenous Peoples
UNEP	United Nations Environment Programme
UNFCCC	United Nations Framework Convention on Climate Change
UNPFII	United Nations Permanent Forum on Indigenous Issues

TABLE OF CASES

NSWLEC

New South Wales Court of Appeal

Other NSW Cases

Other Australian cases

EU

India

Netherlands

New Zealand

Pakistan

United Kingdom

United States

1

The Many Facets of a Cutting-Edge Court: A Study of the Land and Environment Court of New South Wales

THE HON JUSTICE BRIAN J PRESTON

1. Introduction

This book serves two purposes. The first and particular purpose is to study a leading example of an environmental court in action. The Land and Environment Court of New South Wales (the Court) was constituted by the Land and Environment Court Act 1979 (NSW) (the LEC Act). The Court was established as an innovative legal institution as part of progressive environmental law reforms. Over time, the Court has needed to adapt and evolve in response to changes in environmental problems and the regulatory environment in order to fulfil its functions to resolve environmental disputes. The book undertakes a multifaceted examination of the Court as a particular legal institution and the contributions it has made over four decades to law and governance.

The second and more general purpose of the book is to provide a conceptual framework for studying environmental courts as legal institutions. This is done through three different analytical frames: frames that focus on function, doctrine and process. These frames are applied to the Court to study and explore the *functional* role of the Court in contributing to environmental law and environmental protection in New South Wales (NSW) and further afield; the Court's significant *doctrinal* contributions; and how the Court has evolved *processes* to resolve disputes.

This chapter begins the book's exploration of these two purposes and introduces the contributions in the following chapters on the three analytical frames. Section 2 advocates up front the importance of taking a 'thick' approach to a study of the Court. Section 3 delves into the essence of the Court, its roles, competences and expertises. The chapter then turns to the three analytical frames, section 4 addressing the functions of the Court, section 5 the doctrines of the Court, and section 6 the processes of the Court. Section 7 briefly concludes the chapter. This exploration reveals a cutting-edge court with many facets. Like a cut and polished diamond, the many facets of the Court illuminate the inquiry and inspire an appreciation of the Court and its contributions.

2. Studying the Court: The Need for a 'Thick' Analysis

The Land and Environment Court is a hybrid legal institution, being in effect both a superior court of record[1] exercising judicial functions, such as judicial review of administrative decisions and civil and criminal enforcement of laws, and an administrative tribunal exercising merits review of administrative decisions. These hybrid functions are reflected in the classes of the Court's jurisdiction, Classes 4–8 involving judicial functions[2] and Classes 1–3 involving mostly administrative functions.[3] To exercise these different functions the Court has two types of members: judges[4] and expert commissioners.[5] Judges constitute the Court and may hear and dispose of all proceedings in the Court.[6] As a consequence, judges may exercise both judicial and administrative functions in all classes of the Court's jurisdiction.[7] Commissioners can only exercise administrative functions in Classes 1–3,[8] although a commissioner who is an Australian lawyer, referred to as a Commissioner for Mining, can exercise Class 8 of the Court's jurisdiction involving mining matters.[9] Where a judge hears proceedings in Classes 1–4 of the Court's jurisdiction, the judge may be assisted by a commissioner, who may assist and advise but not adjudicate.[10]

The judicial and administrative functions of the Court are diverse, covering a wide array of planning and environmental laws.[11] The exercise of the Court's functions under these planning and environmental laws has provided many opportunities for the Court to contribute to law and governance. As the chapters of the book reveal, the Court has contributed to key areas of law and governance, including planning law, climate law, transnational environmental law and principles, biodiversity law, indigenous law, administrative law, criminal law and access to justice. The Court has also contributed to legal thinking, decision-making and reasoning in environmental law.

In putting together a collection studying the Court an important question arises of how to examine the work of such an institution. Many analyses of environmental law, and most analyses of environmental courts, can be characterised as being 'thin'. Laws and courts are seen in instrumental terms, as being instruments whose worth lies in their regulation and resolution of environmental problems. Such environmental law scholarship can be described as 'immature'.[12] A purely descriptive commentary of environmental laws and regulations, and of environmental courts, aimed primarily at practitioners, is poor scholarship.[13]

[1] Land and Environment Court Act 1979 (NSW) s 5(1).
[2] ibid, ss 20–21C.
[3] ibid, ss 17–19.
[4] ibid, ss 8, 11.
[5] ibid, ss 12, 13.
[6] ibid, s 6(1).
[7] ibid, s 33(1), (2), (2A).
[8] ibid, s 33(1).
[9] ibid, s 33(2A) and s 30(2C).
[10] ibid, s 37(1), (3).
[11] See the large number of statutes listed in Land and Environment Court Act 1979 (NSW) ss 17–21C.
[12] E Fisher et al, 'Maturity and Methodology: Starting a Debate about Environmental Law Scholarship' (2009) 21 *Journal of Environmental Law* 213, 218.
[13] ibid, 223–24.

There can be, and needs to be, a thicker description of environmental law and environmental courts. A thicker analysis includes understanding the historical forces and legal culture that gave rise to, and continue to shape, the law and the legal institutions. Courts adjudicate disputes 'according to their proper role as it is understood in a particular legal culture'.[14] Legal culture is 'one way of describing relatively stable patterns of legally oriented social behaviour and attitudes'.[15] Its identifying elements include particular facts about the law, legal system and legal institutions such as the Court; various forms of behaviour such as litigation; and nebulous aspects of ideas, values, aspirations and legal thinking.[16] In short, Nelken says, 'Like culture itself, legal culture is who we are not just what we do.'[17]

The concept of legal culture can be understood in different ways. It can be seen as an explanatory concept, exploring what and how culture contributes to elements of the law, legal system and legal institutions. It can also be an interpretative concept, treating culture as an aggregating concept, so as to include the elements of the law, legal system and legal institutions as parts of an integrated whole.[18] Both concepts of legal culture are employed in the book. Different chapters draw out different elements of legal culture, sometimes explaining the contributions legal culture makes to the law, including the planning and environmental laws applied by the Court, the legal system in which the Court operates, the Court as a legal institution and the decisions it makes, but other times using legal culture to reveal the historical and societal contexts that influence the interpretation and development of the law.

The Court has adjudicated disputes according to the role considered proper by the legal culture in NSW. Identifying the prevailing legal culture is a large and complex task. Taggart sketched some distinctive elements of Australian legal culture with respect to judicial review of administrative action.[19] These include facts about the constitutional and institutional design of Australian law, legal systems and legal institutions; central ideas and values, such as the principle of the separation of powers between the three branches of government, which bifurcates administrative law into judicial review and merits review of administrative action; the rule of law; and ways of legal thinking and reasoning, such as a devotion to legal formalism.[20] These are distinctive elements of the Court's approach to judicial review.

Some of these elements might also be seen to shape the Court's approach to other areas of the Court's jurisdiction, including merits review of administrative decisions. There are differing conceptions of the scope of merits review, including the intensity of review of the administrative decision and the extent of review enabled by the Court. Judges and commissioners of the Court, embracing a narrower conception of merits

[14] E Fisher and E Scotford, 'Climate Change Adjudication: The Need to Foster Legal Capacity: An Editorial Comment' (2016) 28 *Journal of Environmental Law* 1, 3.

[15] D Nelken, 'Using the Concept of Legal Culture' (2004) 29 *Australian Journal of Legal Philosophy* 1, 1.

[16] ibid.

[17] ibid.

[18] J Webber, 'Culture, Legal Culture, and Legal Reasoning: A Comment on Nelken' (2004) 29 *Australian Journal of Legal Philosophy* 27, 27–28.

[19] M Taggart, '"Australian Exceptionalism" in Judicial Review' (2008) 36 *Federal Law Review* 1.

[20] ibid.

review, see the process and their role in the process as akin to judicial review.[21] This narrower understanding of merits review can lead to legal cultural attitudes to judicial review shaping the process and outcome of merits review.[22] On a wider conception of merits review, as a decision-making process that is a substitute for the original administrative decision, these legal cultural attitudes to judicial review have less relevance.[23]

The difficulty in identifying the elements of legal culture contributing to the law, legal system and the Court is compounded by the evolution of legal culture over the four decades of the Court's life. Legal culture has evolved in response to changing contexts, including changes in the environmental laws and policies, the natural and built environments, the economy, society, and the political environment.[24] In turn, these changes in legal culture have shifted conceptions of what is the proper role of the Court. Key aspects of the role the Court plays have remained constant over time. These include resolving disputes before the Court; facilitating interest representation; providing a forum for public discourse; explaining and upholding values of the laws; and promoting the purposes of the laws. But how the Court should undertake these roles and the weight and priority that should be afforded one role in preference to another have changed over time. As a number of chapters explain, the Court in the last fifteen years has placed greater emphasis on adjudication as a form of expository justice and not merely as a form of dispute resolution. Examples are the Court's exposition of the principles of ecologically sustainable development (ESD), climate law, and restorative and reparative justice in criminal law.[25]

The thicker legal analysis employed by the book can be seen to involve two methodological approaches, termed an internal approach and an external approach. An internal approach involves traditional doctrinal legal analysis 'of legal rules and principles taking the perspective of an insider in the system'.[26] The sources of an internal approach 'are predominantly those that are thrown up by the legal process: principally statutes and decided cases, supplemented where possible with lawyers' literature expounding the rules and occasionally reflecting on them'.[27] As the name suggests, an internal approach to the study of law and legal institutions takes 'the internal participants' point of view', trying 'to grasp the argumentative character of our legal practice by joining that practice and struggling with the legal issues of soundness and truth participants face'.[28] In short,

[21] E Fisher, *Risk Regulation and Administrative Constitutionalism* (Oxford, Hart Publishing, 2010) 57, 126.

[22] An example is *Nicholls v Director General of National Parks and Wildlife Service* (1994) 84 LGERA 397 where Talbot J saw his role in merits review as externally reviewing the original decision, not remaking the decision: see Fisher (n 21) 142.

[23] Examples are *Telstra Corporation Ltd v Hornsby Shire Council* (2006) 67 NSWLR 256; *Bulga Milbrodale Progress Association Inc v Minister for Planning and Infrastructure* (2013) 194 LGERA 347; and *Gloucester Resources Ltd v Minister for Planning* (2019) 234 LGERA 257 where the Court did not review the original decision but instead substituted a fresh decision for the original decision.

[24] See Stein, this volume.

[25] See Scotford (on environmental principles), Peel (on climate law) and White (on environmental crime), this volume.

[26] C McCrudden, 'Legal Research and the Social Sciences' (2006) 122 *Law Quarterly Review* 632, 633.

[27] D Ibbetson, 'Historical Research in Law' in P Cane and M Tushnet (eds), *Oxford Handbook of Legal Studies* (Oxford, Oxford University Press, 2003) 863, 864.

[28] R Dworkin, *Law's Empire* (London, Fontana, 1986) 14.

an internal approach 'explains the practice in the same way that the practice explains itself'.[29] An external approach, in contrast, involves the study 'of the law in practice, or legal institutions at work in society, rather than legal rules existing in a social, economic and political vacuum'.[30]

The studies of the Court that this book undertakes embrace both internal and external points of view. The internal approach is most evident in the study of the Court's doctrinal development of the law. The sources of the doctrinal legal analysis are the planning and environmental statutes and the decisions of the Court interpreting and applying these statutes.[31] There is also to some degree an internal account of the functions and processes of the Court, taking an internal, participants' point of view of what are the functions of the Court and what processes the Court uses to resolve the disputes before it. However, the study also provides an external account of the Court, evaluating it as a legal institution at work in society, an environmental court in action.[32] The Court is studied for the roles it plays and the functions it performs and how successfully it does these things. The combination of an internal and an external account of the Court gives the study its strength. As Dworkin observed: 'Both perspectives on law, the external and internal, are essential, and each must embrace or take account of the other.'[33]

3. The Court: Roles, Competences, Expertises

3.1. Roles

The Court plays at least five roles. First, at a basic level, the role of the Court, common with all courts, is to resolve disputes that come before it, determine claims of right and accusations of guilt, enforce the law both civilly and criminally, and uphold the rule of law. These are the products of the proper exercise of the functions vested in the Court. However, the role of the Court is not merely functional. As Fisher, Lange and Scotford observe:

> [C]ourts are more than the sum of their parts and the judgment of a court has a symbolism and authority that few other legal documents have. The judgment is an 'icon of the rule of law' and a particular case is a 'carefully orchestrated process through which indeterminate aggregations of persons, words, stories, and materials are transformed into facts of intention, causality, responsibility and property'. Law, in the form of a judgment, has a 'homeostatic' quality in which any argument must be integrated into 'the integrity of the legal edifice'. The processes of courts are thus fundamental both to the construction of legal discourse and to the authority of law itself.[34]

[29] SA Smith, 'Taking Law Seriously' (2000) 50 *University of Toronto Law Journal* 241, 252–53.
[30] McCrudden (n 26) 633–34.
[31] Douglas Fisher, this volume.
[32] See Gill, this volume.
[33] Dworkin (n 28) 13–14.
[34] E Fisher, B Lange and E Scotford, *Environmental Law: Text, Cases and Materials*, 2nd edn (Oxford, Oxford University Press, 2019) 184.

Second, the Court facilitates interest representation in administrative decision-making. Over the forty years of the Court's operation, there has been an increasing recognition of the importance of public participation in decision-making under planning and environmental laws.[35] McAuslan identifies public participation as one of the ideologies of planning law.[36] This is evident in the many opportunities for public participation in the Environmental Planning and Assessment Act 1979 (NSW) (the EPA Act), which commenced on the same day as the Court commenced operation. The EPA Act enables the public to gain access to information, participate by way of making submissions on strategic planning and the assessment and approval of developments, and access the Court to appeal or review decisions. The Court's decisions, in both judicial review and merits review of administrative action, have upheld these three pillars of access to justice: access to information, public participation and access to the Court.

Improving interest representation facilitates participatory democracy. Sax has argued that environmental litigation helps to realise a truly democratic process. Citizen actions in the court can force a reluctant or prevaricating executive to make decisions, and to make them in accordance with the law.[37] The availability of the courts means that access to the executive, and securing government accountability, are a reality for the ordinary citizen. A great strength of litigation is that a citizen

> can be heard and that, in a setting of equality, he can *require* bureaucrats and even the biggest industries to respond to his questions and to justify themselves before a disinterested auditor who has the responsibility and the professional tradition of having to decide controversies upon the merits. The citizen asserts rights which are entitled to enforcement, he is not a mere supplicant.[38]

Citizen actions in the courts also provide a means of facilitating citizen access to the legislature:

> Courts are not used as substitutes for the legislative process – to usurp policies made by elected representatives – but as a means of providing realistic access to legislatures so that the theoretical processes of democracy can be made to work more effectively in practice. Citizen initiatives in the Court can be used to bring important matters to legislative attention, to force them upon the agendas of reluctant and busy representatives.[39]

By restraining conduct of the government or industry causing or threatening environmental harm, courts 'can thrust upon those interests with the best access to the legislature the burden of obtaining legislative action'.[40] Sax's insights regarding how litigation can be a form of political mobilisation and realise a truly democratic process have been borne out in public interest litigation in the Court.[41]

[35] Bonyhady, this volume.

[36] Patrick McAuslan, *The Ideologies of Planning Law* (Amsterdam, Elsevier, 1980).

[37] JL Sax, *Defending the Environment: A Handbook for Citizen Action* (London, Vintage Books, 1971) 111–12.

[38] ibid, 112.

[39] ibid, xviii.

[40] ibid, 152.

[41] BJ Preston, 'The Role of Public Interest Environmental Litigation' (2006) 23 *Environmental and Planning Law Journal* 337, 337–40 and BJ Preston, 'The Contribution of the Courts in Tackling Climate Change' (2016) 28 *Journal of Environmental Law* 11, 12.

Third, the Court provides a forum for public discourse, and not just a legal forum.[42] Environmental disputes involve contested ideas, values, aspirations and mentalities of not only what we do but also who we are. The court case provides a forum for a discourse on these questions. Although the central purpose of the court case is the resolution of the legal dimensions of the dispute, the hearing of the case in public also provides a forum for a discourse on these non-legal dimensions of the dispute. This discourse may be of more interest to the public, and more influential generally, than the particular resolution of the legal dispute. The Court's hearing and disposal of cases concerning climate change are illustrative of this role in providing a forum that facilitates public discourse on climate change issues.

Fourth, the Court plays a role in explaining and upholding the values underpinning environmental laws. Values affect the making of environmental laws. All statutes are explicitly normative.[43] Environmental statutes are obviously so. Environmental laws reflect a choice of public values and a conception of identity of our society. Laws express 'what we believe, what we are, what we stand for as a nation'.[44] Environmental laws are founded on different values, which may be influenced by different understandings of environmental problems.[45] In short, different environmental laws will be products of different environmental discourses.[46]

Values influence how environmental laws are understood and applied.[47] Understanding environmental laws involves discerning the values of the laws. As Simmonds observes:

> [I]f we are to have a real understanding of what it [a legal rule] requires of us, so that we can guide our conduct by it, we must be able to grasp the values or objectives that the rule serves and to see how the rule fits intelligibly into some possible pattern of life.[48]

Insofar as environmental laws give decision-makers discretionary powers, such as the manner and extent of regulation of activities that harm the environment, the laws require normative choices to be made, which may be more or less bounded depending on the terms of the laws.[49] The values of the decision-maker influence the application of the laws. Values influence how environmental laws are interpreted, not only for the reasons already advanced but also because values affect judicial decision-making. As Waldron pithily points out, 'the idea of "neutral" or "value-free" decision-making by judges is a non-starter'.[50]

This clash of different values, such as the contradiction between promoting economic and social development whilst ensuring environmental protection, is an inseparable part

[42] Fisher, Lange and Scotford (n 34) 185.
[43] J Waldron, *The Law* (London, Routledge, 1990) 132.
[44] M Sagoff, *The Economy of the Earth* (Cambridge, Cambridge University Press, 1988) 16–17.
[45] Fisher, Lange and Scotford (n 34) 50.
[46] See JS Dryzek, *The Politics of the Earth: Environmental Discourses*, 3rd edn (Oxford, Oxford University Press, 2013).
[47] ibid.
[48] N Simmonds, *Law as a Moral Idea* (Oxford, Oxford University Press, 2007) 163.
[49] E Fisher, 'Towards Environmental Constitutionalism: A Different Vision of the Resource Management Act 1991?' [2015] *Resource Management Theory and Practice* 63, 74–76.
[50] Waldron (n 43) 146.

of environmental law and of the work of the Court. But far from inhibiting the success of environmental laws and the Court, these contradictions are responsible for the creativity and dynamism of environmental laws and doctrinal development of the law by the Court.[51] Consider, for example, the 'cognitive dissonance'[52] involved in determining how to achieve the competing goals of economic development, social development and environmental protection. The creative, integrative solution suggested by the World Commission on Environment and Development was the concept of sustainable development – 'development that meets the needs of the present without compromising the ability of future generations to meet their own needs'. The needs of present and future generations are economic, social and environmental. However, economic and social needs cannot be met continuously in a deteriorating environment. Environmental protection is therefore necessary to ensure the economic and social needs of present and future generations can be secured.[53] The Court has explicated and expanded upon these principles of ecologically sustainable development.

Fifth, the Court plays a role in implementing the purposes of the environmental legislation it applies in resolving disputes before it. A motivation for the establishment of environmental courts has often been said to be to achieve 'greening justice'.[54] One problem with this perspective is that environmental protection is only one goal amongst others when designing a court system. As Lees observes, environmental protection, whilst an important test for the success of the court system, 'is not *necessarily* the only benchmark for a "good" court and that focusing on "environmental" outcomes produces too narrow a consideration of the judiciary in environmental law'.[55]

This debate about the purpose of an environmental court is reflective of the debate about the definition of environmental law.[56] Environmental law is not one-dimensional, reflecting only one purpose. Rather, environmental laws reflect multiple purposes, whether expressly or impliedly. Expressly, objects of much environmental legislation promote conflicting purposes, such as economic development, social development and environmental protection. The task, in administering such legislation, is to strike a balance between these conflicting purposes in the individual case. One purpose, such as environmental protection, cannot necessarily be given overriding priority over other purposes, such as economic development and social development.[57] The task for the Court, in adjudicating disputes, is to construe the purposes and provisions of the laws and supervise that administration is in accordance with the laws.

There is also the problem that pursuit of a purpose of environmental protection at all costs can run up against other purposes, including the internal values of the law, such

[51] See analogously YN Harari, *Sapiens: A Brief History of Humankind* (London, Harper Collins, 2014) 183.
[52] ibid, 184.
[53] BJ Preston, 'The Judicial Development of Ecologically Sustainable Development' in D Fisher (ed), *Research Handbook on Fundamental Concepts of Environmental Law* (Cheltenham, Edward Elgar 2016) 480.
[54] G Pring and C Pring, *Greening Justice: Creating and Improving Environmental Courts and Tribunals* (Washington, DC, The Access Initiative of the World Resources Institute, 2009).
[55] E Lees, 'Adjudication Systems' in E Lees and JE Viñuales (eds), *The Oxford Handbook of Comparative Environmental Law* (Oxford, Oxford University Press, 2019) 797.
[56] Fisher, Lange and Scotford (n 34) 10.
[57] See *Minister for Planning v Walker* (2008) 161 LGERA 423, [52], [55].

as upholding legality.[58] Formal legality is a version of the rule of law.[59] The rule of law assists in the interpretation and application of environmental laws. A potential consequence is that an environmental purpose of a law might not be perceived to be able to be achieved because the law is read down to accord with the principles of legality. This is an illustration of how legal culture can shape the interpretation of the law.

3.2. Competences of the Court

For the Court to achieve these different purposes it needs competences. There are two senses in which the competence of a court can be understood: constitutional competence and institutional competence.[60]

The question of constitutional competence involves a normative assessment of the proper role of institutions in a democracy.[61] For a court, this involves identification of the proper role of a particular court in the government and governance of the polity. This is not simply a question of separation of powers between the legislative, executive and judicial branches of government, to ensure that each does not trespass into the field of competence of the others. The theory is that there should be a separation of legislative, executive and judicial functions, and the conferral on each branch of government of the appropriate function and only that function.[62] The separation of powers is engrained in Australian legal culture and shapes Australian courts' sharp demarcation between judicial review and merits review.

In practice, however, there is overlap in the functions exercised by the three branches of government. This is particularly true in state courts in Australia where the separation of powers doctrine is not constitutionally entrenched to the same extent as it is for federal courts.[63] The Court is a case in point, exercising both judicial functions, such as judicial review, and executive or administrative functions, such as merits review. The day-to-day practice of the Court challenges the legal cultural assumption of the universal applicability of the separation of powers doctrine. In such a court, Warnock observed, 'there is too much blurring of the traditional delineations that a pure approach to the separation of powers relies upon – between law, policy and fact, and between qualitatively different types of decision (the legal and the political) and forms of decision-making'.[64]

[58] E Lees, 'Value in Comparative Environmental Law – 3D Cartography and Analytical Description' in Lees and E. Viñuales (n 55) 40.

[59] BJ Preston, 'The Enduring Importance of the Rule of Law in Times of Change' (2012) 86 *Australian Law Journal* 175, 178–80.

[60] J Jowell, 'Of Vires and Vacuums: The Constitutional Conduct of Judicial Review' [1999] *Public Law* 448, 451.

[61] ibid.

[62] Preston (n 59) 180.

[63] See Australian Constitution, Chapter 3, although the supervisory jurisdiction of state courts over executive conduct is constitutionally entrenched: see *Kirk v Industrial Court (NSW)* (2009) 239 CLR 531.

[64] C Warnock, 'Reconceptualising Specialist Environment Courts and Tribunals' (2017) 37 *Legal Studies* 391, 412.

The question of institutional competence involves a practical evaluation of the capacity of the institutions of government to make certain decisions.[65] For a court, it focuses not on the appropriate role of a court (its constitutional competence) but rather on the inherent limitations of the principal process of decision-making employed by courts, namely adjudication. Fuller's exploration of the limits of adjudication concerns this sense of institutional competence.[66] This limitation arises because 'courts are limited in their capacity to decide matters which admit of no generalised or objective determination'.[67] The adjudicative process has also been suggested to be less suited to deciding polycentric problems.[68] A polycentric problem involves 'a complex network of relationships, with interacting points of influence. Each decision made communicates itself to other centres of decision, changing the conditions, so that a new basis must be found for the next decision.'[69] Climate change is a high-profile example of a polycentric problem. Although polycentricity makes adjudication more difficult, the Court has nevertheless adjudicated polycentric environmental disputes.[70] Importantly, adjudication of polycentric disputes has been facilitated when the Court is exercising administrative functions, in merits review proceedings, rather than judicial functions.

The constitutional and institutional competences of a court influence different functions of a court differently. For example, the constitutional and institutional competences influence judicial review to a greater degree than merits review. Fisher identifies three main influences.[71] First, some issues, such as high-level policy issues, are ruled inappropriate subjects for judicial review. An example is the government's nomination of a site for World Heritage listing, which has been held to be not justiciable.[72] Second, the grounds of judicial review are shaped by the courts' understanding of their competence. Matters of procedure are more likely to be understood as being within the courts' competence than matters of substance. For matters of substance, the process by which a decision was made is more likely to be reviewed than the outcome of the decision. This point is borne out in judicial review by the Court. The Court has more commonly set aside administrative decisions on grounds of illegality and procedural impropriety than irrationality, illustrating the pervasive influence of the legal culture of formalism and legality. Third, the courts' understanding of their competence shapes the intensity of review. Whilst a court might review a decision on a certain ground, for reasons of competence, that review may be limited because the court perceives that the decision is beyond its expertise, finely balanced or polycentric.[73] Examples are where the Court has

[65] Jowell (n 60) 451.

[66] L Fuller, 'The Forms and Limits of Adjudication' (1978) 92 *Harvard Law Review* 353.

[67] Jowell (n 60) 451.

[68] J Jowell, 'The Legal Control of Administrative Discretion' [1973] *Public Law* 178, 197, 213–15; Jowell (n 60) 451; Fuller (n 66) 371, 394–98 and L Fuller, 'Adjudication and the Rule of Law' (1960) 54 *American Society of International Law Proceedings* 1, 4–5. See also BJ Preston, 'Limits of Environmental Dispute Resolution' (1995) 13 *Australian Bar Review* 148, 166–68.

[69] Jowell, 'The Legal Control of Administrative Discretion' (n 68) 213.

[70] For example, see *Bulga Milbrodale Progress Association Inc* (n 23) and *Gloucester Resources Ltd* (n 23).

[71] E Fisher, 'Is the Precautionary Principle Justiciable?' (2001) 13 *Journal of Environmental Law* 315.

[72] *Minister for Arts, Heritage and Environment v Peko Wallsend Ltd* (1987) 15 FCR 274.

[73] Fisher (n 71) 321–22.

sometimes been reluctant to set aside administrative decisions on the ground of failure to consider ecologically sustainable development or climate change.[74]

The courts' understanding of their competence does not have the same influence on merits review, primarily because the functions being exercised in undertaking merits review are different to the functions involved in judicial review. Nevertheless, the legal cultural attitudes of the decision-maker of the court undertaking the merits review – how they conceive their role – influences how they undertake merits review, including fact-finding and policy application.[75]

3.3. Expertise of the Court

Closely related to competence is expertise. In order to discharge its role and functions, the Court needs two types of expertise: contributory expertise and interactional expertise. Contributory expertise refers to the sets of skills, knowledge and experience that are needed to contribute to the development of environmental law, and of the legal institutions administering environmental law, as a discipline. This expertise is legal expertise.[76] Contributory expertise requires broad and deep understandings of what is law and what are the functions and processes of the legal institutions charged with the responsibilities of administering law. Interactional expertise refers to the need to interact with other disciplines, including scientific, social and political scientific, and economic disciplines, that relate to how environmental problems are conceptualised. There is a need to develop linguistic expertise, a literacy, in these other disciplines.[77] Interactional expertise assists in understanding environmental problems and their resolution.

The institutional design of the Court incorporates both contributory and interactional expertise by providing for two types of specialist decision-makers: judges, and technical and conciliation assessors (later termed commissioners).[78] The judges are to be judges of a superior court of record or lawyers of at least seven years' standing[79] and preferably have knowledge and expertise of planning and environmental law. The commissioners are to have special knowledge and expertise in areas such as local government administration; town, country or environmental planning; environmental science, protection or assessment; land valuation; architecture, engineering, surveying or building construction; natural resource management; Aboriginal land rights and disputes involving Aboriginal people; urban design or heritage; and law.[80] The qualifications

[74] On ESD, see *Drake – Brockman v Minister for Planning* (2007) 158 LGERA 349 and *Aldous v Greater Taree City Council* (2009) 167 LGERA 13, and on climate change, see *Wollar Progress Association Incorporated v Wilpinjong Coal Pty Ltd* [2018] NSWLEC 92 and *Australian Coal Alliance Incorporated v Wyong Coal Pty Ltd* [2019] NSWLEC 31.

[75] P Cane, 'Merits Review and Judicial Review – The AAT as Trojan Horse' (2000) 28 *Federal Law Review* 213, 239–42.

[76] E Fisher, 'The Rise of Transnational Environmental Law and the Expertise of Environmental Lawyers' (2012) 1 *Transnational Environmental Law* 43, 48.

[77] ibid, 50; see also Fisher, Lange and Scotford (n 34) 232.

[78] BJ Preston, 'Operating an Environmental Court: The Experience of the Land and Environment Court of New South Wales' (2008) 25 *Environmental and Planning Law Journal* 385, 387–88.

[79] Land and Environment Court Act 1979 (NSW) s 8(2)(c).

[80] ibid, s 12(2), (2AA).

required for appointment as either a judge or commissioner, gained through academic study or training, involve explicit knowledge, while experience in practice involves tacit knowledge.[81]

The contributory and interactional expertises of the judges and commissioners can increase as they adjudicate environmental disputes before the Court. Judges develop knowledge in disciplines other than law; expert commissioners develop knowledge in the planning and environmental laws. This continuing professional development is to some extent explicit knowledge but to a greater extent is tacit knowledge. The development in knowledge might not attain the status of being 'expertise', but it nevertheless better equips the judges and commissioners to adjudicate issues involving these areas of expertise.

This institutional design of the Court, to comprise judicial and expert members, creates a new 'epistemic community' within the court system.[82] Gill's observations about the benefits of a similarly constituted institution in India, the National Green Tribunal, are equally applicable to the Court:

> This multifaceted and multi-skilled body encourages a coherent and effective institutional mechanism to adjudicate complex laws and principles in a consistent manner while simultaneously reshaping the approach to environmental problem-solving rather than being limited to predetermined remedies.[83]

The contributory and interactional expertises of the Court influence the Court's understanding of its constitutional and institutional competences and its exercise of its different functions. For judicial review, whilst sometimes the Court has been reluctant to intervene in administrative decisions perceived to be political and polycentric, other times the Court has intervened in such decisions, enabled not only by its contributory expertise in environmental law, but more importantly by its interactional expertise in disciplines other than law. The functional pluralism of the Court fosters interactional expertise. A judge who is well-versed in disciplines other than law by undertaking merits review of administrative decisions under a range of planning and environmental laws can deploy that interactional expertise in judicial review of similar administrative decisions under the same laws.

4. The Functions of the Court

With this explanation of the institutional structure of the Court as a background, I consider the first of the three analytical frames for thinking about the Court: the functional role of the Court. The Court exercises many functions. At an overarching level is

[81] E Fisher and S Shapiro, *Administrative Competence: Reimagining Administrative Law* (Cambridge, Cambridge University Press, 2020) 72.

[82] GN Gill, 'The National Green Tribunal, India: Decision-Making, Scientific Expertise and Uncertainty' (2017) 29 *Environmental Law and Management* 82, 83; GN Gill, *Environmental Justice in India: The National Green Tribunal* (Abingdon, Routledge, 2017) 223.

[83] Gill, *Environmental Justice in India* (n 82) 74.

the function of adjudication of the disputes that come before it. The nature and features of any adjudication will differ depending on the legal nature of the proceedings, which is revealed by the jurisdiction the Court is exercising.

4.1. The Adjudicative Function

All of the functions of the Court involve adjudication. Adjudication, as a dispute resolution process, 'presents itself in many mixed forms'.[84] In broad terms, adjudication includes 'triadic forms of dispute resolution, which may involve some application of legal norms'.[85] By 'triadic' is meant two parties and an adjudicator. Of course, the number of parties can be increased but without effect on the nature of adjudication.

Adjudication can be understood in at least two ways – as a form of dispute resolution and as a form of expository justice.[86] The first is the most common way to conceptualise adjudication. The primary function of adjudication is the resolution of disputes between parties. The hallmark of adjudication in this form is its explicit rationality: rationality in both the presentation of reasoned arguments by the parties to the dispute[87] and rationality in the determination of the dispute.[88] The giving of reasons for the decision establishes that the judge has understood and taken into account the parties' reasoned arguments.[89] The Court's decisions always involve adjudication in this sense of determination of the dispute.

The second way of understanding adjudication is as a form of expository justice. Fisher, Scotford and Barritt explain that:

> On this model, the role of judges is not simply to resolve disputes; they are also to 'tell us how to conform our behaviour to our fundamental values'. It is less important that there are specific victims or claimants who require the resolution of a particular dispute, since adjudication is understood to concern norm setting and compliance, and with providing judgments or precedents for the community at large.[90]

In expressing norms for a community, adjudication may fill a gap left by the failure of other institutions, such as regulatory agencies responsible for environmental protection.[91] Adjudication can also play a deeper set of roles, including holding valuable symbolic significance for a community, as Fisher, Scotford and Barritt illustrate by reference to the problem on climate change:

> In particular, climate change adjudication 'legitimises concerns' over climate change by stating not only what the law is, but also what the facts are. The narrative of climate change litigation has been a narrative of making climate change 'real' within communities and case

[84] Fuller, 'Adjudication and the Rule of Law' (n 68) 1.
[85] E Fisher, E Scotford and E Barritt, 'The Legally Disruptive Nature of Climate Change' (2017) 80 *Modern Law Review* 173, 175.
[86] ibid, 197.
[87] Fuller (n 66) 364, 369; see also Fuller, 'Adjudication and the Rule of Law' (n 68) 2, 3, 5.
[88] Fuller (n 66) 367.
[89] ibid, 388.
[90] Fisher, Scotford and Barritt (n 85) 198.
[91] ibid.

> law has played an important role in that process, often irrespective of who ultimately 'wins' the case. As Jasanoff argues, litigation practices are 'deeply institutionalized modes of achieving pragmatic closures around epistemic claims and controversies that science alone could not have settled'. Climate change adjudication is an arena in which an understanding of social and factual issues are co-produced and settled.[92]

The Court's decisions can involve adjudication in this sense of expository justice, by doctrinally developing environmental law. The judgments are an authoritative statement in finding, interpreting and applying the relevant law. Many of the chapters in this book identify decisions of the Court that have developed legal doctrine. The Court's decisions have also provided an authoritative understanding of the facts. As Birks notes, adjudication plays an important role in 'stabilising' the facts.[93] In deciding the legal aspects of the case, the Court has also authoritatively found the necessary facts. As Fisher, Scotford and Barritt note: 'This function is especially important in relation to environmental problems since the facts are particularly disputed and often require expert analysis – one of the main arguments for a specialist court or tribunal is that they would be a competent specialist finder of facts.'[94] The Court's factual findings have often had greater impact than its legal findings in the same decisions. A topical example is the Court's decisions in climate litigation.[95] In these ways, adjudication by the Court legitimises concerns about environmental problems, especially 'hot' problems such as climate change, by stating what the law is and what the facts are.[96]

4.2. The Court's Jurisdiction

The Court is a statutory court with the jurisdiction vested in it by the LEC Act and other planning and environmental legislation.[97] The jurisdiction is grouped administratively into eight classes.[98] The functions the Court exercises in these classes of jurisdiction fall into two main categories: administrative functions and judicial functions.

In Classes 1, 2 and 3, the Court exercises mainly administrative functions, as the Court engages in merits review of decisions of administrative decision-makers under planning and environmental laws. Class 1 includes environmental planning and protection appeals against decisions of public authorities or officials.[99] The most common types of appeal in Class 1 are appeals against decisions of consent authorities to refuse applications for development consent or to modify development consents under the EPA Act.[100] Class 2 includes local government and miscellaneous appeals and applications

[92] ibid.

[93] P Birks, 'Adjudication and Interpretation in the Common Law: A Century of Change' (1994) 14 *Legal Studies* 156, 158.

[94] Fisher, Lange and Scotford (n 34) 184.

[95] Two examples are *Gray v Minister for Planning* (2006) 152 LGERA 258 and *Gloucester Resources Ltd* (n 23).

[96] E Fisher, 'Climate Change Litigation, Obsession and Expertise: Reflecting on the Scholarly Response to *Massachusetts v EPA*' (2013) 35 *Law and Policy* 236, 240–43.

[97] Land and Environment Court Act 1979 (NSW) s 16(1).

[98] ibid, s 16(2).

[99] ibid, s 17.

[100] EPA Act (NSW) ss 8.7 and 8.9, referred to in Land and Environment Court Act 1979 (NSW) s 17(d).

against decisions of public authorities or officials.[101] Class 3 is a diverse class of land tenure, valuation, rating and compensation matters.[102] Most are appeals against a decision of a public authority or official and involve a form of merits review by the Court.

The role and approach of the Court in merits review differs depending on the decision being reviewed, the statutory framework regulating the review, the issues or grounds of review and the approach to fact-finding, amongst other matters. Care must therefore be taken not to generalise about the role of the Court in fulfilling the court function of merits review. There are at least four dimensions.[103]

The first dimension relates to the intensity and extent of the Court's review of the administrative decision. The appeal reviewing the decision is by way of re-hearing[104] and the Court has all the functions and discretions that the person or body whose decision is the subject of the appeal had in respect of the matter that is the subject of the appeal.[105] However, the Court is not the same type of institution as the original decision-maker and the Court exercises the administrative function in a different manner to how the original decision-maker exercised the function.[106]

The second dimension concerns the issues that the Court takes into account in carrying out merits review. In a broad sense, the legislative framework regulating the administrative decision dictates the relevant matters that must be considered in exercising the administrative function. However, the degree to which and the way in which these relevant matters will be considered by the Court differs from the original decision-maker's consideration of these matters. First, although the appeal is to be conducted by way of re-hearing, the Court does not carry out an original investigation and decide for itself the issues to be determined. The appeal is decided on the issues joined between the parties.[107] Second, the Court is constrained in its fact-finding on the issues. The Court does not conduct its own investigation but is dependent on and responsive to the parties' investigations of the facts. Third, the extent to which and the way in which the Court takes into account government policy differs from the original decision-maker's consideration of policy.[108]

The third dimension concerns the procedures by which the Court hears an appeal. The LEC Act gives some general guidance for the hearing of merits review appeals. The appeal is to be conducted 'with as little formality and technicality, and with as much

[101] Land and Environment Court Act 1979 (NSW) s 18.

[102] ibid, s 19.

[103] E Fisher, 'Administrative Law, Pluralism and the Legal Construction of Merits Review in Australian Environmental Courts and Tribunals' in L Pearson, C Harlow and M Taggart (eds), *Administrative Law in a Changing State: Essays in Honour of Mark Aronson* (Oxford, Hart Publishing, 2008) 325, 333.

[104] ibid, s 39(3).

[105] Land and Environment Court Act 1979 (NSW) s 39 (2).

[106] See *Ku-Ring-Gai Council v Bunnings Properties Pty Ltd* (2019) 236 LGERA 35, [155]–[163].

[107] *Segal v Waverley Council* (2005) 64 NSWLR 177, [42], [44], [99]; *Botany Bay City Council v Pet Carriers International Pty Ltd* (2013) 201 LGERA 116, [101].

[108] See Cane (n 75) 236–38; Andrew Edgar, 'Policy, Morality and the Land and Environment Court' (2006) 14 *Australian Journal of Administrative Law* 38, 47–49, 52–54; BJ Preston 'The Role of Courts in Relation to Adaptation to Climate Change' in T Bonyhady, A Macintosh and J McDonald (eds), *Adaptation to Climate Change: Law and Policy* (Alexandria, Federation Press, 2010) 157, 190–93; *Terrace Tower Holdings Pty Ltd v Sutherland Shire Council* (2003) 129 LGERA 195, [81]; *Stockland Development Pty Ltd v Manly Council* (2004) 136 LGERA 254, [86]–[92].

expedition, as the requirements of this Act and of every other relevant enactment and as the proper consideration of the matters before the Court permits'.[109] The Court 'is not bound by the rules of evidence but may inform itself on any manner in such manner as it thinks appropriate and as the proper consideration of the matters before the Court permits'.[110] The LEC Act gives more particular guidance for the hearing of particular types of merits review appeals. For instance, for certain types of proceedings, an on-site hearing is to be conducted.[111] The Court's Practice Notes for particular types or classes of proceedings specify the manner in which those proceedings are to be conducted.[112]

The fourth dimension concerns the acceptance of evidence. Procedures have been developed for the receiving of evidence of laypersons, such as at an on-site hearing, and of experts, such as by joint conferencing and report to the Court and the giving of evidence concurrently at the hearing. These four dimensions of the Court's function of merits review interrelate and influence the Court's exercise of the administrative function. Because the dimensions will differ depending on the particular administrative function being exercised, the Court's exercise of a function in one merits review appeal will differ compared to the Court's exercise of another function in a different merits review appeal.

In Classes 4–8 of the Court's jurisdiction, the Court exercises judicial functions, adjudicating disputes under both civil and criminal law. In Class 4 the Court exercises supervisory functions, judicially reviewing administrative decisions and conduct[113] and civilly enforcing breaches of planning and environmental laws.[114] These supervisory functions were previously exercised by the Supreme Court of NSW. In Classes 5–7, the Court exercises functions under the criminal law, hearing and disposing of, in a summary manner, proceedings for environmental offences in Class 5,[115] and appeals relating to environmental offences dealt with in the Local Court of NSW in Classes 6 and 7.[116] These criminal law functions were previously exercised by the District Court of NSW or the Supreme Court of NSW. Class 8 is the Court's mining jurisdiction,[117] exercising the jurisdiction transferred to the Court in 2009 on the abolition of the Mining Warden's Court. The Court exercises civil law functions to adjudicate disputes including about rights to mine, use water, and access and occupy land for mining, and contractual disputes involving mining.[118]

4.3. Influence of Competences and Expertise on Functions

The different court functions exercised by the Court involve different competences and expertises. As noted earlier, the constitutional and institutional competences influence

[109] Land and Environment Court Act 1979 (NSW) s 38 (1).
[110] ibid, s 38 (2).
[111] ibid, ss 34A and 34B.
[112] The Practice Notes are available at: www.lec.nsw.gov.au/lec/practice-and-procedure/practice-notes.html.
[113] Land and Environment Court Act 1979 (NSW) s 20(1)(e), (2) and s 20(3).
[114] ibid, s 20(1).
[115] ibid, s 21.
[116] ibid, ss 21A and 21B.
[117] ibid, s 21C.
[118] Mining Act 1992 (NSW) s 293 and Petroleum (Onshore) Act 1991 (NSW) s 112B.

different functions of the Court differently. Aspects of constitutional competences will more sharply delineate the boundaries within which the Court can properly exercise its judicial functions, primarily in Classes 4–8, than they will affect how the Court can exercise its administrative functions in Classes 1–3. Conversely, issues of institutional competence will arise more in the exercise of administrative functions in proceedings in Classes 1–3, which involve to a greater extent polycentric and multidisciplinary issues,[119] than in the exercise of judicial functions in proceedings in Classes 4–8, which involve primarily legal issues. Contributory or legal expertise is more needed in the exercise of judicial functions while interactional or interdisciplinary expertise is more needed in the exercise of administrative functions.

5. Doctrines of the Court

In exercising its functions the Court develops doctrine. This section explains the sources of law on which the Court draws to develop doctrine, the process involved in developing doctrine, and the types of substantive law and procedural law doctrines that the Court has developed.

5.1. The Sources of Law for Developing Doctrine

In developing doctrine, the Court draws on multiple sources of law, principally in the domestic law of NSW but supplementarily in international law or foreign law. First, there are multiple statutory laws, both primary (statutes) and secondary (regulations, rules and statutory instruments). These sources of statutory law may cover the same field, be inconsistent with one another, or be ambiguous in meaning or application to a factual situation. Statutory interpretation is necessary to identify the rule applicable to the case at hand.[120]

Second, the common law supplements statutory law. There is the dependent common law, the judicial decisions premised on statutory law. There is administrative law that is common law in origin. In NSW, judicial review is under the common law, not a statutory scheme.[121] The common law rules of procedural fairness regulate the exercise of all court functions. The common law may also be the basis for and inform the interpretation of statutory provisions. Statutory terms may be 'given precision over time through the development of, and reliance on, well-established common law principles'.[122]

Third, statutory law, and administrative decision-making thereunder, need to be interpreted in accordance with the rule of law and principles of legality. The function

[119] An example is *Bulga Milbrodale Progress Association Inc* (n 23).
[120] See Douglas Fisher, this volume.
[121] See Elizabeth Fisher, 'Administrative Law Expertise', this volume.
[122] E Lees, 'Allocation of Decision-Making Power Under the Habitats Directive' (2016) 28 *Journal of Environmental Law* 191, 218.

of the rule of law has been described in different ways.[123] It has been described as 'the most important of the general principles of law' and as 'absolutely fundamental'.[124] The rule of law 'is the foundational norm and ultimate principle of legality, by which all laws ultimately stand to be judged'.[125] The rule of law involves a set of principles. At its most basic, the rule of law involves rule by law, that 'all government action must have formulation in law, must be authorised by law'.[126] Rule by law is a necessary part of the rule of law, but is insufficient in itself.[127] The rule of law also involves formal legality. Formal legality involves a number of principles that fall into three groups: the standards of laws, the machinery to enforce the law and realisation of the rule of law.[128] One function of the rule of law is setting standards against which laws can be evaluated. Waldron similarly refers to this function: 'the rule of law doctrine is a critical and demanding standard for evaluating the form of positive law'.[129] This function of the rule of law as a yardstick – a set of principles – with which law is expected to comply does not make the rule of law outside the law and legal system. To the contrary, the rule of law is an integral part of the law and legal system. As Simmonds observes, 'we can see that a form of governance constitutes a legal system only by its approximation to the particular moral ideal (the ideal that we call "the rule of law")'.[130]

Fourth, previous judicial decisions influence present judicial decision-making by way of precedent. There are binding precedents. The rule of stare decisis is that appellate courts are bound by their own previous decisions and that each court is bound by the decisions of a court above it in the hierarchy of courts. There are persuasive precedents. Previous judicial decisions that are not binding need not be followed by a subsequent court, but it may choose to do so. The subsequent court will take the previous decision into consideration and give it such weight as it thinks proper. If the court chooses to follow the previous decision, it will be because the decision has persuaded the court by its merits or reasoning, not because it is authoritative.[131] There is judicial comity. This principle requires that a judge of first instance should follow the decision of another judge of first instance unless convinced that it is wrong. The principle applies to the ratio decidendi but not the obiter dictum of the previous decision.[132]

It is to these four sources of domestic law – statutory law, common law, the rule of law including legality, and previous judicial decisions – that the Court will usually look to adjudicate the case at hand and, in doing so, develop doctrine. In some cases,

[123] D Fisher, *Legal Reasoning and Environmental Law: A Study of Structure, Form and Language* (Cheltenham, Edward Elgar 2013) 8.

[124] M Arden, 'The Changing Judicial Role: Human Rights, Community, Law and the Intention of Parliament' (2008) 67 *CLJ* 487, 491.

[125] P Joseph, 'The Rule of Law: Foundational Norm' in R Ekins (ed), *Modern Challenges of the Rule of Law* (Wellington, LexisNexis NZ, 2011) 47, 73.

[126] J Raz, *The Authority of Law* (Oxford, Clarendon Press, 1979) 212.

[127] J Spigelman, 'The Rule of Law in the Asian Region' in T Castle (ed), *Speeches of a Chief Justice: James Spigelman 1998–2008* (Sydney, CS2N Publishing, 2008) 54.

[128] Preston (n 59) 178–86.

[129] Waldron (n 43) 36–37.

[130] Simmonds (n 48) 192.

[131] DM Walker, *The Oxford Companion to Law* (Oxford, Clarendon Press, 1980) 977–78.

[132] *Rivers SOS Inc v Minister for Planning* (2009) 178 LGERA 347, [90].

however, the Court may need to look further afield. Two further sources can be identified. One is international law and the other is environmental principles and policies.

In a dualist legal system, such as Australia's, international law does not directly apply but needs to be incorporated into domestic law. If it is incorporated, it operates not as international law but as domestic law. International law can, however, have an 'inspirational relationship'[133] with domestic law and judicial decision-making in other ways. International law can influence statutory interpretation of domestic law to promote consistency and harmony with international law and it can guide the development of the common law.[134] Domestic courts can flesh out and build on international legal principles to make them work at national and sub-national levels.[135] One illustration is the Court's application and elaboration of the principles of ecologically sustainable development.[136] Another is the Court's use of international climate law, including the terms and norms of the Paris Agreement.[137]

Environmental principles and policies can also perform legal functions in environmental law. Environmental principles 'are primarily policy ideas concerning how environmental protection and sustainable development ought to be pursued'.[138] They include the well-known principles of ecologically sustainable development, such as the precautionary principle, the principles of intergenerational equity and intragenerational equity, and the polluter-pays principle. Environmental policy refers to 'a course of action adopted to secure, or that tends to secure, a state of affairs in relation to environmental matters that is conceived to be desirable'.[139] Environmental policy serves two roles: it has legal effects and it imposes legal constraints.[140] The setting of policy can have legal effects, such as structuring the exercise of discretionary powers or being a relevant matter needing to be considered in administrative decision-making.[141] The setting of policy can also be legally constrained, including by a statute that empowers the making of policy and by intensive judicial review of policy such as on grounds of legality.[142] The Court has had regard to environmental principles in its doctrinal development of the law.[143]

[133] Fisher, Lange and Scotford (n 34) 414.

[134] BJ Preston and C Hanson, 'The Globalisation and Harmonisation of Environmental Law: An Australian Perspective' (2013) 16 *Asia Pacific Journal of Environmental Law* 1, 18–21.

[135] See Boer, this volume.

[136] ibid, 21–22. See also BJ Preston, 'The Role of the Judiciary in Promoting Sustainable Development: The Experience of Asia and the Pacific' (2005) 9 *Asia Pacific Journal of Environmental Law* 109. The Court's decision in *Telstra Corporation Ltd v Hornsby Shire Council* (n 23) is an example.

[137] An example is *Gloucester Resources* (n 23); see further BJ Preston, 'The Influence of the Paris Agreement on Climate Litigation: Legal Obligations and Norms (Part 1)' (2021) 33(1) *Journal of Environmental Law* 1 and BJ Preston, 'The Influence of the Paris Agreement on Climate Litigation: Causation, Corporate Governance and Catalyst (Part 2)' (2021) 33(2) *Journal of Environmental Law* 227.

[138] E Scotford, *Environmental Principles and the Evolution of Environmental Law* (Oxford, Hart Publishing, 2017) 6.

[139] Fisher, Lange and Scotford (n 34) 244.

[140] ibid.

[141] One recent example of this legal effect of policy is in *R (on application of Plan B Earth) v Secretary of State for Transport* [2020] All ER(D) 170; [2020] EWCA (Civ) 214 reversed in *R (on the application of Friends of the Earth Ltd) v Heathrow Airport Ltd* [2021] 2 All ER 967; [2020] UKSC 52; and another is in *Bushfire Survivors for Climate Action Incorporated v Environment Protection Authority* (2021) 250 LGERA 1; [2021] NSWLEC 92.

[142] Fisher, Lange and Scotford (n 34) 246–47.

[143] Scotford (n 138) ch 5, 202–59.

5.2. The Process of Developing Doctrine

The Court, in exercising its various functions to adjudicate cases, produces doctrine. A judicial decision involves substantive legal reasoning. Indeed, as noted earlier, a hallmark of judicial adjudication is its explicit rationality, manifested in the reasons for judgment. A judicial decision may influence the doctrinal development of environmental law by the nature and strength of the legal reasoning involved.[144]

The judicial development of the law occurs through the court finding, interpreting and applying the law on a case-by-case basis. The Court's decision at each of the steps in the Court's reasoning process may develop the law. The Court applies this syllogistic reasoning process in the exercise of all of its court functions, although the manner in which the Court undertakes each step varies depending on the court function being exercised. Let me expand briefly on these three steps to illustrate how doctrinal development of the law occurs.

The first step of identification of the applicable law involves isolating the legal rule or rules to be applied. The legal rule or rules will be drawn from the multiple sources of law, discussed earlier. It may be one or more statutory provisions, a rule of the common law or a principle of the rule of law, such as the principle of legality. There may be more than one legal rule that is potentially applicable, or none of the existing legal rules may be appropriate and a new one needs to be developed.[145] Choices may need to be made as to what is or should be the legal rule to be applied to the legal problem or dispute. Cardozo suggested different methods to choose or develop the legal rule to be applied to the case at hand. The legal rule may be developed along the line of logical progression (what Cardozo called the rule of analogy or the method of philosophy), the line of historical development (called the method of evolution), the line of customs of the community (called the method of tradition), or the line of justice, morals and social welfare (called the method of sociology).[146] Choices are involved in selecting the method and in applying the selected method. An example of the Court's doctrinal development of the law at the first step is the Court's use of the rule of analogy to hold that the principles of ecologically sustainable development are relevant matters to be considered in determining an application for consent to carry out development likely to impact the environment.[147]

The second step in the reasoning process is interpreting the legal rule identified. All legal rules require interpretation. There will be some clear cases where a rule certainly applies but many where there is doubt as to when and how the rule applies.[148] The language in which legal rules are expressed is often indeterminate and open textured.[149] Rules can never in advance govern every case. It is impossible to have either a complete

[144] ibid, 399.

[145] BJ Preston, 'The Art of Judging Environmental Disputes' (2008) 13 *Southern Cross University Law Review* 103, 109; H Dagan, 'The Realist Conception of Law' (2007) 57 *University of Toronto Law Journal* 607, 617.

[146] BN Cardozo, *The Nature of the Judicial Process* (New Haven, CT, Yale University Press, 1921) 30–31.

[147] See *Leatch v National Parks and Wildlife Service* (1993) 81 LGERA 270; *Carstens v Pittwater Council* (1999) 111 LGERA 1; *BGP Properties Pty Ltd v Lake Macquarie City Council* (2004) 138 LGERA 237 and *Telstra Corporation Ltd* (n 23), amongst other decisions and see Preston (n 145) 115–21.

[148] HLA Hart, *The Concept of Law*, 2nd edn (Oxford, Oxford University Press, 1994) 123.

[149] ibid, 128.

legislative provision in advance covering every case or authoritative extra-judicial interpretation.[150] There is thereby uncertainty in the applicability of a rule to the circumstances at hand. Rules may use very general standards, such as reasonableness, fairness or what is just and equitable, thereby incorporating extra-legal norms into the law. These standards are predicated on 'fact-value complexes, not on mere facts'.[151] The use of these standards enables changes in society's values to be incorporated into the law,[152] and thereby, for the law to be relative and attuned to the time and place.[153] Legal rules may also gain and change meaning from their social context. A broad understanding of the social context in which legal rules gain practical meaning helps judges in settling the interpretation and application of legal rules to the dispute at hand.[154]

Legal rules will also be interpreted in accordance with forms of moral association such as the rule of law.[155] Fuller proposed eight desiderata of the rule of law. The quest of laws and legal systems to achieve these desiderata gives rise to the inner morality of the law.[156] As Waldron observes, judges will hold the values associated with the rule of law and these are bound up with a particular outlook on politics, society and freedom.[157] Judges will draw on these values in interpreting laws. Interpreting laws to be consonant with, rather than discordant with, the rule of law may result in the laws bearing a meaning different to the literal meaning of the words in the text of the law. The same desire for an interpretation that is consonant with the rule of law may lead the judge to look beyond the particular statute to the rest of the law. Dworkin argues that, where there are two or more interpretations of a statutory provision, judges should favour the one that allows the provision to sit most comfortably with the rest of the law as a whole and with the principles and ideals of law and legality in general.[158]

An example of the Court's doctrinal development of the law in the interpretation of the law is the Court's resolution of the linguistic uncertainty in statutory provisions that made it an offence to take or kill protected fauna.[159] Taking fauna was defined to include disturbing fauna. The Court interpreted the statutory provisions against taking fauna holistically and consistently with the ESD principle of the conservation of biodiversity and ecological integrity, so as not to be confined to the direct and intended consequences of conduct constituting the taking of fauna, but to include also indirect consequences such as disturbance of habitat of fauna.[160]

[150] Roscoe Pound, *The Spirit of the Common Law* (Piscataway, NJ, Transaction Publishers, 1999) 179 and see 174. See also R Pound, *An Introduction to the Philosophy of Law* (New Haven, CT, Yale University Press 1922) 51.

[151] J Stone, *Legal System and Lawyers' Reasoning* (Maitland Publications, 1964) 264.

[152] J Stone, *The Province and Function of Law* (Associated General Publications, 1947) 144.

[153] Pound, *The Spirit of the Common Law* (n 150) 172.

[154] K Llewellyn, 'A Realistic Jurisprudence – The Next Step' (1930) 30 *Columbia Law Review* 431, 446–47; W de Been, *Legal Realism Regained: Saving Realism from Critical Acclaim* (Stanford, CA, Stanford University Press, 2008) 82.

[155] Simmonds (n 48) 152.

[156] L Fuller, *The Morality of Law*, rev edn (New Haven, CT, Yale University Press, 1969).

[157] Waldron (n 43) 123.

[158] Dworkin (n 28) 6, 9.

[159] National Parks and Wildlife Act 1979 ss 98 and 99.

[160] *Corkill v Forestry Commission of New South Wales* (1991) 73 LGERA 126, 136–40. See further Adam, this volume.

The third step in the reasoning process is to apply the law so identified and interpreted to the facts of the case. The finding and interpretation of the law establish the major premise in the syllogistic reasoning process of 'formal logic'. Finding the facts establishes the minor premise. The tasks of finding and interpreting the law (the major premise) and finding the facts (the minor premise) are 'full of hazards and uncertainties, but the hazards and uncertainties are ordinarily concealed by the glib use of formal logic'.[161] Correspondence between the facts of the case and the relevant legal rule is almost never a straightforward matter. The judge deciding the case has latitude in fitting the facts to the relevant legal rule. Consequently, the idea that the logical application of legal rules will make law certain and predictable is a chimera.[162]

Application of the major premise (the law) to the minor premise (the facts) determines whether a breach of law has occurred. If so, there will often be discretion as to the remedy or relief that ought to be granted. A range of considerations will be relevant, pertaining to the private interests of the parties to the dispute or third parties, as well as the public interest.[163] Moral considerations may be as relevant as legal ones. As I have noted earlier, the Court plays a role in explaining and upholding the values underpinning, and the purposes of, environmental laws. The Court will have regard to these in exercising its discretion to remedy any breach in the laws. The duty of the Court, in the exercise of its discretion as to what remedy, relief or punishment, if any, is to be granted, is to exercise its moral judgment as to what is right, just, equitable or reasonable in the case.[164] The Court's moral judgment will evolve over time in response to changes in society and in the environment. For example, the Court found an important consideration in the exercise of discretion to remedy illegal development in a national park was that 'national parks are held by the State in trust for the enjoyment and benefit of its citizens, including future generations'.[165]

This process of finding, interpreting and applying the law involves judicial law-making, although this is interstitial and incremental. In fulfilling this role, courts have been described as the 'judicial partner in the legislative project'.[166] This process is especially important for environmental legislation, which can be drawn as a skeletal framework of rules expressed at a high level of generality, using terms containing 'multiple concealed references'[167] and 'terminology that is both factually descriptive and legally evaluative'.[168] The Court can, by interpreting and applying the legislation, flesh out the skeletal framework, both in meaning and application to the facts of the dispute before it.[169] Warnock's description of the role the New Zealand

[161] J Frank, *Law and the Common Mind* (Anchor Books, 1963) 72; see also K Llewellyn, *In the Bramble Bush: On Our Law and Its Study* (Oceans Publications, 1960) 72.

[162] de Been (n 154) 143.

[163] See *Warringah Shire Council v Sedevcic* (1987) 10 NSWLR 335, 339–41.

[164] PJ Fitzgerald, *Salmond on Jurisprudence*, 12th edn (London, Sweet & Maxwell, 1966) 68–69, 70–71.

[165] *Willoughby City Council v Minister Administering the National Parks and Wildlife Act* (1972) 78 LGERA 19, 34.

[166] A Barak, *The Judge in a Democracy* (Princeton, NJ, Princeton University Press, 2006) 4.

[167] Stone (n 151) 246.

[168] C Warnock, 'Environment and the Law: The Normative Force of Content and Constitutional Challenges' (2020) *Journal of Environmental Law* 1, 9.

[169] Preston, 'The Role of Public Interest Environmental Litigation' (n 41) 15.

Environment Court plays in statutory interpretation and application is equally apposite to the Court:

> [T]he Court plays a critical role in crafting a legal meaning to statutory terms that capture complex ideas and reflect 'competing understandings' but nevertheless have to be translated into something that is meaningful in order for people to regulate their behaviour and resolve disputes.[170]

The jurisprudence so produced by the Court is 'dependent common law', involving 'the creation of norms generated during adjudication as a by-product of the application of statutory and constitutional norms'.[171]

5.3. Developing Substantive Law

The body of statutory environmental laws comprises two broad categories of legal rules: rules of competence and rules of limitation. Rules of competence enable the exercise of power whereas rules of limitation control the exercise of power.[172] The two categories of rules are linked: power must exist before its exercise can be controlled.[173]

Rules of competence in statutory laws acknowledge an existing power (such as power at common law) or grant power (such as the power of the legislature to make delegated legislation and statutory instruments, the power of the executive to execute and implement the laws, or the power of the judiciary, constitutionally and institutionally, to adjudicate a dispute under the laws).[174]

Rules of limitation control the exercise of power and include strategic rules, regulatory rules, liability rules and market rules.[175] Rules of strategy indicate at a high level of abstraction what the exercise of power should achieve. They state the direction for environmental management for the future and sometimes the criteria according to which environmental management in the past is to be judged.[176] Rules of regulation prescribe how and for what purpose strategic planning and regulatory decisions must be made. A statutory provision prohibiting or restricting the carrying out of a particular activity, either at all or only with prior approval, is a type of regulatory rule, imposing a negative duty.[177] Most environmental laws employ regulatory rules as the primary means to manage the environment. Rules of liability prescribe standards of conduct or behaviour and the consequences for failure to comply. Liability rules address non-compliance with regulatory rules. They provide for administrative, civil or criminal liability.[178] Rules for markets describe the requirements for establishing and managing trade and commerce in environmental services.[179]

[170] Warnock (n 168) 15–16. See also Ceri Warnock's chapter in this book.
[171] P Cane, *Controlling Administrative Power: An Historical Comparison* (Cambridge, Cambridge University Press, 2016) 333.
[172] Fisher (n 123) 5.
[173] D Fisher, *Australian Environmental Law: Norms, Principles and Rules*, 2nd edn (Lawbook, 2010) 211.
[174] ibid, 229.
[175] ibid, 203.
[176] ibid, 234.
[177] ibid, 256.
[178] ibid, 264.
[179] ibid, 204.

The Court, in adjudicating the cases before it, has developed jurisprudence on these rules of competence and limitation. The Court has determined questions of competence – who has what power in what circumstances. Questions of competence particularly arise in planning law, especially in more recent times with devolution and distribution of powers for strategic planning and development assessment and consent to disparate public authorities, bodies and officials. More generally, the statutory power conferred on a public authority to approve an activity that the statute prohibits without first obtaining approval is a rule of competence. The Court regularly reviews the exercise of such statutory power.

The bulk of the work of the Court, however, has concerned rules of limitation, primarily strategic, regulatory and liability rules and less so market rules. The Court's articulation of the principles of ecologically sustainable development has doctrinally developed rules of strategy.[180] As noted earlier, environmental laws primarily use regulatory rules to manage the environment. The most common form of regulation is to prohibit some activity but confer power on a public authority or official to approve the otherwise prohibited activity. The Court regularly reviews these rules of regulation and linked rules of competence.

Failure to comply with liability rules may give rise to administrative, civil or criminal liability. The Court enforces liability rules in administrative appeals, civil enforcement proceedings and criminal prosecutions. In these proceedings, the Court has expounded on the rules of liability and the sanctions for their breach. The Court's articulation of sentencing principles for environmental offences is an example.[181]

5.4. Developing Procedural Law

The body of environmental law also comprises procedural laws. Procedural laws include laws regulating access to environmental information, public participation in environmental decision-making and access to justice, including access to review procedures before the Court to challenge decision-making or impairment of rights of access to information or public participation. Together these elements constitute procedural justice.[182] The Court's decisions have doctrinally developed these elements of procedural justice. The Court has upheld statutory provisions entitling public access to environmental information,[183] public participation in environmental decision-making[184] and access to the Court.[185]

[180] ibid, 244–45, 246–53.

[181] See cases in BJ Preston, 'Principled Sentencing for Environmental Offences – Part 1: Purposes of Sentencing' (2007) 31 *Criminal Law Journal* 91 and BJ Preston, 'Principled Sentencing for Environmental Offences – Part 2: Sentencing Considerations and Options' (2007) 31 *Criminal Law Journal* 142.

[182] BJ Preston, 'The Effectiveness of the Law in Providing Access to Environmental Justice' in P Martin et al (eds), *The Search for Environmental Justice* (Cheltenham, Edward Elgar, 2015) 23, 34–38. See also Smith and Higginson, this volume.

[183] An example of failure to publicly exhibit a development application is *Monaro Acclimatisation Society v The Minister* (NSWLEC, Stein J, 31 October 1986).

[184] Examples of inadequate public notification of a development application include *Nelson v Burwood Municipal Council* (1991) 75 LGERA 39; *Curac v Shoalhaven City Council* (1993) 81 LGERA 124; *Simpson v Wakool Shire Council* (2012) 190 LGERA 143.

[185] Examples of decisions upholding the standing of applicants include *Rowley v New South Wales Leather Trading Co Pty Ltd* (1980) 46 LGRA 250; *Building Owners and Managers Association (Aust) Ltd v Sydney City*

Procedural laws also include laws regulating practice and procedure in the Court. These laws include the LEC Act and Court Rules and the Court's Practice Notes. These procedural laws can have an important influence on litigation, especially public interest litigation. Rules can inhibit public interest litigation such as the requirements for standing, to provide an undertaking for damages as the price of an interlocutory injunction, to provide security for costs, and for the unsuccessful party to pay the successful party's costs of the litigation. The Court Rules go some way towards assisting public interest litigation. The Court may decide, if it is satisfied the proceedings have been brought in the public interest, not to make an order for the payment of costs against an unsuccessful applicant, not to require an applicant to give security for the respondents' costs or not to require an applicant to give an undertaking as to damages.[186] The Court's decisions have also assisted in lowering these procedural barriers to public interest litigation.[187]

6. The Processes of the Court

So far, I have outlined the different functions the Court performs in the exercise of its jurisdiction and explained how in doing so the Court develops doctrinally environmental law and jurisprudence. The process by which the Court does these things differs, depending primarily on the function being exercised. As with many aspects of the law, although ends are important, so too are the means by which the ends are achieved. This section outlines the means – the processes – by which the Court resolves the disputes before it.

6.1. Different Dispute Resolution Processes

The Court employs different processes to resolve the disputes before it. The choice of dispute resolution process depends on, on the one hand, the inherent nature and characteristics of the type of dispute resolution process and, on the other hand, the nature and characteristics of the dispute and disputants in the case at hand. The first can be described as 'the forum' and the second as 'the fuss'.[188] The goal of appropriate dispute resolution is to match the forum to the fuss.[189]

In order to achieve this goal of appropriate dispute resolution, the Court offers a variety of types of dispute resolution processes, including both non-consensual and

Council (1984) 53 LGERA 54 (LEC); (1985) 55 LGRA 444 (CA); *Residents Against Intermodal Development Moorebank Inc v Minister for Planning* (2017) 228 LGERA 15.

[186] Land and Environment Court Rules 2007 (NSW) ('Court Rules') r 4.2.

[187] See cases in BJ Preston, 'Judicial Review in Environmental Cases' (1993) 10 *Australian Bar Review* 147; PL Stein, 'The Role of the Land and Environment Court in the Emergence of Public Interest Law' (1996) 13 *Environmental and Planning Law Journal* 179; BJ Preston, 'The Role of Public Interest Environmental Litigation' (2006) 23 *Environmental and Planning Law Journal* 337; *Caroona Coal v Coal Mines Australia Pty Ltd (No 3)* (2010) 173 LGERA 280; *Hill Top Residents Action Group Inc v Minister for Planning (No 3)* (2010) 176 LGERA 20.

[188] FEA Sander and SB Goldberg, 'Fitting the Forum to the Fuss: A User-Friendly Guide to Selecting an ADR Procedure' [1994] *Negotiation Journal* 49.

[189] Walker, this volume.

consensual mechanisms. The non-consensual mechanism is adjudication. Adjudication involves the Court determining the whole or a part of a dispute before the it by making an order or judgment. The determination of the Court is authoritative and binding on at least the parties to the dispute (judgment in personam) and sometimes, in the case of judicial decisions, against the whole world (judgment in rem). Although all disputes in the Court can be determined by adjudication, not all disputes are because another dispute resolution process might be more appropriate than adjudication.

Consensual mechanisms are mechanisms of resolving disputes which depend on the consensus or agreement of the parties to the dispute. They include negotiation between the parties without the assistance of a third party (negotiation) and well as negotiation with the assistance of a third party (conciliation and mediation). Where a third-party facilitator is used, the facilitator will have process expertise – expertise in the process of assisting the parties to negotiate a consensual resolution of the dispute. Where the facilitator has and uses subject matter expertise – special knowledge and expertise in the subject matter and issues involved in the dispute – the process is referred to as conciliation; otherwise the process is referred to as mediation.[190]

Conciliation is provided for all matters in Classes 1–3 of the Court's jurisdiction.[191] For appeals concerning small-scale residential development, a streamlined conciliation process is provided.[192] Both types of conciliation are hybrid processes involving, first, conciliation and then, if the parties are not able to agree at the conciliation, adjudication.[193] Mediation offered in the Court is the same process as is offered for civil proceedings in other courts in NSW.[194] Neutral evaluation is another consensual mechanism, involving evaluation by a third party of the relative strengths and weaknesses of each party's case and offering of an opinion to the parties as to the likely outcome of the proceedings.[195]

In offering a variety of dispute resolution processes, the Court is operating as a form of multi-door courthouse. The concept of the multi-door courthouse is that of a dispute resolution centre offering intake services and an array of dispute resolution processes in one institution. The idea is to match the appropriate dispute resolution process (the forum) to the particular dispute (the fuss). The intake services comprise screening, diagnosis and referral of a dispute to the appropriate dispute resolution process.[196]

6.2. Limits and Forms of Dispute Resolution Processes

The concepts of appropriate dispute resolution and a multi-door courthouse are based on the limits and forms of the dispute resolution processes employed. The question of limits involves identification of the essential characteristics of each dispute resolution

[190] BJ Preston, 'The Land and Environment Court of New South Wales: Moving Towards a Multi-Door Courthouse – Part II' (2008) 19 *Australasian Dispute Resolution Journal* 144, 145–46.

[191] Land and Environment Court Act 1979 (NSW) s 34.

[192] ibid, s 34AA.

[193] See BJ Preston, 'Conciliation in the Land and Environment Court of New South Wales: History, Nature and Benefits' (2007) 13 *Local Government Law Journal* 110.

[194] Civil Procedure Act 2005 (NSW) s 26.

[195] Preston (n 190) 146, and see Land and Environment Court Rules 2007 r 3.8.

[196] Preston (n 190) 147–150.

process and its inherent capacity to resolve certain types of disputes. The question of forms involves examination of the ways in which each dispute resolution process can be organised and conducted. Although a dispute might be of a kind that in theory can properly be resolved by a particular dispute resolution process, that is to say the dispute is within the limits of that dispute resolution process, the effectiveness of the selected dispute resolution process in practice may depend on the manner in which it is organised and conducted. In short, the form in which it is organised and conducted will be important.[197]

Answering the limits question involves understanding the inherent nature of each of the dispute resolution processes offered by the Court – adjudication, conciliation, mediation and neutral evaluation – and their appropriateness to resolve the particular dispute at hand. Answering the forms question involves tailoring the different types of dispute resolution processes so as to improve their effectiveness to resolve particular types of disputes.

For adjudication, the Court organises and conducts differently hearings for different types of disputes. To a large extent, the differences in adjudication correspond with the differences in the court functions being exercised. Merits review is organised and conducted differently to judicial review, for example. Further differences can be seen within categories of court functions. Different types of merits review appeals are organised and conducted differently. Again, these differences largely correspond with the different administrative functions being exercised, but they also relate to the subject matter of the dispute and what is at stake.

There are certain types of merits review appeals to which on-site hearing procedures apply.[198] These proceedings are to be dealt with by means of an on-site conference to be heard and disposed of by one or more commissioners.[199] Other types of proceedings can be dealt with by a court hearing,[200] although before disposing of a court hearing matter, the Court must make an inspection of the site of the proposed development, except in limited circumstances.[201] Small-scale residential development matters are dealt with by a different procedure, involving mandatory conciliation and adjudication.[202]

This adjustment of the forms in which the dispute resolution process is organised or conducted extends to how the Court receives evidence. The Court is a specialist institution and can inform itself as it thinks fit in proceedings in Classes 1–3 of its jurisdiction.[203] This enables the Court to take advantage of its contributory and interactional expertise. It also facilitates access to justice, levelling the scales between parties who cannot afford access to expert evidence and those who can.

The Court has adopted special procedures for receiving evidence, both lay and expert, at hearings. Lay evidence can be received on-site, more informally than in a court hearing. Members of the community who object to a proposed development can

[197] Preston (n 68) 148.
[198] Land and Environment Court Act 1979 (NSW) s 34A(1).
[199] ibid, s 34B(1).
[200] ibid, s 34C.
[201] ibid, s 34D.
[202] ibid, s 34AA.
[203] ibid, s 39(2).

tell their story in their own words in familiar surroundings. Experts ordinarily will be required to confer and prepare a joint expert report identifying the areas in which they agree, the areas in which they disagree and, where they disagree, their reasons for their disagreement. The joint expert report is provided to the Court. At the hearing, the experts' evidence is given concurrently, a procedure that reduces partisanship and improves impartiality.[204] By this bespoke tailoring of the forms in which a particular dispute resolution process is organised and conducted, the Court facilitates individualised access to justice.

7. Conclusion

Lord Carnwath, after surveying judicial decisions on the protection of the environment across time and place, observed that:

> [T]he courts have for more than 150 years been seeking to mould the law to respond to the environmental challenges of a developing world. … It is true of course that our primary job is to decide the cases before us, and we search for the most suitable legal tools to enable us to do so within our own legal systems.[205]

These observations ring true for the Court. The Court, over forty years, has sought to respond to the environmental challenges of the time. It has searched for the most suitable legal tools to enable it to do so. The search has been in its functions and processes. The Court has reflected on the nature and features of its functions and how these functions can best be exercised to resolve the environmental problems in dispute. The Court has adaptively managed its dispute resolution processes so as to enable it to better exercise its functions. One result has been the doctrinal development of environmental law, both substantive and procedural. The Court has thereby evolved as an institution, adapting to an ever-changing environment but also building a system of common laws of the environment.[206]

This adaptation and evolution of the Court, in terms of function, doctrine and process, has produced a Court of many facets. The value of the Court and its contributions is to be appreciated not from viewing any one facet, but instead by viewing all of its facets, from different perspectives, revealing an institution as a whole that is greater than the sum of its parts.

[204] See Justice PD McClellan, 'Expert Witness – The Recent Experience of the Land and Environment Court' (2005) 17(10) *Judicial Officers' Bulletin* 83; Justice PD McClellan, 'Expert Evidence: Aces Up Your Sleeve' (2007) 8 *The Judicial Review* 215.

[205] Lord Carnwath, 'Judges and the Common Laws of the Environment – At Home and Abroad' (2014) 26 *Journal of Environmental Law* 177, 187.

[206] ibid, 177, 187.

PART I

Function

2

From Reactive to Proactive Decision-Making by the Land and Environment Court of New South Wales

DOUGLAS FISHER

1. Introduction

The contribution of the Land and Environment Court of New South Wales (the Court) to the development of environmental law is a reflection of the dynamic nature of environmental law. The function of the law is to ensure compliance by all persons – individual, corporate and institutional – with the standards of behaviour and decision-making required of them. These standards assume the form of a range of criteria within a framework of multifunctional rules. The nature of these rules varies in accordance with the function they are designed to perform. The functions include prescribing standards of individual behaviour, enabling decisions to be made, prescribing how decisions are to be made and stating the outcomes that decisions are to achieve. The substance of these rules is not static. They evolve from time to time in accordance with the policies and values enacted by the legislature.

The judiciary has a vital part to play in the administration of these rules. It adjudicates upon civil disputes and upon breaches of criminal law. It reviews the legality of decisions made by the executive branch of government. It reviews the merits of decisions made by the executive. The nature of the reasoning required of the judiciary in undertaking these responsibilities depends upon the structure, form and language of the relevant rules. In some cases, the rules reflect what has happened in the past. Their application involves reactive decision-making. In other cases, they reflect what should happen in the future. Their application involves proactive decision-making. The Court engages in all of these forms of judicial reasoning. This chapter describes the legal architecture according to which the Court engages in both reactive and proactive decision-making.

2. Environmental Governance as a Challenge for the Court

2.1. The Functions of the Court

The name of the Court – Land and Environment – reveals that it is concerned with the use and development of land, the management of natural resources, the conservation of the natural and built environments and the protection of the environment at large: hereinafter collectively termed environmental governance. The legislation for which the Court is responsible includes all of these matters. The prescribed objects of each statute are often controversial and potentially in conflict – in other words multifaceted legislation. The jurisdiction of the Court includes civil and criminal proceedings,[1] judicial review[2] and merits review.[3]

The legislation administered by the Court comprises provisions that state: (1) the activities that are to be authorised or prohibited; (2) rules that prescribe the processes for creating these rights and duties – regulatory rules; (3) rules that create criminal or civil liability for breach of the duties so created – liability rules; (4) the intended outcomes of the decision-making processes – substantive rules; and (5) how these decisions are to be made – methodological rules. Together these rules answer the questions of what and how. The functions of the Court in this context include interpreting and applying the rules, reaching a decision, engaging in reasoning to justify the decision, reviewing decisions on their merits and solving complex problems. It will be informative at this stage to discuss the functions of these rules and to review the decision-making and reasoning processes of the Court.

2.2. The Functions of the Rules[4]

The way in which the rules are formulated reflects their function. The adjudication of civil and criminal disputes revolves around liability rules. They are in the form of enforceable duties. The judicial responsibility for adjudicating upon such an issue is not complicated. It is to apply a liability rule to a substantiated set of facts – as in the following example.

Section 120(1) of the Protection of the Environment Operations Act 1997 (NSW) states that a person who pollutes any waters is guilty of an offence. This is a rule creating criminal liability. The language of this rule does not in terms impose a duty. However, 'while seemingly trite, implicit in the words "a person who pollutes any waters is guilty of an offence" is the imposition of a duty … not to pollute waters'.[5] It is a duty that the Court has the responsibility to enforce.

[1] Land and Environment Court Act 1979 (NSW), ss 20, 21, 21A and 21B.
[2] ibid, s 20(2) and (3).
[3] ibid, ss 17 and 21C.
[4] See generally DE Fisher, *Australian Environmental Law: Norms, Principles and Rules*, 3rd edn (London, Thomson Reuters, 2014).
[5] *Blue Mountains Conservation Society Inc v Delta Electricity (No 3)* (2011) 81 NSWLR 407, 414.

A regulatory rule enables the authorisation of an activity otherwise prohibited. For example, section 4.2(1) of the Environmental Planning and Assessment Act 1979 (NSW) (the EPA Act) regulates the use of land by controlling development. If an environmental planning instrument provides that specified development requires development consent, then the carrying out of the development requires consent. The implicit duty is not to carry out the development rather than not to develop. The Act goes on to prescribe how the decision to consent to the carrying out of the development is to be made.

A substantive rule prescribes the direction of decision-making in implementing regulatory rules. The direction of decision-making stated in section 2A(1)(a) of the National Parks and Wildlife Act 1974 (NSW) is the conservation of nature in general and more specifically the conservation of habitat, ecosystems and ecosystem processes, biological diversity, landforms, landscapes, and natural features. This substantive rule contains several complementary and potentially competing elements – not an uncommon characteristic of environmental legislation.

A methodological rule states how a regulatory rule is to be implemented. In other words, how the decision is to be made. In practice these are the most difficult rules to interpret and apply. The criteria for decision-making include the objects of the Act, the matters for consideration, any relevant principles and the public interest. For example, section 5.5(1) of the EPA Act states in summarised form that all matters affecting the environment by reason of the proposed activity shall be taken into account. The Court in addition is required by section 39(4) of the Land and Environment Court Act 1979 (NSW) to have regard to three matters, including the public interest. The responsibility of the Court is to interpret and apply these complex sets of related rules.

2.3. Reviewing Decisions on their Merits

The jurisdiction of the Court includes both judicial review and merits review. Judicial review determines the legality of decisions made executively in the past. Merits review is fundamentally different. The Court is invited to determine the issues on their merits by applying all the relevant legal rules to its decision-making process. Its function is to decide proactively what is the best outcome for the future. Accordingly, the relationship between substantive and methodological rules on the one hand and the function of proactive decision-making on the other hand has become critical in the context of the exercise by the Court of its merits review jurisdiction. Significantly, the same rules apply to both judicial and merits review. Consequently, how the rules are interpreted and applied by the Court – whether reactively or proactively – are mutually relevant in each area of judicial responsibility.

The distinction between judicial review and merits review is easy to state. It raises, however, a number of issues. The Court of Appeal has recently commented on some of these issues in the context of the EPA Act. First, 'the primary decision-maker, being the consent authority, does not hold hearings (as would a tribunal) or make findings of fact'.[6] Second, 'nor does it provide a reasoned justification for a particular outcome'.[7]

[6] *Ku-ring-gai Council v Bunnings Properties Pty Ltd* (2019) 236 LGERA 35, [42].
[7] ibid, [42].

Third, 'the Court performs the statutory function of the consent authority to determine the development application … by granting or refusing consent'.[8] Fourth, 'the question for the determination of the Court is whether the decision was the correct or preferable one on the material before the Court'.[9] Fifth, 'unlike a consent authority, the Court is not within the executive; it remains external to the executive'.[10] These comments neatly indicate the nature of merits review.

2.4. Solving Complex Problems

A glance at the substantive rules in any of the statutes for which the Court is responsible demonstrates the wide range of interests – both human and environmental – that are to be accommodated. Although adjudication and judicial review may raise several issues, it is suggested that the response is to address one issue at a time: for example, whether the activities constitute an offence. Merits review addresses several issues at the same time: for example, the economic, the social and the environmental. The methodological rules indicating how the decision about the outcome stated in the substantive rules is to be made are equally complex.

Reactive decision-making has been the conventional method of adjudication. The wide range of interests involved in environmental governance requires a different approach. The answer is not monocentric but polycentric decision-making. A decision seeking to accommodate all of these interests 'requires consideration, weighing and balancing of the environmental, social and economic impacts'.[11] Consequently:

> The range of interests affected, the complexity of the issues and the interdependence of the issues means that decision-making involves a polycentric problem. A polycentric problem involves a complex network of relationships, with interacting points of influence. Each decision made communicates itself to other centres of decision, changing the conditions, so that a new basis must be found for the next decision.[12]

The solution to a polycentric problem accordingly requires a polycentric approach to decision-making. What is the nature of this approach? The response:

> This spontaneous transformation of the nature and scope of the issues in resolving polycentric problems makes classic forms of adjudication out of place and instead resolution by exercise of managerial authority, a form of executive action, more appropriate.[13]

The adoption of this approach must be consistent with all the rules for decision-making prescribed by the relevant legislation. The Court has responded by interpreting and applying the provisions of the legislation for which it is responsible.

[8] ibid, [150].
[9] ibid, [153].
[10] ibid, [160].
[11] *Bulga Milbrodale Progress Association Inc v Minister for Planning and Infrastructure* (2013) 194 LGERA 347, [31].
[12] ibid, [31].
[13] ibid, [34].

2.5. Reasoning to Justify a Decision[14]

Attention now turns to the decision-making processes involved in ensuring compliance with these rules and to the reasoning used to justify the decision. Adjudication responds to the following questions: what activity has taken place? Have any rules been breached? If so, what remedy or sanction will be appropriate? Two in the past tense; the third in the future tense. Judicial review responds to the following questions: what decision has been made? How was that decision made? Have any rules been breached? If so, what remedy will be appropriate? Three in the past tense; the fourth in the future tense. Merits review responds to the following questions: what activity will be undertaken? What substantive and methodological rules will be applied? What will be the final decision? All in the future tense. Responses to questions in the past tense involve reactive decision-making: looking backwards. Responses to questions in the future tense involve proactive decision-making: looking forwards.

Adjudication, judicial review and merits review perform different functions. Reactive and proactive decision-making are intrinsically different. Do they involve different forms of legal reasoning – particularly in the context of environmental governance? This is a complex issue.[15] Adjudication is a three-step process: a statement of the rule; a statement of the substantiated facts; a conclusion. Identifying the rule and the facts may be simple or difficult. Reaching the conclusion – again either simple or difficult – is generally an example of syllogistic logic.

What is the nature of syllogistic reasoning?[16] A syllogism consists of a statement of a major premise, a minor premise and a conclusion. The major premise is the rule of law; the minor premise is a statement of fact or circumstance; and the conclusion automatically follows by applying the major premise to the minor premise.[17] For example, every person who pollutes the environment commits a punishable offence; this person has polluted the environment; therefore this person has committed a punishable offence. This is based upon the assumption that the major premise states a valid rule of law and that the minor premise is in fact true. If neither premise is valid, then the conclusion is invalid. Judicial review is similar: the rule, the decision and the conclusion. Theoretically, syllogistic reasoning is simple but often very difficult in practice. It is the form of reasoning usually applicable in reactive decision-making by the judiciary.

Merits review – a form of proactive decision-making – is fundamentally different. It involves what may be described as a form of teleological reasoning. Teleology is the doctrine of final causes. In other words, 'developments are due to the purpose

[14] See generally DE Fisher, *Legal Reasoning in Environmental Law: A Study of Structure, Form and Language* (Cheltenham, Edward Elgar, 2013). For a detailed analysis, see BJ Preston, 'The Art of Judging Environmental Disputes' (2008) 12 *Southern Cross University Law Review* 103, in particular 108–13.

[15] See generally ibid.

[16] The material in this paragraph is sourced directly from ibid, 13.

[17] E Feteris, *Fundamentals of Legal Argumentation: A Survey of Theories on the Justification of Judicial Decisions* (Dordrecht, Kluwer, 1999) 28–29.

that is served by them'.[18] For example, in the context of environmental governance, if a development is proposed, what purpose is to be achieved by its implementation?

Increasingly, this question is answered by a number of interacting legal rules.[19] These often include the outcome to be achieved by the decision-maker. In the case of merits review, this is the Court. The purpose underlying the legal rule, or the purpose stated in the legal rule, becomes one of the most important elements in the methodology of decision-making when the function of the rule is to set standards for future activities rather than to apply standards to past activities. It has been suggested that this process of reasoning is particularly appropriate in relation to 'polycentric' decisions rather than 'single-issue' decisions.[20] The question then becomes whether and to what extent the Court has engaged in syllogistic reasoning in performing adjudication and in teleological reasoning in performing merits review.

3. The Nature of Reasoning in Relation to Environmental Governance

The reasoning of the Court in *Willoughby City Council*[21] demonstrates how reactive decision-making operates in accordance with a set of regulatory and substantive rules. The Court analysed a number of provisions in the National Parks and Wildlife Act 1974 (NSW) and in a range of planning instruments under the EPA Act. Section 47B of the 1974 Act enables the minister to reserve land as a state recreation area for the purpose of public recreation and enjoyment. An area of land within a state recreation area may be leased with the consent of the minister. The Local Environmental Plan provided that development permissible under the 1974 Act was permissible without development consent in a relevant state recreation area zone and that all other development in that zone was prohibited. The issue was whether the development in question was permissible under the 1974 Act.

A lease had been approved by the minister in relation to a single-storey building in a state recreation area. The building included a kiosk, tea-room, and boat and bike hire. The lease later included permission to carry out private catering functions such as weddings, musical performances and Christmas carols. Building work commenced without development consent. If the development was permissible under the 1974 Act, then development consent was not required. The Court decided that the development was not permissible under the Act, principally because use for private functions was not authorised in a state recreation area. It was accordingly prohibited under the Local Environmental Plan.

The Court reasoned:

> The National Parks and Wildlife Act does not expressly set forth the purposes for which a lease may be granted within a State recreation area. The power of leasing will therefore be

[18] 'Teleology', *The Concise Oxford Dictionary* (1989).

[19] The material in this paragraph is sourced directly from Fisher (n 14) 32.

[20] J Bell, *Policy Arguments in Judicial Decisions* (Oxford, Clarendon Press, 1983) 242. See also Fisher (n 14) 51.

[21] *Willoughby City Council v Minister Administering National Parks and Wildlife Act* (1992) 78 LGERA 19: a judicial review case.

> controlled by the purpose and scope of the legislation. They are powers which must advance and be consistent with the objects of the statute. The purposes will be limited to those which promote and are ancillary to the use and enjoyment of the land as a State recreation area.[22]

The Court referred specifically to section 47B(1) enabling the minister to reserve land as a state recreation area 'for the purpose *of public* recreation and enjoyment'. It was concluded:

> It follows that any purpose which is not for public recreation or enjoyment, or which will ipso facto inhibit or exclude public recreation and enjoyment is not permissible.[23]

The Court answered the questions – what had been decided and had any rules been breached. The Minister had decided to approve the lease, but the minister had approved by implication a use not permitted by section 47B of the 1974 Act. In this way, the Minister had applied a relevant rule – the power to approve a lease – to enable the carrying out of private catering functions – a purpose not permitted by the legislation. This amounted essentially to a form of syllogistic reasoning: namely, three major premises, two minor premises and a conclusion.

The major premises were in the form of legal rules derived from the range of multifunctional rules in the various statutes and statutory instruments. These rules included substantive rules – in particular, the rule that the purpose of a state recreation area was public recreation and enjoyment – and the methodological rules that indicated the connections between all of the rules. The reasoning of the Court began with conventional but complex syllogistic reasoning. It concluded with critical references to the purpose of a recreation area. This was an indirect use of teleological reasoning – namely 'developments are due to the purpose that is served by them'. Although this was a judicial review of the decision of the minister, the nature of the relevant rules involved the Court in an analysis of the objects of the legislation. This points in many respects to what will emerge as the paradigm of proactive decision-making in the exercise of the Court's merits review jurisdiction.

4. The Relationships between Multifunctional Rules

4.1. Introduction

The foregoing paragraphs have discussed the challenges facing the Court in administering its statutory responsibilities in relation to environmental governance. Attention now turns to an analysis of how the Court has interpreted the multifunctional rules contained in the relevant legislation. This is a critical part of the decision-making processes engaged in by the Court.

[22] ibid, 26.
[23] ibid, 26.

4.2. The Rules Indicating the Relationship between Objects and the Public Interest

It will be informative at the outset to identify the ways in which the methodological rules interact. The decision of the Court in *Carstens* is instructive.[24] One of the objects stated in section 5(a)(vii) of the EPA Act was 'to encourage' ecologically sustainable development (ESD). The matters to be 'taken into consideration' did not include ESD but did include 'the public interest'. The question for the Court was whether the Commissioner had erred in deciding that the 'principles' of ESD 'must be a factor in an assessment of the impact on the environment' of the development application.[25]

The Court noted 'the matters that must be taken into consideration' and continued:

> That subsection … does not exclude from consideration matters not listed and which may be of relevance to the particular development application and which further the objects of the Act. That is to say, it is not an irrelevant consideration for the decision maker to take into account a matter relating to the objects of the Act. One of those objects is to encourage ecologically sustainable development. Moreover, one of the considerations expressly mentioned … is … the 'public interest'. In my opinion it is in the public interest, in determining a development application, to give effect to the objects of the Act.[26]

Significant are the references to these expressions: 'further the objects'; 'give effect to the objects'; 'take into account a matter relating to the objects'; and 'in the public interest to give effect to the objects'.

Accordingly, the objects of the Act perform a number of distinct functions in decision-making. Moreover, even in the absence of a specific reference to the public interest, it is arguable that a statutory statement of the objects of the Act constitutes a declaration by the legislature of what it considers to be in the public interest. In any event, it seems clear that the objects of the Act are at least a relevant – perhaps a mandatory – matter for consideration.

The notion that statements of objects reflect what the legislature perceives to be in the public interest receives some support from the decision of the Court in *Patra Holdings*.[27] This case involved not one but two sets of objects: those of the EPA Act and those of the Native Vegetation Conservation Act 1997 (NSW) (NVC Act). The case was about an application for development consent to clear native vegetation. The EPA Act required a consideration of the public interest. As the Court noted:

> Although the term 'public interest' is not defined in either the [EPA Act] or the NVC Act, it must be applied, in the determination of an application for the clearing of native vegetation, having regard to the scope and purpose of those statutes.[28]

These words imply two duties: to apply the public interest and to have regard to the objects of the Acts. The Court then proceeded to do precisely that.

[24] *Carstens v Pittwater Council* (1999) 111 LGERA 1: a judicial review case. See Fisher (n 14) 411.

[25] *Carstens v Pittwater Council* (n 24) 25. For a discussion of this form of analogical reasoning, see Preston (n 14) 115–21.

[26] ibid, 25.

[27] *Patra Holdings Pty Ltd v Minister for Land and Water Conservation* (2011) 119 LGERA 231: a judicial review case. See Fisher (n 4) 275–76.

[28] *Patra Holdings Pty Ltd v Minister for Land and Water Conservation* (n 27) [11].

In considering the public interest, the Court decided that it was legitimate to consider the ultimate use to which the site was to be put.[29] Hence a review of the objects of both statutes. The relevant object stated in section 5(a)(ii) of the EPA Act was the orderly and economic use and development of land, and that stated in section 3(b) of the NVC Act was the promotion of native vegetation management in the social, economic and environmental interests of the state. The word 'economic' appeared in both of these objects. As the Court explained:

> The exercise of the discretion of the consent authority (or the Court on appeal) … includes consideration of the promotion of native vegetation management in the economic interests of the State and the orderly and economic use and development of land. In that context and to the limited extent encompassed by those statutory objects, economic considerations (to use a neutral term) as a component of the public interest may be relevant to the exercise of the discretion.[30]

In effect, therefore, the relationship between objects, considerations and the public interest.

4.3. The Rules Indicating the Relationship between Objects and Considerations

The relationship between objects and considerations was an issue for the Court in *Coffs Harbour City Council*.[31] In this case the rules were contained in the applicable local environmental plan. The land in question adjoined a marine park. The plan contained two relevant provisions: clause 22(4)(a) and (b). The grant of development consent was prohibited in relation to land adjoining the marine park, first, unless the consent authority had taken into account a number of the objectives of the Marine Parks Act 1997 (NSW), and, second, without consulting the relevant marine park authority if certain conditions were satisfied. In relation to the first point:

> The mandatory effect of cl 22(4)(a) is that in terms it prohibits a determination to grant consent unless the objectives of the Marine Parks Act are considered where the land adjoins the Park.[32]

This is a duty to consider the relevant objectives.

In relation to the second point:

> Clause 22(4)(b) requires the council as consent authority to consider whether the proposal is likely to have an impact on flora and fauna within the Marine Park and its habitat for the purpose of determining whether consultation with the Park Authority is required. The council's failure in this respect amounts to a failure to take into account relevant matters for the purposes of the determination under s 79C [of the EPA Act]. The council failed to ask

[29] ibid, [9].
[30] ibid, [13].
[31] *Coffs Harbour City Council v Arrawarra Beach Pty Ltd* (2006) 148 LGERA 11: a judicial review case. See Fisher (n 4) 294–95.
[32] *Coffs Harbour City Council v Arrawarra Beach Pty Ltd* (n 31) 22.

> itself the relevant question, thereby constructively failing to properly exercise the discretion to determine the development application.
>
> The chapeau to cl 22(4) is expressed in the context of a prohibition not to grant consent unless (a) and (b) are satisfied. The council totally ignored the direction. Accordingly the decision to grant consent is also invalid on that account.[33]

The first point concerned a failure to comply with a methodological rule; the second with a failure to comply with a liability rule. The consequence of a breach of these rules was an invalid decision.

The relationship between objects and considerations was similarly fundamental to the decision in *Village McEvoy*.[34] The Commissioner had taken into account the objectives stated in the EPA Act in determining to refuse a development application – including the promotion of the orderly and economic use and development of land. It was argued that the Commissioner in doing so had 'converted the objects of the Act into a de facto test or consideration required to be satisfied in order for the development to be approved'.[35] This was rejected. The Commissioner had not 'measured the development against the objects of the Act as a matter relevant to be considered'.[36]

According to the Court, what the Commissioner had done was to consider

> whether the proposed development met the objects of the Act given that it did not represent the orderly and economic use of land 'and in relation to strategic town planning considerations, would not be in the public interest'. In so concluding, the Commissioner was not requiring that the proposed development positively satisfy this object, rather he was stating that it did not further it.[37]

Perhaps this translates into an encouragement but not a duty to further the objects of the Act by taking them into consideration. In other words, the objects are not a standard or test against which the validity of a decision is determined. Rather they are considerations relevant to the decision-making process.

4.4. The Rules Indicating How to Achieve Outcomes

The foregoing discussion reveals how important is the verb that links its subject and its object. The verb in a statement of objects usually includes an object – in the grammatical sense – but not a subject. The subject by implication is the decision-making authority. The object in the grammatical sense is the intended outcome of the decision-making process: for example, production, development, conservation or protection. Such terms are critical to the outcome of any decision-making process. Perhaps even more important is the verb preceding the intended outcome.

Take as an example the achievement of ESD. The Court has noted that 'the need for development to be ecologically sustainable is no longer seriously in debate. The principles

[33] ibid, 23.

[34] *Village McEvoy Pty Ltd v Sydney City Council (No 2)* (2010) 176 LGERA 119: a judicial review case. See Fisher (n 4) 303–04.

[35] *Village McEvoy Pty Ltd v Sydney City Council* (n 34) 141.

[36] ibid, 142.

[37] ibid, 142.

of ecologically sustainable development are reasonably settled.'[38] How might it be achieved? In this way:

> In order to achieve sustainability, however, hortatory statements of principle and aspirational goals are insufficient; the grand strategy must be translated into action. This involves not only institutionalising the principles of ecologically sustainable development in policies and laws, but also ensuring that functions under those policies and laws are exercised in a way so as to promote and implement the principles of ecologically sustainable development.[39]

The verb 'implement' is significant. It could also be 'facilitate', 'further', 'give effect to' or even 'achieve' ESD. The legislature, and by implication the Court, have for the most part been reluctant to create or recognise a duty to achieve ESD that might be implicit in this terminology. It has already been seen that the response of the legislature and of the Court has been to permit or require the objects of the Act to be considered in the decision-making process rather than an obligation to do so.

5. The Rules Defining Consideration[40]

5.1. The Meaning of 'Consider'

The methodological rules enacted in the legislation include not only the expressions analysed in the preceding paragraphs but also the verb 'consider'. It is now appropriate to undertake an analysis of what has been described generically as the deliberative duty – to consider. This in addition indicates the relationship between all of the other methodological rules.

The deliberative duty – as originally enacted – in section 90(1) of the EPA Act was subjected to detailed scrutiny by the Court of Appeal in *Hale*.[41] The section provided in summary form that 'in determining a development application, a consent authority shall take into consideration' a range of matters: clearly a duty. The Court described the 'obligation' as 'direct and specific' and defined in 'positive terms'.[42] The argument that the relevant matters could be considered and then rejected was itself rejected. The Court went further:

> The requirement of s 90(1) to consider carries with it an indirect obligation, which rests upon the authority to acquaint itself with such material as will permit it to consider such s 90(1) matters as are in fact material.[43]

[38] *Hub Action Group Inc. v Minister for Planning* (2008) 161 LGERA 136, [1]. See Fisher, *Australian Environmental Law* (n 4) 338–39.

[39] *Hub Action Group Inc v Minister for Planning* (n 38) [2].

[40] For a recent authoritative summary of these rules, see *Palm Beach Protection Group Incorporated v Northern Beaches Council* (2020) 250 LGERA 212; [2020] NSWLEC 156, [260]–[261].

[41] *Parramatta City Council v Hale* (1982) 47 LGRA 319. See Fisher (n 4) 315.

[42] *Parramatta City Council v Hale* (n 41) 339.

[43] ibid, 340.

So the duty to consider carries with it a duty to obtain all the material necessary to discharge the primary duty – an objective rather than a subjective test. The Court, finally, made this comment:

> Section 90 does not prescribe the decision to be come to. It merely dictates to what the authority shall apply its mind in deciding.[44]

There is, accordingly, no duty to achieve an outcome – only an obligation to make a decision in a specified way. The reference to the 'mind' categorises the process as intellectual.

What intellectual processes are involved in considering relevant matters? This was the response of the Court of Appeal in *Weal*:[45]

> Taking relevant matters into consideration called for more than simply adverting to them. There had to be an understanding of the matters and the significance of the decision to be made about them, and a process of evaluation, sufficient to warrant the description of the matters being taken into consideration.[46]

The three essential elements are understanding, contextual significance and evaluation. The relative simplicity of this formulation has been complicated by the suggestion that the process of consideration should in addition be 'proper, genuine and realistic'.[47] This has been criticised because it would essentially involve the Court in a merits review rather than a judicial review.[48] In other words, the nouns 'understanding' and 'evaluation' describe the intellectual processes in reaching a decision, while the adjectives 'proper', 'genuine' and 'realistic' relate to the substantive quality of the decision.

Which approach is currently favoured by the Court? The Court of Appeal in *Anderson*[49] preferred the accepted meaning of consideration without the addition of adjectives. The idea of evaluation found favour with the Court of Appeal:

> Whether or not it can be judged that a matter has been considered is essentially an evaluative process based exclusively on what the decision-maker has said or written.[50]

Essentially, therefore, to consider is simply to understand and to evaluate.

5.2. Performing the Function of Consideration

The general duty to 'consider' environmental impacts is amplified by two rules. The first is the duty imposed on the determining authority by section 5.5(1) of the EPA Act to 'examine and take into account to the fullest extent possible all matters affecting or likely to affect the environment'. The second is the duty imposed on the determining authority by section 5.7(1)(a) to examine and consider an environmental impact statement (EIS)

[44] ibid, 345.
[45] *Weal v Bathurst City Council* (2000) 111 LGERA 181. See Fisher (n 4) 312, 316, 319.
[46] *Weal v Bathurst City Council* (n 45) 201.
[47] For a detailed discussion of how this happened, see Fisher (n 4) 315–16.
[48] *Kindimindi v Lane Cove Council* (2006) 143 LGERA 277, 298.
[49] *Anderson v Director-General, Dept of Environment and Climate Change* (2008) 163 LGERA 400. See Fisher (n 4) 317, 345–46.
[50] *Anderson v Director-General, Dept of Environment and Climate Change* (n 49) 421.

in respect of 'an activity that is likely to significantly affect the environment'. The terminological structure of these sections is subtly different. The former refers generally to 'all matters affecting or likely to affect the environment'. The latter refers specifically to 'an activity likely to significantly affect the environment'. The duty in section 5.5(1) is 'to examine and take into account to the *fullest extent possible*'. The duty in section 5.7(1)(a) is 'to examine and consider' the environmental impact statement.

The first question is the meaning of 'to the fullest extent possible'. The Court of Appeal answered this question in *Guthega*.[51] After stating that the requirements of section 5.5(1) – then section 111 – were mandatory, the Court proceeded:

> The phrase 'to the fullest extent possible' would present an insoluble problem to an administrator since it would be necessary to search the aggregated knowledge of the experts of the world in order to discharge the almost limitless burden imposed by the word 'possible'. 'Possible' is of a similar kind to 'foreseeable', a word etched in the professional core of common lawyers and capable of very extensive application indeed. Accordingly, in my view, some element of reasonableness must be introduced and may be achieved by reading the section as if the word 'reasonably' was inserted before 'possible'.[52]

It was accordingly concluded that the duty imposed by section 5.5(1) was to consider to the fullest extent reasonably practicable matters likely to affect the environment.

The second question is to determine the standard required of an EIS, which is the principal mechanism for identifying and assessing the environmental impacts of an activity. Once again, a concept of reasonableness was indicated. 'The possibility of a superficial, subjective or non-informative environmental impact statement' was rejected.[53] This would satisfy the obligation:

> Provided an environmental impact statement is comprehensive in its treatment of the subject matter, objective in its approach and meets the requirement that it alerts the decision-maker and members of the public and the Department of Environment and Planning to the effect of the activity on the environment and the consequences to the community inherent in carrying out or not carrying out of the activity, it meets the standards imposed by the regulations.[54]

In short, it must be comprehensive, objective and informative: a sufficient basis on which a consideration of the environmental effects of a proposed development can be undertaken.

5.3. The Meaning of 'Must'

The deliberative rule is often accompanied by other rules. How are they interpreted? This was one of the issues for the Court of Appeal in *Desane*.[55] A Proposed Acquisition Notice (PAN) was issued under the Land Acquisition (Just Terms Compensation)

[51] *Guthega Development Pty Ltd v Minister Administering the National Parks and Wildlife Act 1974* (1986) 7 NSWLR 353.
[52] ibid, 366.
[53] *Prineas v Forestry Commission of New South Wales* (1983) 49 LGRA 402, 417.
[54] ibid, 417.
[55] *Roads and Maritime Services (NSW) v Desane Properties Pty Ltd* (2018) 98 NSWLR 820.

Act 1991 (NSW). Section 15(a) of the Act stated that a PAN 'must be in the form … approved by the Minister'. The PAN in this case departed in some respects from the approved form. On its face, the PAN was invalid. It was suggested that section 80(1) of the Interpretation Act 1987 (NSW) applied. It provides that, if a form is approved under an Act or statutory rule, strict compliance with the form is not necessary but substantial compliance is sufficient. The Court held that section 80(1) applied and that the PAN substantially complied with the approved form.

The reasoning of the Court is illuminating:

> We have concluded that s 80 of the Interpretation Act applies to the PAN in this case. It may be accepted that the word 'must' is used in s 15 of the Just Terms Act. Mandatory language such as that used in s 15, however, does not determine the question. If s 80 of the Interpretation Act only applied in circumstances where permissive language about the use of a form was used in the relevant statute, the circumstances in which it would operate would be few. As the High Court has observed about a similar question … the fact that a requirement is expressed by use of the term 'must' is not conclusive.[56]

Accordingly, whether a word such as 'must' is mandatory or not is interpreted in the context of the totality of the legislation.

The Court was confronted by a similar question in *Satmell*.[57] Clause 26 of the Environmental Planning and Assessment Regulations 2000 asked the question in what form must a contributions plan be prepared. Subclause (1) responded:

> A contributions plan must be prepared having regard to any relevant practice notes adopted for the time being by the Planning Secretary.

The Court noted that the Commissioner had decided that the contributions plan had to be made 'in accordance with' the practice note.[58] It will be recalled that the regulation used the words 'must be prepared having regard to'.

The Court continued:

> The language of 'having regard to' is less prescriptive and less onerous than the language of 'in accordance with'. While there is no question that the Practice Note was a 'relevant practice note' for the purpose of cl 26(1) … and moreover that the Contributions Plans 'must' be prepared in the manner prescribed, cl 26(1) does not mandate compliance with the Practice Note.[59]

This interpretation was confirmed when the Court stated that 'the words "having regard to" did not transmogrify an obligation to take into account the Practice Note into a requirement that its contents be adhered to'.[60]

These cases contain an instructive judicial analysis of the interaction among the four expressions 'must', 'have regard to', 'in accordance with' and 'be adhered to'. The judicial message is clear. Each is subtly different from the others. Perhaps the statutory context is the determining factor in deciding what each expression means and how it is to be applied.

[56] ibid, [227].
[57] *Satmell Holdings Pty Ltd v Blacktown City Council* (2019) 239 LGERA 178.
[58] ibid, [109].
[59] ibid, [109].
[60] ibid, [119].

6. The Integration of Multifunctional Rules in Decision-Making by the Court

6.1. Introduction

The rules governing environmental governance – particularly those in the legislation administered by the Court – reflect the multifaceted nature of the legislation. These rules are themselves multifunctional. Proactive decision-making in the context of merits review requires a polycentric approach. The notion of multiplicity accordingly applies to the legislative outcomes, the statutory rules and the issues demanding a solution. It is ultimately the responsibility of the Court to integrate in its decision-making processes all of these multiple factors.

6.2. Determining Sanctions for Environmental Crime

The approach adopted by the Court in *Walker Corporation*[61] illustrates how proactive decisions are made in the context of sentencing for environmental crime. In effect the Court was guided by the purposes of sentencing stated in the Crimes (Sentencing Procedure) Act 1999 (NSW), the matters required to be considered by the Protection of the Environment Operations Act 1997 (NSW), and the principles of totality and even-handedness. Effectively, an example of teleological reasoning by applying a number of multifunctional rules.

The Court examined in detail a large amount of factual information about, for example, the nature of the offence, harm to the environment, future risk of harm and lack of prior criminality.[62] This was the conclusion:

> I take account of the need to impose a sentence that achieves the purposes of denouncing the conduct of Walker, ensuring that Walker is adequately punished for the offence, making Walker accountable for its actions, recognising the harm done to the environment by commission of the offence and preventing crime by deterring other persons from committing similar offences.[63]

The use of the words 'achieves the purposes' emphasises the teleological nature of the reasoning. This is consistent with the structure, form and language of the legislation. The Court was looking to the future based upon what had happened in the past. The Court in this way solved a polycentric problem by adopting a polycentric approach to proactive decision-making.[64]

[61] *Corbyn v Walker Corporation Pty Ltd* [2011] NSWLEC 119. See Fisher (n 4) 624–25.
[62] *Corbyn v Walker Corporation Pty Ltd* (n 61) 448–54.
[63] ibid, 456.
[64] For similar reasoning, see *Environment Protection Authority* v *Hanna* (2018) 235 LGERA 114, *Environment Protection Authority v Signium Pty Ltd* (2018) 239 LGERA 1 and *Environment Protection Authority v Whitehaven Coal Mining Ltd* (2019) 239 LGERA 31.

6.3. Planning and Ecologically Sustainable Development

The merits review function of the Court is performed when it reviews the decision of a consent authority under the EPA Act. Accordingly, issues related to planning, ecologically sustainable development and environmental protection arise. The company BGP Properties Pty Ltd applied for development consent under the EPA Act to subdivide land for industrial use and storage purposes in an area of environmental sensitivity. It was refused and the merits appeal to the Court was dismissed.[65]

The Court clarified three matters. First, what the Act described as the 'encouragement' of ESD as one of its objects. Second, the requirement to take into consideration the public interest. Third, section 6(2) of the Protection of the Environment Administration Act 1991 (NSW) which stated that ESD can be achieved through the 'implementation' of the principles of ESD:

> By requiring a consent authority (including the court) to have regard to the public interest, [s 79C(1)(e) of the EPA Act] obliges the decision-maker to have regard to the principles of ecologically sustainable development. This will have a consequence that … consideration must be given to matters of intergenerational equity, conservation of biological diversity and ecological integrity. Furthermore, where there is a lack of scientific certainty, the precautionary principle must be utilised.[66]

This brings together in the proactive decision-making process: the public interest; the objects of the Act; ESD; and the principles of ESD. Consideration of the principles, however, did not preclude approval 'where the overall benefits of the project outweigh the likely environmental harm'[67] – essentially, the balancing process intrinsic to solving a polycentric problem.

How the principles of ESD should be 'implemented' was considered in detail by the Court in *Telstra*[68] – a decision under the EPA Act. The issue was whether telecommunications equipment and a base station should be constructed on the roof of a local recreational club. Members of the community were concerned that there would be emissions of 'electronic energy' and that these would harm the health and safety of residents and the environment.[69] These concerns were regarded as subjective perceptions. The claims of the residents were unsubstantiated and without evidentiary foundation. There was no basis on which the Court could refuse the application.

The detail of the reasoning by the Court is instructive. These paragraphs describe the methodology prescribed by the Act:

> It expressly states that one of the objects of the Act is to encourage ecologically sustainable development: s 5(a)(vii). The Act defines ecologically sustainable development as having the same meaning as it has in s 6(2) of the Protection of the Environment Administration Act.

[65] *BGP Properties Pty Ltd v Lake Macquarie City Council* (2004) 138 LGERA 237. See Fisher (n 4) 339–41, 351, 358.

[66] *BGP Properties Pty Ltd v Lake Macquarie City Council* (n 65) 262.

[67] ibid, 262.

[68] *Telstra Corp Ltd v Hornsby Shire Council* (2006) 67 NSWLR 256. See Fisher, *Legal Reasoning in Environmental Law* (n 14) 413–16 and Fisher (n 4) 342, 359–61.

[69] More specifically 'the effect of radiofrequency electromagnetic energy emitted from the proposed base station'.

> Section 79C(1) of the Act, which sets out the relevant matters which a consent authority must take into consideration, does not expressly refer to ecologically sustainable development. Nevertheless, it does require a consent authority to take into account 'the public interest' in s 79C(1)(e). The consideration of the public interest is ample enough, having regard to the subject matter, scope and purpose of the Act, to embrace ecologically sustainable development.
>
> Accordingly, by requiring a consent authority (or on a merits review appeal the Court) to have regard to the public interest, s 79C(1)(e) of the Act obliges the consent authority to have regard to the principles of ecologically sustainable development in cases where issues relevant to those principles arise.[70]

Given the mandatory relevance of these principles, the Court went on to explain in detail six of them. In summary form: sustainable use; effective integration; precaution; intergenerational and intragenerational equity; biological diversity and ecological integrity; and internalisation of environmental costs. What functions do they perform? Certainly, they afford guidance. However, they 'are to be applied when decisions are being made under any legislative enactment or instrument which adopts the principles'.[71] The precautionary principle was relevant in this case, discussed in detail and then 'applied'.

The issue, it will be recalled, was whether the residents would be exposed to 'electronic transmissions' detrimental to their health and safety: more specifically, 'the effect of radiofrequency electromagnetic energy emitted from the proposed base station'.[72] Australian Standard RPS3 set the standard of emission levels of radiofrequency electromagnetic energy. The standard had been set after adopting a precautionary approach. There was, therefore, no reason to apply the precautionary principle in this case. The proposed development could go ahead. Essentially three reasons were decisive: the subjective perceptions of the residents; claims without evidence; and compliance with RPS3.

6.4. Energy-Related Development

The decision of the Court in *Taralga*[73] responded to an application under the EPA Act for the construction of sixty-nine wind turbines and associated infrastructure works on land zoned as general rural. It was a state-significant development and a designated development. An environmental impact statement was required. After the application was granted, a group of local residents appealed to the Court. The contested issues were the aesthetic and cultural impact of wind turbines on a non-industrial community and the desirability of generating less electricity from fossil fuel sources and generating more electricity from renewable sources. The Court expressed it in these words:

> Resolving this conundrum – the conflict between the geographically narrower concerns of the Guardians [the applicants for review] and the broader public good of increasing the

[70] *Telstra Corp Ltd v Hornsby Shire Council* (n 68) 37–38.
[71] ibid, 37.
[72] ibid, 35.
[73] *Taralga Landscape Guardians Inc v Minister for Planning* (2007) 161 LGERA 1. See Fisher (n 14) 416–19 and Fisher (n 4) 347, 638, 667–69.

> supply of renewable energy – has not been easy. However, I have concluded that, on balance, the broader public good must prevail.[74]

The cultural and environmental impacts of the proposal were undoubtedly relevant under the EPA Act. The Act said nothing about greenhouse gas emissions, climate change or renewable energy. How could their relevance be justified? By considering the 'policy framework' within which the Act operated. There were four aspects to this framework: climate change; the energy industry; sustainable development; and renewable energy.[75]

The relevance of climate change was based upon factual circumstances derived from a series of international and national reports. The relevance of the energy industry was justified by its large contribution to greenhouse gas emissions. The principles of ESD were relevant under the Act – in particular the principle of intergenerational equity. The relevance of renewable energy was supported by the initiatives taken by the Commonwealth and by New South Wales: particularly the Renewable Energy (Electricity) Act 2000 (Cth) and the Electricity Supply Act 1995 (NSW). Wind assets emerged as potentially important sources of energy. The Court considered these wider issues together with the cultural and environmental impacts of the proposal and decided to grant development consent subject to conditions to protect the local community.

6.5. Mining-Related Development

A polycentric approach to proactive decision-making, as earlier noted, was canvassed by the Court in *Bulga*.[76] This concerned a major project application under the EPA Act for project approval to extend existing operations at an open-cut coal mine. It would involve: a road closure; clearing an extensive area of habitat of four types of endangered ecological communities; removal of significant landform; and emplacement of overburden at an adjacent mine.

A complex set of environmental, economic and social matters emerged for consideration. The decision-making process would involve four steps: identifying the relevant matters to be considered; fact finding for each relevant matter; determining how much weight to give each relevant matter; and balancing the weighted matters to arrive at a managerial decision.[77]

To some extent, this is a reflection of the obligation imposed on the Court by section 39(4) of the Land and Environment Court Act 1979 (NSW). It is, however, the fourth step that points to a polycentric approach:

> The fourth step requires the weighted matters to be balanced, each against the others. Because all of the matters may not be, or be capable of being, reduced to a common unit of measurement, such as money, balancing of the weighted matters is a qualitative and not a quantitative exercise. The ultimate decision involves an intuitive synthesis of the various matters.[78]

[74] *Taralga Landscape Guardians Inc v Minister for Planning* (n 73) 3.
[75] ibid, 10–13.
[76] *Bulga Milbrodale Progress Association v Minister for Planning and Infrastructure* (2013) 194 LGERA 347. See Fisher (n 4) 366–67, 448–49.
[77] *Bulga Milbrodale Progress Association v Minister for Planning and Infrastructure* (n 76) [36].
[78] ibid, [41].

The Court implied that it would proceed in this way when it set the following order for giving its reasons: the merits review task on appeal; impacts on biological diversity; noise and dust impacts; social impacts; economic issues; the balancing of the factors[79] – essentially, in other words, an application of the principles of ESD. One of the associated issues in this case was distributive justice. This 'involves the just distribution or allocation of the benefits and burdens of economic activity'.[80] Once the Court had deliberated in this way, the 'preferable decision was to disapprove of the carrying out of the Project'.[81]

The Court of Appeal was invited to consider the lawfulness of the decision of the Court.[82] A large number of submissions were presented to the Court of Appeal. Three are relevant: the relevance of a polycentric approach; the function rather than the meaning of 'consider'; and the relationship between the planning and the mining legislation.

It was argued that a polycentric approach, in effect, diverted the Court from performing its statutory functions. This was the first response:

> Although his Honour spent some time expounding upon the theoretical bases for the resolution of a polycentric problem, for the most part he used the concept as a catchphrase to describe the multifaceted nature of the issues that had to be determined.[83]

There was no criticism of the nature of the issues. But the corollary was that:

> His Honour, having identified the decision-making process as involving a polycentric problem, with issues being interdependent, then determined each of the issues relating to offset packages, noise impacts and air quality, in a way that was adverse to the approval of the project prior to undertaking a consideration and weighing of all relevant matters. The consequence, on this submission, was that the question of approval had in effect been determined by these matters without there being a proper balancing of all matters in determining whether it was in the public interest that the Project be approved or not.[84]

In other words, the obligation to consider all relevant matters had been bypassed by deciding what, fundamentally, would be in the public interest. This argument was rejected.

The Court of Appeal then reviewed in detail how this obligation should be implemented in accordance with the extensive range of judicial authority:

> These cases do not state an inflexible legal rule of construction as to the weight to be accorded to all statutory provisions which require a particular matter to be considered or taken into account by a decision-maker. The result in each case was dependent upon the terms of the legislation and the particular circumstances in which the legislation was applied.[85]

Finally, the Court of Appeal examined precisely how the Court had in this case implemented this obligation. As a result, the argument that the Court had failed to consider all relevant matters, to give them appropriate weight and to engage in the necessary balancing process was rejected.

[79] ibid, [23].
[80] ibid, [486].
[81] ibid, [499].
[82] *Warkworth Mining Ltd v Bulga Milbrodale Progress Association Inc* (2014) 86 NSWLR 527.
[83] ibid, [170].
[84] ibid, [174].
[85] ibid, [225].

A significant issue was the relevance of the Mining Act 1992 (NSW). Section 39(4) of the Land and Environment Court Act 1979 (NSW) required the Court to have regard to any relevant Act. It was argued that the Court had failed to have regard to the Mining Act and the mining leases granted under that Act. In addition, according to the relevant planning instruments, mining was permissible with development consent. The Court of Appeal looked at the operative provisions of the Mining Act, noted the objects of the Act and the range of matters to be considered – including environmental matters – and concluded that they 'do not deal with the grant of development consent for mining activities'.[86] The provisions of the planning and the mining legislation overlapped in some respects. The mining legislation was 'directed to the means by which mining may be facilitated and undertaken'.[87] Even if the mining legislation were relevant under section 39(4), a failure to have regard to it would 'not have vitiated the decision'.[88] The appeal was dismissed.[89] Hence, here we have an example of the achievement of multi-faceted objectives by means of proactive decision-making in response to a polycentric problem.

7. Conclusion

The functions of the Court reviewed in this chapter are varied and extensive. While they include adjudication and judicial review, the focus has been the review of the substantive merits of decisions made by the executive branch of government and a determination of the substantive issues raised in the context of the review. The functions of adjudication and judicial review are based upon an analysis of past activities and of decisions already made: reactive decision-making. The determination of a remedy or sanction and the determination of the decision in a merits review relate to what is appropriate for the future: proactive decision-making. Each function is performed in accordance with the complex sets of multifunctional rules that apply to each part of the decision-making process. These rules are variously procedural, methodological or substantive.

The challenge for the Court has been the interpretation and application of these complex rules – particularly in the performance of its merits review function which addresses polycentric problems. The rules – which apply to both judicial review and merits review – state variously the intended outcomes of the decision-making process and the methodological criteria according to which the decision is to be made. The relevant legislation is multifaceted: hence the need for a considered balancing of all the relevant facets in accordance with these multifunctional rules. This requires a totally integrated approach to decision-making: legally, rationally and intellectually. The several reasoning processes are a critical element of this approach to integration.

[86] ibid, [320].
[87] ibid, [322].
[88] ibid, [323].
[89] Similar issues arose for determination by the Court in *Gloucester Resources Ltd v Minister for Planning* (2019) 234 LGERA 257. The Court refused development consent. Its reasoning was very similar to that adopted in the earlier cases. A detailed review of *Gloucester* is undertaken in Chapter 4.

The significance of an integrated approach has been recognised by the international community in the Draft Global Pact for the Environment[90] which states that: 'Parties shall integrate the requirements of environmental protection into the planning and implementation of their policies.'[91] Out of all of these disparate but integrated elements of the system for environmental governance there emerge clues that suggest the method of reasoning required to make the final decision – a combination of syllogistic and teleological reasoning. This has become the rational process engaged in by the Court in performing the function of proactive decision-making in the context of its merits review jurisdiction. This chapter has demonstrated how positively the Court has performed this function over the last four decades.

[90] Available at http://globalpactenvironment.org.
[91] See Art 3.

3

The Place of the Land and Environment Court in the Planning System of New South Wales

LESLIE STEIN

1. Introduction

The planning system of New South Wales has meandered through numerous substantive reforms since the enactment of the Environmental Planning and Assessment Act 1979 (NSW) (the EPA Act). This chapter focuses on how the Land and Environment Court of NSW (the Court) in its planning jurisdiction[1] has found its place in this ever-changing planning regime over the last forty years.

The place that the Court occupies in the planning system of NSW is best understood through an analysis of four factors that take account of its past, its present and its potential future. The first factor is the effect of the original form of the Court as a judicial body with Supreme Court status, distinct from other planning courts and tribunals in Australia. The second is the manner in which the Court conceptualised its own jurisdiction in light of evolving planning theory. The third is how it is presently perceived, as evaluated by its influence and the reputation it has established in planning law in Australia. The fourth factor is the future possibility of the Court stabilising the NSW planning system that has lost its way.

There is a thread that runs through all of these factors: the Court seeking to maximise its potential as a unique experiment in planning law. From the very first judicial appointment to the present, all judges have shown pride in its status as a superior court that has led to a specialist commitment to unravel the nuances of planning law, exhibited by scholarship and the careful reasoning of its decisions. There is no other planning court or tribunal in Australia that has therefore had as much influence on the refinement of the doctrines of this area of the law.

[1] Land and Environment Court Act 1979 (NSW), ss 17 and 20, Class 1 appeals and Class 4 proceedings.

2. The Form of the Court

2.1. Historical Influences

The circumstances of the creation of the Court as a judicial body with Supreme Court status are particularly important to understand its current place in the NSW planning system. The structure was not random but was the result of its formation at a particular, noteworthy time in the history of planning. The Court became operational in 1980 during an intense period of neoliberalism that had commenced in the 1970s through the New South Wales government's orientation to the imperative of economic growth. Neoliberalism is perhaps best defined as an ideology that wealth creation through growth is the primary task of government, to be carried out by policies that prioritise economic development by means of reducing barriers to that growth. It is not a specific platform that is articulated in legislation or policy but rather is an ideology that became particularly identified with the policies of Thatcher and Reagan. The emphasis of this ideology, as it applies to planning in Australia,[2] has been to focus the planning regime on promoting land development as the highest priority, as it is the basis of economic growth. This is to be implemented by reducing regulations and therefore delays in the planning approval process that stand in the way of rapid development.

It should not be underestimated how neoliberal ideas changed the planning culture through the 1970s. As an example, at the start of that period, before neoliberalism took hold as the prevalent ideology, the Land Development Contribution Act 1970 (NSW) was symbolic of a clear social welfare statement that the profits of development belonged in part to the state and a percentage was therefore to be captured by a levy. This betterment charge, as it was called, was repealed in 1973, ostensibly because it was unpopular,[3] but also because many aspects of a social welfare orientation were inimical to rapid economic growth. The Australia of the early 1970s – a complex mix of anti-Vietnam war sentiments and Fabian social democracy – was rapidly influenced by neoliberal ideas of national economic growth and reducing the impediments to development.[4] Justice Else-Mitchell, who had just retired as a Judge of the Land and Valuation Court, noted in 1975 the shift at that time from the historic sovereignty of private property rights, evidenced by full compensation for compulsory acquisition, to the emerging idea of economic progress that required a weakening of legal constraints in order to advance development.[5]

If a more specific marker of this change of prioritising economic growth above other concerns in planning is needed, it is the introduction of development corporations as governance bodies under the Growth Centres (Development Corporations) Act 1974 (NSW). The Development Corporations were based upon the neoliberal idea of using a business efficiency governance model to be able to accelerate growth. This idea of a

[2] T Sager, 'Neo-liberal Urban Planning Policies: A Literature Survey 1990–2010' (2011) 76 *Progress in Planning* 147.

[3] N Gurran, *Australian Urban Land Use Planning: Principles, Systems and Practice*, 2nd edn (Sydney, Sydney University Press, 2011) 64.

[4] J Jupp, *Party Politics: Australia 1966–1981* (London, Allen & Unwin, 1982).

[5] R Else-Mitchell, 'Legal Constraints in Planning' (1975) 13 *Royal Australian Planning Institute Journal* 22.

neoliberal, entrepreneurial governance model for land use issues was taken up in NSW because it dovetailed squarely with the idea that distinct growth centres are the primary form for the zoning and development of Greater Sydney. The core of all New South Wales planning has followed this form of prioritising the economic growth of centres, such as the County of Cumberland Plan in 1951, the Sydney Region Outline Plan of 1968, the 1988 Metropolitan Strategy ('Sydney into Its Third Century') and the 'City of Cities 2005' Metropolitan Strategy. The clear orientation of these and subsequent strategies has been to service nominated growth centres in the Greater Sydney metropolitan area so they become economically viable.

The early adjudicative response to the economic imperative to encourage the growth and development of centres, as well as reducing barriers, was to replace planning appeals to the Land and Valuation Court with appeals to the Local Government Appeals Tribunal. This Tribunal, established in 1971, was created for the purpose of speeding up development approvals for private developers by rejecting a legal model, reducing legal representation and instead using lay members – thereby encouraging less formality and quicker decisions. The judicial model had been, up until that time, the Land and Valuation Court, and the argument for the creation of the Tribunal to replace the Court was that formal judicial proceedings were a barrier to economic growth. This idea was strongly rejected during the Second Reading Speech for the creation of the Tribunal by Neville Wran,[6] who stressed the necessity of precedent and judicial decision-making in the planning process. His sound argument was rejected primarily because the system had become slow and cumbersome, as the Land and Valuation Court, which dealt with less than 5 per cent of planning appeals, was part of a confused appeals system that included the State Planning Authority and other bodies where decisions were inconsistent.[7] Over other considerable objection to the loss of judicial input, the Bill was passed, and the Appeals Tribunal started to function, to be finally repealed by the EPA Act.

In the 1970s, the substantive changes to planning thus focused primarily on creating economic growth. In introducing the Environmental Planning and Assessment Bill and the related Land and Environment Court Bill in April 1979, it was stated in the Legislative Assembly that '[the Bills] will indicate clearly the importance that the Government places on planning, fostering and encouragement of economic developments in the interests of the community'.[8] A key aspect of the Bills, in line with efficient economic development, was to 'wind down inevitable delays that have occurred to date'[9] by creating an efficient court that would relieve the 'costly appeals which must at the present time go before the Local Government Appeal Tribunal',[10] as well as bringing together disparate planning appeal jurisdictions of the Land and Valuation Court, the Valuation Boards of Review, and the Supreme Court and District Court.

The need for regulatory efficiency to encourage economic growth was served by combining jurisdictions, thereby reducing confusion and delay, along with the realisation that efficiency through consistent decision-making can be advanced by the

[6] Hansard, *NSW Parliamentary Debates*, Legislative Council, 2 December 1971, 3719.
[7] ibid, 3724 (Mr Vickery).
[8] Hansard, *NSW Parliamentary Debates*, Legislative Assembly, 17 April 1979, 4278 (Mr Rogan).
[9] ibid, 4286 (Mr Hatton).
[10] ibid, 4280 (Mr Rogan).

application of the rule of law. This idea appears critical to the forces behind the creation of the Court. Another significant reason for the foundation of the Court was consistency with the early evolution of concerns for the environment in NSW.[11] However, in terms of planning law, the role of the Court in undertaking merits reviews was specifically required to provide reliability and efficiency in order to promote economic growth through a 'one-stop shop'. This was to be accomplished by efficient procedures, following precedent established in judicial review proceedings, providing an orientation to common issues in merit appeals, and producing well-reasoned determinations. Accordingly, the Court's very creation depended on it expediting economic growth that had been hindered by the failure of the Tribunal to provide any certainty to the process, as explained clearly upon the introduction of the Land and Environment Court Bill into Parliament:

> Possibly the greatest criticism that could be levelled at the tribunal is that it was not bound by precedent but that each application that came before it was to be judged on its merits. Of course, results depended on which particular panel dealt with the application. There was no certainty as to what the result would be. Consequently, councils could never be sure how applications before them would be dealt with when such applications eventually came before the Local Government Appeals Tribunal. With the setting up of the Land and Environment Court the element of speculation, which has been so much the subject of decisions of the Local Government Appeals Tribunal, will be eliminated and, it is hoped, we shall once more achieve a degree of certainty in this important aspect of local government.[12]

This need for efficiency in the planning system and reliability in decision-making is an explicit, originating purpose of the Court's role in planning law that came of age in the late 1970s because of the neoliberal paradigm requiring a reduction of barriers to encourage economic growth. This overwhelming need for a sense of authoritative certainty – for a superior court – was particularly necessary in Greater Sydney as the planning regime for the growth centres was confusing and uncertain. This was primarily because the choice of which growth centre to activate and in what order was not explicitly addressed by legislation, but only through ever-changing state planning policies coming from a siloed Department of Planning. In addition, the planning for these growth centres was to be carried out by councils that were subject to corruption, as the councils were placed under intense pressure by developers to have their land chosen for profitable development. The idea of a superior court offering certainty in planning is grounded in legal theory,[13] as the most important aspect of regulatory efficiency is uniform and consistent standards or principles, because decisions based on the rule of law are critical to certainty in the marketplace.

This idea that a confusing planning system and lack of certainty promoted the use of a superior court is best understood by a comparison with Melbourne, which employed a tribunal for merit appeals rather than a court. Melbourne's population growth and the pressure for development of greenfield sites for housing was considerably less than

[11] M Pearlman, 'The Land and Environment Court of New South Wales: A Model for Environmental Protection' (2000) 123 *Water, Air, Soil Pollution* 395.

[12] Hansard, *NSW Parliamentary Debates*, Legislative Assembly, Mr Wilde, 17 April 1979, 4282–83.

[13] H Latin, 'Ideal versus Real Regulatory Efficiency: Implementation of Uniform Standards and "Fine-tuning" Regulatory Reforms' (1985) 37 *Stanford Law Review* 1267.

that of Sydney throughout the 1970s.[14] More importantly, Melbourne, by the 'Planning Policies for the Melbourne Metropolitan Region 1971', did not rely on growth centres. The emphasis in Melbourne was instead on linear, corridor growth between green wedges and development confined within existing urban zones in a more organised statutory and strategic planning system. The need for certainty in Melbourne was delivered by the planning system itself and the need for a court was not therefore as immediate as in Sydney, where the planning system was unclear and the push for economic development opportunities in dispersed growth centres was much greater.

Even though the pressing need for certainty through judicial reasoning, the bedrock of the rule of law, was the *spiritus rector* behind the creation of the Court, the confusing planning system did not necessarily require a superior court. Other jurisdictions chose a tribunal that was chaired by a lawyer, such as the Town Planning Appeals Tribunal of Victoria, which began hearing appeals in 1969, and the Town Planning Appeal Tribunal of Western Australia, which started with a Town Planning Court in 1970. Where there has been a need for judicial officers for a merits review body, they could be appointed at District Court level, such as the New Zealand Environment Court and the Queensland Planning and Environment Court. At its inception, the NSW Court was unique in having judges of Supreme Court status dealing with merit appeals from the refusal or delay of development permission as well as judicial review proceedings. This was not a foregone conclusion as the Law Reform Commission had, in fact, recommended the Land and Valuation Court be abolished and the jurisdiction transferred to the District Court.[15]

2.2. The Need for Supreme Court Status

The idea of using a specialist court with Supreme Court status to hear planning merit appeals, as well as judicial review proceedings, was a novelty internationally in 1980. The underlying concerns that could have led to an argument against this arrangement were several: the introduction of a formal Supreme Court process implied cost, it would lead to a legalistic approach to what are essentially policy decisions, it would be removed from the real-world realities of planning, and it would create an intimidating environment for relatively minor issues.

The use of a superior court in NSW to decide land disputes was already a convenient and familiar idea when the status of the NSW Court was considered, as there had been a Land Court whose determinations were given the force of a Supreme Court decision under the Crown Lands Act 1889 (NSW) in relation to the distribution of Crown land. That approach of using a superior court was maintained for Crown land when it was renamed to the Land Appeal Court in 1913,[16] and it then became the Land and Valuation Court in 1921. The continuity of Supreme Court status for merits appeals added to the jurisdiction for judicial review, was a natural consequence for the NSW Court.

[14] Australian Historical Population Statistics (cat no 3105.0.65.001).
[15] NSW Law Reform Commission, *Land and Valuation Court* (Report 23, 1975).
[16] Its history is discussed in R Else-Mitchell, 'Mr Justice Roper and the Land Jurisdiction' (1996) 70 *Australian Law Journal* 902.

At its inception, the case for the Court as a specialist, superior court must have caused concern for the development industry because the judges of the Land and Valuation Court had been clearly tentative as to their role as decision-makers in merit appeals. This hesitation was apparent in two instances: the explicit support of judges for local government decisions, and a reluctance to enter planning policy issues. The Court's proclivity to support a council's views on planning issues was confusing for the planning system as it promoted the idea that, in an appeal, the council's view that was the catalyst for the appeal had the greatest weight: 'The Court has no jurisdiction to sit in judgment upon those town-planning decisions. Its task is to have regard to them in deciding an appeal.'[17] In terms of avoiding planning policy determinations, the decision in *Pitt-Mullis v Sydney City Council*[18] is typical. Hardie J, in the Land and Valuation Court, refused to accept the submission of the Council that the negative effect on young customers of attending a nightclub on William Street should be considered a relevant consideration. He suggested that this was a policy question that should be referred to a specialist body.

A specialist court had greater potential to makes its own merit and policy decisions, An emphasis on the status of Supreme Court judges being available to sit on merits appeals as well as deciding applications for judicial review, so that the NSW Court could develop unique, specialist expertise in planning matters, was very much in the mind of the legislators. The idea was therefore rejected that the Court become merely a division of the Supreme Court, as suggested by the New South Wales Bar Association on the basis that if it was randomly staffed by any Supreme Court judge, it could not claim that expertise. As well, the idea was also raised and rejected that the Court should only deal with merit reviews, leaving judicial review to the Supreme Court.

Obtaining both judicial review and merits appeals jurisdiction therefore made it incumbent upon the Court from its inception to stake out its jurisdiction in judicial review cases, as well as to firmly establish the position it was to take on merit reviews. Although its judicial review jurisdiction followed naturally from its Supreme Court status, there are early decisions of the Court that signal how it would now approach its jurisdiction as a separate, specialist court carrying out merit reviews, and not merely a lesser form of Supreme Court, as perhaps the Land and Valuation Court was considered. As one example, in *Trazlo Pty Ltd v Waverley Municipal Council*,[19] three months after his appointment, Cripps J, a foundation judge of the Court, later appointed as Chief Judge and then to the NSW Court of Appeal, created an independent voice for the Court. The appellant sought a merits review from the refusal of development consent under an Interim Development Order to carry out the use of a 'video amusement centre' in Bondi Junction. The Council opposed the use because of a fear that it would attract 'undesirable elements'. Cripps J stated that he rejected the assumption of the Council: 'The Council has undertaken no study of the matter and the anecdotal evidence presented does not greatly assist me in the resolution of the problem.'[20] This differed significantly

[17] *Skerrett v Blacktown Shire Council* (1959) 5 LGRA 72, 77.
[18] *Pitt-Mullis v Sydney City Council* (1964) 10 LGRA 242.
[19] *Trazlo Pty Ltd v Waverley Municipal Council* (1980) 41 LGRA 429.
[20] ibid, 433.

from the Land and Valuation Court approach of deferring to the local knowledge and town planning expertise of the local council.

While only one example, it quickly set a markedly different tone to that of the Land and Valuation Court. The historical development that led to the Court having judges of Supreme Court status impelled the impression that the place of the Court in the planning system was to undertake an authoritative, substantive, and specialist role in establishing certainty of approach, without any of the equivocation of the Land and Valuation Court or the inconsistency of the Tribunal. Although not made explicit, it defined the approach of the Court from its inception and conferred on it a purpose, pride, and a boldness to make clear the legal basis upon which decisions are made. This is the context in which the Court is to be understood and the leitmotiv behind the certainty it brings to the legal structure of planning in NSW.

3. Conceptualising its Jurisdiction

Planning theory is constantly evolving, seeking ways to accommodate different interests and theories, as well as changing social and economic circumstances. This theory is not brought to the attention of the Court unless it is presented in the circumstances of a case, which has not often occurred. The Court is unable to conduct its own research to understand the current importance of a planning initiative and its consistency with theory, such as the emphasis on quality-of-life considerations that are now viewed as critical in contemporary planning theory. There are no other means by which the Court is informed about current strategic planning directions or planning theory unless they are reduced to Environmental Planning Instruments. The consequence is that decisions of the Court are not explicitly oriented to current urban theories, no matter how important they have become. The Court has the imperative to devise the scope of planning considerations it will take into account based on statutory interpretation of the provisions of the Act and Regulations. However, these provisions may fail to breathe life into what are the important relevant considerations in theory and in practice. In commenting on the statutory consideration of 'public interest', Cripps CJ, the Chief Judge of the Court in 1991,[21] explained:

> Judges of the Land and Environment Court are mandated by Parliament to have regard to the 'public interest' although it won't tell us what that interest is. The direction is part of the same legislative whimsy which directs us to inform ourselves on all relevant aspects of development and denies us any budgetary allocation to pursue our enquiries … the focus of its work is directed toward what might be loosely called 'public interest' considerations.

As an example of this problem, the Greater Sydney Region Plan (GSRP) of 2018, 'A Metropolis of Three Cities', the overarching strategic planning document for Greater Sydney, introduces the concept of 'liveability', a key element to address social concerns

[21] Mr Justice JS Cripps, 'Environment; Courting the Public Interest' (1991) 2 *Polemic* 40.

arising from growth. This concept is at the very core of contemporary urban planning theory. The definition of 'liveability' can be expressed as:[22]

> Community livability is constructed by the sum of the physical and social characteristics experienced in places – including the natural environment and a walkable and mixed-use built environment, economic potential near diverse housing options, and access to a broad range of services, facilities, and amenities – that add up to a community's quality of life.

The essence of liveability in urban planning theory is that every development must address these issues on an equal footing to economic growth and sustainability. The current ideal of quality-of-life considerations is that social interactions will foster a network within a community, leading to a sense of well-being. The idea is related to the formation of 'social capital': the concept that only when a community has cohesion and there are meaningful interactions between its members, can the goals of planning be fulfilled.[23] This social level is not an afterthought or tentative idea, but is now an essential platform of contemporary planning theory.[24]

The range of considerations the Court takes into account in deciding a merits appeal could therefore become inconsistent with the manner in which aspects of planning, such as liveability, are conceptualised by non-statutory policies of the state or may be at odds with contemporary planning theory. This, however, has not been the case because the Court has provided a liberal interpretation of the relevant considerations it is bound by under the EPA Act. This has effectively closed the gap between adjudication and planning theory by concentrating on the rational planning outcome and not the limitation of the words of the Act. This is well illustrated in respect of the Court's treatment of 'social' and 'public interest' considerations under the Act. How this has occurred is reflective of the manner in which the Court orients itself in a changing planning environment and conceptualises its jurisdiction.

The treatment of social considerations in the EPA Act has a general and specific dimension. The current, general objects of the Act (section 1.3(a)) include 'to promote the social and economic welfare of the community'. In evaluating an application for development permission, a consent authority, more specifically, must consider 'social and economic impacts in the locality' (section 4.15(1)(b)). The EPA Act is only providing general words that lack specificity as to the relevant matters that can be taken into account by a consent authority, under the umbrella of 'social and economic' considerations. The problem this leaves is then determining under what circumstances these considerations are applicable – a problem well expressed in a decision of the Victorian Planning Appeals Tribunal, which stated that 'the Act did not assist in determining what circumstances would justify a responsible authority or the Tribunal considering the social and economic effects of the proposal'.[25]

[22] M Gough, 'Reconciling Livability and Sustainability: Conceptual and Practical Implications for Planning' (2015) 25 *Journal of Planning Education and Research* 145, 147.

[23] C Osborne, C Baldwin and D Thomsen, 'Contributions of Social Capital to Best Practice Urban Outcomes' (2016) 34 *Urban Policy and Research* 212.

[24] K Lloyd, S Fullagar and S Reid, 'Where Is the "Social" in Constructions of "Liveability"? Exploring Community, Social Interaction and Social Cohesion in Changing Urban Environments' (2016) 34 *Urban Policy and Research* 343.

[25] *Shaw & Ors v St Kilda SC & Mandalay Gardens Pty Ltd* (1988) 2 AATR 102, citing *Venus Pty Ltd & Ors v City of South Melbourne & Ors* [1988] 1 AATR 2.

Historically, the Land and Valuation Court struggled with defining the range of relevant considerations to be taken into account in a merits appeal. It grounded relevancy on a distinction between 'town planning considerations' and other, general social or economic considerations, thus negating quality-of-life issues. This limitation was in line, at that time, with a narrow view of the nature of planning as concerned with the efficient layout of streets, roads, housing and compatible land uses, with little attention to social issues and economic productivity.

At the time of the commencement of the Court, there was a developing shift in planning theory that viewed the urban environment as including social welfare. Although this sentiment had not yet been specifically named in and incorporated into the planning strategies in Australia, the reason for its inclusion in the EPA Act appears in the parliamentary debates:

> In the past, due to lack of consideration of social and economic effects many inequities have occurred. Through the operation of such plans as the Sydney Region Outline Plan social inequities have occurred because of lack of appreciation of the effect of plans on people.[26]

The initial reception of the new relevant considerations of social and economic impacts, then in section 90(1)(d) of the EPA Act, by the Court's Chief Judge McClelland in *Bauer Holdings Pty Ltd v Sydney City Council*, was not enthusiastic:

> However, the fact that the words of s 90(1)(d) are novel in planning legislation gives them no greater weight than the other words in the section. The social and economic effect of a development in a locality is only one of a long list of matters which the court is directed by the legislature to take into consideration in determining a development application. … I do not read the words of s 90(1)(d) to mean that, if an adverse social and/or economic effect on certain people living in a locality can be demonstrated to be the likely result of a proposed development, that conclusion per se is fatal to the grant of consent to such a development. The result postulated might be outweighed by other considerations of which the court is directed to take account.[27]

There was no acceptance, at least in 1981 in NSW, that social and economic considerations, as they are now understood, were to be considered relevant considerations at the very core of planning. This was exacerbated by the lack of clarity among local governments as to what were the social concerns that were relevant in a decision relating to the use and development of land. There was no essential urban planning theory or practice at that time revealed in international literature or that could be found in the planning documents of this period that supported the idea that planning did have an impact on the social fabric of a community. In *Lirimo Pty Ltd v Sydney City Council*,[28] Cripps J accordingly considered evidence of social and economic effects too vague and irrelevant in a case that was to be determined on the law as it was before the EPA Act.

The manner in which the jurisdiction of the Court evolved thereafter on this issue did not immediately recognise the importance of social considerations, most likely because the ideas continued to remain vague. For example, in *Meriton Apartments Pty*

[26] Hansard, *NSW Parliamentary Debates*, Legislative Assembly, 21 November 1979, 3379.
[27] *Bauer Holdings Pty Ltd v Sydney City Council* (1981) 48 LGRA 356, 365.
[28] *Lirimo Pty Ltd v Sydney City Council* (1981) 66 LGRA 47.

Ltd v Minister for Urban Affairs and Planning,[29] the Local Environmental Plan (LEP) for the relevant area, Green Square, contained a provision supporting affordable housing and that there should be 'diversity' in housing, defined as:

> This applies to the development of a mix of land uses, a range of building types, diverse public spaces, and employment and housing choices, which will support a socially diverse community, underpinning a vibrant city that offers complex experiences and social contact.

The affordable housing requirements of the LEP were challenged by the applicant on the basis that the EPA Act, which mentioned social welfare as an object, did not authorise such a provision. Cowdroy J agreed and, in finding it invalid, stated:

> The reference in s 5(a)(i) of the Act to the promotion of 'the social and economic welfare of the community' is not in itself an object of the Act. Rather it is the desired consequence intended to result from the development with which the objects of such Act are concerned. Such words relate to the betterment of the community as a whole which is to flow from the sound development and planning required by the Act. No particular class of the community is identified for special benefit, nor is it an object of the Act to create a 'social mix' (cl 2.1 of the DCP) within any sections of the community.[30]

He concluded that the Legislative Debates in 1979 that led to the inclusion of social and economic welfare in the Act were directed to the reform of town planning more generally and 'not to the provision of welfare for the community'.[31]

It is understandable why this lack of attention to matters of social welfare occurred through a narrow reading of the provisions of the Act: the width and breadth of social considerations appear to fall outside what traditionally are town planning matters. Social considerations could potentially go too far, such as the mental health of members of the community, the way in which residents interact, the proximity of the elderly to health services or even the income mix of a community. However, ignoring these considerations denies that there should be an emphasis on quality-of-life issues. The vagueness of the content of social considerations, given the planning theory, must still be given a place in the decisions of the Court, and this required a bold and liberal interpretation of this relevant consideration.

This wider inclusion of social considerations by the Court occurred by three related factors: the inventiveness of the judiciary, the scope of the 'public interest' consideration under the EPA Act and the wide interpretation given to the principles of ecologically sustainable development. An example can be found in the decision of Preston CJ in *Gloucester Resources v Minister for Planning*.[32] The case dealt with an open-cut mine and is better known for the relevance of the downstream consequences of greenhouse gas emissions. As the proposal had environmental consequences, an Environmental Impact Statement (EIS) was required under the EPA Act and the Environmental Planning and Assessment Regulation 2000 (NSW) (the EPA Regulation). Section 4.15(1)(b) of the EPA Act required consideration of the 'social and economic impacts in the locality'

[29] *Meriton Apartments Pty Ltd v Minister for Urban Affairs and Planning* (2000) 107 LGERA 263.
[30] ibid, [33].
[31] ibid, [36]; subsequent amendments to the EPA Act (Division 7.2) provided a more fulsome consideration of matter relating to affordable housing.
[32] *Gloucester Resources v Minister for Planning* (2019) 234 LGRA 257.

and clause 7(1)(f) of Schedule 2 to the EPA Regulation required the EIS to include reasons justifying the carrying out of the development in the manner proposed, having regard to, among other things, 'economic and social considerations'. A 'Social Impact Assessment' was produced to satisfy this requirement of the EPA Regulation and the impact considerations under section 4.15(1) of the EPA Act. It was found by the Chief Judge that the project would create significant social issues because of its visual impact, the effect on the community's way of life, reduced access to infrastructure and services, issues of health and well-being, as well as fears and lost aspirations. This was not the first such case and social considerations, as in this case, have also been examined in prior decisions of the Chief Judge[33] on the basis of the social impact on the existing community that resulted in an alignment with planning theory.

The manner in which the Court has broadened its approach has closed the gap with planning theory in relation to the social impact of a proposed development. The issue of social capital has not, however, arisen for consideration and there is no reason why it cannot be included in the determination of the merits of a development by section 4.15(1)(d) in the future as a matter of the 'public interest'. Through the wide scope of public interest, the Court can enter the same room to consider all aspects of social considerations including social capital and interactions, but by a different door.

This is possible because from the very beginning of the operation of the Court, the relevant consideration of 'public interest' received immediate attention and has been most useful in providing a wide jurisdiction in merit appeals. In a decision three months after the Court commenced hearing appeals, Chief Judge McClelland, in *McDonald Industries Ltd v Sydney City Council*,[34] was reviewing a decision that refused development consent for a residential flat building in Darlinghurst, then described by a witness as 'one of the artistic and social cradles of Australia'.[35] His Honour considered that this was 'one of the best endowed building sites' in a deteriorated area: 'Not to put too fine a point on it, a lot of the area has run to seed.'[36] He stated: 'It is important, in my view, not to construe "the public interest" in the narrow sense of the interest of the public of Darlinghurst even though their interest must, of course, be considered.'[37] His decision turned on social considerations:

> It is unquestionably in the public interest that this outstanding site be developed as soon as possible. … But in an era when it is the general policy of municipal authorities to foster and encourage the 'repeopling' of inner city areas, it is contrary to the public interest that the outstanding opportunity afforded by this site to contribute to the achievement of this aim be wasted.[38]

The concept of 'public interest' has, in fact, been expanded to include all relevant planning considerations. Mason P in *Tower Holdings Pty Ltd v Sutherland Shire Council*[39] explained that the court could use this consideration to go beyond the matters specified

[33] *Bulga Milbrodale Progress Association Inc v Minister for Planning and Infrastructure and Warkworth Mining Ltd* (2013) 194 LGERA 347.
[34] *McDonald Industries Ltd v Sydney City Council* (1980) 43 LGRA 428.
[35] ibid, 433.
[36] ibid, 411.
[37] ibid, 411.
[38] ibid, 440.
[39] *Tower Holdings Pty Ltd v Sutherland Shire Council* (2003) 129 LGERA 195.

in an environmental planning instrument, such as an LEP, to determine the public interest. Most significantly for the range of considerations is also the critical addition of 'ecologically sustainable development' (ESD) to section 6(2) of the EPA Act in 2005. It was stated by Hodgson JA in *Minister for Planning v Walker*[40] that, as the Act includes ESD, the Court must consider these principles where they arise.

Sustainability, one of the pillars of ESD, has become the umbrella under which all aspects of planning and the environment can shelter, as it is a balancing of social as well as economic and environmental considerations. One commentator[41] suggests that the three be replaced by 'quality of life' and 'sustainable livelihoods' as these are, in essence, the real bases of sustainability. In this way, the extent of relevant social considerations and their use in the planning process to implement social goals is wide and consistent with contemporary planning theory.

The open door suggested by sustainability offers the Court an opportunity to examine not only any aspect of productivity in economic or environmental terms, but all aspects of what makes an area liveable, including social concerns and social capital. This arises because the scope of ESD by section 6(2) of the EPA Act includes not only balancing economic considerations with environmental issues, but it also includes the precautionary principle that encompasses intergenerational equity to ensure health, diversity and productivity for future generations.

Carstens v Pittwater Council[42] suggests the approach that the Court is going to take in the future, as it was decided that the range of relevant considerations are to be interpreted liberally and not confined to the list in the EPA Act. Instead, the considerations in section 4.15 must relate to the broad objects of the Act (section 1.3) that include the promotion of the social and economic welfare of the community. The result is that a consent authority and the Court on a merits review can take into account matters of planning beyond the mandatory relevant considerations provided they are not irrelevant considerations. This makes the range of relevant considerations consistent with the orientation of planning theory towards creating better communities, having regard to all aspects of ESD and the broad objects of the EPA Act.

The conclusion can be drawn that the Court has conceptualised its jurisdiction in a manner that has not confined its potential, such that it can approach any relevant concept that is germane to an appeal by reliance on ESD and the objects of the EPA Act. In this sense, it has conceptualised its jurisdiction as wide and able to align with planning policy. This incorporation of relevant planning theory has been achieved by the inventiveness and expertise of the judiciary, the manner in which it continues to conceptualise its jurisdiction and the position taken by the Court to be clear about the ESD principles under the Act.

[40] *Minister for Planning v Walker* (2008) 161 LGERA 423, [42]–[43]. See also *Telstra Corporation Pty Ltd v Hornsby Shire Council* (2006) 146 LGERA 10, [121]–[124]; and B Preston, 'The Judicial Development of Ecologically Sustainable Development' in D Fisher (ed), *Research Handbook on Fundamental Concepts of Environmental Law* (Cheltenham, Edward Elgar, 2016).

[41] E Miller, 'Economization and Beyond: (Re)composing Livelihoods in Maine, USA' (2014) 46 *Environment and Planning A* 2735.

[42] *Carstens v Pittwater Council* (1999) 111 LGERA 1, [20]–[25].

4. Influence of the Court

The influence of the Court cannot be fully understood solely as a planning merit appeal court or even a judicial review forum for planning law issues. This is because it has achieved most attention as a significant court in Australia and internationally in relation to the development of environmental law. In terms only of planning law, it is useful to turn to the objective criteria of the citation metrics and statistics analysis in the AustLII Database[43] that indicate that decisions of the Court are indeed cited very frequently in other jurisdictions in Australia. The decisions are used in providing guidance to other courts and tribunals in relation to complex planning issues that arise on merit appeals, such as the relevance of view sheds, how to approach design excellence and the weight to be given to non-statutory policy.

It is clear that when the planning decisions of the Court are cited in other Australian jurisdictions, it is because the Court's refinements of relevant considerations and legal reasoning are taken as the authoritative voice of a superior court. There are many examples in all states. In *Robertson and City of Albany*,[44] for example, the State Administrative Tribunal of Western Australia referred to the Court's decision in *Telstra Corporation*[45] on the extent of ESD as 'seminal'. This tendency to rely on the reasoning of the Court as highly persuasive is common, as in the Resource Management and Planning Appeal Tribunal of Tasmania in *R Brown and T Shaw v Launceston City Council and Bullock Consulting*,[46] where the Tribunal's interpretation of the term 'consistent with' in a planning appeal relied on the reasoning of the Court. The Tribunal noted 'We respectfully agree with, and adopt, the Court's observations' which can be found in planning cases in South Australia.[47] Not all decisions of the Court are followed when it has been found that the planning law in other jurisdictions differs: 'If the New South Wales cases, however correct they may be in relation to New South Wales planning law and practice, are advanced to me as persuasive of Victorian planning law, I remain unpersuaded.'[48]

The greatest influence of the Court in planning matters has been by clarifying the law through judicial review and merits appeals for lawyers and planners, but not necessarily for the public. The NSW planning system is a maze that only an expert can navigate, and it is a rare lay person who will understand the interaction of multiple planning bodies. This makes the 'Planning Principles' created by the Court Commissioners in 2003 of great importance and more generally useful. A former Chief Judge, McClellan CJ, explained: 'I have no doubt this will assist in the application by those bodies of appropriate principles to the decisions which they must make.'[49] The Principles set out the relevant cases of the Court on basic issues of planning, such as the degree of access to sunlight and the use of landscaping to protect privacy. The Court has used this general

[43] http://classic.austlii.edu.au/austlii/metstats/au/cases/nsw/NSWLEC/2018/12/ (last accessed 16 February 2020.

[44] *Robertson and City of Albany* [2019] WASAT 3, [175].

[45] *Telstra Corporation* (n 40).

[46] *R Brown and T Shaw v Launceston City Council and Bullock Consulting* [2014] TASRMPAT 15.

[47] For example, *St Ann's College Inc v The Corporation of the City of Adelaide* [2019] SAERDC 20, [128].

[48] *NBH Business Park Ltd v Whittlesea CC and Ors (No 2)* [2012] VCAT 968, [144].

[49] Cited in P Williams, 'The Land and Environment Court's Planning Principles: Relationship with Planning Theory and Practice' (2005) 22 *Environmental and Planning Law Journal* 401.

concept of Planning Principles to explain earlier significant decisions on merits review, such as the weight to be given to non-statutory Development Control Plans or how views should be shared. Together the Principles created by the Commissioners and expanded on by the Court create certainty for the public on merits appeals. McClellan CJ, on being sworn in, stated about the Court that: 'Its continuing legacy rests on the consistency of decision-making in accordance with recognised principles.'[50]

The influence of the Court is based, as well, on other factors that are more amorphous but provide a sense of how the court is perceived. One particular factor is the fact that the judges have contributed to the academic analysis of environmental law. Each Chief Judge has written scholarly works that go beyond that normally seen by judges sitting in the Supreme Court. This has been a pattern from the time of the appointment of the first Chief Judge and is a practice not echoed to this extent in other planning tribunals or courts in Australia. The Chief Judge of the Court has emphasised that the specialist knowledge and competency of judges includes their continuing professional education.[51] This both adds a level of respect from the profession and an understanding by practitioners and the public that these issues are constantly being scrutinised and refined.

5. Stabilising the Planning System

The introduction of 'strategic planning' into NSW has destabilised the planning system and now needs the Court to make it functional. This is an excellent illustration of the place of the Court in the NSW planning system and its likely future.

In 2017, the EPA Act was amended to add the new Division 'Strategic Planning' (now Division 3.1). This followed the Greater Sydney Commission Act 2015 (NSW), where the Greater Sydney Commission (GSC) was established and charged with strategic planning for the Greater Sydney Region. In 2017, by agreement with the Minister, the GSC undertook to prepare the Greater Sydney Region Plan (GSRP) and District Plans. This was the start of strategic planning in NSW and the beginning of a new dimension in planning.

The concept of strategic planning is that the vision of the state as to how development should progress is to be echoed in all planning documents, especially the Local Environmental Plan (LEP). The critical idea is that there is to be a line of sight from the LEP back to the District Plan and up to the GSRP so the nature of a zone or the designation of use classes and discretionary uses can be understood. As they are 'strategic', all plans (except for the LEP) are highly aspirational and contain broad goals as to what is to be achieved. The GSRP has thirty-eight broad objectives that seek to dictate the direction of land-use planning for four decades. The GSRP divides the region into three districts, and each has its own aspirational District Plans listing many priorities that follow the objectives of the GSRP.

[50] CJ McClellan, 'Swearing in of Justice Peter McClellan as Chief Judge of the Land and Environment Court' (25 August 2003) 10.

[51] B Preston, 'Characteristics of Successful Environmental Courts and Tribunals' (2014) 26 *Journal of Environmental Law* 365.

Each local government is required by the EPA Act (section 3.9) to prepare a Local Strategic Planning Statement (LSPS) in line with the GSRP and District plans. Each LSPS is also highly aspirational and verbose; for example, the City of Parramatta LSPS is eighty-seven pages long. These verbose and aspirational plans, directed to the planning of the local government for a twenty-year period, are to finally result in an LEP that will zone land and allocate uses. The idea is that the GSRP aspirations and District and local visions will somehow create the reasons for the zoning and land uses in the LEP.

The significant problem, perhaps unforeseen, is that the GSC has not provided any guidelines of how the broad LSPS will be converted to a legal LEP: a major failing. The GSC has thereby destabilised the planning system. This is a particular problem for NSW because in other places strategies are usually published with the legal controls so there are no doubts about how a particular zoning or discretionary use fits into the strategic matrix. In NSW, strategies have never been incorporated into the legal instrument and stand apart, making their importance or the manner in which land use choices are made very uncertain.

This lack of connection between metropolitan policies and the final legal instrument, the LEP, can be seen in all earlier plans. The County of Cumberland Scheme of 1948 was the first attempt by the state to orient Sydney to a regional rather than a local growth pattern by concentrating that growth away from the central core. The plan, however, was considered inflexible and ineffective and was not enforced, which led to the Sydney Region Outline Plan in 1968. That plan was not prescriptive and was promoted as a 'strategic' plan[52] designed to set out the strategies to develop new growth areas. There were, however, no enforcement mechanisms to carry out its objectives because the plan itself did not override or control LEPs. In 1980, at the time of the commencement of the operation of the EPA Act, the flaws resulting from designation of growth through a metropolitan policy without statutory recognition led to the Outline Plan being considered ineffective.[53] This pattern of new strategies with no concordance with legal controls at the local level remained, causing continuous confusion, and was meant to be cured by the addition of statutory recognition of strategic planning in the Act in 2018. It required the GSRP and resulting District Plans to be taken into account by each council by preparing an LSPS, deriving principles from the GSRP and District Plans, as the basis for a new LEP. However, the strategic documents remain outside the LEP and are too vague and aspirational to directly indicate what led to a zoning or use classification in the LEP. This situation was exacerbated by an announcement of the outgoing Minister for Planning in December 2021[54] that all planning consider these new principles, leaving the status of other strategic plans in doubt.

This form of strategic planning of the GSRP, District Plans and the LSPS, made part of the planning process in the Act, means that decisions as to development consent should, ideally, be looked at through the lens of the strategic layering of plans – Region, District and local as well as in accordance with the new Planning Principles. The list of matters for consideration in the EPA Act (section 4.15) does not, however, directly

[52] State Planning Authority of NSW 1968, *Sydney Region Outline Plan* (SPA, 1968).
[53] NSW Planning and Environment Commission, *Review: Sydney Region Outline Plan* (PEC, 1980).
[54] NSW Government, *The Minister's Planning Principles: A Plan for Sustainable Development in NSW.* (December 2021).

include the strategic planning process, its goals and objectives, but relies on the unarticulated assumption that the LEP is the end result of the strategic process through the LSPS, encapsulating the strategic decisions of the GSRP and District Plans.

This recitation may seem to be of a highly technical matter, but it is fundamental to understanding the effectiveness of strategic planning in NSW, the appropriate range of relevant considerations for the Court and the Court's likely future jurisdiction. The strategic plans do not effectively explain the LEP because it is not an easy inquiry as to why a particular use or zone was created resulting from the plans. The main difficulty in linking back to the GSRP and its categories of productivity, sustainability and liveability is that they are not explained anywhere in the documents and can only be understood by inference from the set of actions proposed as strategic directions. There are only a few objective indicators such as housing targets for different areas set out in the District Plans; the rest are unclear. As one example, 'liveability', without express explanation of what is required in the LSPS, may possibly be an empty term, unrelated to planning theory. A developer putting forward an application for a rezoning is forced to address the GSRP and District Plans (and now the Planning Principles) without an understanding of what the objectives mean, so that the application is inevitably vague and only self-serving.

These strategic documents are the essence of planning in NSW; they are the system in practice and cannot be said to be of lesser importance once there is an LEP. However, they offer no clear relevant considerations for use by the Court in a merit appeal. This can be contrasted with a State Environmental Planning Policy (SEPP), a formal planning instrument made under the EPA Act that provides a range of matters for a council and the Court to consider, as in the case of the SEPP (Housing for Seniors or People with a Disability) 2004. These SEPPs are not strategic plans as they provide no overarching plan that provides a line of sight.

There is no direct basis for the Court to consider the GSRP, District Plans, LSPSs and the Minister's Planning Principles. In terms of the District Plans, even though they must accord with the strategic planning direction of the GSRP, the Court has taken into account these critical Plans in only a few instances, and even then not as a determinant of the appeal. In a decision of a Commissioner in *DA Number 7 Pty Ltd v Waverly Council*,[55] for example, it was noted that a proposal will allow the Council to meet housing targets set out in the District Plan. This was mentioned as one of the considerations that supported the development, but the nature of those targets and their significance was not analysed.

Although they are the most critical plans for the Greater Sydney region, the GSRP and District Plans are not taken into account by the Court because they are perceived as 'non-statutory' instruments.[56] This is the case even though the LEP must be consistent with the Plans by the EPA Act, and they are also the basis for rezoning decisions. A rare example where there is a cross-over between the strict words of the LEP and the strategic planning process in NSW can be found in one case: *Kingsland Developments Australia Pty Ltd v City of Parramatta Council*.[57] An application for thirty-three apartments built

[55] *DA Number 7 Pty Ltd v Waverly Council* [2020] NSWLEC 1039, [91].
[56] *Pista Pty Ltd v Parramatta City Council* [2019] NSWLEC 1627, [31].
[57] *Kingsland Developments Australia Pty Ltd v City of Parramatta Council* [2018] NSWLEC 1241, [45]–[46].

over retail and commercial uses did not comply with the LEP, but there was a capacity to vary the restrictions by clause 4.6 of every LEP. The applicants had raised that the development would be consistent with the economic corridor referenced in the GSRP, in which the land was included. This raised the issue of whether the dictates of that Plan could become a relevant consideration. Consideration was given to the fact that the site as a strategic location under the GSRP supported the density sought.

This is not a failing of the Court but rather of a highly confused state government's set of policies and neglect by the GSC as to how to make the strategies work in practice and to create a bridge from the strategic documents to the LEP. It has made NSW one of the most confusing planning systems in the world. Every attempt at correcting the confusion has added further complexities. An example is that an application by an individual to amend the LEP and thereby effect a rezoning, called a 'Planning Proposal', is appealable to state government-appointed Joint Regional Planning Panels in Sydney and Regional Panels, but not to the Court. The Panels undertake a merit assessment of the Planning Proposal that must take into account the strategic planning principles of the GSRP and the District Plans.[58] This necessarily makes a merits review of a rezoning focused on these strategic planning documents. The decision on review, if successful, is sent back to the Department with a recommendation to proceed. This process fails to yield any consistency of approach as to the meaning of various strategies or how to understand objectives and concepts in the strategies, and there is therefore no basis upon which a developer can clearly evaluate the principles that stand behind decisions of the Panels. It is a chaotic system because the Department itself has to make a decision to progress the Proposal and that decision is not appealable.

From the viewpoint of the Court, when an LEP establishes a zone based on the strategic plans, the nature of the zone will be considered.[59] However, while the Court does not decide rezoning appeals, very many developments require rezoning. There are no legal precedents or consistency of approach for considering rezonings, but the developer, Panels and the Department must return to the strategic planning documents to somehow decipher the objectives and ideas, in order to determine what is appropriate and within the aspirational objectives for that area. Strategic issues are always relevant considerations and excluding the Court from their consideration, even on a merits review, makes little sense because the suitability of a discretionary use is best understood in the context of the strategic plans that prompted its permissibility.

A government announcement in July 2020 states that the role of the Court should be expanded to include appeals for rezonings. This is part of a 'Planning Reform Action Plan' that will see, if ever implemented, a new class of appeals for rezoning to the Court with the appointment of two new commissioners that will allow approximately 150 more matters to be considered each year.[60] The role of inculcating stability into the system should naturally fall to the Court because of its reputation, its capacity for

[58] NSW Planning Circular: Independent reviews of plan making decisions, PS 18-012, 14 December 2018.
[59] *BGP Properties Pty Limited v Lake Macquarie City Council* (2004) 138 LGERA 237, [117].
[60] Planning NSW: www.planning.nsw.gov.au/Policy-and-Legislation/Planning-reforms/Planning-Reform-Action-Plan (accessed 9 September 2020).

reflective precedent and its existence as the only island of certainty. Without it, the planning system is mired in delay and confusion.

It is, in fact, a novel idea for Australia to have an appeal system for rezonings because a rezoning has been conceived historically as a legislative act rather than a judicial or quasi-judicial act that is reviewable. The idea that a rezoning decision be classified as quasi-judicial is, however, part of early planning theory[61] and could have suggested the Court at an earlier time as a model for rezoning appeals, but the mood was to have independent bodies to replace council decision-making because councils could be corrupt – a result of high-profile cases before the Independent Commission Against Corruption.[62]

The review system in NSW that brings rezoning before a state-appointed Planning Panel that makes a recommendation exists entirely by the minister's fiat[63] on the basis that, as the minister has the final say on rezonings, the pass to that door (the 'gateway') can be reviewed prior to a final decision. The process is not authorised by statute and has critical problems, but when the Department submitted to a review of this process in 2016[64] it was surprisingly affirmed that it should continue with the means of reviewing a rezoning must include a merits assessment having regard to the strategic plans.

The result has been to establish two forms of planning reviews in NSW: the Court in terms of development permissions without direct reliance on the statutory strategic documents, and rezoning reviews to the Planning Panels, dependent on those documents and not reliant on the Court's decisions. This is understandable historically as the Court at its inception was never mandated to examine strategic planning documents, such as the GSRP, as an express consideration under the EPA Act, and the Planning Panels were specifically directed to make those documents the basis of their recommendations.

It has become clear by the July 2020 press release that the Court is the indeed the right venue for these rezoning appeals. The idea that the Court now consider rezoning appeals reflects the early reasons that created it in the first place. It establishes that the Court is the only guiding hand that can stabilise a confusing system and can offer a sense of security to the development industry and the public. It is the correct idea because the Court has already carefully dealt with the strategic pillars of the GSRP as it has provided clear jurisprudence on ESD that consists of those same pillars. It is obviously the most equipped and competent adjudicator. The rezoning review process at present does not provide any certainty, as well as having no predetermined principles, and is greatly diminished in comparison to the consistency and precedent of the Court.

[61] For example, WE Lyons, 'Making Judges out of Legislators: Rezoning on a Quasi-judicial Model' (1983) 8 *Legislative Studies Quarterly* 673.

[62] Independent Commission Against Corruption, Annual Report 2010–2011 (2011); Independent Commission Against Corruption, Anti-corruption Safeguards and the NSW Planning System (ICAC Report, 2012).

[63] Explained in *Henroth Investments Pty Ltd v Sydney North Planning Panel* [2018] NSWLEC 112.

[64] Department of Planning and Environment, Rezoning Reviews: Final Review Report, (August 2016). The entire system of planning panels is analysed in Y Stone, 'Council Decision Making and Independent Panels' (The Henry Halloran Trust Research Report, 2014).

6. Conclusion

The Court does not stand above the planning system but is embedded in a fluid, dynamic, although confusing, regime. Its decisions influence the other actors in the system, such as councils, developers, planners and lawyers, and the use of land is allocated and the marketplace affected by its deliberations. It has a distinct place in that system because of the reasons for which it was created, its status as a superior court, the liberal manner in which it has worked with the scope of its jurisdiction, judicial inventiveness in bringing practical solutions to abstract policy issues, and its reputation resulting from the manner in which the judges contribute to the understanding of planning law. In a difficult, ever-evolving system that is always in a continuous state of reform, it stands as the only institution in NSW that has remained consistent in the manner in which it operates and approaches planning law.

The inclusion of the Court into rezoning appeals is an essential part of planning in NSW because there is always a lag in amending an LEP and land may need to be rezoned in order to be used in a manner that was not anticipated. This will be the necessary culmination of forty years of success. This is called for because the Court can bring to bear the same standards and principles around strategic planning principles that would remove doubt as to the manner in which development is to take place in the state and especially the Greater Sydney Region. Ignoring the Court to date in strategic planning and rezoning appeals has made the planning system too unstable, and it is only the Court that has the ability to solve this dilemma.

4

The Land and Environment Court of New South Wales and the Transnationalisation of Climate Law: The Case of *Gloucester Resources v Minister for Planning*

JACQUELINE PEEL*

1. Introduction

In February 2019, Justice Brian Preston, Chief Judge of the Land and Environment Court of New South Wales (the Court) delivered judgment in the case of *Gloucester Resources v Minister for Planning*.[1] At one level the ruling was unremarkable.[2] It confirmed the decision of the (then) State Planning Assessment Commission,[3] as the Minister for Planning's delegate, that a medium sized, new coal mine in a scenic rural area of the Gloucester Valley should not go ahead, principally due to its visual, amenity and social impacts on the surrounding community and environment. At another level, however, Preston CJ's judgment was extraordinary. Not only did it refuse consent for a coal mine – a rarity in

* I would like to thank my wonderful research assistant, Ms Rebekkah Markey-Towler, for her assistance with referencing.

[1] *Gloucester Resources Ltd v Minister for Planning and Another* (2019) 234 LGERA 257. Gloucester Resources Ltd filed a Notice of Intention to Appeal the Land and Environment Court's decision to the NSW Court of Appeal but later decided not to pursue the appeal: see http://envlaw.com.au/gloucester-resources-case/ (accessed 13 August 2021).

[2] E Johnson, M Floro and J Brown, '*Gloucester Resources Ltd v Minister for Planning*: A Decision for the Right Place – at the Right Time' (2019) 34(2) *Australian Environment Review* 38, 38: describing the decision as 'certainly groundbreaking, [although] anything but radical. Rather, it is a logical development in the law that applies established legal principles to the science of climate change.'

[3] On 1 March 2018, the Planning Assessment Commission was replaced by the Independent Planning Commission (IPC) of NSW, which operates as a standalone agency under Part 2, Division 2.3 of the Environmental Planning and Assessment Act 1979 (NSW).

Australian environmental jurisprudence[4] – but in so doing it also provided a comprehensive response to questions that have dogged climate change litigation around the world.[5] These questions included whether an assessment of the environmental impact of a coal project needs to encompass downstream greenhouse gas (GHG) emissions from the coal when burned, how to understand the significance of the contribution of a single mine's carbon footprint in the context of the global problem of climate change, the relevance of the international goals of the Paris Agreement[6] in construing domestic planning and environmental laws, and the adequacy of arguments about market substitution and carbon leakage in justifying a particular coal mining proposal.

This chapter argues that the *Gloucester Resources* decision exemplifies the cross-cutting function played by the Court's jurisprudence in the emerging field of climate change law.[7] In weaving together existing climate case law from Australia and other jurisdictions, together with the findings of climate science and climate litigation scholarship, the *Gloucester Resources* judgment illustrates how the Court contributes to the transnationalisation of climate law. Transnationalisation of law – where the mainstream binary division of law into either national law or international law is challenged by the generation of transcendental norms[8] – is particularly important in the field of climate law. It helps mediate between the global nature of the problem of GHG pollution and the largely local scale at which decisions on polluting projects take place.[9]

While the Court's reasoning in *Gloucester Resources* made clear that the development application for the coal mine at issue could have been refused on the basis of its local impacts alone,[10] the project's GHG emissions and their likely contribution to adverse impacts on the global climate system added 'a further reason for refusal'.[11] It is on this basis that the case has been labelled 'a landmark judgment on climate change in Australia'[12] and 'a significant contribution to the growing body of climate change

[4] An early example was another decision of Preston CJ refusing consent for the Warkworth coal mine: *Bulga Milbrodale Progress Association Inc v Minister for Planning and Infrastructure and Warkworth Mining Limited* (2013) 194 LGERA 347. The Land and Environment Court's decision was upheld by the NSW Court of Appeal: *Warkworth Mining Ltd v Bulga Milbrodale Progress Association Inc* (2014) 86 NSWLR 527. The *Gloucester Resources* case, however, was 'the first time, a proposed open-cut coal mine has been rejected by a court in Australia on environmental grounds that include the projected carbon emissions that would arise from its operation and from the down-stream burning of its coal' (Rob Fowler, 'Case-note: *Gloucester Resources Limited v Minister for Planning*' (31 July 2019, IUCN News)). A burgeoning jurisprudence applying Preston CJ's reasoning in *Gloucester Resources* is emerging, including the decisions and appeals refusing KEPCO Bylong Australia Pty Ltd's application for development of a coal mine in the Bylong Valley.

[5] J Peel, 'Issues in Climate Change Litigation' (2011) 1 *Carbon & Climate Law Review* 15. See also V McGinness and M Raff, 'Coal and Climate Change: A Study of Contemporary Climate Litigation in Australia' (2020) 37 *Environmental and Planning Law Journal* 87.

[6] Paris Agreement (adopted 12 December 2015, entered into force 4 November 2016) 55 ILM 740 (Paris Agreement).

[7] J Peel, 'Climate Change Law: The Emergence of a New Legal Discipline' (2008) 32 *Melbourne University Law Review* 922.

[8] V Heyvaert and L-A Duvic-Paoli, 'The Meanings of Transnational Environment Law' in V Heyvaert and L-A Duvic-Paoli (eds), *Research Handbook on Transnational Environmental Law* (Cheltenham, Edward Elgar, 2020) 4.

[9] HM Osofsky, 'The Continuing Importance of Climate Change Litigation' (2010) 1 *Climate Law* 3.

[10] *Gloucester Resources* (n 1) 380, [556].

[11] ibid.

[12] Johnson, Floro and Brown (n 2) 38. See also S Little, '"Dire Consequences": NSW Coal Mine Refused on Climate Change Grounds' [2020] *Native Title Newsletter*, issue 1, 12.

judicial rulings emerging across the world'.[13] The decision provides a treasure trove from which environmental authorities, advocacy groups and other courts may draw in scrutinising future proposals for coal mines and other developments involving the extraction and use of fossil fuels.

The chapter begins with a discussion of the transnationalisation of climate law and the role that courts are playing in that process through the medium of domestic climate litigation. It then analyses the treatment of climate change issues in the *Gloucester Resources* decision as an example of the way in which the Court has contributed to the development of transcendental climate law norms. The direct application of *Gloucester Resources* as a precedent in future lawsuits may be limited by distinctive features of the case – such as that it involved a merits review appeal[14] under planning laws and affirmation of an existing refusal of development consent – as well as specific changes to NSW planning law proposed in the aftermath of the decision.[15] However, this does not diminish the significance of its contribution to the wider field of global climate litigation and to the broader transnationalisation of climate law.[16]

2. Courts and Transnational Climate Law

The law of climate change – dealing with legal responses to problems of GHG emissions reduction, adaptation to climate change impacts, and loss and damage stemming from climate harms – has been identified as a 'prime arena' for the development of transnational law.[17] Although much of climate law has its roots in the treaties of the international climate change regime, such as the United Nations Framework Convention on Climate Change (UNFCCC), the Kyoto Protocol and the Paris Agreement,[18] its branches and shoots extend into several other areas of law, at multiple levels of governance, and affect a wide range of actors.[19] This polycentric legal

[13] Fowler (n 4).

[14] As explained by the Court on its website, merits review 'involves the Court re-exercising the administrative power previously exercised by the original local or State government decision-maker. The Court has the same functions and discretions as the original decision-maker.' By contrast, the majority of Australian climate change cases have involved judicial review: McGinness and Raff (n 5) 99. Judicial review challenges to coal mine proposals have achieved less success, as the decision of *Australian Coal Alliance Incorporated v Wyong Coal Pty Ltd* [2019] NSWLEC 31 (which closely followed *Gloucester Resources* in March 2019) demonstrated. Moore J was careful to distinguish this case from *Gloucester Resources*: [33]–[41].

[15] The Environment Planning and Assessment Amendment (Territorial Limits) Bill 2019 (NSW) in the NSW Parliament proposed a prohibition on imposing conditions on a development consent regulating downstream emissions and seeks to remove the specific requirement under the Mining SEPP to consider Scope 3 emissions; see further below (n 63).

[16] Fowler (n 4). See also C Covington et al, 'Is Rocky Hill the Tipping Point? Implications of the NSW Land and Environment Court's Decision in *Gloucester Resources Ltd v Minister for Planning*' (2019) 34(3,4) *Australian Environment Review* 68; G Medici-Colombo, 'Presupuesto de Carbono y Autorización de Proyectos de Producción de Combustibles Fósiles: el Caso *Gloucester Resources Ltd v Minister for Planning*' (2020) 11(1) *Revista Catalana de Dret Ambiental* 1 (translation on file with author).

[17] T Etty et al, 'Transnational Climate Law' (2018) 7 Transnational Environmental Law 191, 191.

[18] United Nations Framework Convention on Climate Change (adopted 9 May 1992, entered into force 21 March 1994) 1771 UNTS 107 (UNFCCC); Kyoto Protocol to the United Nations Framework Convention on Climate Change (adopted 11 December 1997, entered into force 16 February 2005) 2303 UNTS 148; Paris Agreement (n 6).

[19] Etty et al (n 17) 191.

structure is a response to the multidimensional nature of the climate problem, which is simultaneously global and local in its causes and effects.[20] Such polycentricism is also implicitly endorsed by the 'hybrid architecture' of the 2015 Paris Agreement.[21] The Agreement combines nationally determined contributions (NDCs) to the global climate change response with an international transparency and oversight mechanism,[22] and recognises 'the importance of the engagements of all levels of government and various actors' in addressing climate change.[23]

In the multidimensional arrangement that represents current climate governance,[24] courts can play a key role in facilitating fluid interaction between different levels and layers of legal requirements. As Hari Osofsky notes, this fluidity 'comes not from the tribunals themselves', which are 'constituted at specific, fixed scales', but rather 'from the multiscalar nature of the problem of climate change and regulatory efforts to address it'.[25] Climate litigation disputes, such as the *Gloucester Resources* case, often raise arguments about the appropriate locus of resolution, with those who want less action 'claiming that climate change is too big a problem for local, state, and even national regulation', while those who want more action 'tend to scale down, and focus on the ways in which emissions, impacts, and adaptation take place at smaller spatial and temporal scales'.[26] Through their decisions on such questions, courts become 'an important part of the transnational regulatory dialogue over climate change'.[27]

There are a number of ways in which courts deciding climate cases may contribute to a transnational regulatory dialogue on climate change. Courts may cross-cite to other climate cases arising outside their own jurisdiction as authority for a particular legal position.[28] They may apply international treaty norms, for instance, from the Paris Agreement, in the interpretation of domestic rules.[29] They may employ existing transnational environmental law principles,[30] such as precaution and intergenerational equity, to guide decision-making on climate issues.[31] Or courts may help to

[20] A Jordan et al, 'Emergence of Polycentric Climate Governance and its Future Prospects' (2015) 5 *Nature Climate Change* 977.

[21] D Bodansky, J Brunnée and L Rajamani, *International Climate Change Law* (Oxford, Oxford University Press, 2017) 23–27, 214.

[22] Paris Agreement (n 6), Arts 2 (temperature goals), 4 (mitigation), 13–15 (transparency and global stocktake).

[23] ibid, Preamble.

[24] Jordan et al (n 20). See also J Peel, L Godden and RJ Keenan, 'Climate Change Law in an Era of Multi-level Governance' (2012) 1 *Transnational Environmental Law* 245.

[25] Osofsky (n 9) 15.

[26] ibid, 15.

[27] ibid, 27.

[28] O Perez and O Stegmann, 'Transnational Networked Constitutionalism' (2018) 45(1) *Journal of Legal Studies* S135, S143–S144.

[29] L Wegener, 'Can the Paris Agreement Help Climate Change Litigation and Vice Versa?' (2020) 9(1) *Transnational Environmental Law* 17. In dualist legal systems, such as Australia's, international law does not form part of domestic law unless 'transformed' by statute. The use of international law norms in legislative interpretation is an important avenue for international law to influence domestic decision-making: see G Cranwell, 'Treaties and Australian Law – Administrative Discretions, Statutes and the Common Law' (2001) 1(1) *Queensland University of Technology Law & Justice Journal* 49.

[30] Heyvaert and Duvic-Paoli (n 8) 6.

[31] *Gloucester Resources* (n 1) 365–66, [488] referring to the principles of ESD, including precaution and intergenerational equity. See, more generally, BJ Preston, 'The Contribution of the Courts in Tackling Climate Change' (2016) 28 *Journal of Environmental Law* 11.

embed widely accepted non-legal norms, such as the findings of climate science assessments produced by the Intergovernmental Panel on Climate Change (IPCC), into the legal sphere.[32]

While not all courts play these roles in all climate cases, it is a noticeable trend across the field, and particularly in the climate jurisprudence of a specialist environmental court such as the Land and Environment Court. Through consistent citation to, and application of, particular principles or shared interpretations of the law in climate cases, national courts and judges are arguably 'co-producing a new and emergent body of transnational environmental law and jurisprudence'.[33] Prominent examples in global climate jurisprudence that illustrate this transnational norm-generating role of courts include the US Supreme Court's decision in *Massachusetts v EPA*;[34] the Dutch Supreme Court's decision in the *Urgenda* case;[35] Justice Shah's decisions in the case of *Leghari v Federation of Pakistan*;[36] and the decision of the English Court of Appeal in the *Heathrow Third Runway* case.[37] As the next section of the chapter discusses, the Land and Environment Court decision in *Gloucester Resources* is a worthy addition to this group of rulings as an exemplar of judicial transnationalisation of climate law.

[32] Reports of the IPCC have become a scientific baseline in climate disputes as they provide an authoritative synthesis and assessment of current scientific knowledge on climate change. For example, in *Gloucester Resources*, Preston CJ cited ((n 1) 351 [431]) the IPCC's finding that it is extremely likely (95–100 per cent confidence) that the increase in global average temperatures is due to anthropogenic activity: see IPCC, *Climate Change 2014: Synthesis Report. Contributions of Working Groups I, II and III to the Fifth Assessment Report of the Intergovernmental Panel on Climate Change* (IPCC, 2014) 48. This trend – tying legal arguments closely to the latest climate science – has been a feature of recent climate jurisprudence: Jacqueline Peel and Rebekkah Markey-Towler, 'Recipe for Success?: Lessons for Strategic Climate Litigation from the Sharma, Neubauer, and Shell Cases' (2021) 22 *German Law Journal* 1181, 1192–93.

[33] G Ganguly, 'Judicial Transnationalization' in Heyvaert and Duvic-Paoli (n 8) 301.

[34] *Massachusetts v Environmental Protection Agency* 549 US 497 (2007). In interpreting the term 'air pollutant' in the US Clean Air Act, a majority of the Court found that GHG emissions from domestic motor vehicles could be characterised as such (at 532), enlivening the Environmental Protection Agency's (EPA) regulatory mandate. In refuting the EPA's reasons for its failure to regulate, the majority also held that US motor vehicle GHG emissions make a meaningful contribution to GHG concentrations despite only being a relatively small proportion of worldwide carbon emissions (at 525).

[35] *State of the Netherlands v Urgenda Foundation* No 19/00135, 20 December 2019, ECLI:NL:HR:2019:2007. The Supreme Court, affirming decisions of lower courts, found that by failing to reduce GHG emissions by at least 25 per cent by the end of 2020, the Dutch government was acting unlawfully in contravention of its duty of care under Arts 2 and 8 of the European Convention on Human Rights. Reasoning building on the landmark *Urgenda* decisions was subsequently used by the Hague District Court in *Milieudefensie et al. v. Royal Dutch Shell plc* No C/09/571932 / HA ZA 19-379, 26 May 2021, ECLI:NL:RBDHA:2021:5339 finding a private corporation (Shell's) contributions to climate change violated its duty of care under Dutch law and human rights obligations.

[36] *Ashgar Leghari v Federation of Pakistan* WP No 25501/2015, 4 September 2015. In this decision and a supplemental ruling on 14 September 2015, Judge Shah found that failures of national adaptation policy gave rise to a violation of the constitutionally enshrined right to life in Pakistan.

[37] *Plan B Earth v Secretary of State for Transport* [2020] EWCA Civ 214. The Court of Appeal ruled that the UK government's Paris Agreement commitments needed to be taken into account in designation of its Airports National Policy Statement under the Planning Act 2008. However, leave to appeal to the Supreme Court was granted to Heathrow Airport Limited and Arora Holdings in May 2020, and on 16 December 2020, the Supreme Court overturned the Court of Appeal decision.

3. Transcendental Climate Norms in the *Gloucester Resources* Case

Compared with the high-profile rulings of national appellate courts, a merits appeal heard by a state-level environmental court, examining a refusal issued for an open-cut coal mine in the Hunter Valley region of NSW, might seem like an unlikely forum for pronouncements on transnational climate law. The *Gloucester Resources* case is one in a line of Australian climate cases that have featured challenges to fossil fuel projects, such as coal mines.[38] By comparison with other proposed coal mines that have been the focus of court challenges, such as the Adani Carmichael mine in the Galilee Basin of Queensland,[39] the Gloucester Resources Ltd (GRL) proposal was of a relatively modest size. The Court noted it would not be one of largest coal mines in Australia and had a projected production (21 million tonnes over sixteen years) that was about one-third that of the average coal mine in NSW.[40] In addition, the mine was intended to produce coking coal used in the manufacture of steel, rather than the more clearly climate-detrimental purpose of mining thermal coal for combustion to generate energy.[41]

GRL's proposal had been rejected by the Planning Assessment Commission not on climate change grounds but rather on the basis of more general planning considerations relating to the contravention of objectives specified for particular land zonings, the proposal's likely visual impact and the fact that approval of the proposal was not considered to be in the public interest.[42] The mine, in the 'idyllic' Rocky Hill valley close to the rural-residential town of Gloucester, had attracted significant community objections, focused particularly on the proposal's likely amenity impacts.[43] In GRL's merits appeal to the Court of the minister's refusal, the local community representative group, Groundswell Gloucester, which had objected to the Rocky Hill mining proposal, was granted leave to join the proceeding.[44] In addition to amenity concerns, Groundswell Gloucester contended that the Rocky Hill Coal Project should be refused because its

[38] McGinness and Raff (n 5) 92–93, 99. While many of these cases have involved judicial review of coal mines, more recent cases have explored more 'novel' legal avenues including the success at first instance of the litigants in *Sharma by her litigation representative Sister Marie Brigid Arthur v Minister for the Environment* (2021) 391 ALR 1; [2021] FCA 560.

[39] The Carmichael mine is proposed to extract approximately sixty million tonnes of coal per annum over an operating life of sixty years. The mine has attracted significant opposition, with various legal challenges brought in Queensland and Federal courts including *Adani Mining Pty Ltd v Land Services of Coast and Country Inc & Ors* [2015] QLC 48; *Australian Conservation Foundation Inc v Minister for the Environment* (2016) 251 FCR 308; *Australian Conservation Foundation Incorporated v Minister for the Environment* [2021] FCA 550.

[40] *Gloucester Resources* (n 1) 379–80, [556].

[41] GRL emphasised this distinction, arguing that while there were other fuel substitutes for thermal coal, typically burned for electricity generation, there were limited substitutes for coking coal used in steel production. Preston CJ rejected the argument as being overstated: *Gloucester Resources* (n 1) 378-379, [546]–[549].

[42] NSW Planning Assessment Commission Determination Report Rocky Hill Coal Project (SSD 5156) (14 December 2017).

[43] Ninety per cent of submissions to the Department opposed the mining development, with 72 per cent of objectors raising visual impacts and 66 per cent raising the location of the mine and its proximity to other land uses: *Gloucester Resources* (n 1) 268, [20].

[44] Pursuant to s 8.15(2) of the Environmental Planning and Assessment Act 1979 (NSW).

GHG emissions would adversely impact measures limiting dangerous anthropogenic climate change.[45]

The Court ultimately accepted these arguments, finding that the development application for the Rocky Hill mine should be refused because its costs – including its indirect environmental impacts in contributing to climate change – outweighed its potential benefits.[46] A judicial decision to refuse a coal mine in Australia in and of itself would have been a significant ruling. However, as the following sections discuss, arguably what makes Preston CJ's judgment in *Gloucester Resources* truly remarkable in the evolution of global climate litigation is less its result than its clearly reasoned responses to questions that are common to many climate disputes. It is these responses, and the way they build from existing, diverse precedents and other knowledge sources, that contribute to the decision's development of transcendental climate norms, which have the capacity to resonate beyond the fixed jurisdictional boundaries of the Land and Environment Court.

3.1. Downstream Coal Emissions

A key issue that has arisen in challenges to coal projects in Australia and other countries is whether the assessment of the environmental impact of these projects may take account of the GHG emissions arising when the coal (or other fossil fuel) is burned, often at a site geographically remote from that of the project.[47] These downstream emissions from a coal project are often called 'Scope 3 emissions', following the World Resources Institute Protocol that distinguishes such emissions from on-site emissions resulting directly from the project (Scope 1 emissions) and emissions associated with energy supplied to the project (Scope 2 emissions).[48] As a major coal exporter, Scope 3 emissions from coal are a significant contributor to Australia's overall carbon footprint. Indeed, in 2018, emissions produced from the coal extracted by Australia's top six producers amounted to 551 $MtCO_2$-eq, exceeding Australia's projected domestic emissions (524 $MtCO_2$-eq) for that year.[49]

The problem of whether Scope 3 emissions are a permissible matter for decision-makers to consider in assessing coal projects is exacerbated by international legal structures that assign state responsibility for GHG emissions based on territorial control.[50] It has thus been common in climate litigation concerning coal projects for

[45] *Gloucester Resources* (n 1) 349, [422].

[46] ibid, [8].

[47] Peel (n 5) 21–22. See also N Rogers, 'Making Climate Science Matter in the Courtroom' (2017) 34 *Environmental and Planning Law Journal* 475; K Parker, 'Litigating at the Source: Attributing Climate Impacts to Coal Mines' (2020) 37 *Environmental and Planning Law Journal* 67; J Bell-James and C Forrest, 'Ecologically Sustainable Development and the Great Barrier Reef – A Delicate Balance of Interests' (2019) 36 *Environmental and Planning Law Journal* 97.

[48] World Resources Institute (WRI) and World Business Council for Sustainable Development (WBCSD), *Greenhouse Gas Protocol: A Corporate Accounting and Reporting Standard* (2004) https://ghgprotocol.org/sites/default/files/standards/ghg-protocol-revised.pdf (accessed 16 September 2020).

[49] J Moss and P Fraser, *Australia's Carbon Majors* (Practical Justice Initiative, UNSW, 2019) 4.

[50] J Peel, 'Climate Change' in A Nollkaemper and I Plakokefalos (eds), *The Practice of Shared Responsibility in International Law* (Cambridge, Cambridge University Press, 2017).

defendants to argue that Scope 3 emissions ought not to be considered in environmental impact assessment (EIA) as these emissions should only be 'counted' in the place where the coal is burned, often offshore in developing countries. If accepted, this argument acts to minimise assessments of a coal project's environmental impact by excluding from consideration the most significant source of associated GHG emissions. For example, for the Rocky Hill Coal Project, the environmental impact statement (EIS) submitted by the proponent estimated the total Scope 1 and Scope 2 emissions to be about 1.8 $MtCO_2$-eq over the life of the mine, whereas the Scope 3 emissions were estimated to be at least 36 $MtCO_2$-eq.[51] Excluding the consideration of such 'downstream emissions' in EIA runs counter to the recognition of climate change as a global problem with widespread effects that are not confined to the particular territorial location where emissions occur.[52]

In climate cases decided by the Court prior to *Gloucester Resources*, there had already been judicial pronouncements accepting the relevance of Scope 3 emissions for EIA of coal projects.[53] A notable, early example was Pain J's decision in *Gray v Minister for Planning*, involving a judicial review proceeding brought in respect of the Anvil Hill coal mine proposal.[54] In *Gray*, Pain J drew on principles of ecologically sustainable development (ESD) – a foundation of much Australian environmental law[55] – to justify inclusion of both direct and indirect impacts, including Scope 3 emissions, in the EIA undertaken for the mine.[56] Courts in the United States have also supported this position when reviewing environmental studies prepared for the approval of fossil fuel projects.[57] Following these cases, it has become fairly standard for proponents of coal projects to include information on Scope 3 emissions in the EIS they prepare for the purposes of approval processes, as was the case with the EIS prepared by GRL for the Rocky Hill Coal project. In NSW, moreover, the State Environmental Planning Policy for the mining industry (the Mining SEPP), in clause 14(2), refers to consideration of the assessment of GHG emissions, including downstream emissions.[58]

[51] *Gloucester Resources* (n 1) 365, [486]–[487]. The Court noted that the estimated Scope 3 emissions did not include transportation emissions, eg from shipping associated with moving the coal from the site of extraction to the site of combustion.

[52] ibid.

[53] *Australian Conservation Foundation v Latrobe City Council* (2004) 140 LGERA 100, [46]–[47], [49]; *Coast and Country Association of Queensland Inc v Smith* [2016] QCA 242, [11], [45], [51]; *Wollar Progress Association Inc v Wilpinjong Coal Pty Ltd* [2018] NSWLEC 92, [180]–[183]. See discussion in, for example, J Peel, 'The Role of Climate Change Litigation in Australia's Response to Global Warming' (2007) 24 *Environmental and Planning Law Journal* 90; K Bennett, 'Australian Climate Change Litigation: Assessing the Impact of Carbon Emissions' (2016) 33 *Environmental and Planning Law Journal* 538; McGinness and Raff (n 5).

[54] *Gray v Minister for Planning* (2006) 152 LGERA 258.

[55] G Bates, *Environmental Law in Australia* (London, LexisNexis Butterworths 2019) 171.

[56] *Gray* (n 54), [126], [130].

[57] *Border Power Plant Working Group v Department of Energy v Department of Energy* 260 F Supp 2d 997 (2003); *Mid States Coalition for Progress v Surface Transportation Board* 345 F 3d 520 (2003); *Montana Environmental Information Center v US Office of Surface Mining* 274 F Supp 3d 1074 (2017); *Sierra Club v Federal Regulatory Commission* 867 F 3d 1357 (2017); *San Juan Citizens Alliance v United States Bureau of Land Management* 326 F Supp 3d 1227 (2018).

[58] State Environmental Planning Policy (Mining, Petroleum Production and Extractive Industries) 2007 (NSW), cl 14(2).

Despite these trends, the inclusion of Scope 3 emissions in the assessment of a coal project's environmental impact continues to be contested in climate litigation.[59] For example, GRL contended before Preston CJ that the Scope 3 emissions of the Rocky Hill Coal Project could not be taken into consideration by the Court on the basis that Australia's international climate change obligations only require accounting for Scope 1 and 2 emissions.[60] In the 2018 case of *Wollar Progress Association Inc v Wilpinjong Coal Pty Ltd*, Sheahan J rejected a judicial review challenge to a coal mining proposal, which included a ground concerning the application of clause 14(2) of the Mining SEPP by the Planning Assessment Commission.[61] His Honour accepted that the Commission had given 'close consideration' to an assessment of GHG emissions, including downstream emissions, in its determination and indicated his preference for the submission of Wilpinjong Coal, which had argued that 'Clause 14(2) does not introduce a standalone requirement for consent authorities to consider whether to stop the development of coal mines'.[62] Clause 14(2) of the Mining SEPP itself was also targeted for amendment following the *Gloucester Resources* decision in order to remove the reference to downstream emissions, such that this is no longer a mandatory requirement in the assessment of coal mining projects.[63]

By contrast, Preston CJ's decision in *Gloucester Resources* affirmed the notion that Scope 3 emissions are a relevant matter to be considered in assessing a new coal mine proposal.[64] His Honour might have done so simply on the basis of consideration of the proponent's EIS and applicable planning instruments, such as the NSW Mining SEPP; however, the decision went further in a number of ways.

First, the judgment linked its finding on Scope 3 emissions to broader developments in NSW and Australian environmental law. This included the Federal Court's leading environmental decision in *Nathan Dam*, interpreting project impacts as including 'indirect impacts'.[65] Preston CJ also relied on decisions of the Land and Environment Court, such as *Gray*, holding that consideration of the 'public interest' includes reference to principles of ESD, particularly the precautionary and intergenerational equity principles, which in turn can involve consideration of the impact of a development on climate change.[66]

[59] Regulatory requirements for corporate disclosure of these emissions are also lacking, with the focus of legislation in G20 countries on Scope 1 and 2 emissions, which is the case for Australia's National Greenhouse and Energy Reporting Act 2007 (Cth): OECD/CDSB, *Climate Change Disclosure in G20 Countries: Stocktaking of corporate reporting schemes* (2015) 30.

[60] *Gloucester Resources* (n 1) 359, [453].

[61] *Wollar Progress Association Inc v Wilpinjong Coal Pty Ltd* [2018] NSWLEC 92.

[62] ibid, [145], [180].

[63] Environment Planning and Assessment Amendment (Territorial Limits) Bill 2019 (NSW) (n 15) was introduced in October 2019 and went to inquiry: A Smith, 'NSW Government Says New Planning Laws Give Certainty for Mines' *Sydney Morning Herald*, 22 October 2019. Parliament shut down soon after the report was delivered due to COVID 19, recommending that the Bill not proceed in its current form: A Smith, 'NSW Parliamentary Inquiry Finds New Mining Laws Should Not Go Ahead' *Sydney Morning Herald*, 6 March 2020. See further BJ Preston, 'Contemporary Issues in Environmental Impact Assessment' (2020) 37 *Environmental and Planning Law Journal* 423, 433–34.

[64] *Gloucester Resources* (n 1) 365, 370, [487], [513].

[65] *Minister for Environment and Heritage v Queensland Conservation Council Inc* (2004) 139 FCR 24, [53]. See discussion in L Godden and J Peel, 'The Environment Protection and Biodiversity Conservation Act 1999 (Cth): Dark Sides of Virtue' (2007) 31 *Melbourne University Law Review* 106.

[66] *Gloucester Resources* (n 1) 367, [498].

Second, the Court situated its finding on Scope 3 emissions within the broader landscape of Australian and US climate litigation.[67] Drawing on these authorities, the judgment noted:

> Many courts have held that indirect, downstream GHG emissions are a relevant consideration to take into account in determining applications for activities involving fossil fuel extraction or combustion or electricity generated by fossil fuel combustion.[68]

This analysis identifies the consideration of downstream (and potentially also upstream)[69] GHG emissions from fossil fuel projects as part of a wider trend in the case law to assess the impacts of such projects fully. This norm transcends the specific context in which planning instruments, such as the Mining SEPP, apply, helping to bridge between the localised scale of project assessment and implementation, and the broader scales at which related climate change effects take place.

3.2. Addressing the 'Drop in the Ocean' Problem

Alongside the question of whether downstream emissions can be included in environmental assessments of coal projects, one of the arguments most frequently raised by proponents of their exclusion when these projects are challenged is the so-called 'drop in the ocean' issue.[70] The argument most commonly takes the form that a particular project or action cannot be considered to have a significant impact in the global context of the climate change problem, as its emissions contribution is small. While this argument was not directly raised by GRL in the *Gloucester Resources* case, the company's submissions on the economic and social rationale for the mine touched on this point. In particular, GRL argued that the economic benefits of mining for coking coal, coupled with local social benefits associated with the proposal, such as employment, needed to be taken into account and 'weighed against the uncertain, long-term impacts of carbon emissions produced by the mine'.[71]

If the 'drop in the ocean' argument is allowed to stand in climate litigation, it gives rise to another well-known environmental challenge, that of 'a death by a thousand cuts'.[72] In essence, as climate change is a problem of cumulative environmental impact from anthropogenic additions of GHG emissions to the atmosphere over time and space, there is a strong argument that effective climate change mitigation efforts require

[67] Australian cases referred to in nn 53–54; US cases cited in n 57.

[68] *Gloucester Resources* (n 1) 367, [499].

[69] M Burger and J Wentz, 'Downstream and Upstream Greenhouse Gas Emissions: The Proper Scope of NEPA Review' (2017) 41 *Harvard Environmental Law Review* 109.

[70] Peel (n 5) 16–17.

[71] *Gloucester Resources* (n 1) 365, [484].

[72] See R Nelson, 'Breaking Backs and Boiling Frogs: Warnings from a Dialogue between Federal Water Law and Environmental Law' (2019) 42 *University of New South Wales Law Journal* 1179; JT Dales, 'Death by a Thousand Cuts: Incorporating Cumulative Effects in Australia's Environment Protection and Biodiversity Conservation Act' (2011) 20(1) *Pacific Rim Law and Policy Journal* 149.

assessment of the impact of any GHG-producing project in light of its cumulative contribution to the overall problem.[73]

The necessity for cumulative impact assessment in respect of fossil fuel projects is well-supported by climate science.[74] This point was emphasised by prominent climate scientist Professor Will Steffen in a report prepared for Groundswell Gloucester in the litigation. Professor Steffen stated:

> All emissions are important because cumulatively they constitute the global total of greenhouse gas emissions, which are destabilising the global climate system at a rapid rate. Just as many emitters are contributing to the problem, so many emission reduction activities are required to solve the problem.[75]

Preston CJ referred to Professor Steffen's evidence in reaching his conclusion that: 'The direct and indirect GHG emissions of the Rocky Hill Coal Project will contribute cumulatively to the global total GHG emissions.'[76] His Honour characterised the Scope 1, 2 and 3 emissions over the life of the project (at least 37.8 $MtCO_2$-eq) as 'a sizeable individual source of GHG emissions'.[77] However, in the Chief Judge's view, it was not the relative size of the project's emissions compared with the global total of GHG emissions that was critical. Rather, following the approach of climate science recognising GHG pollution as a cumulative impact problem, his Honour emphasised the need for the global problem of climate change 'to be addressed by multiple local actions to mitigate emissions by sources and remove GHGs by sinks'.[78]

The Court's finding was reinforced through the links Preston CJ drew to global climate jurisprudence on this question.[79] This included references to two highly cited climate cases from the United States and Europe mentioned earlier: the US Supreme Court's decision in *Massachusetts v EPA*[80] and the decisions of Dutch courts in the *Urgenda* case.[81] Both precedents, in very different settings, recognise the importance of treating climate change as a cumulative impact problem in assessing the sufficiency of any single mitigation action. In *Gloucester Resources*, the Court used these cases to demonstrate a broader transnational judicial trend whereby '[m]any courts have recognised this point that climate change is caused by cumulative emissions from a myriad of individual sources, each proportionally small relative to the global total of GHG emissions, and will be solved by abatement of the GHG emissions from [this] myriad of individual sources'.[82]

[73] Preston (n 63) 436–40.

[74] The 'carbon budget' approach, discussed below, is commonly used to determine whether states' efforts will be cumulatively sufficient to meet the Paris Agreement's temperature goals. This has implications for the rate of emissions reductions required towards the phasing out of fossil fuels. Current estimates suggest the world is on the cusp of missing the opportunity to limit warming to 1.5°C: *Emissions Gap Report 2019* (United Nations Environment Programme, 2019).

[75] *Gloucester Resources* (n 1) 358, [450].

[76] ibid, 370, [515].

[77] ibid.

[78] ibid.

[79] ibid, 371–73.

[80] *Massachusetts v Environmental Protection Agency* (n 34).

[81] Reference was made to the District Court and Court of Appeal decisions in *Urgenda* only, as the Supreme Court decision (n 35) was handed down after *Gloucester Resources* in December 2019.

[82] *Gloucester Resources* (n 1) 371, [516].

This analysis allows a refocusing of the assessment process away from the size of a particular coal project or the mitigation contribution of any one individual action, towards a more holistic consideration of how individual actions link together to produce the overall climate change problem and its consequences. As Preston CJ summarised in the judgment:

> There is a causal link between the Project's cumulative GHG emissions and climate change and its consequences. The Project's cumulative GHG emissions will contribute to the global total of GHG concentrations in the atmosphere. The global total of GHG concentrations will affect the climate system and cause climate change impacts. The Project's cumulative GHG emissions are therefore likely to contribute to the future changes to the climate system and the impacts of climate change. In this way, the Project is likely to have indirect impacts on the environment, including the climate system, the oceanic and terrestrial environment, and people.[83]

3.3. Role of the Paris Agreement

Since the conclusion of the Paris Agreement at the end of 2015, international climate law has operated under a new 'hybrid' framework that seeks to harness the 'nationally determined' climate change actions of parties towards the achievement of the Paris Agreement's collective objectives.[84] These collective objectives include the Paris Agreement's long-term temperature goal to hold increases in global average temperatures to 'well below' 2°C above preindustrial levels and to 'pursue efforts' to contain temperature rises to 1.5°C.[85] In addition, in Article 4.1 of the Paris Agreement, parties articulated a collective aim to achieve peaking of global GHG emissions as soon as possible and to undertake rapid reductions thereafter in order to achieve a 'balance' between anthropogenic emissions by sources and removals by sinks in the second half of the century. A growing number of governments and corporate actors have responded to this goal with commitments to achieve 'net zero' emissions by 2050.[86] For example, the state of NSW has a 2020–2030 climate change plan that includes a goal to reach net zero emissions in the state by 2050.[87]

The long-term temperature goal of the Paris Agreement allows scientific calculations to be made about the remaining CO_2-eq emissions that can be released to the

[83] ibid, 373, [525].

[84] Combining 'bottom-up' substance (parties' NDCs) with a 'top-down' process (provisions on progression, highest possible ambition, accounting, transparency, stocktake and compliance): Bodansky, Brunnée and Rajamani (n 21) 214.

[85] Paris Agreement (n 6) art 2(1)(a).

[86] Especially following the IPCC's special report in 2018, which concluded that in pathways with limited or no overshoot of 1.5°C, global net anthropogenic CO_2 emissions must decline by approximately 45 per cent from 2010 levels by 2030 and reach net zero around 2050: V Masson-Delmotte et al (eds), *Global Warming of 1.5°C: An IPCC Special Report on the Impacts of Global Warming of 1.5°C above Pre-industrial Levels and Related Global Greenhouse Gas Emission Pathways, in the Context of Strengthening the Global Response to the Threat of Climate Change, Sustainable Development, and Efforts to Eradicate Poverty* (IPCC, 2018) 12.

[87] Which was updated after Preston CJ's decision on 28 September 2021: NSW Government, *Net Zero Plan Stage 1: 2020–2030* (2020). In advance of COP26, under much international pressure, the Australian Federal government finally committed to net zero emissions by 2050: Australian Government, *Australia's Long-Term Emissions Reduction Plan* (2021).

atmosphere from anthropogenic sources without exceeding temperature thresholds – the so-called 'carbon budget'.[88] These calculations are possible because of the essentially linear relationship that exists between cumulative GHG emissions and temperature increases.[89] In the *Gloucester Resources* case, Professor Steffen gave evidence, based on IPCC reports,[90] that to have a 66 per cent probability of restricting global average temperature rises to no more than 2°C, the remaining carbon budget is around 215 Gt.[91] On present emission rates this budget would be expended in two decades, meaning that GHG emissions need to net out at zero before 2050 to prevent unsustainable temperature rises.[92] In turn, the emissions reduction trajectory to achieve net zero by 2050 is dependent on the peaking year for global GHG emissions. Scientists estimate that 2020 is about the latest GHG emissions can peak before declining to ensure an emissions reduction trajectory that is technologically and economically feasible.[93]

The question that this has raised in climate litigation concerning coal and other carbon-intensive projects is what role the Paris Agreement goals – and the carbon budget/emission reduction trajectories that they imply – play in decision-making on authorisation of such projects. In turn, there is increasing interest in the contribution domestic climate litigation makes to implementation of the Paris Agreement and overall climate governance.[94] From a scientific viewpoint, the conclusion to this enquiry is straightforward. Professor Steffen's report in *Gloucester Resources* advised, for instance, that the 'clear message from any carbon budget analysis' was that 'fossil fuel combustion must be phased out quickly'. In his expert view, meeting the Paris Agreement's goals would require leaving most of the world's existing fossil fuels 'in the ground, unburned', with 'no new fossil fuel developments … allowed'.[95]

From a legal standpoint, however, the role that the Paris Agreement plays in domestic decision-making on GHG-emitting projects is a more complicated question, not least because it contains no enforcement mechanism and articulates its climate mitigation goals in collective, aspirational terms.[96] In addition, although parties are bound as a matter of international law by its provisions,[97] the Agreement contains

[88] *Gloucester Resources* (n 1) 355, [441].

[89] ibid.

[90] Including T Stocker et al, *Climate Change 2013: The Physical Science Basis. Contribution of Working Group I to the Fifth Assessment Report of the Intergovernmental Panel on Climate Change* (IPCC, 2013); Masson-Delmotte et al (n 86).

[91] *Gloucester Resources* (n 1) 355, [443].

[92] ibid, 356, [443].

[93] Rapid and far-reaching changes across all sectors, unprecedented in terms of scale, are required to limit warming to 1.5°C: Masson-Delmotte et al (n 86) 15.

[94] See Wegener (n 29); A-J Saiger, 'Domestic Courts and the Paris Agreement's Climate Goals: The Need for a Comparative Approach' (2020) 9 *Transnational Environmental Law* 37; OpenGlobalRights, 'Litigating the Climate Emergency' (2020).

[95] *Gloucester Resources* (n 1) 357–58, [445]–[447], [449].

[96] The Agreement 'aims to' hold temperatures to 'well below 2°C' while pursuing efforts to limit the increase to 1.5°C; 'Parties aim to reach global peaking of greenhouse gas emissions as soon as possible': Paris Agreement (n 6) Arts 2(1)(a), 4(1). See also L Rajamani, 'Ambition and Differentiation in the 2015 Paris Agreement: Interpretative Possibilities and Underlying Politics' (2016) 65 *ICLQ* 493.

[97] The Paris Agreement (n 6) is a treaty within the meaning of the Vienna Convention on the Law of Treaties (adopted 23 May 1969, entered into force 27 January 1980) 8 ILM 679, Art 1(a). It contains hard, soft and non-obligations: L Rajamani, 'The Paris Agreement: Interplay Between Hard, Soft and Non-obligations' (2016) 28 *Journal of Environmental Law* 337. In dualist systems, such as Australia's, international treaties, once

no specification about how its goals are to be met; the principal binding obligation on parties is to prepare, communicate and maintain successive NDCs.[98] Australia's present NDC commits the nation to a 26–28 per cent reduction in GHG emissions below 2005 levels by 2030 but proposes a vague set of policies and measures to facilitate the deployment of new and emerging low-emissions technologies to drive emission reductions and support economic growth, rather than clearly indicating the particular climate mitigation measures or pathways to be adopted nationally, or at the state level, to achieve this target.[99] As Lennart Wegener points out, this arrangement means that the mechanisms and norms of the Paris Agreement are 'rarely directly justiciable in national proceedings', which can lead to their 'legal value' being easily neglected.[100] However, he argues that this should not prevent use of these norms by courts in domestic climate change jurisprudence 'as a means of interpretation and guidance'.[101]

In recent years, such instances of courts referencing the Paris Agreement's goals in interpreting the requirements of domestic law are steadily growing. For example, in the New Zealand case of *Thomson v Minister for Climate Change Issues* – concerning a challenge to the government's failure to update the country's 2030 and 2050 emissions reduction targets following the release of the IPCC's Fifth Assessment Report – the High Court found that the Minister's statutory discretionary powers under the Climate Change Response Act had to be construed consistently with New Zealand's international climate obligations.[102] It held that those obligations, while not expressly requiring review of New Zealand's domestic emissions reduction targets when an IPCC report is published, nevertheless

> underline[d] the pressing need for global action, that global action requires all Parties individually to take appropriate steps to meet the necessary collective action, and that Parties should do so in light of relevant scientific information and update their individual measures in light of such information.[103]

More recently,[104] in the *Heathrow Third Runway* case, the English Court of Appeal interpreted a reference in the Planning Act 2008 to consideration of 'government policy' relating to climate change when designating a national policy statement as clearly

ratified, bind a country on the international plane but do not take direct effect in the country's legal system. On the different situation applying in 'monist' systems, such as in the Netherlands, see G van der Schyff and A Meuwese, 'Dutch Constitutional Law in a Globalizing World' (2013) 9(2) *Utrecht Law Review* 1.

[98] Paris Agreement (n 6) Art 4(2)(3)(9).

[99] *Australia's Nationally Determined Contribution* (Australian Government, 2021) 5. Under the Glasgow Climate Pact, concluded at COP26 in Glasgow 2021, countries like Australia who failed to communicate new or updated NDCs are being urged to do so 'as soon as possible' in advance of COP27 at the end of 2022. In addition, the Pact requests Parties 'to revisit and strengthen the 2030 targets in their nationally determined contributions as necessary to align with the Paris Agreement temperature goal by the end of 2022, taking into account different national circumstances': Glasgow Climate Pact (adopted 13 November 2021), Decision -/CMA.3, Arts 28-29.

[100] Wegener (n 29) 23.

[101] ibid.

[102] *Thomson v Minister for Climate Change Issues* [2017] NZHC 733 [88].

[103] ibid, [91].

[104] See also, for example, *Friends of the Irish Environment v. Ireland* [2020] IESC 49; *Notre Affaire à Tous and Others v France*, No. 1904967, 1904968, 1904972, 1904976/4-1, Paris Administrative Court (3 February 2021); *Neubauer v Germany*, Bundesverfassungsgericht [BVERFG], 1 BvR 2656/18, Federal Constitutional Court (24 March 2021).

encompassing the UK government's 'commitment to the Paris Agreement'.[105] While the Court of Appeal found the UK government was not bound to conform to those policy commitments in designating a national policy statement regarding development of Heathrow Airport, it was nevertheless required to take them into account and explain how it had done so.[106]

In *Gloucester Resources*, the Court approached the question of the relevance of the Paris Agreement's provisions for its decision on the Rocky Hill coal mine project through a lens of assessing the causal link between the project's likely emissions and climate change impacts. The Court noted that the Paris Agreement, and NSW Climate Change Policy Framework (as it was at the time) that builds on its requirements, do not proscribe emissions-intensive activities such as new coal mines.[107] As Preston CJ pointed out in a later part of the judgment, a decision that the Paris Agreement or carbon budget considerations requires no new fossil fuel developments would be akin to a 'policy decision', which might raise justiciability concerns similar to those that have constrained the actions of other courts in climate cases.[108]

Instead, the Court emphasised that exploitation and burning of a new fossil fuel reserve, which would increase GHG emissions, 'cannot assist' in meeting the Paris Agreement's long-term temperature and net zero objectives and would be 'likely to run counter to the actions that are required to achieve peaking of global GHG emissions as soon as possible and to undertake rapid reductions thereafter in order to achieve net zero emissions … in the second half of this century'.[109] Preston CJ tied these conclusions about the inconsistency with the requirements of the Paris Agreement of approving the mine to the carbon budget analysis presented by Professor Steffen that 'achieving [Paris] goals implies phasing out fossil fuel use within that time frame'.[110]

As Lennart Wegener has eloquently argued, this kind of analysis by courts provides a way of synchronising domestic actions with 'the ambitious and dynamic character of the overall objectives under the Paris Agreement and the UNFCCC' by 'defining and reducing executive or legislative discretion in view of evolving science or evolving international agreement'.[111] Such decisions provide the transnational glue between the aspirational goals of climate mitigation adopted internationally and the local actions needed to realise those goals. In particular, the *Gloucester Resources* decision illustrates how the Paris Agreement's goals can be translated into parameters guiding the scope of reasonable executive decision-making on projects and actions that increase global GHG emissions.

3.4. Rebutting Market Substitution Arguments

In *Gloucester Resources*, the end point of Preston CJ's analysis of the implications of the carbon budget approach was that this would tend to militate against the burning

[105] *Plan B Earth v Secretary of State for Transport* (n 37) [228].
[106] ibid, [231].
[107] *Gloucester Resources* (n 1) 373, [526].
[108] ibid, 379, [552].
[109] ibid, 373 [526].
[110] ibid, 373 [527].
[111] Wegener (n 29) 26.

of further fossil fuel reserves. GRL raised several arguments as to why the Rocky Hill coal mine should nonetheless be one of the fossil fuel reserves permitted to be exploited and burned.[112] These arguments turned on the so-called 'market substitution assumption'[113] (MSA) that has been a common feature of Australian climate cases, particularly those adjudicated in Queensland.[114]

The MSA is 'the assertion that the rejection of a coal mine in a particular location will make no material difference to global greenhouse gas emissions and resulting climate change, because other coal mines resulting in equal emissions will be developed elsewhere in its stead to cater for global demand for coal'.[115] This argument is often deployed in conjunction with contentions of potential 'carbon leakage' on the basis that market demand for coal will be met from countries where coal mining results in greater emissions due to less stringent environmental standards.[116] In *Gloucester Resources*, GRL buttressed its MSA/carbon leakage submissions by pointing to the strong projected demand, and more limited substitutes, for coking coal in steel production.[117]

The success of the MSA in previous Australian climate cases has turned to a large extent on courts' uncritical acceptance of economic evidence asserting that the global coal market is 'demand-driven', such that a reduction in supply (through refusal of a particular coal mine) will not affect overall demand (which will be met by other suppliers).[118] In *Gloucester Resources*, Preston CJ followed the trend of US courts[119] to examine more closely the evidentiary underpinnings of this argument. His Honour found that there was 'no certainty' of market substitution from new coal mines in other countries if the project was refused, especially given the trend of increasing regulation of coal in large developing countries to meet climate mitigation and air pollution control objectives.[120] The Court also rejected the carbon leakage argument on similar evidentiary grounds, noting that a parallel finding had been made by the Dutch Court of Appeal in the *Urgenda* case.[121] The Court held that GRL had failed to substantiate that the 'risk of carbon leakage will actually occur if approval for the Rocky Hill Coal Project were not to be granted'.[122]

Although no mention of the precautionary principle was made by the Court in this section of its judgment, this reasoning might be described as precautionary.[123] In the

[112] In addition to market substitution/carbon leakage arguments, these included arguments that emissions from the mine could be offset by actions elsewhere and that refusal of the mine was not the least cost abatement action. Both arguments were rejected by the court: *Gloucester Resources* (n 1) 374–75, [529]–[533].

[113] J Bell-James and B Collins, '"If We Don't Mine Coal, Someone Else Will": Debunking the "Market Substitution Assumption" in Queensland Climate Change Litigation' (2020) 37 *Environmental and Planning Law Journal* 167.

[114] J Bell-James and S Ryan, 'Climate Change Litigation in Queensland: A Case Study in Incrementalism' (2016) 33 *Environmental and Planning Law Journal* 515.

[115] Bell-James and Collins (n 113) 169.

[116] *Gloucester Resources* (n 1) 376, [536]–[537].

[117] Preston CJ did not accept though that demand could not be met from other Australian coking coal mines: ibid, [536].

[118] Bell-James and Collins (n 113) 175–76.

[119] *WildEarth Guardians v US Bureau of Land Management* 870 F 3d 1222 (2017).

[120] *Gloucester Resources* (n 1) 376, [538].

[121] ibid, 376 [536]–[537].

[122] ibid, [536].

[123] See also Bell-James and Collins (n 113) 183.

face of serious and potentially irreversible threats to the global climate system posed by the proposed mine's GHG emissions, the Court effectively found that the burden lay with the proponent to produce evidence substantiating the position that there would be no additional harm caused by authorising the proposal.

Preston CJ's judgment in *Gloucester Resources* also exposed the 'morally problematic'[124] nature of the MSA. His Honour pointed to the responsibility, urged by the international climate regime,[125] for developed countries to 'take the lead' in combating climate change – a responsibility which is linked to the fact that 'the largest share of historical and current global emissions of greenhouse gases has originated in developed countries'.[126] Rather than prompting an inevitable course of approval of new coal mines elsewhere, the Court opined that refusal of a coal mine in Australia might be seen as a demonstration of the nation 'taking the lead' in climate policy, which could encourage other developing countries in the region to embrace stronger controls on new fossil fuel developments in their NDCs.[127]

Finally, the Court relied on the critical assessment of the MSA in the climate litigation literature to highlight its logical flaws.[128] In essence, the use of the MSA in justifying coal projects creates a false equivalence between defined actions with certain climate harms and hypothetical projects with uncertain consequences. As Justine Bell-James and Briana Collins have argued: 'There are few other contexts where a harmful behaviour or action is excused purely because another entity would have otherwise caused the harm.'[129] In *Gloucester Resources*, the Court gave its judicial imprimatur to this reasoning, noting:

> If a development will cause an environmental impact that is found to be unacceptable, the environmental impact does not become acceptable because a hypothetical and uncertain alternative development might also cause the same unacceptable environmental impact. The environmental impact remains unacceptable regardless of where it is caused. The potential for a hypothetical but uncertain alternative development to cause the same unacceptable environmental impact is not a reason to approve a definite development that will certainly cause the unacceptable environmental impacts.[130]

4. Conclusion: The Land and Environment Court and the Transnationalisation of Climate Law

Decisions of domestic courts in climate cases inevitably depend on local legal conditions and hence constitute 'a heterogenous phenomenon'.[131] The Court's decision in *Gloucester Resources* reflects these constraints to the extent that it involved an assessment on the

[124] ibid, 181.
[125] Paris Agreement (n 6) Art 4(4); UNFCCC (n 18) Art 3(1).
[126] UNFCCC (n 18) Preamble.
[127] *Gloucester Resources* (n 1) 376, [539].
[128] Bennett (n 53); Bell-James and Ryan (n 114).
[129] Bell-James and Collins (n 113) 185.
[130] *Gloucester Resources* (n 1) 378, [545].
[131] Wegener (n 29) 22.

merits of the legal and factual arguments for approving or refusing a new coal mine. The job of the Court, as articulated by Preston CJ, was to undertake a qualitative balancing exercise through an 'intuitive synthesis of the relevant factors' to determine whether the impacts of the project outweighed its benefits.[132] The result of the Court's assessment was that the balance in this case lay in favour of refusal of the project, or as Preston CJ eloquently put it, 'an open cut coal mine in this part of the Gloucester valley would be in the wrong place at the wrong time'.[133]

Although the result reached in *Gloucester Resources* may not be replicated in subsequent coal litigation,[134] the case still stands as an important example of how judicial reasoning in climate litigation can generate normative understandings of critical issues that are capable of transcending the particular jurisdictional confines and legal context of the decision. Decisions of courts in different countries referencing similar principles, doctrines and precedents, while also drawing on a common scientific understanding of the climate problem, can be seen as a 'transnational feature of climate change governance'.[135] These decisions help connect the global context of GHG pollution and its consequences to the myriad of actions taken at a local scale that can address or exacerbate the problem.

This chapter has argued that the findings of the Land and Environment Court on climate issues in its *Gloucester Resources* decision exemplify the transnational role courts are increasingly playing in a polycentric system of climate governance. The Court's rulings on matters such as the relevance of assessment of downstream emissions, the need to understand climate change as a cumulative impact problem to which all sources of emissions contribute, the role of the aspirational goals of the Paris Agreement in shaping domestic decision-making, and the evidentiary, moral and logical flaws of MSA/carbon leakage arguments provide a comprehensive set of responses to some of the most contested issues in climate litigation: a feat rivalled by few other climate precedents. The case is already having an important impact on the way that other coal mining proposals in NSW are being considered and assessed by planning authorities and courts.[136]

[132] *Gloucester Resources* (n 1) 401, [687]. This was described as assessment on a relative basis. The Court did indicate that there might be a project so large that refusal of the development could be seen to make a meaningful contribution to remaining within the carbon budget and achieving the long-term temperature goal: [555]–[556].

[133] ibid, [699].

[134] See literature assessing the decision: E Aydos et al, 'Rocky Hill: A Legal Breakthrough in the Consideration of Climate Change and Social Impacts of Coal Mines' (2020) 14(2) *Carbon and Climate Law Review* 98, 105–06; E Johnson and R Chick, 'The Ripple Effect of Rocky Hill: One Year On' (2020) 34(9,10) *Australian Environment Review* 194, 195–97; L Hughes, 'The Rocky Hill Decision: A Watershed for Climate Change Action?' (2019) 37 *Journal of Energy and Natural Resources Law* 341, 348–50; Covington et al (n 16); Medici-Colombo (n 16).

[135] Wegener (n 29) 18.

[136] Subsequent assessments of coal mines in NSW by the IPC have referred to *Gloucester Resources*, eg in September 2019 the IPC refused approval for Kepco's Bylong coal project, including following Preston CJ's reasoning that a new coal mine 'cannot assist' global climate change efforts: *Bylong Coal Project (SSD 6367) Statement of Reasons for Decision* [691]–[693]. The decision has been upheld on appeal by the Land and Environment Court of New South Wales and the NSW Court of Appeal. At the time of writing, KEPCO had further sought leave to appeal to the High Court of Australia: J Lapham, 'KEPCO to seek leave to appeal Bylong Valley coal mine refusal in High Court' *ABC News*, 14 October 2021.

More broadly, as climate litigation continues to grow and expand globally,[137] there are increasing opportunities for courts to contribute to a transnational law of climate change that transcends jurisdictional boundaries and the structural constraints of localised legal systems to address the shared issues that arise in these cases. In this respect, the *Gloucester Resources* decision charts a way forward for other courts seeking to reconcile local fossil fuel developments with international legal requirements under the Paris Agreement and scientific imperatives to reduce GHG emissions in order to ensure the prospect of a safe climate future.[138]

[137] J Setzer and C Higham, *Global Trends in Climate Change Litigation: 2021 Snapshot* (Grantham Research Institute on Climate Change and the Environment, 2021).

[138] See, for example, the case of *Waratah Coal Pty Ltd v Youth Verdict Ltd & Ors* [2020] QLC 33 concerning objections to applications for a coal mine in the Galilee Basin by Waratah Coal. Part of the contention being made is that existing coal mines will exceed the world's carbon budget and therefore 'no new fossil fuel development is consistent with meeting the Paris Agreement climate targets', going further than the reasoning of Preston CJ (www.youthverdict.org.au/our-objection, accessed 18 September 2020). See also the decision in *Sharma by her litigation representative Sister Marie Brigid Arthur v. Minister for the Environment* (2021) 391 ALR 1; [2021] FCA 560 finding at first instance that the Federal Environment Minister owes Australian children a duty of care to avoid causing harm when considering approval for a coal mine. At the time of writing, the decision has been appealed to the Full Bench of the Federal Court of Australia.

5

Transnational Dimensions of the Land and Environment Court of New South Wales

BEN BOER

1. Introduction

On my arrival at Macquarie University in 1979, I was asked to develop a course in environmental law, focused on the new suite of environmental legislation that was just being enacted, and which heralded the establishment of the Land and Environment Court of New South Wales (the Court). The task of designing such a course was daunting.[1] It involved understanding the complex history and politics of planning and associated law in the state, and rapidly gaining some comprehension of the brand-new legislation, which had emerged from a rather different cultural and social milieu to that with which I was familiar in Victoria. I also endeavoured to absorb the Australian federal environmental legislation that had been passed from 1974 onwards, as well as to seek guidance from then more-advanced jurisdictions in the field, namely the United States and Canada. Working with the new legislation and its associated institutions, I have been privileged to observe the Court, albeit at a distance, from the very earliest stages of its development; over the years I have interacted with a variety of its judges and commissioners, as well as many practising and academic lawyers and other experts within Australia and across the world who have been involved in the field. The preparation of this chapter has thus involved both academic and personal reflections on the development of the Court over the past four decades.

While the establishment of the Court can in part be seen as a product of the political, economic, social and cultural fabric of Australia, and in particular of the state of New South Wales, there is a need to understand the broader global stage from which

[1] The task was made easier by the fact that Donna Craig, then my new colleague at Macquarie University, had taken a course in Environmental Law at the University of New South Wales, and she graciously lent her expertise to the task of designing the first course, before leaving me to teach it for the first time while she pursued graduate studies in environmental law in Canada. Happily, on her return we continued our collaboration and established the Macquarie Centre for Environmental Law, which still thrives.

the Court emerged, and with which, over time, it has increasingly merged. It has now forged a leading role for itself within the constellation of specialist environmental courts in an increasingly interconnected world. With these points in mind, the aim of the chapter is to understand the development of the Court in terms of its transnational dimensions.

In order to gain some perspective on how the Court's establishment might be understood from the point of view of its transnational dimensions, the chapter first explores the meaning of transnational environmental law, and then sketches the international and national context of the 1960s and 1970s. Part of that picture involves contemplating the political and social policy issues that stimulated the development of international environmental law and the related global institutions around that time. It examines the influence of those movements on Australian law, government and institutions, and looks in particular at the transnational law influences on the Court. A short exposition of the legal responses stimulated by the environment movement, focusing on New South Wales, is also included. The chapter examines the international significance of the Court, and its role as a transnational model for environmental courts and tribunals in other jurisdictions. It also focuses on the internationally established concept of sustainable development and associated principles, as well as the emerging concept of the environmental rule of law. Further, it briefly canvasses the work of the Court in the area of climate change. It then looks at the importance of public litigation, legal aid and open standing in our environmental law system, and then the role of the Court in transnational capacity building. It concludes that the Court, being recognised as a global leader, has an ethical responsibility to continue to promote improved decision-making on the environment and the ecologically sustainable exploitation of natural resources around the world through its expertise, its jurisprudence and its procedural practices.

2. The Meaning of Transnational Environmental Law

The concept of transnational environmental law can be apprehended in a variety of ways.[2] It involves, first and foremost, an understanding of the global nature of environmental issues. This means that specialist environmental courts, including the Land and Environment Court, cannot work in isolation, but must deal with many of the legal issues before them in their international and national legal context. It entails some comprehension of different legal cultures and the political, economic and social contexts that underlie other legal systems. Transnational environmental law can incorporate the idea of vertical transfers of knowledge concerning legal instruments, jurisprudence and procedural mechanisms as well as principles and concepts between international, regional and national levels. It draws also on the development of international environmental law and is related to the work of United Nations bodies, especially the law and

[2] A more in-depth discussion of the complexities of transnational environmental law is found in E Fisher, 'The Rise of Transnational Environmental Law and the Expertise of Environmental Lawyers' (2012) 1 *Transnational Environmental Law* 43.

policy arms of the United Nations Environment Programme (UNEP) and the United Nations Development Programme,[3] organisations such as the International Union for Conservation of Nature,[4] and the jurisprudence of global decision-making bodies such as the International Court of Justice and the Law of the Sea Tribunal. Just as importantly, the process of 'transnationalising' environmental law can also involve horizontal transfers of approaches and concepts between national jurisdictions, as part of ongoing processes of globalisation[5] and regionalisation.[6] In the Asian and Pacific regions, legal cultures differ, sometimes markedly, not only because of the differences between civil law, common law and the sharia Islamic legal system, but also because of the different understandings of the functions of law and the idea of the 'rule of law'.[7]

Transnational environmental law has clearly become relevant to the work of the courts, and raises the issue of the need for judges to understand the wider implications of their decisions, especially in particular areas of environmental law. The most obvious fields in this respect are climate change and biodiversity loss, taken both separately and together, as well as every type of pollution.

A further transnationally important dimension is that of human rights, especially concerning the right to life, livelihood and shelter, the right to food and water, and the right to culture. There has also been a longstanding debate concerning the right to a clean, healthy and sustainable environment, a form of which was first recognised in the Stockholm Declaration in 1972.[8] The most significant development of this dimension is the Human Rights Council resolution of 2021 with respect to recognition of the human right to a clean, healthy and sustainable environment.[9] Based on years of work by successive United Nations Special Rapporteurs on Human Rights and the Environment,[10] the resolution is likely to have far-reaching repercussions with respect

[3] See B Boer, 'The Globalisation of Environmental Law: The Role of the United Nations' (1995) 20 *Melbourne University Law Review* 101.

[4] The work of the IUCN World Commission on Environmental Law is particularly relevant in terms of developing international environmental law instruments, declarations and institutions; see www.iucn.org/commissions/world-commission-environmental-law/about/history.

[5] See RV Percival, 'The Globalization of Environmental Law' (2009) 26 *Pace Environmental Law Review* 451.

[6] See B Boer, 'The Rise of Environmental Law in the Asian Region' (1999) 32 *University of Richmond Law Review* 1503, 1508.

[7] For examples in the Asian region, see R Peerenboom, *Asian Discourses of Rule of Law: Theories and Implementation of Rule of Law in Twelve Asian Countries, France and the US* (London, Routledge, 2004); P Barresi, 'The Role of Law and the Rule of Law in China's Quest to Build an Ecological Civilization' (2017) 1 *Chinese Journal of Environmental Law* 9; B Boer et al, *The Mekong: A Socio-legal Approach to River Basin Development* (London, Routledge 2016).

[8] Declaration of the United Nations Conference on the Human Environment, Stockholm, UN Doc A/CONF 48/14.Rev 1 Principle 1. The right to a clean, healthy and sustainable environment (or similar formulations) has now been recognised in more than 150 countries, in constitutions and or national legislation: UNGA A/73/188 (2018) UN Human Rights Obligations relating to the Enjoyment of a Safe, Clean, Healthy and Sustainable Environment, para 29; J May and E Daly, *Global Judicial Handbook on Environmental Constitutionalism*, 3rd edn (UNEP, 2019) 18; B Boer, 'Environmental Principles and the Right to a Quality Environment' in L Krämer and E Orlando (eds), *Principles of Environmental Law* (Cheltenham, Edward Elgar, 2018) 52–75.

[9] Human Rights Council 'The human right to a clean, healthy and sustainable environment' A/HRC/RES/48/13, adopted 8 October 2021.

[10] Office of the High Commissioner on Human Rights, https://www.ohchr.org/en/Issues/environment/SRenvironment/Pages/SRenvironmentIndex.aspx#:~:text=About%20the%20mandate&text=John%20Knox%20was%20appointed%20the,(resolution%2028%2F11).

to the future development of international and domestic environmental law. Another emerging aspect of human rights is the increasing occurrence of intimidation and harassment of, and violence directed towards, environmental human rights defenders around the world, including in the Asian and Pacific region,[11] and even in Australia.[12]

All of these dimensions are becoming increasingly relevant to courts at national and subnational levels. Their importance is underlined by a variety of declarations and statements issued by high-level meetings and conferences of judges in the area of environmental law.[13] Such documents call on judges around the world to respond. For example, the Kunming Declaration states (in summary) that judges should: enhance the judicial response to the environmental crisis, and in particular to address climate change and conserve biodiversity; actively adopt preventive judicial measures; preferentially apply restorative judicial measures; explore and improve the public interest litigation system; encourage the use of diversified dispute resolution methods; promote the professional development of environmental justice; enhance the professional capacity of environmental justice; increase the application of information technology; and deepen international cooperation and exchanges.[14] While such declarations and statements do not legally bind the judges involved in their drafting and endorsement, they do reach into the judiciaries of every jurisdiction represented; arguably there are clear moral obligations to take judicial notice of them. They should certainly be seen as relevant to decision-making in specialised bodies such as the Land and Environment Court.

3. Transnational Law Influences on the Court

Understanding the context for the establishment of the Land and Environment Court in its transnational dimensions must necessarily include identifying the growth of significant global concern with respect to the degradation of the environment, the depletion of natural resources, and the deterioration of the cultural and natural heritage. Increasing concern for protection of the natural and cultural environment grew as a result of the ravages of the Second World War. The initiation of UNESCO in 1945[15] and the establishment of the International Union for Conservation of Nature and Natural Resources (IUCN) in 1948[16] were two early indicators of that concern.

[11] See United Nations Environment Programme, Issue Brief, *SDG 16: Human Rights and the Environmental Rule of Law* (2021) www.unep.org/resources/factsheet/human-rights-and-environmental-rule-law.

[12] 'Moree shooting: Farmer Ian Turnbull jailed for 35 years for murdering environmental officer' ABC News 23 June 2016, https://www.abc.net.au/news/2016-06-23/moree-shooting-ian-turnbull-sentenced-over-murder/7535808 concerns the murder in 2015 of a compliance official of the New South Wales Office of Environment and Heritage who was investigating illegal clearing of native vegetation.

[13] Recent examples include the Statement of the Asia-Pacific Judicial Conference on Climate Change: Adjudication in the Time of Covid-19, Asian Development Bank and United Nations Environment Programme Conference, 11 December 2020, www.ajne.org/event/asia-pacific-judicial-conference-climate-change-adjudication-time-covid-19#quicktabs-event_tabs=5, and the Kunming Declaration of the World Judicial Conference on Environment. The conference was entitled 'The Role of the Judiciary in Advancing Ecological Civilization: Building a Shared Future for All Life on Earth' 27 May 2021, full text at www.xinhuanet.com/2021-05/28/c_1127500735.htm (translated).

[14] Kunming Declaration (n 13).

[15] United Nations Educational, Cultural and Scientific Organization established in London in 1945.

[16] See M Holgate, *The Green Web: A Union for World Conservation* (London, IUCN Earthscan, 1999).

In the decades after the Second World War, and in particular from the 1960s onwards, the processes of decolonisation around the world[17] led to increasing awareness of the need for recognition of the sovereign rights of the newly independent countries over their natural resources and demands for a seat at the table.[18] The voices of a much wider range of states, especially developing states, began to be heard.[19]

The emerging environmental movement and the growing awareness by governments and civil society of the causes and effects of environmental degradation led to the world's first global environmental political gathering at the Stockholm Conference on the Human Environment in 1972. The influential Stockholm Declaration[20] mirrored some of this movement, setting out a range of ground-breaking environmental principles. These have continued to resonate in the drafting of multilateral environmental treaties, becoming part of the environmental debate from the level of the United Nations down to national and subnational decision-making. As a result, the modern international environmental law regime emerged, becoming an inherent and increasingly significant part of the broader international legal order. There are now literally hundreds of bilateral and multilateral treaties concerning the environment,[21] as well as a number of important conventions relating to various aspects of the cultural and environmental heritage.[22] These developments inevitably had ramifications on the growth of environmental law regimes at national level, as well as at subnational level in federally organised countries such as Australia. They can be characterised as vertical or top-down transfers of transnational legal knowledge.

Australian national governments have generally been strong supporters of this burgeoning international regulatory regime, which has demonstrably influenced the development of environmental law. Many of these treaties have become part of Australian federal law, necessarily through legislative enactment at federal level.[23] As noted by Gerry Bates:

> To be effective in this country … international law must be translated into Australian law by domestic legislators, federal and state. The majority of federal environmental legislation, in

[17] Manifested, inter alia, by the United Nations Decolonisation Resolution UNGA Res 1514 (XV) 1960.

[18] See United Nations Permanent Sovereignty Resolution, UNGA Res 1803 (XVII) 1962.

[19] Some of this history is traced in P Hassan, 'Role of the South in the Development of International Environmental Law' (2017) 1 *Chinese Journal of Environmental Law* 133, 157.

[20] Stockholm Declaration (n 8).

[21] Early examples include: Convention on Wetlands of International Importance especially as Waterfowl Habitat (adopted 2 February 1971, entered into force 21 December 1975) 996 UNTS 245: Convention on International Trade in Endangered Species of Wild Fauna and Flora (adopted 3 March 1973, entered into force 1 July 1975) 993 UNTS 243. UN Convention on the Law of the Sea (adopted 10 December 1982, entered into force 16 November 1994) 1833 UNTS 397. For full lists of these treaties, see P Sands and J Peel, *Principles of International Environmental Law*, 4th edn (Cambridge, Cambridge University Press, 2018); JE Viñuales and P-M Dupuy, *International Environmental Law*, 2nd edn (Cambridge, Cambridge University Press, 2018).

[22] These include: Convention and Protocol for the Protection of Cultural Property in the Event of Armed Conflict (adopted 14 May 1954, entered into force 7 August 1956) 249 UNTS 215; Convention Concerning the Protection of the World Cultural and Natural Heritage (adopted 16 November 1972, entered into force 17 December 1975) 1037 UNTS 151; Convention on the Protection of the Underwater Cultural Heritage 41 ILM 40 (2002); Convention for the Safeguarding of the Intangible Cultural Heritage (adopted 17 October 2003, entered into force 20 April 2006) 2368 UNTS 3; Convention on the Protection and Promotion of the Diversity of Cultural Expressions (adopted 20 October 2005, entered into force 18 March 2007) 2440 UNTS 311.

[23] These include the suite of Australian federal laws enacted in the mid-1970s: the Environment Protection (Impact of Proposals) Act 1974, the Australian Heritage Commission Act 1975, the Australian National Parks

fact, reflects the content of international agreements; there is very little federal environmental law that does not spring from international obligations.[24]

Although international law does not directly bind the Australian states and territories, the influence of environmental treaties can nevertheless be discerned both directly and indirectly. This is both in terms of specific mechanisms such as environmental impact assessment as well as the concept of sustainable development and associated principles such as the precautionary principle, found in state and territory legislation,[25] which were directly derived top-down from the international level as well as horizontally from other national jurisdictions.[26]

4. Legal Responses to the Environment Movement

These transnational influences are of course not the only forces that shaped environmental law in Australia in the 1970s. The federal, state and territory governments legally responded in a variety of ways to address the issues that were being highlighted by national and state conservation organisations as well as local groups of concerned citizens. The social movement that developed the Green Bans were bent on conserving the built and natural environment.[27] Sadly, Green Bans continue to be relevant today.[28] The Australian Conservation Foundation, a national organisation, and bodies such as the Nature Conservation Council and the Total Environmental Centre at NSW state level also shaped the legal responses.

The Wran government's suite of environment and heritage legislation dramatically altered the decision-making processes on these issues at both state government and local council level, especially with regard to the demands for public participation and legal remedies.[29] The Heritage Act 1977 (NSW) (originally intended to be part of the same legislative package) was joined two years later by the Environmental

and Wildlife Conservation Act 1975, followed by the World Heritage Properties Conservation Act 1983. This legislation was subsumed by the Environment Protection and Biodiversity Conservation Act 1999.

[24] G Bates, *Environmental Law in Australia*, 10th edn (LexisNexis, 2019) 2.61; for the direct connection between federal environmental legislation and international environmental treaties see, ibid, Table 3.1 Application of external affairs power, 3.13.

[25] See RJ Fowler, "Environmental principles in Australia' in Krämer and E Orlando (n 8) 476–493 for a detailed exposition of the development and adoption of these principles.

[26] ibid, ch 4 'Ecologically Sustainable Development: The Template for Environmental Management'. In New South Wales, the relevant legislation includes the Protection of the Environment Administration Act 1991 (NSW), s 6(2), and, by reference, the Environmental Planning and Assessment Act 1979 (NSW), s 1.4 and the Protection of the Environment Operations Act 1997 (NSW), s 47.

[27] The story of the Green Bans is told in J Mundey, *Green Bans and Beyond* (Sydney, Angus and Robertson, 1981); RJ Roddewig, *Green Bans: The Birth of Australian Environmental Politics* (Sydney, The Conservation Foundation and Hale & Iremonger, 1978); and M Burgmann and V Burgmann, *Green Bans, Red Union: The Saving of a City*, 2nd edn (Montgomery, AL, NewSouth Books, 2017).

[28] See 'Green Bans – Action Now', www.greenbans.net.au/now, concerning removal and resituating of 'Willow Grove' in Parramatta in 2021 to make way for the Powerhouse Museum; this was also the subject of an action in the Land and Environment Court, *North Parramatta Residents Action Group v Infrastructure NSW* [2021] NSWLEC 60, and the Court of Appeal, *North Parramatta Residents' Action Group Inc v Infrastructure New South Wales* (No 2) [2021] NSWCA 146.

[29] Also see Stein, this volume.

Planning and Assessment Act 1979 (NSW) and the Land and Environment Court Act 1979 (NSW), together with the Coastal Protection Act 1979 (NSW) (now the Coastal Management Act 2016 (NSW)) and the Historic Houses Act 1980 (NSW). It fell to the newly established Land and Environment Court to preside over these fields as well as over the early pollution control legislation (and over time, several dozen other laws).[30] The new laws and the new Court also spawned, in a similar way to earlier developments in the United States and Canada, the establishment of the Environmental Law Association of New South Wales in 1980,[31] followed by the establishment of the National Environmental Law Association in 1982 and the Environmental Defenders Office in 1984.[32]

With increasing knowledge and concern about increasing global environmental degradation and cultural loss, especially for First Nations peoples,[33] the Court can thus be seen as reflecting a demand for greater accountability for environmental decision-making. But international environmental law was already definitely in the mix. A consideration of Australian cases from the 1970s onwards indicates that international environmental law obligations found in international conventions as well as policies concerning the environment have influenced the decisions of both federal and state courts.[34] At federal level, the World Heritage Convention[35] has been litigated a number of times.[36] The most important of these instances was the *Tasmanian Dam* case[37] in the High Court. The Ramsar Convention on Wetlands[38] was the subject of a case in the Federal Court.[39] As Bates notes 'Australian courts … are prepared to interpret domestic legislation and even the Constitution, in a way that fulfils Australia's international legal responsibilities. Indeed, where there is a choice, courts would prefer such a construction.'[40]

As hinted at above, Australian environmental law and its legal culture has also clearly been influenced by developments in other jurisdictions, representing a horizontal transfer of concepts and mechanisms. The steps taken in the United States from

[30] See Land and Environment Court Act 1979 (NSW), ss 16–21 (where the jurisdiction of the Court was listed at that time).

[31] Now known as the Environmental and Planning Law Association, New South Wales; Murray Wilcox QC served as its first president; I was its first vice-president).

[32] Originating in New South Wales, it is now a national body.

[33] The Court has specifc jurisdiction concerning First Nations peoples under the Aboriginal Land Rights Act 1983 (NSW): see Land and Environment Court Act 1980 ss 19, 20, 36, and 37.

[34] DR Rothwell and B Boer 'The Influence of International Environmental Law on Australian Courts' (1998) 7 *Review of Community and International Environmental Law* 31.

[35] Convention Concerning the Protection of the World Cultural and Natural Heritage 1972 (n 22).

[36] See B Boer, 'World Heritage Disputes in Australia' (1992) 7 *Journal of Environmental Law and Litigation* 247, 260; B Boer and G Wiffen, *Heritage Law in Australia* (Oxford, Oxford University Press, 2006), ch 3, 'The World Heritage Convention in Australia'.

[37] *Commonwealth v Tasmania* (1983) 158 CLR 1.

[38] Convention on Wetlands of International Importance especially as Waterfowl Habitat 1971 (n 22).

[39] *Greentree v Minister for Environment and Heritage* (2005) 144 FCR 388; see further DR Rothwell and B Boer, 'From the Franklin to Berlin: the Internationalisation of Australian Environmental Law and Policy' (1995) 17 *Sydney Law Review* 242 and D Fisher, 'The Impact of International Law upon the Australian Legal System' (1999) *Environmental and Planning Law Journal* 372; see also B Boer 'The Globalization of Environmental Law' (2000) 76 *Reform* 33 (Australian Law Reform Commission Journal).

[40] Bates (n 24) 4.46.

the 1970s, with the introduction of the National Environmental Policy Act[41] and the setting up of the President's Council on Environmental Quality, became well known in Australia. One significant aspect was the introduction of public interest environmental actions, known in the United States as 'citizen suits', based on the idea of open standing.[42] This has been particularly important for the Land and Environment Court, as a number of environmental laws in NSW allow for 'any person' to bring an action for breach of the legislation,[43] a concept that was 'readily embraced' in this jurisdiction.[44] This was despite the expressed fear that litigation floodgates would be thereby opened, a notion rejected by Stein J, based on the experience of the Court over many years, that the open standing provision 'has produced little more than a modest flow barely wetting the wellies'.[45]

5. Ecologically Sustainable Development in the Land and Environment Court

The concept of sustainable development and its associated principles became a central driver for cases in the Land and Environment Court from an early stage. The concept was generated in the 1980s, beginning with the World Conservation Strategy.[46] It was popularised around the world through the Brundtland Commission report *Our Common Future*[47] in 1987 and with *Caring for the Earth*[48] in 1991. Since the 1992 Earth Summit in Rio de Janeiro, with its resulting *Agenda 21* and the Rio Declaration on Environment and Development,[49] sustainable development has become a catch-cry of high-level intergovernmental environmental policy, especially within UNEP and the United Nations Development Programme, as well as in national jurisdictions around the world.[50]

[41] National Environmental Policy Act of 1969, 42 USC § 4321; for an overview of fifty years of the National Environmental Policy Act, see D Binder, 'NEPA at 50: Standing Tall' (2019) 23 *Chapman Law Review* 3–51 and D Binder, 'The Pillars of Modern American Environmental Law' (2020) 24 *Chapman Law Review* 1, 3.

[42] A pioneering enactment with regard to a very wide application of locus standi was the Michigan Environmental Protection Act 1970. Based on the Michigan law, I first advocated for the 'any person' provision to apply even more broadly than the New South Wales open standing provision, as part of an argument for an ecological ethic in B Boer 'Social Ecology and Environmental Law' (1984) 2 *Environmental and Planning Law Journal* 233, 252.

[43] Including the Environmental Planning and Assessment Act 1979 ss 9.45 and 9.46; Heritage Act 1977 ss 153 and 154; National Parks and Wildlife Act 1974 s 193.

[44] P Ryan 'Court of Hope and False Expectations; The Land and Environment Court 21 Years On' (2002) 14 *Journal of Environmental Law* 301, 304 citing *Rowley v NSW Leather Company* (1980) 46 LGRA 250.

[45] *Oshlack v Richmond River Council*, (1994) 82 LGERA 236 at 245.

[46] See World Conservation Strategy: Living Resource Conservation for Sustainable Development (IUCN, 1980); the 1983 National Conservation Strategy for Australia, based on the global strategy, was the subject of critique by a leading member of the New South Wales land and environment bar, Murray Wilcox QC (speaking in his then capacity as President of the Australian Conservation Foundation); see DC Frecker, 'National Conservation Strategy for Australia; Draft Report on Canberra Conference' (1983) 2 *AMPLA Bulletin* 41.

[47] World Commission on Environment and Development (Brundtland Report), *Our Common Future* (Oxford, Oxford University Press, 1987).

[48] David Munro, *Caring for the Earth: A Strategy for Sustainable Living* (IUCN, UNEP, WWF, 1991).

[49] Rio Declaration on Environment and Development, UN Doc. A/CONF.151/26. Rev.1.

[50] The Sustainable Development Goals of 2015, contained in the 'Transforming our World: The 2030 Agenda for Sustainable Development', are the latest major iteration of UN policy in this field.

In 1989, the Australian federal government, at the urging of Prime Minister Hawke, initiated a series of reports focusing on a wide range of environmental and natural resources issues that had the effect of introducing the concept of *ecologically* sustainable development (ESD) into the Australian environmental law realm. ESD and its associated principles quickly became the subject of legislation at federal, state and territory levels in Australia,[51] being adopted into their environmental laws with an enthusiasm not reflected in many other countries.[52] Government departments, planning bodies, courts and tribunals thus became obliged to consider the concept in their decision-making.[53]

As a consequence, a significant challenge with respect to the development of the jurisprudence has been the need to understand and implement the legislated ESD principles,[54] some of which are based on international developments. Several of them were incorporated in Australian federal legislation[55] and NSW legislation.[56] The Court has therefore had to interpret and implement them in a wide range of cases. The precautionary principle is the most prominent of these. In the early 2000s, Justice Stein[57] surveyed a number of the early cases that dealt with the precautionary principle,[58] including *Leatch*,[59] *Nicholls*[60] and *Greenpeace*.[61] Later analyses have examined further cases and their reasoning in some detail.[62] Nicolas de Sadeleer says

[51] P Stein and S Mahony, 'Incorporating Sustainability Principles in Legislation' in P Leadbeter, N Gunningham and B Boer (eds), *Environmental Outlook No 3: Law and Policy* (Alexandria, Federation Press, 1999) 58.

[52] For early analysis, see B Boer, 'Institutionalising Ecologically Sustainable Development: The Roles of National, State, and Local Governments in Translating Grand Strategy into Action' (1995) 31 *Willamette Law Review* 307; B Boer, 'Institutionalising Ecologically Sustainable Development' (1995) 2 *Judicial Review* 243; for more recent comment, see BJ Preston, 'The Judicial Development of the Precautionary Principle' (2018) 35 *Environmental and Planning Law Journal* 123, 123–26.

[53] See Boer, 'Institutionalising Ecologically Sustainable Development' (n 52); B Boer, 'Environmental and Resource Law in Australia' (1993) 31 *Osgoode Hall Law Journal* 327.

[54] See Scotford, this volume.

[55] The Environment Protection and Biodiversity Conservation Act 1999 (Cth) incorporates five principles for ecologically sustainable development in s 3A; in summary,: (a) the principle of integration, (b) the precautionary principle, (c) the principle of intergenerational equity, (d) the conservation of biological diversity and ecological integrity, and (e) promotion of improved valuation, pricing and incentive mechanisms.

[56] The Environmental Planning Assessment Act 1979 (NSW) refers to ESD as set out in the Protection of the Environment Administration Act 1991 (NSW) together with four associated principles; in summary: (a) the precautionary principle, (b) intergenerational equity, (c) conservation of biological diversity and ecological integrity, and (d) improved valuation, pricing and incentive mechanisms.

[57] P Stein, 'Are Decision-Makers Too Cautious with the Precautionary Principle?' (2000) 17 *Environmental and Planning Law Journal* 3–23.

[58] P Stein, 'Specialist Environmental Courts: The Land and Environment Court of New South Wales, Australia' (2002) *Environmental Law Review* 4, 5, 18; see also a critique of these cases by J Peel, *The Precautionary Principle in Practice: Environmental Decision-Making and Scientific Uncertainty* (Alexandria, Federation Press 2005) 203–10. Peel also critiqued the well-known case *Telstra Corporation Limited v Hornsby Shire Council* (2006) 67 NSWLR 256, decided after her book was published: J Peel 'When (Scientific) Rationality Rules: (Mis)Application of the Precautionary Principle in Australian Mobile Phone Tower Cases' (2007) 19 *Journal of Environmental Law* 103–20; see response to the Peel critique by Preston (n 52).

[59] Stein J in *Leatch v National Parks and Wildlife Service* (1993) 81 LGERA 270.

[60] Talbot J in *Nicholls v National Parks and Wildlife Service* (1994) 84 LGERA 397.

[61] Pearlman CJ in *Greenpeace v Redbank Power Co* (1994) 86 LGERA 143.

[62] For example, E Fisher, *Risk Regulation and Administrative Constitutionalism* (Oxford, Hart Publishing, 2007) ch 1; E Scotford, *Environmental Principles and the Evolution of Environmental Law* (Oxford, Hart Publishing, 2017); BJ Preston, 'The Role of the Judiciary in Promoting Sustainable Development' (2005) 9(2–3) *Asia Pacific Journal of Environmental Law* 109.

of these developments: 'Australian courts have been at the forefront in implementing the principle; Australian case law thus contains a range of citations on its contents and legal application.'[63]

ESD as a concept has thus necessarily become infused into the judgments of the Court, and that jurisprudence has been the subject of some specialised studies. One of the most comprehensive of these is the work of Eloise Scotford,[64] which traces the evolution of ESD principles.[65] Scotford recognises the importance of international law in moulding the Court's jurisprudence:

> The NSWLEC uses ESD principles to push doctrinal boundaries in NSW law, in a conscious bid to aid what it recognises as a broader project of developing a 'global jurisprudence' in relation to environmental principles. The Court uses this appeal to international law to give authority to its novel reasoning, drawing on transnational influences to develop its jurisprudence on ESD principles. This outward-looking attitude to environmental law globally is part of the NSWLEC legal culture that shapes its ESD doctrine, along with a range of jurisdictional and doctrinal factors that are particular to the NSW legal system.[66]

Significantly, in the context of this chapter, Scotford goes on to say: 'The openness of the Court to transnational legal influences is an important feature of the Court's culture, allowing it to draw inspiration and authority from international sources to support and inform localised legal developments.'[67]

6. Environmental Rule of Law

As demonstrated by the experience with ESD, a characteristic of the field of environmental law is the ongoing development of new concepts and principles. Statements of environmental principles issued by international institutions have proven to be very useful for developing domestic jurisprudence in appropriate cases in the past decade. An umbrella term for these principles is the concept now known as the environmental rule of law (EROL). EROL was developed with the participation of some of the world's leading environmental judges and lawyers. It is quintessentially an outcome of intense transnational interactions, and has become internationally known as a result of the UNEP's focus on this concept. In 2013, UNEP's governing body adopted Decision 27/9, on Advancing Justice, Governance and Law for Environmental Sustainability. This decision is the first legal recognition of the concept at UN level. The resolution called on UNEP's executive director

> to lead the United Nations system and support national Governments upon their request in the development and implementation of environmental rule of law with attention at all

[63] N de Sadeleer, *Environmental Principles: from Slogans to Legal Rules*, 2nd edn (Oxford, Oxford University Press, 2020) 188; one example is the Victorian Supreme Court in *Brown Mountain Environment East Gippsland Inc v VicForests* (2010) 30 VR 1 (*Brown Mountain*) [188], [190], [195], where Osborne J accepted the analysis of the precautionary principle as stated by Preston CJ in *Telstra Corporation Limited* (n 58).

[64] For example, Scotford (n 62). See also Scotford, this volume.

[65] Scotford (n 62) ch 5.

[66] ibid, 203, footnotes omitted.

[67] ibid, 231.

> levels to mutually supporting governance features, including information disclosure, public participation, implementable and enforceable laws, and implementation and accountability mechanisms including coordination of roles as well as environmental auditing and criminal, civil and administrative enforcement with timely, impartial and independent dispute resolution.[68]

UNEP sees EROL as central to sustainable development, by integrating 'environmental needs with the essential elements of the rule of law, and provides the basis for improving environmental governance. It highlights environmental sustainability by connecting it with fundamental rights and obligations'.[69] However, it is the courts that will continue to be critical to achieving this integration:

> The judiciary ... plays a vital role as the guarantor of the protective benefits of environmental law. Moreover, what judges treat as important, a society comes to judge as important. Thus, the courts' response to environmental problems can have a powerful transforming effect across society, with the seriousness of judicial attention and response projecting to the regulated community and the public at large the importance of environmental quality and the unacceptability of behaviors that jeopardize the environment. *The judicial response can serve as a powerful catalyst toward the solidification of the environmental rule of law and the development of an environmental ethic* – an ethic that, once it takes hold, can engender a sense of responsibility in all sectors of society, inspire citizens to think green and buy green, and encourage businesses to respond to green consumer demand and to their own emergent corporate environmental conscience.[70]

In 2013, UNEP set out seven guiding principles as core elements of EROL:[71]

1. Fair, clear and implementable environmental laws.
2. Access to information, public participation and justice.
3. Accountability and integrity of institutions and decision-makers.
4. Clear and coordinated mandates and roles, across and within institutions.
5. Accessible, fair, impartial, timely and responsive dispute resolution mechanisms.
6. Recognising the mutually enforcing relationship between rights and the environmental rule of law.
7. Specific criteria for courts to interpret environmental law.

The emergence of EROL was reinforced by the IUCN World Commission on Environmental Law through the IUCN World Declaration on the Environmental Rule of Law.[72] The Declaration envisages EROL as a fundamental aspect of the role of judges and courts: 'The environmental rule of law is understood as the legal framework of

[68] 27th Session of UNEP Governing Council/Global Ministerial Environment Forum www.informea.org/en/decision/advancing-justice-governance-and-law-environmental-sustainability.

[69] UNEP, Environmental Rule of Law, www.unep.org/explore-topics/environmental-rights-and-governance/what-we-do/promoting-environmental-rule-law-0.

[70] S Fulton and A Benjamin 'Foundations of Sustainability' (2011) 28(6) *Environmental Forum* 32, 36 (emphasis added).

[71] See UNEP, 'Environmental Rule of Law: Critical to Sustainable Development' (Issue Brief 2015) www.unep.org/resources/report/environmental-rule-law-critical-sustainable-development, and *The Environmental Rule of Law: First Annual Report* (UNEP 2019) 1.3.

[72] IUCN World Declaration on the Environmental Rule of Law (Rio De Janeiro, 2016) www.iucn.org/commissions/world-commission-environmental-law/wcel-resources/wcel-important-documentation/environmental-rule-law.

procedural and substantive rights and obligations that incorporates the principles of ecologically sustainable development in the rule of law.' The preamble states in part:

> Observing the essential role that judges and courts play in building the environmental rule of law through the effective application of laws at national, sub-national, regional, and international levels, and through fair and independent decision-making that accords all parties equal access and consideration regardless of power or privilege.[73]

The Declaration includes a list of thirteen principles, some already established, and some emerging.

Courts around the world, including the Land and Environment Court, have absorbed some of the long-established principles that are now identified under EROL.[74] One example of the application of an emerging principle, listed in the Declaration, is *in dubio pro natura*,[75] first adopted in some Latin American jurisdictions,[76] but now beginning to be adopted transnationally, along with an even newer principle, *in dubio pro aqua*.[77] Both of these were incorporated into Pakistani law in *D G Khan Cement Company Ltd v Government of Punjab* in 2021.[78]

In due course, it can be expected that lawyers will add some of the new and emerging principles to their arguments before the Land and Environment Court, and its judges will find it appropriate to absorb them into their judgments.

7. The Land and Environment Court as a Transnational Model

The Land and Environment Court, as the earliest example in the world of a superior court of record specialising in environmental law, is 'universally viewed as one of the very best operationally independent environmental courts' and 'recognised as one of the most visionary and successful, based on its innovations, best practices and advising of other ECs [environmental courts] around the world'.[79] The significance of its

[73] ibid, Preamble, para 11.

[74] Smith and Higginson identify some of these decisions on access to justice in their chapter in this volume, although the principles referred to are not identified as EROL principles as such.

[75] Principle 5, *in dubio pro natura*: 'In cases of doubt, all matters before courts, administrative agencies, and other decision-makers shall be resolved in a way most likely to favour the protection and conservation of the environment, with preference to be given to alternatives that are least harmful to the environment. Actions shall not be undertaken when their potential adverse impacts on the environment are disproportionate or excessive in relation to the benefits derived therefrom': IUCN World Declaration (n 72).

[76] In Brazil, Chile, Costa Rica and Ecuador; see A Olivares and J Lucero, 'Content and Development of the Principle in Dubio Pro Natura: Towards Comprehensive Protection of the Environment' (2018) 24(3) *Ius et Praxis* 619; N Bryner 'In Dubio Pro Natura: A Principle for Strengthening Environmental Rule of Law' (2015) 78 *Revista de Direito Ambiental* 245.

[77] The Brasília Declaration of Judges on Water Justice in 2018, Principle 6: *in dubio pro aqua*: 'Consistent with the principle *in dubio pro natura*, in case of uncertainty, water and environmental controversies before the courts should be resolved, and the applicable laws interpreted, in a way most likely to protect and conserve water resources and related ecosystems'; www.iucn.org/commissions/world-commission-environmental-law/wcel-resources/wcel-important-documentation/brasilia-declaration-judges-water-justice.

[78] Justice Syed Mansoor Ali Shah, CP1290-L/2019, Supreme Court of Pakistan 2021.

[79] G Pring and C Pring, *Environmental Courts and Tribunals: A Guide for Policymakers* (United Nations Environment Program, 2016) 21; an updated version is forthcoming produced by the Asia Pacific Centre for Environmental Law at the University of Singapore in collaboration with UNEP.

establishment must be viewed in a transnational context, as the number of specialised environmental courts and tribunals (ECTs) around the world has now grown to nearly 1,500. They include specialist divisions of the general courts at national and subnational level, for example in China,[80] green benches, environmental certification of judges and a variety of other configurations, as set out in the study by Pring and Pring.[81] That study makes clear that the various ECTs that have sprung up over the past couple of decades are a result of transnational interactions and cross-fertilisation across jurisdictions, through conferences, capacity-building programmes and international visits, in which the Land and Environment Court has been a long-term actor.

It is against this background that the Court must be understood, developing from the 1980s into what it is today. While its geographical jurisdiction is necessarily limited to decision-making in the state of New South Wales, the Court has become globally known, not only as the first court of its kind, but also because of the breadth of its legal jurisdiction, its innovative procedures, the quality of its judges and their judgments, the modern and streamlined nature of its operation, and the unique status of its commissioners in making decisions on a wide range of expert matters.

Over the years, the Court has exerted increasing influence around the world through its judgments, and the outreach of its judges at international, national and subnational levels. This includes not only through dozens of papers at international conferences,[82] but also the regular involvement of some of its judges and commissioners in transnational capacity-building and training initiatives in collaboration with the Australian government as well as global and regional organisations such as UNEP, the Asian Development Bank and the IUCN Academy of Environmental Law, particularly in the Asian and Pacific regions.[83] Several judges of the Court were also engaged in the establishment of the Global Judicial Institute for the Environment in 2016 and continue to be engaged in the work of that organisation.[84]

The Court has been identified by other systems as a model both in terms of scope of jurisdiction as well as its procedures. For example, in reflecting on the establishment of the National Green Tribunal in India,[85] Amirante stated:

> While Europe and the US showed a considerable reticence in establishing independent green judges, the first models of environmental courts came from Oceania, with the experience of the Land and Environment Court of New South Wales, Australia (established in 1979), and the New Zealand Environment Court (1996). The 'Australasian model' is very relevant to the study of the recent development of green justice in India because both the Supreme Court

[80] Some 1,270 ECTs have been established in China at provincial, regional and city levels as of 2021.

[81] Pring and Pring (n 79).

[82] Land and Environment Court, Judicial Speeches and Papers, https://lec.nsw.gov.au/lec/publications-and-resources/judicial-speeches-and-papers.html.

[83] For example, Indonesia–Australia Specialised Training Project, Environmental Law and Enforcement Program; AUSAID 1999–2004; the Asian Development Bank and UNEP Round Tables; and the Asian Judicial Network on the Environment.

[84] The Institute's mission is to 'support the role of courts and tribunals in applying and enforcing environmental laws and in promoting the environmental rule of law and the fair distribution of environmental benefits and burdens' (Statute of the Global Judicial Institute for the Environment, Art 1).

[85] Also see Gill, this volume.

> and the Law Commission of India, which described these experiments as 'ideal', have relied heavily on them to define the proposed Environmental Courts system.[86]

Amirante also noted that the idea of a specialised court was contemplated by the Indian Supreme Court as far back as 1999, in a discussion regarding the need for specialised experts:

> [T]he Court recommends a model, identified in the Land and Environment Court of New South Wales (Australia), because 'its jurisdiction combines appeal, judicial review and enforcement functions … such composition in our opinion is necessary and ideal in environmental matters'.[87]

The Court was also favourably cited by Chinese researchers when investigating the best models from around the world for the establishment of specialist environmental courts in the People's Republic of China.[88] Further, Kenya saw the Court as a model for its Environment and Land Court.[89] In addition, the United Kingdom has long looked at the example of the Land and Environment Court in discussions concerning the establishment of a specialist environment court, so far without any progress.[90] The Court is also often mentioned in articles and books focusing on environmental adjudication in other countries, with one commentator stating: '[W]ith its long-established history, the court has an outstanding international and national reputation. It is successful and acts as a role model for other ECTs.'[91] It has also been the subject of transnational comparative study.[92]

Since the early days of its existence, the Court has regularly hosted visits from a wide range of jurisdictions. Judges and officials from inter alia Bhutan, Brazil, Canada, China, Indonesia, Japan, Kenya, New Zealand, Philippines, Russian Federation, Thailand, the United Kingdom, the United States and Vietnam, often on officially arranged study

[86] D Amirante, 'Environmental Courts in Comparative Perspective: Preliminary Reflections on the National Green Tribunal of India' (2012) 29 *Pace Environmental Law Review* 441.

[87] ibid, quoting *AP Pollution Control Board v Nayudu* (1999) 1 SCC 140, 156 (India).

[88] R Wang and W Zeng, 'Research on the Establishment of Environment Protection Division in Chinese Court' (2009) 4 *Journal of Cambridge Studies* 59.

[89] DW Kaniaru, 'Environmental Courts and Tribunals: The Case of Kenya' (2012) 29 *Pace Environmental Law Review* 566, 570.

[90] M Grant, *Environmental Court Project: Final Report* (UK Department of Transport, the Environment and the Regions, 2000).

[91] G Gill, *Environmental Justice in India: The National Green Tribunal* (London, Routledge, 2016) 24; reference to the Court at 208. See further U Tandon, 'Environmental Courts and Tribunals: A Comparative Analysis of Australia's LEC and India's NGT' [2016] *Indian Yearbook of Comparative Law* 477; P Jaderojananont, 'The Establishment of [an] Environmental Court in Thailand: Possible Lessons from Australian Experience', International Conference on Advancement of Development Administration (2013) (Bangkok National Institute of Development Administration,); T Lin et al, *Green Benches: What Can the People's Republic of China Learn from Environment Courts of Other Countries?* (Mandaluyong, Asian Development Bank, 2009) 11, 16, 17, 18 and 19; JD Zhang, 'A Thesis on the Establishment of Specialized Environmental and Resources Courts in China', IOP Conference Series: Earth and Environmental Science, Vol 354 (Bristol, IOP Publishing, 2019); W Kisworo, *A Framework for the Establishment of an Environmental Court in Indonesia: Opportunities and Challenges* (PhD thesis, Macquarie University, 2019).

[92] For example, with the Environmental Court of New Zealand; see C Warnock, *Environmental Courts and Tribunals: Powers, Integrity and the Search for Legitimacy* (Oxford, Hart Publishing, 2020); see also review of this book by of the Land and Environment Court's Justice Nicola Pain: (2021) 5 *Chinese Journal of Environmental Law* 109.

tours but also individual visits, have interacted with members of the Court.[93] In the same vein, over the years, judges and commissioners of the Court in addition to giving papers to a wide range of conferences in other countries,[94] they have participated in the drafting of a variety of internationally significant environmental declarations.[95]

8. Climate Change Litigation and the Land and Environment Court

Climate change litigation is a relatively recent but now burgeoning global phenomenon, which has become a specialised aspect of environmental litigation, and thus deserves particular mention in the context of this discussion of the transnational aspects of the Court. Climate change litigation is now extensively monitored and documented by a range of organisations, including UNEP,[96] international financial organisations,[97] universities[98] and specialist environmental law organisations such as Our Children's Trust.[99] New cases are emerging on a regular basis.[100]

It is becoming obvious around the world that the issue of climate change is reaching far beyond the realm of politics, and that where major disputes occur, either within nations or between nations, the courts will have an increasingly important role to play, as so clearly articulated by Justice Benjamin of the National High Court of Justice of Brazil:

> We should include courts in the climate change picture because we have no other option. No substitute exists for the court system. If judges are in charge of deciding all sorts of conflicts about life, death, love, human rights, and national security, it makes no sense to leave climate change outside the courtroom.[101]

The International Bar Association (IBA) has traditionally been a relatively conservative body, but one that has not hesitated to adhere to its mandate: '[T]he IBA was born out of the conviction that it could contribute to global stability and peace through the

[93] Land and Environment Court, *Annual Reviews from 2003 to 2020:* https://lec.nsw.gov.au/lec/publications-and-resources/annual-reviews.html; see also n 82.

[94] ibid.

[95] For example, the IUCN World Declaration on the Environmental Rule of Law (n 72) and the Brasília Declaration of Judges on Water Justice (Brasília 2018) https://www.iucn.org/commissions/world-commission-environmental-law/wcel-resources/wcel-important-documentation/brasilia-declaration-judges-water-justice.

[96] *UNEP Status of Climate Change Litigation: A Global Review* (2017); *Global Climate Litigation Report: 2020 Status Review* (UNEP and Sabin Centre for Climate Change Law, Columbia University, 2021).

[97] For example, Asian Development Bank, *Climate Change, Coming Soon to a Court Near You, Report 2: Climate Litigation in Asia and the Pacific and Beyond* (2020) https://www.adb.org/publications/climate-litigation-asia-pacific.

[98] Such as the Sabin Center, Columbia University. See http://climatecasechart.com/us-climate-change-litigation/ and Grantham Institute at Imperial College London.

[99] Our Children's Trust, which documents US and global cases, www.ourchildrenstrust.org/juliana-v-us.

[100] Some of the latest cases include: *Milieudefensie et al v Royal Dutch Shell*, District Court, The Hague, Netherlands, 26 May 2021, case no C/09/571932 / HA ZA 19–379; *Sharma by her litigation representative Sister Marie Brigid Arthur v Minister for the Environment* (2021) 391 ALR 1; [2021] FCA 560; *Sharma by her litigation representative Sister Marie Brigid Arthur v Minister for the Environment* (No 2) [2021] FCA 774.

[101] Asian Development Bank (n 97) x.

promotion and protection of the rule of law.'[102] The IBA's work on climate change is now well known.[103] In May 2020, it issued its Climate Crisis Statement, which recognised that lawyers have an important role to play in addressing the climate crisis and its consequences, including by supporting their clients' efforts to do so.[104]

The latest global count of climate change cases in a wide range of jurisdictions is now over 1,840.[105] There have been some 123 cases to date across Australia.[106] The Land and Environment Court has dealt with thirty-eight of those cases, beginning with Pearlman CJ's judgment in *Redbank v Greenpeace* in 1994.[107] The New South Wales climate case of *Gloucester Resources Ltd v Minister for Planning* in 2019[108] should be highlighted here because of the international response to the judgment.[109] It stands out as an example of the need for the Court to consider Australia's international obligations with respect to climate change, notwithstanding the fact that New South Wales is not directly bound by the Climate Change Convention and the 2015 Paris Agreement.[110]

In late 2020, *KEPCO Bylong*, a judicial review case regarding the upholding of an Independent Planning Commission decision to refuse development consent for a coal mine, cited *Gloucester Resources Ltd* favourably.[111] Significantly, from the point of view of this chapter, Pain J referred to the applicable policies that the Independent Planning Commission must consider in its deliberations, pursuant to section 4.15(1)(a) of the Environmental Planning and Assessment Act. This includes the New South Wales Climate Change Policy Framework,[112] which contains a section on the international context, and refers to the national obligations of the Paris Agreement on climate change. It includes the aim: '… to maximise the economic, social and environmental well-being of NSW in the context of a changing climate and current and emerging *international and national policy settings* and actions to address climate change'.[113] In 2021, the *Bushfire*

[102] International Bar Association: https://www.ibanet.org/.

[103] One of the most significant of its reports is 'Achieving Justice and Human Rights in an Era of Climate Disruption' (IBA, 2014): https://biotech.law.lsu.edu/blog/Climate-Change-Justice-and-Human-Rights-Report-FULL.pdf.

[104] Climate Crisis Statement of 2020, www.ibanet.org/article/D1E68796-A00F-460E-9B24-0AB1D8D07B5C. The IBA has also produced a model statute on climate change: www.ibanet.org/Climate-Change-Model-Statute.

[105] As of May 2021; see J Setzer and C Higham, *Global Trends in Climate Change Litigation: 2021 Snapshot* (London, Grantham Research Institute on Climate Change and the Environment and Centre for Climate Change Economics and Policy, London School of Economics and Political Science, 2021).

[106] Sabin Center for Climate Change Law, Columbia University http://climatecasechart.com/non-us-jurisdiction/australia/.

[107] *Greenpeace v Redbank Power Co* (n 61).

[108] Preston CJ, in *Gloucester Resources Ltd v Minister for Planning* (2019) 234 LGERA 257, examined in detail BJ Preston, 'The End of Enlightened Environmental Law?' (2019) 31 *Journal of Environmental Law* 399.

[109] See Peel, this volume.

[110] See D Adler, 'Big Climate Win Down Under: Australian Court Blocks Coal Mine Citing Negative Impacts of Greenhouse Gas Emissions' Climate Law Blog (Sabin Center for Climate Change Law, Columbia Law School, 19 February 2019).

[111] Pain J, *KEPCO Bylong Australia v. Independent Planning Commission and Bylong Valley Protection Alliance (No 2)* (2020) 247 LGERA 130.

[112] New South Wales Climate Change Policy Framework 2016, 3.

[113] *KEPCO Bylong* (n 111) para 6.14.2 (emphasis added).

Survivors Case[114] also attracted a great deal of attention around the world with respect to the duty of public authorities to put into place policies and plans to combat climate change.

The Court has clearly become a global leader in this area of litigation, as documented in journal articles,[115] books,[116] blogs,[117] and extra-judicial writings and speeches.[118] Its judgments on climate change will continue to be looked at with particular interest and cited in jurisdictions within and outside Australia. Equally, its judges will no doubt remain cognisant of the emerging concepts and principles associated with climate change law being developed elsewhere.

9. Legal Aid and the Land and Environment Court

In discussing the transnational dimensions of the Court, it is relevant to mention the importance to the work and development of the Court of the availability of legal aid for environmental matters, and in particular the establishment of the Environmental Defenders Office (EDO) in the early 1980s.[119] The setting up of the EDO itself has transnational dimensions, being inspired in part by the initiatives of several North American public interest environmental law offices, including the Natural Resources Defense Council, the Environmental Defense Fund and the Sierra Club Legal Defense Fund (now Earthjustice Legal Defense Fund) in the United States and the Canadian Environmental Law Association in Canada. It is also important to note the part that was played by the Legal Aid Commission of New South Wales in setting up a system of legal aid funding for environmental issues that went beyond the more traditional approach of merely assessing the financial means of the plaintiffs as if they were

[114] Preston, CJ, *Bushfire Survivors for Climate Action Incorporated v Environment Protection Authority* (2021) 250 LGERA 1; [2021] NSWLEC 92.

[115] J Peel and J Lin, 'Transnational Climate Litigation: The Contribution of the Global South' (2019) 113 *American Journal of International Law* 679, 722; referring to the *Urgenda* and *Gloucester* cases, Smith opined: '[T]he world witnessed two landmark judicial decisions that have the possibility to remake the legal landscape with respect to climate change litigation', DC Smith, 'Landmark Climate Change-Related Judicial Decisions Handed Down in the Netherlands and Australia: A Preview of What's to Come?' (2019) 37 *Journal of Energy and Natural Resources Law* 145.

[116] For example, J Peel, HM Osofsky and A Foerster, '"Next Generation" Climate Change Litigation in Australia' in J Lin and D Kysar (eds), *Climate Change Litigation in the Asia Pacific* (Cambridge, Cambridge University Press, 2020) 175–206; and Scotford (n 62).

[117] Climate Law Blog (n 110) affiliated with the United Nations Environment Programme, stands out.

[118] For example, the Chief Judge has delivered more than fifteen speeches and conference papers on the subject of climate change since 2008, some also published as articles or book chapters; eg B Preston, 'The Contribution of the Courts in Tackling Climate Change' (2016) 28 *Journal of Environmental Law* 11; and B Preston, 'The Evolving Role of Environmental Rights in Climate Change Litigation' (2018) 2 *Chinese Journal of Environmental Law* 131. See also R Pepper, 'Turning a Ripple into a Torrent: Riding the Waves of Climate Change Litigation', paper presented at Clayton Utz seminar, Climate Change Litigation (Sydney, 26 March 2021).

[119] See Smith and Higginson, this volume. For a history of the EDO, see Murray Hogarth, *Law of the Land: Rise of the Environmental Defenders* (Environmental Defenders Office, 2015). The beginnings of the EDO are also traced in B Boer, 'Legal Aid in Environmental Disputes' (1986) 3 *Environmental and Planning Law Journal* 22; I was the Convenor of the EDO at that time. See also D Robinson and J Dunkley (eds), *Public Interest Perspectives in Environmental Law* (Wiley Chancery 1995).

representing their own private interests in disputes. Discussions at the time included the experience of North American public interest bodies that were bringing citizen suits under environmental statutes in order to protect the public interest. This was part of the context in which the legal aid system for environmental matters became established in New South Wales.

The Legal Aid Commission Act 1979 had been enacted some eight months before the Environmental Planning and Assessment Act 1979 was passed. In introducing the Legal Aid Commission Bill, D Paul Landa, the Minister for Planning and the Environment, stated:

> [T]he Bill makes specific provision for the Commission's power to grant legal aid and to relax any stated means tests, in environmental litigation, relator suits, test cases and statutory inquiries … the Commission will not be choked by rigid rules as to what kind of legal aid may be made available and who is to provide it. Subject to the availability of funds, it will be able to ensure the expansion of legal aid as this becomes socially necessary and to guide this expansion along practical and well-planned lines.[120]

In order to establish an assessment system for provision of environmental legal aid, the Legal Aid Commission initiated a Special Consultative Committee to assess applications and make recommendations.[121]

10. Conclusion

In the past four decades, the Court has been a highly significant element in decision-making at both local and state level in New South Wales, but also a leader in the growing cohort of specialist courts globally. That expectation of leadership is consistent with the 2021 Kunming Declaration of the World Judicial Conference on the Environment,[122] which included a statement that 'countries around the world should enhance the judicial response to the environmental crisis so as to address climate change and its effects, conserve biodiversity, and prevent and control environmental pollution'.[123]

It is clear from this brief overview that the Court enjoys high standing around the world, with governments, courts, lawyers and academicians in other jurisdictions seeing it as a model to emulate. This global reputation could not have been predicted when I began teaching, researching and writing in the area of environmental law forty years ago, but it is more than evident today. The Court has demonstrated its capacity, competence and willingness to make some very significant contributions. While it plainly draws on transnational environmental law, it is also a contributor to it, in a two-way process that will be a continuing theme of its existence. Given its resources, both intellectual and

[120] *NSW Hansard*, Legislative Council, 23 April 1979, 4770.
[121] Fortuitously, the chair of the Legal Aid Commission at that time was Justice Jerrold Cripps of the Land and Environment Court. The details of these negotiations and arrangements can be found in Boer (n 118).
[122] Kunming Declaration (n 13).
[123] ibid.

physical, and the recognition that it is a world leader in the realm of specialist courts, as recorded here and in other chapters of this book, it also has an ethical responsibility to continue with these endeavours in order to promote improved decision-making on the environment and the ecologically sustainable exploitation of natural resources. Environmental law still has much work to do in addressing the polycentric environmental crises with which Australia, along with the rest of the world's nations and their communities, are increasingly confronted.

6

The International Outreach of the Land and Environment Court of New South Wales: Diffusion in India

GITANJALI NAIN GILL

1. Introduction

Environmental courts and tribunals (ECTs) play a leading role in ensuring fair, transparent and dependable environmental adjudication based upon the environmental rule of law.[1] ECTs are presented as 'organisations'[2] with public value and a duty to operate within the 'new public management' (NPM) paradigm.[3] NPM, a powerful but diffuse paradigm, structures the 'scholarly discussion of contemporary changes in the organization and management'[4] of public sector organisations by focusing on the 'importation of private sector practices to the internal workings of public administrations, and introduction of management ideas in public policy domains'.[5] It encompasses a 'critique of monopolistic forms of service provision and an argument for a wider range of service providers and a more market-oriented approach to management'.[6] Increasingly, NPM is reconfigured to fit the public value approach

[1] UNEP, *Environmental Rule of Law: First Global Report* (United Nations Environment Programme, 2019) ch 5.

[2] An organisation is an organised or cohesive group of people working together to achieve their agreed mission, values and strategic goals. See JM Allen and R Sawhney, *Administration and Management in Criminal Justice: A Service Quality Approach* (Thousand Oaks, CA, SAGE, 2018) 4.

[3] GY Ng, *Quality of Judicial Organisation and Checks and Balances* (Cambridge, Intersentia, 2011) 11; S Van de Walle and G Hammerschmid, 'The Impact of the New Public Management: Challenges for Coordination and Cohesion in European Public Sectors' (2011) 12 *Halduskultuur – Administrative Culture* 190.

[4] E Mak, 'The European Judicial Organisation in a New Paradigm: The Influence of Principles of "New Public Management" on the Organisation of the European Courts' (2008) 14 *European Law Journal* 718, 724.

[5] V Lapuente and S Van de Walle, 'The Effects of New Public Management on the Quality of Public Services' (2020) 33 *Governance* 461, 462; see also J Alford and O Hughes, 'Public Value Pragmatism as the Next Phase of Public Management' (2008) 38 *American Review of Public Administration* 130; P Dunleavy and C Hood, 'From Old Public Administration to New Public Management' (1994) 14(3) *Public Money and Management* 9.

[6] J O'Flynn, 'From New Public Management to Public Value: Paradigmatic Change and Managerial Implications' (2007) 66(3) *Australian Journal of Public Administration* 353, 354.

being 'substantively valuable to the citizenry, politically legitimate, feasible and sustainable, and operationally possible and practical'.[7] Public value is described as a 'multi-dimensional construct – a reflection of collectively expressed, politically mediated preferences consumed by the citizenry – created not just through "outcomes" but also through processes which may generate trust or fairness'.[8]

NPM focuses on quality, namely 'achieving the full potential that one is capable of with the resources one has',[9] by exercising a 'client-oriented approach'.[10] In the context of ECTs, NPM quality involves the key values of effectiveness, efficiency and transparency[11] that lead to fairness and public trust. Factors including time, competency, consistency, accessibility, accuracy and responsiveness provide direction and help in assessing the quality of service provided by ECTs.[12] Realising this quality requirement contributes towards operationalising the ECTs' key characteristics and associated benefits in two ways. First, ECTs strengthen societal trust by exercising and displaying good governance. Second, by recognising the need for 'adaptive management that strives for organisational excellence that is continually looking, learning, changing and improving'.[13]

This chapter presents the Land and Environment Court of New South Wales (the Court) through the lens of functionality and the Court's overseas reach and impact in India. The NPM paradigm is employed to test the practical application of functionality in the Court and in the National Green Tribunal (NGT) in India. Section 2 briefly introduces the principle of functionality. Functionality offers 'better solutions' through the command of legal materials and its deeper understanding to discover similarities and substitutes. Environmental problems are global and associated disputes are polycentric, multidisciplinary, complex and often political.[14] There is an ongoing need to promote transformative adjudicatory institutions that provide effective environmental justice and uphold the environmental rule of law.

In this context, section 3 analyses the Court's influential contribution as an 'ideal model' to the establishment of the NGT in 2010 as the first specialised environmental tribunal in a developing country. The Land and Environment Court, a free-standing

[7] ibid, 359.

[8] ibid, 358; see also A Hefetz and M Warner, 'Privatization and its Reverse: Explaining the Dynamics of the Government Contracting Process' (2004) 14(2) *Journal of Public Administration Research and Theory* 171; G Stoker, 'Public Value Management: A New Narrative for Networked Governance?' (2006) 36(1) *American Review of Public Administration* 41.

[9] Ng (n 3) 29.

[10] ibid, 11–12. For example, see Client Service Charter for NSW Courts and Tribunal Services.

[11] Mak (n 4) 735; M Visser, R Schouteten and J Dikkers, 'Controlling the Courts: New Public Management and the Dutch Judiciary' (2019) 40(1) *Justice System Journal* 39; D Piana, 'Reforming the Judiciary Through Standards; Agency Empowerment and Centre (Re)Building in Italy 2001–2015' (2017) 83(4) *International Review of Administrative Sciences* 757; R Mohr and F Contini, 'Judicial Evaluation in Context: Principles, Practices and Promises in Nine European Countries' (2007) 1(2) *European Journal of Legal Studies* 1. These articles argue that the NPM paradigm influences European judicial organisations to solve questions in liberal democracies.

[12] J Petrick and W Lindsay, *Total Quality and Organization Development* (Boca Raton, LA, CRC Press, 1996) 55.

[13] BJ Preston, 'Benefits of Judicial Specialization in Environmental Law: The Land and Environment Court of New South Wales as a Case Study' (2012) 29 *Pace Environmental Law Review* 396, 440.

[14] Ceri Warnock, 'Environment and the Law: The Normative Force of Context and Constitutional Challenges' (2020) *Journal of Environmental Law* 1, 4–5.

environmental court 'often called a Rolls Royce model',[15] is recognised as 'one of the most visionary and successful, based on its innovations, best practices and advising of other [environmental courts] around the world'.[16]

Section 4 selectively explores, through the NPM paradigm, Preston CJ's 'desirable dozen' institutional characteristics that are successfully embedded in the Court. The NPM paradigm includes three quality values: effectiveness, efficiency and transparency. This trio incorporates and tests the 'desirable dozen'. Preston's 'desirables' are also reflected in the working practices of the NGT, although systematic cloning did not occur. The chapter identifies direct and indirect parallels with working practices found both in the Court and the NGT. The concluding section acknowledges the need for continuously adopting 'better solutions' arising out of successful models such as the Court, thereby promoting specialised and responsive environmental adjudication capable of global application.

2. The Principle of Functionality: Better Solutions

Konrad Zweigert and Hein Kötz's classic work on functionalism provides an elaborate and robust perspective to understand and resolve legal and social conflicts through better solutions.[17] Functionality not only defines the problem but in its 'applied version' provides advice to solve the problem within given social and economic situations.[18] Functionalism both as 'mantra and *bête noire* of comparative law'[19] is an '"école de verité" that extends and enriches the supply of solutions … and offers the opportunity of finding the "better solution" in given time and place'.[20]

Zweigert and Kötz assert that 'incomparables cannot usefully be compared, and in law the only things which are comparable are those which fulfil the same function'.[21] The premise is based upon *praesumptio similitudnis* – the presumption of similarity. The presumption is that every legal system faces the same or similar problems and resolves them in independent ways that result in the same or similar practical outcomes.[22]

[15] G Pring and C Pring, *The ABCs of the ECTs: A Guide for Policy Makers for Designing and Operating a Specialised Environmental Court or Tribunal* (Nairobi, United Nations Environment Programme, 2016) 20–21.

[16] ibid.

[17] K Zweigert and H Kötz, *An Introduction to Comparative Law*, trans T Weir (Oxford, Oxford University Press, 1998) 15.

[18] ibid, 11.

[19] R Michaels, 'The Functionalist Method of Comparative Law' in M Reimann and R Zimmermann (eds), *The Oxford Handbook of Comparative Law*, 1st edn (Oxford, Oxford University Press, 2006) 339, 340.

[20] Zweigert and Kötz (n 17) 15; see also J Ellis, 'General Principles and Comparative Law' (2011) 22(4) *European Journal of International Law* 949, 959–61; CA Whytock, 'Legal Origins, Functionalism, and the Future of Comparative Law' (2009) *Brigham Young University Law Review* 1879, 1883; J Hill, 'Comparative Law, Law Reform and Legal Theory' (1989) 9 *OJLS* 101, 102. For a critique on functionality, see Michaels (n 19); P Legrand, 'The Same and the Different' in P Legrand and R Munday (eds), *Comparative Legal Studies: Traditions and Transitions* (Cambridge, Cambridge University Press, 2003).

[21] Zweigert and Kötz (n 17) 34.

[22] ibid, 40; J De Coninck, 'The Functional Method of Comparative Law: "Quo Vadis"?' (2020) 74 *Rabel Journal of Comparative and International Private Law* 318.

In respect of institutions and rules, functionalism as *tertium comparationis* offers a response from a comparable common point of reference. Institutions are thought to be 'comparable because they fulfil the same (or equivalent) function(s), because they relate to the same problem'. This provides 'meta-nationally or cross-culturally'[23] valid points of common institutional denominators in the pursuit of better solutions. Accordingly, functionalism provides lessons of experience and neutral responses to 'look at different systems of the world [that] offer a greater variety of solutions'.[24]

Functionality fosters international understanding, exchange of legal ideas and reforms, thereby promoting the domestic development of legal institutions and rules.[25] The principle is particularly helpful for developing countries where legal, procedural and regulatory systems are underdeveloped or slow to respond to socioeconomic crises. Those countries are encouraged to address common environmental challenges and support the development of better solutions at the national level. This results in facilitating the 'trans-frontier mobility of law'[26] for 'structural and discursive changes',[27] thereby improving the law and promoting globalisation discourse.

The environmental rule of law underpins the principle of functionality being a comparable common point of reference that reflects shared purpose or *tertium comparationis.*[28] It is indispensable for environmental justice and sustainable development. In its 'unique' context, the environmental rule of law 'integrates critical environmental needs with the elements of rule of law [fair, just and accountable laws], thus creating a foundation for environmental governance that protects rights and enforces fundamental obligations'.[29] In this context, the environmental rule of law experiences articulation in institutional values and practices in an optimal manner. Globally, ECTs provide a strong institutional framework for environmental protection, diligent enforcement and effective access to justice by upholding the environmental rule of law. Strong and effective institutions are especially important because the 'benefits of environmental rule of law are diffused across society'.[30] The achievement of normative legitimacy lies in the realisation of environmental justice through the identification of common institutional denominators (values) resulting in better solutions for sound governance and social inclusion. ECTs such as the Land and Environment Court that display the NPM's quality values – effectiveness, efficiency and transparency – help uphold the environmental rule of law. The Court is an example for other jurisdictions, including India, that helps shape the adjudicatory landscape and offers an 'enhanced opportunity to learn from the experience of those who went before, as legal systems

[23] De Coninck (n 22) 323.

[24] Zweigert and Kötz (n 17) 15.

[25] Whytock (n 20) 1883. See also RB Schlesinger et al, *Comparative Law: Cases, Text and Material*, 6th edn (Mineola, NY, Foundation Press, 1998) 22.

[26] E Örücü, 'Infusion of the Diffused: Four Cycles of Diffusion Infusing the Legal System of Turkey' in S Farran, J Gallen and C Rautenbach (eds), *The Diffusion of Law: The Movement of Laws and Norms Around the World* (Farnham, Ashgate, 2015) 7.

[27] ibid.

[28] M Prityi et al, 'Locating Environmental Law Functions Among Legislative, Judicial, and Implementation Bodies' in KW Junker (ed), *Environmental Law Across Cultures: Comparisons for Legal Practice* (London, Routledge, 2020) 73.

[29] UNEP (n 1) 8.

[30] ibid, 37.

borrow and learn from one another, while also bringing their own perspectives to bear to make improvements'.[31]

3. The Influence of the Land and Environment Court: Genesis of the NGT

The inauguration of the Court on 1 September 1980 introduced a specialised environmental court that embraced a flexible mechanism for dispute resolution.[32] The vanguard status of the Court, described as a 'superb [environmental court] model',[33] and its judicial leadership increased international interest in specialised environmental adjudication.

The Court's outreach was witnessed when India's senior judiciary recognised the need to protect and improve the environment because of the Bhopal disaster in 1984.[34] The complex and uncertain scientific risks with shared environmental concerns influenced both the Supreme Court and subsequently the Law Commission of India to promote the establishment of a specialised environmental court. The Supreme Court, in three important judgments, advocated the establishment of environmental courts. In *MC Mehta v Union of India*,[35] *Indian Council for Enviro-Legal Action v Union of India*[36] and *AP Pollution Control Board v Professor MV Nayudu (I and II)*,[37] the Supreme Court expressed judicial concern about its ability to evaluate and incorporate scientific input in complex environmental cases. Uncertainty becomes a problem when scientific knowledge, claims and counterclaims are institutionalised into policy-making as a basis for decision-making. Accordingly, as environmental cases frequently involve assessment of scientific data, it was desirable to establish regional environmental courts with a legally qualified judge and two experts, to undertake relevant adjudication as part of a faster judicial process.

In this context, the Land and Environment Court was described as an 'ideal' model for India, providing appropriate judicial and scientific inputs rather than leaving complicated disputes regarding environmental pollution to officers drawn from the executive. The Supreme Court stated:

> [The] NSWLEC could be ideal. It is a superior Court of record and is composed of four Judges and nine technical and conciliation assessors. Its jurisdiction combines appeal, judicial review and enforcement functions. Such a composition in our opinion is necessary and ideal in environmental matters.[38]

Additionally, specialised environmental courts would recognise the principle of good governance and maintain the rule of law. Good governance in environmental

[31] ibid, 29.
[32] Land and Environment Court Act 1979 (NSW) (the NSWLEC Act).
[33] Pring and Pring (n 15) 22.
[34] *Union Carbide Corporation v Union of India* (1989) 2 SCC 540.
[35] *MC Mehta v Union of India* (1986) 2 SCC 176.
[36] *Indian Council for Enviro-Legal Action v Union of India* (1996) 3 SCC 212.
[37] *AP Pollution Control Board v Professor MV Nayudu (I and II)* (1999) 2 SCC 718 and (2001) 2 SCC 62.
[38] ibid, (1999) 735.

matters includes effective state institutions, transparency and accountability in public affairs, respect for human rights and the meaningful participation of citizens including the scientific community. Accordingly, the Supreme Court suggested that the Law Commission examine the establishment of a specialised environmental court.

Following these powerful judicial statements, the Law Commission undertook the recommended study. Ultimately, in its 186th Report 'Proposal to Constitute Environment Courts', it strongly advocated the establishment of environmental courts by examining courts in foreign jurisdictions.[39] The Law Commission was influenced by the Land and Environment Court and observed its 'broad features commend themselves to us'.[40] For instance, the Court's composition of judicial and expert members influenced the Law Commission in its recommendations. The Law Commission decided on a similar balanced complement. Environmental courts with legal and scientific inputs were thought to be better placed to reach a determination. Such courts could have wide powers to make on-the-spot inspections and hear oral evidence from resident panels of environmental scientists. The Law Commission followed the Court's practice and recommended a qualified statutory panel of technical/scientific personnel called Commissioners to assist the proposed court. The Commissioners would advise and assist the court in analysing and assessing scientific or technological issues.[41]

On the issue of standing the Law Commission recommended the Land and Environment Court's approach as a good practice exemplar.[42] Any person or organisation who or which has an interest in the subject matter or in the public interest should be able to approach the court. Further, the Court's practice of conducting proceedings with reduced formality and technicality and with as much expedition, mediation and conciliation as possible should be encouraged and adopted in the Indian context.[43]

The Law Commission's recommendations resulted in the Green Tribunal Bill. It was debated in Parliament[44] where the NGT was described as 'one element of a reformist approach to environmental governance',[45] thereby acknowledging the importance of NPM quality values. The Bill received presidential assent in 2010 and became the National Green Tribunal Act 2010 (the NGT Act).[46] The Land and Environment Court as an 'ideal' model helped India introduce and shape the design and content of the NGT as a specialised body to act as a forum offering greater plurality for environmental justice. The Court's institutional values and practices are illustrative of the better solution instinct of the applied functionality principle, thereby promoting the environmental rule of law. An improved justice system (such as ECTs) that provides steadfast foundations for resolving environmental disputes and enforcing environmental law through NPM quality values – namely effectiveness, efficiency and transparency – optimises the environmental rule of law.

[39] Law Commission of India, *186th Report on Proposal to Constitute Environment Courts* (Government of India, 2003) 50–86.

[40] ibid, 54, 63.

[41] ibid, 154.

[42] ibid, 152.

[43] ibid, 62, 148.

[44] The Bill was introduced in Parliament on 31 July 2009; passed in Lok Sabha (the Lower House) on 30 April 2010 and in Rajya Sabha (the Upper House) on 5 May 2010.

[45] Statement made by Jairam Ramesh, former Minister of Environment and Forests, April 2010.

[46] The National Green Tribunal Act 2010, Gazette of India Extraordinary (No 19, 2010).

However, the Land and Environment Court was not cloned in India. The NGT's differences are an illustration of 'transposition and tuning … the transposition occurring to suit the particular socio-legal culture and needs of the recipient'.[47] The NGT's transposition and tuning is based upon the legal context and system, the nature of socioeconomic assessments, and coordination and synergies between existing regulatory institutions and their processes, including human and technical capacity constraints. For example, the Law Commission recommended a simpler procedure for the Indian environmental court.[48] It found the Court's classification of cases and its various proceedings too complicated. The Law Commission also excluded criminal jurisdiction to avoid the constitutional conflict that would result if the criminal appellate jurisdiction of the High Court were removed and vested in a tribunal staffed by retired judges.[49] The Commission's position was upheld by Parliament because 'criminal adjudication requires a hierarchy of courts and the tribunal system does not fit into the architecture of criminal courts'.[50] Neither did the Commission recommend the prospective tribunal be made a superior court of record with the power of judicial review.[51] It is settled constitutional law that tribunals only have a 'supplemental not a substitutional role and merely have the trappings of a court'.[52] The constitutional courts (Supreme Court and High Courts) have the power of judicial review which cannot be ousted or excluded. Vesting the power of judicial review in a tribunal would lead to constitutional confusion and complexity. The position of the Law Commission was upheld by the Supreme Court in *TN Pollution Control Board v Sterlite Industries*,[53] wherein the court declared it would be 'fallacious to state that the NGT has the power of judicial review akin to the High Court. … It is a statutory tribunal set up under NGT Act.'[54]

Despite differences in structure and substance between the Land and Environment Court and the NGT, functionality through NPM quality values helped the NGT in its 'internalisation and increased its own receptivity by making a significant adaptation of the foreign formal legal order to initial [internal] conditions'.[55] Functionality works best when the problems are similar and there is clarity about the goals and the new ways of working. The NGT benefited through adopting those qualities of the Court identified as the 'desirable dozen' (as discussed in Section 4) that are clear, auditable and secure legal

[47] Esin Örücü, 'Law as Transposition' (2002) 51 *ICLQ* 205, 207.

[48] Law Commission of India (n 39) 63.

[49] ibid, 156. The Law Commission examined the criminal jurisdiction matter in detail and observed that appeals/revisions from the trial courts as filed in High Courts – whether in case of conviction or acquittal under environmental laws – could be shifted to the Environment Court. However, there was no special law that transferred the criminal appellate jurisdiction of the High Court to another court at the state level. Hence, it is not fit to touch the criminal jurisdiction.

[50] Parliament of India, *Two Hundred and Third Report on the NGT Bill 2009* (Rajya Sabha Secretariat, 2009).

[51] The NGT in *Wilfred J v MoEFCC* and *Kalpavriksh v Union of India* (Judgments 17 July 2014) used textual ambiguity to expand its jurisdiction and claim the power of judicial review. See N Chowdhury and N Srivastava, 'The National Green Tribunal in India: Examining the Question of Jurisdiction' (2018) 21(2) *Asia Pacific Journal of Environmental Law* 190.

[52] *L Chandra Kumar v Union of India* (1997) 3 SCC 261, 302; Gopal Krishna, 'When Tribunals Undermine the Judiciary' *Rediff.com* (Delhi, 25 October 2013).

[53] *TN Pollution Control Board v Sterlite Industries* 2019 SCC OnLine SC 221.

[54] ibid, [52].

[55] Örücü (n 47) 208.

continuity by promoting the environmental rule of law. The pervasive influence and positive outcomes of the Court provide greater justification and serve as an entryway for its acceptance by countries that are creating or refining ECTs.

4. The Land and Environment Court's 'Desirable Dozen': Reflections in the NGT

The recognition of the Court as a 'bold and brave experiment'[56] and being an innovative court is fulsome and positive. Justice Preston, Chief Judge of the Court, in illuminating articles and speeches, identifies twelve key characteristics, the 'desirable dozen', required for the successful operation of an ECT.[57] These characteristics are rationalisation and centralisation, scientific and technical specialisation, multi-door courthouse, superior court of record, independence from the government, responsiveness to environmental problems, facilitation of access to justice, development of environmental jurisprudence, flexibility and innovation, better court administration, value-adding function, and unifying ethos and mission. The 'desirable dozen' constitutes a characteristic framework capable of being tested through the NPM quality value paradigm.

The NPM paradigm operationalises the quality of justice through institutional values respectful of the environmental rule of law in judicial organisations including ECTs. These values – effectiveness, efficiency and transparency – are 'essential components of organisational culture … adherence to high-level public service values can generate substantial public trust and confidence'.[58] Interlinked, interdependent and overlapping, these institutional values are given 'focus, structure and visibility'[59] through powerful statements, strategic goals and objectives that ensure elements of good judicial governance and sound decision-making. In this regard, 'development of standards … elaboration of benchmarks … diffusion of good practices … [and] innovation'[60] facilitate and improve the quality of justice. The NPM in ECTs infuses accountability in an instrumental form to deliver 'good services to the users (citizens)'[61] thus responding to and satisfying societal and environmental needs. The Court reflects the NPM quality values in the 'best interests of the public, the litigants and the environment'.[62] The Court's purpose is to safeguard and maintain the rule of law (including equality before the law); access to justice; fairness, impartiality and independence in decision-making;

[56] Justice Neal Bignold, 'The Land and Environment Court: Its Contribution to Australia's Development of Environmental Law' (National Environmental Law Association Conference, Fremantle, September 2000).

[57] BJ Preston, 'Characteristics of Successful Environmental Courts' (2014) 26(3) *Journal of Environmental Law* 365.

[58] European Commission, *Quality of Public Administration: A Toolbox for Practitioners* (European Commission's Inter-service group on Public Administration Quality and Innovation, 2017) 18.

[59] ibid, 19.

[60] Piana (n 11) 760–61.

[61] ibid.

[62] Justice Terry Sheahan, 'Use of ADR in the New South Wales and in the Land and Environment Court' (Australasian Conference of Planning and Environment Courts and Tribunals, September 2010).

transparency, timeliness and certainty; accountability; and competency and personal integrity of its judges, commissioners and support staff.[63]

In this context, the Court's 'desirable dozen' as NPM quality values and their ultimate diffusion are reflected in the NGT's structure and working practices. The principal NPM headings of effectiveness, efficiency and transparency are discussed below.

4.1. Effectiveness

Effectiveness concerns the extent to which high-level objectives and societal needs have been or should be achieved due to the organisation's activities. From a quality justice standpoint, it includes 'adequate material and human resources, accessibility of justice to citizens, putting in place assessment tools, and using quality standards'.[64]

In regard to *rationalisation and centralisation* (the first of the desirable dozen), a strong institutional framework for environmental protection, diligent enforcement and effective access to justice is fundamental in supporting the environmental rule of law. The Land and Environment Court is a 'one stop shop'[65] – a dedicated environmental court with an integrated, wide-ranging jurisdiction.[66] The rationalisation and centralisation of the Court created a 'critical mass'[67] for a new style of environmental governance.

Rationalisation and centralisation in the Court facilitates improved quality and innovative decision-making in the substantive and procedural aspects of the wide subject-matter coverage, ensures effective enforcement, increases awareness of the end-users, and reduces litigation and associated costs.[68] Thus, it provides a predictable and steadfast foundation to seek redress of grievances and enforcement of legal rights and obligations.

Likewise, the NGT is 'one element of a reformist approach to environmental governance'.[69] It is a specialised body equipped with the expertise necessary to handle environmental disputes. It is considered as a contributor to a more coherent and effective system of environmental governance and regulation.[70] The NGT aims to provide

[63] Land and Environment Court, www.lec.justice.nsw.gov.au/Pages/about/about.aspx (accessed 30 January 2021).

[64] European Commission (n 58) Theme 7 (quality of justice systems); see also the EU Justice Scoreboard available at https://ec.europa.eu/commission/presscorner/detail/en/ip_20_1316 (accessed 30 January 2021).

[65] Paul L Stein, 'Specialist Environmental Courts: the Land and Environment Court of New South Wales, Australia' (2002) 4 *Environmental Law Review* 5, 8.

[66] The Land and Environment Court has an appellate and a review jurisdiction in relation to planning, building, environmental, mining and ancillary matters. It also exercises summary criminal jurisdiction and appellate criminal jurisdiction in relation to environmental offences. The jurisdiction is exercised by reference to the subject matter of the proceedings (Classes 1–8).

[67] Preston (n 57).

[68] ibid.

[69] Ramesh (n 45).

[70] GN Gill, *Environmental Justice in India: The National Green Tribunal* (London, Routledge, 2017); S Shrotia, 'Environmental Justice: Is the National Green Tribunal of India Effective?' (2015) 17(3) *Environmental Law Review* 169; D Amirante, 'Environmental Courts in Comparative Perspective: Preliminary Reflections on the National Green Tribunal of India' (2012) 29 *Pace Environmental Law Review* 441.

access to the tribunal through its principal bench in Delhi and four regional benches.[71] Additionally, to become more accessible in remote areas, the NGT followed the circuit procedure of courts going to people and not people coming to the courts.[72]

In 2015, five years after the creation of the NGT, the Supreme Court of India reviewed its own environmental case-load, and again acknowledged its limited environmental expertise. The Supreme Court in *Bhopal Gas Peedith Mahila Udyog Sangathan v Union of India*[73] and *TN Godavarman Thirumulpad v Union of India*[74] transferred all environmental cases, both active and prospective, to the NGT to render expeditious and specialised judgments, reduce the burden and cost of litigation in the higher courts, and avoid the likelihood of conflicts of orders between High Courts and the NGT.

The NGT has wide jurisdiction (original, appellate and special) over all civil cases concerning substantial environmental questions if such matters arise from the legislation listed in Schedule I.[75] The jurisdiction is expansive and may be exercised *ex debito justitiae*.[76] This 'one stop shop' tribunal developed innovative solutions, remedies and enforcement, thereby promoting the environmental rule of law.

In regard to *scientific and technical specialisation*, environmental decision-making may involve science; consequently, scientific and technical expertise may provide appropriate solutions to technical or complicated environmental problems.[77] The importance and involvement of experts is recognised because

> experts define the regime of truth; they tell us what the world looks like, identify and quantify relevant variables, provide statistical measurements and risk analyses, and solve the equations that indicate the path towards increasing the aggregate level of well-being … experts define the system.[78]

Diverse scientific and technical expertise alongside a specialised and experienced judiciary lends credence to the environmental legitimacy of the Land and Environment Court and acts as a guardian of the environmental rule of law. The Commissioners or assessors in the Court advise and assist judges, decide appropriate

[71] MoEFCC, Government of India, Notification, 17 August 2011, SO 1908 E. The regional benches found their bases in Bhopal (central zone), Chennai (south India), Pune (western territory) and Kolkata (eastern region).

[72] Ramesh (n 45).

[73] *Bhopal Gas Peedith Mahila Udyog Sangathan v Union of India* (2012) 8 SCC 326.

[74] *TN Godavarman Thirumulpad v Union of India* Supreme Court Order, 5 November 2015.

[75] NGT Act 2010 s 14. The enactments in Schedule I include: Water (Prevention and Control of Pollution) Act 1974; Water (Prevention and Control of Pollution) Cess Act 1977; Forests (Conservation) Act 1980; Air (Prevention and Control of Pollution) Act 1981; Environment (Protection) Act 1986; Public Liability Insurance Act 1981; and Biological Diversity Act 2002. Furthermore, section 15 of the NGT Act 2010 provides the Tribunal with special jurisdiction to order relief and compensation to victims of pollution and other environmental damage arising under the enactments specified in Schedule I, for restitution of damaged property and the environment in such areas as the Tribunal may think fit.

[76] *Wilfred J v Ministry of Environment and Forests* (n 51).

[77] PM Haas, *Epistemic Communities, Constructivism, and International Environmental Policy* (London, Routledge, 2016); A Gupta et al, 'Science Networks' in F Biermann and P Pattberg (eds), *Global Environmental Governance Reconsidered* (Cambridge, MA, MIT Press, 2012) 69; Robin Feldman, *The Role of Science in Law* (Oxford, Oxford University Press, 2009).

[78] J Lawrence, 'The Structural Logic of Expert Participation in WTO Decision-Making Processes' in M Ambrus et al (eds) *The Role of 'Experts' in International and European Decision-Making Processes: Advisors, Decision Makers or Irrelevant Actors?* (Cambridge, Cambridge University Press, 2014) 173, 186.

disputes (such as merits review)[79] and undertake alternative dispute resolution (ADR) such as mediation and conciliation.[80] The epistemic qualities of the Commissioners, as competent individuals, are recognised in a range of environmental areas.[81] According to Bignold J, the Commissioners undertake the Court's work with 'considerable competence and efficiency … this enables speedy determination'.[82]

In addition, the Court may appoint experts or order the parties to select a single expert to provide expert evidence.[83] The Court may also obtain assistance from a specially qualified adviser on any matter arising in the proceedings and act on the adviser's opinion.[84] According to Preston CJ, the Court's processes involving expert evidence result in: reduced costs; the potential for partisan and biased testimony from external experts; a more efficient use of time and money; facilitation of a less adversarial and more flexible, problem-solving-based approach; and the provision of greater assistance to judges and Commissioners when reviewing the evidence given by experts on discrete issues.[85]

The NGT's 'scientifically legal' composition was influenced by the Land and Environment Court. The adjudicative process involves an interdisciplinary bench that harmonises legal norms with scientific knowledge. A unique feature of the NGT's adjudicative process engages legal judges and scientific experts with environmental knowledge as joint decision-makers of equal standing. The experts are 'central', not 'advisers', within the NGT's normative structure. The tribunal has contributed to the development of environmental jurisprudence not only through legal doctrine but also via science-based knowledge, resulting in domain-specific solutions.[86] This multifaceted, multiskilled body produces a coherent and effective institutional mechanism to apply complex laws and principles in a uniform and consistent manner.[87] It simultaneously reshapes the approach to solving the environmental problem at its source rather than being limited to predetermined remedies. The NGT's willingness to offer scientifically based structural policies that respond creatively to weak, ineffective or absent regulation reflects an accountability-based approach. For example, NGT's creativity includes the preparation and recommendation of policies on biomedical waste,[88] tyre burning,[89] emission standards for clamp-type traditional brick kilns[90] and translocation of trees.[91] Unbiased, in-house, scientific knowledge becomes an integral part

[79] NSWLEC Act Classes 1–3 proceedings.

[80] NSWLEC Act ss 34–38.

[81] NSWLEC Act ss 12. Non-legally trained Commissioners are qualified in areas such as town planning, environmental science, land valuation, architecture, engineering and heritage.

[82] Justice Neal R Bignold, 'Overview of Court – Constitution, Jurisdiction and Procedures' (NSW Young Lawyers Seminar, February 2001).

[83] Uniform Civil Procedure Rules 2005 Rule 31.46.

[84] ibid, Rule 31.54.

[85] Preston (n 57).

[86] ibid.

[87] GN Gill, 'Environmental Justice in India: The National Green Tribunal and Expert Members' (2016) 5(1) *Transnational Environmental Law* 175; GN Gill, 'The National Green Tribunal of India: Decision-Making, Scientific Expertise and Uncertainty' (2017) 29 (2–3) *Environmental Law and Management* 82.

[88] *Haat Supreme Wastech Limited v State of Haryana* NGT Judgment 28 November 2013.

[89] *Asim Sarode v Maharashtra Pollution Control Board* NGT Judgment 6 September 2014.

[90] *Sonyabapu v State of Maharashtra* NGT Judgment 24 February 2014.

[91] *KD Kodwani v District Collector* NGT Judgment 25 August 2014.

that produces judicially binding decisions by adopting both a problem-solving and policy-creation approach.

The availability of merits review to the NGT allows the experts as primary decision-makers to undertake technical in-depth scrutiny that involves not only law but also the technical evaluation underpinning the decision. It promotes the effective application of the precautionary principle.[92]

However, in 2019, the Supreme Court critically commented on the failure of the NGT to carry out a merits review when it discharged in a perfunctory paragraph its adjudicatory function concerning vital technical evaluation in the grant of an environmental clearance.[93]

A full bench is a sine qua non for the decision-making process. Since 2017, the NGT has been experiencing an acute shortage of legal and scientific bench judges. Section 4 of the NGT Act requires a full-time chairperson and at least ten, but not exceeding twenty, judicial and expert members at all times. In 2021, the NGT has only five judicial and four expert members.[94] The current expert judges are specialists in forest-related matters; the previously wide spectrum of scientific expertise has been lost.[95] This limited expertise impacts on the effectiveness of delivering environmental justice. As a consequence of the increasing shortage of bench experts, the NGT, since 2019, has outsourced work to over 175 ad hoc committees to review and monitor compliance with environmental laws, and to submit status reports to the NGT.[96] The truism that committees take minutes, but may waste years, is illustrated by these committees. An abrogation of responsibility alongside a failure to meet statutory fixed deadlines for disposal of cases is a consequence of the mushrooming of these committees and their tardiness in reporting promptly to the NGT.

In August 2020, the Supreme Court directed the appropriate authorities to fill the bench vacancies resulting from the shortfall of scientific and legal expertise. A full bench offering a scientific and technical perspective generates hypotheses about environmental events and processes. It provides an evaluative statement to compare possible options in support of sound decision-making that upholds the environmental rule of law.

The *development of environmental jurisprudence* is related to scientific and technical specialisation. It requires the engagement of judges as constructive scholars. They develop environmental jurisprudence that ensures recognition of the mutually reinforcing relationship between rights, justice and the environmental rule of law. The Court's

[92] Through a series of NGT judgments and upheld by the Supreme Court of India, the NGT is vested with the power of merit review through the NGT Act 2010 (with special reference to ss 2, 14–20). See *Rajeev Suri v DDA* 2021 SCC OnLine SC 7; *Mahendra Pandey v Union of India* NGT Judgment 8 December 2017; *M/S Sterlite Industries v Tamil Nadu Pollution Control Board* Judgment 8 August 2013. See also GN Gill, 'Precautionary Principle, its Interpretation and Application by the Indian Judiciary: "When I Use a Word It Means Just What I Choose It to Mean – Neither More Nor Less" Humpty Dumpty' (2019) 21(4) *Environmental Law Review* 292.

[93] *Hanuman Laxman Aroskar v Union of India* 2019 SCC OnLine 441, [148]. See also *Tamil Nadu Pollution Control Board v Sterlite Industries* (2019) 19 SCC 479 where the Supreme Court found that the NGT passed an order outside its statutory power and without jurisdiction.

[94] https://greentribunal.gov.in/ (accessed 8 August 2021).

[95] https://greentribunal.gov.in/expert-present-members (accessed 10 August 2021).

[96] R Nair and N Pandey, 'NGT Decisions Causing Loss to Industry, Need to Look at its Mandate – Ministerial Panel' *The Print* (Delhi, 10 December 2020); M Ramesh, 'Turning a Decade Old, NGT Faces Some Tough Questions?' *The Hindu* (Chennai, 16 October 2020).

specialised adjudication has developed environmental jurisprudence in aspects of 'substantive, procedural, restorative, therapeutic and distributive justice'.[97] Substantive justice covers principles of ecologically sustainable development (ESD) within the context of both judicial review proceedings and in merits appeals.[98] For Pain J, the ESD principles reflect a 'human rights concern'.[99] Procedural aspects include relaxed standing, interlocutory injunctions and costs rules.[100] The distributive aspects cover inter- and intragenerational equity,[101] and the balancing of public–private rights and responsibilities.[102] Restorative justice includes victim–offender mediation[103] and the polluter-pays principle for environmental crime.[104] Therapeutic justice focuses on litigant welfare by improving court practices that include accessibility.[105]

The NGT also developed an environmental jurisprudence and its practical application by preserving the link between life and a healthy environment and by successfully placing human rights within environmental discourse. In judicial pronouncements, the right to a healthy environment has been construed as a part of the right to life under Article 21 of the Constitution.[106] The derivative application of principles of international law are read in conjunction with the domestic constitutional right to a wholesome environment.[107] This offers a framework for reinforcing and strengthening the environmental rule of law by protecting vital environmental interests and claims.

Effectiveness also *facilitates access to justice.* Access to environmental justice is a pillar of democratic governance. It promotes just and equitable outcomes, thereby supporting the environmental rule of law. Participatory mechanisms address issues of 'inequality and recognition'[108] concerning access to justice. 'Participatory parity' comes with the satisfaction of two conditions: 'that institutionalised cultural patterns of interpretation and evaluation express equal respect for all participants and ensure equal opportunity' and 'the resources to enable participation'.[109]

[97] Preston (n 57).

[98] Protection of the Environment Administration Act 1991 (NSW) Part 6. See *Telstra Corporation Limited v Hornsby Shire Council* (2006) 67 NSWLR 256; *Gray v The Minister for Planning* (2006) 152 LGERA 258; *BT Goldsmith Planning Services Pty Ltd v Blacktown City Council* [2005] NSWLEC 210.

[99] Justice N Pain, 'Human Rights and Environmental Rights: A Role for Domestic Courts? – An Australian Perspective' (GNHRE Spain, June 2014).

[100] Preston (n 57).

[101] *Gloucester Resources Limited v Minister for Planning* (2019) 234 LGERA 257; *Anderson v Director-General of the Department of Environment and Climate Change* (2008) 163 LGERA 400; *Warkworth Mining Limited* (2013) 194 LGERA 347.

[102] *Taralga Landscape Guardians Inc v Minister for Planning and RES Southern Cross Pty Ltd* (2007) 161 LGERA 1.

[103] *Chief Executive, Office of Environment and Heritage v Clarence Valley Council* (2018) 236 LGERA 291; *Garrett v Williams* (2007) 151 LGERA 92.

[104] *Environment Protection Authority v Waste Recycling and Processing Corp* (2006) 148 LGERA 299.

[105] Preston (n 57).

[106] *Federation of Rainbow Warriors v Union of India* Order 21 August 2018; *Citizens for Green Doon v Union of India* Order 8 October 2018; *Tribunal on its Own Motion v Secretary of State* Judgment 4 April 2014.

[107] NGT Act s 20. The principles include the precautionary and polluter-pays principles, sustainable development, inter- and intragenerational equity, and public trust. See *L G Polymers v Union of India* 2020 SCC OnLine NGT 129; *Westend Green Farms Society v. Union of India* Order 2 November 2018; *Aditya N Prasad v Union of India* Order 1 November 2018; *Anjani Kumar v. State of UP* 2017 SCC OnLine NGT 979.

[108] D Schlosberg, *Defining Environmental Justice: Theories, Movements and Nature* (Oxford, Oxford University Press, 2007) 25–29.

[109] N Fraser, 'Recognition Without Ethics?' (2001) 18(2–3) *Theory, Culture and Society* 21, 29–30.

The role of the Land and Environment Court is to 'administer justice in the adjudication and resolution of disputes'[110] and it is 'critical that [its] dispute resolution mechanisms adopt appropriate procedures'.[111] In this context, the Court's approach covers both 'its substantive decisions and its practices and procedures'.[112] The substantive decisions uphold the statutory rights that include public access to information,[113] public participation,[114] review and appeal of legislative and administrative decisions,[115] and citizens having access to the courts to remedy or restrain breaches of public law, including environmental law.[116]

The Court has devised progressive practices and procedures applicable to public interest litigation (PIL) to provide access to environmental justice. Public interest, a 'multi-faceted concept'[117] but simultaneously a 'nebulous concept',[118] involves 'public and not private rights, and something more'[119] represented by parties to the litigation. The Court offers a public forum to those affected by environmental issues and the opportunity to express their concerns and claims.[120] Accordingly, the Court's relaxed procedural prescriptions facilitate access to environmental justice as 'judges should not fetter judicial discretions with self-imposed rigid rules'.[121] This relaxation includes broad and liberal standing requirements,[122] not making an order for the payment of costs against an unsuccessful applicant in any proceedings,[123] not requiring security for the costs of the proceedings,[124] not to require an undertaking for damages as a prerequisite for granting interlocutory injunctive relief,[125] and the limited relevance of the equitable defences of laches, acquiescence and delay.[126] Further, use of technology and online services promote participatory mechanisms to access environmental justice.[127]

[110] Chief Justice Mahla L Pearlman AM, 'Celebration of 20 Years of the Land and Environment Court' (Royal Australian Planning Institute Congress Conference, October 2000).

[111] Chief Justice McClellan, 'Environmental Issues – How Should We Resolve Disputes?' (National Environmental Law Association, Canberra, July 2005).

[112] Preston (n 57).

[113] *Environment Protection Authority v Hargraves* [2002] NSWLEC 113; *Brooklyn Resort Pty Ltd v Hornsby Shire Council* (1999) 105 LGERA 208.

[114] *Reulie Land Co Pty Limited v Lee Environmental Planning Pty Limited* [2019] NSWLEC 194; *Stockland Development Pty Ltd v Manly Council* (2004) 136 LGERA 254.

[115] *Gibson v Mosman Municipal Council* (2001) 116 LGERA 397.

[116] *Oshlack v Richmond River Council* (1994) 82 LGERA 236, 238; *Anderson v Jali Local Aboriginal Land Council (No 2)* [2009] NSWLEC 222.

[117] *Ruddock v Vadarlis (No 2)* (2001) 115 FCR 229; *Engadine Area Traffic Action Group v Sutherland Shire Council (No 2)* (2004) 136 LGERA 365, (15).

[118] *Caroona Coal Action Group Inc v Coal Mines Australia Pty Ltd and Another (No.3)* (2010) 173 LGERA 280.

[119] ibid, [60].

[120] BJ Preston 'The Contribution of the Courts in Tackling Climate Change' (2016) 28 *Journal of Environmental Law* 11, 12.

[121] *Gibson v Mosman Municipal Council* (n 115), [11].

[122] Open standing provisions 'reflect the high social importance of protecting the environment by the processes of law' (Stein (n 65) 14); Environmental and Planning Assessment Act 1979 (NSW) s 123; *Haughton v Minister for Planning and Macquarie Generation* (2011) 185 LGERA 373; *Anderson v Jali Local Aboriginal Land Council* (n 116).

[123] NSWLEC Rules 2007 part 4 rule 4.2; *Friends of Hay Street v Hastings Council* (1995) 87 LGERA 44; Schlosberg (n 108).

[124] ibid (Rules) Part 4 Rule 4.2; *Byron Shire Business for the Future v Byron Shire Council* (1994) 83 LGERA 59.

[125] ibid (Rules); *Tegra (NSW) Pty Ltd v Gundagai Shire Council* (2007) 160 LGERA 1; *Ross v State Rail Authority (NSW)* (1987) 70 LGRA 91.

[126] Preston (n 57).

[127] ibid; www.lec.nsw.gov.au/ (accessed 5 August 2020).

Thus, the Court's jurisdictional and geographical accessibility practices strengthen the environmental rule of law and ensure justice is realised equitably and equally.

Some of the Court's procedures reappear in the NGT and facilitate access to justice. The NGT's environmental dispute litigation approach is not solely adversarial. It is also quasi-investigative and quasi-inquisitorial.[128] The NGT developed and expanded its procedures and powers through participatory mechanisms that express equal respect and opportunity for all participants. The tribunal created receptive, accessible opportunities for the affected, the dispossessed and the representative non-governmental organisations (NGOs), through the encompassing term 'aggrieved person',[129] the genesis of which is derived from the Supreme Court's public interest litigation.[130] In *Samir Mehta v Union of India*,[131] the NGT observed that:

> [A]n 'aggrieved person' is to be given a liberal interpretation … the person has to show that he is directly or indirectly concerned with adverse environmental impacts … the construction that will help in achieving the cause of the Act should be accepted and not the one which would result in deprivation of rights created under the statute.[132]

The adoption of an on-the-spot investigative procedure involving the inspection of affected sites by expert members allows the comparison of contradictory claims, positions and reports filed by the parties.[133] The stakeholder consultative process engages the diversity of stakeholders, ensures information sharing is effective, and employs techniques that help the submission of time-bound, clear-cut proposals and suggestions for the effective enforcement of environmental laws.[134] It is applicable to cases of wider significance involving Pan-Indian issues such as river cleaning or air pollution. The use of *suo motu* (on its own motion) is an integral part of the NGT.[135]

The NGT also employs technology to facilitate quick access to justice. This includes the use of geotagging, e-petition throughout India, videoconferencing technologies and a user-friendly website with detailed information about cases, reports and guidance documents.[136] However, technology can work both for the benefit and to the detriment of parties. For example, recently video conferences have been cancelled without notice or given insufficient time.[137] Shockingly, it is reported that lawyers have been put on 'mute settings' while presenting their arguments from regional benches.[138] Such regressive practices coupled with the absence of proper hearings

[128] *Forward Foundation v State of Karnataka* Judgment 10 September 2015; *MoEFCC v Nirma Ltd*, Supreme Court Order 4 August 2014.

[129] NGT Act s 18(2); *Kishan Lal Gera v State of Haryana* (2015) All (I) NGT Reporter (2) (Delhi) 286; *Sri Ranganathan v Union of India* (2014) All (I) NGT Reporter (2) (SZ) 1.

[130] *State of Uttranchal v Balwant Singh Chaufal* 2010 3 SCC 402; *In re Noise Pollution* AIR 2005 SC 3136; G Sahu, 'Implication of Indian Supreme Courts Innovation for Environmental Jurisprudence' (2008) 4 *Law, Environment and Development Journal* 377; L Rajamani, 'Public Interest Litigation in India: Exploring Issues of Access, Participation, Equity, Effectiveness and Sustainability' (2007) 19 *Journal of Environmental Law* 29.

[131] NGT Judgment 2 August 2016.

[132] ibid, [31]–[32].

[133] Gill (n 70) 166.

[134] ibid, 167–68.

[135] *EAS Sarma v Union of India* NGT Order 1 June 2020; Gill, 'Environmental Justice in India' (n 87).

[136] Green Tribunal, https://greentribunal.gov.in/ (accessed 30 January 2020).

[137] G Sahu, 'Whither the NGT?' *Down to Earth* (Delhi, 23 September 2019).

[138] R Dutta, 'Woes of the NGT: Are the Recent Appointments Unconstitutional?' *Bar and Bench* (Delhi, 17 December 2019).

strike at the very heart of the NGT's mandate to offer environmental justice, increased public confidence and the promotion of the environmental rule of law.

Finally, in relation to effectiveness, it is worth considering the *value-adding* function of the Land and Environment Court and the NGT. NPM effectiveness involves a 'process in which a feedback loop is represented by using standards of performance, measuring system performance, comparing that performance with standards, feeding back information about unwanted variances in the system, and modifying the system'.[139] The Court is the first court to implement the International Framework for Court Excellence to improve its performance and administration.[140] Effectiveness is measured through quantitative and qualitative indicators (affordability, accessibility, responsiveness to the needs of users, and timeliness and delay measured by a backlog indicator and compliance with time standards).

However, the NGT has not endorsed an evaluative performance framework. There is no public evidence that this measure is under consideration. The absence of a feedback loop raises questions about the quality and effectiveness of justice. Since 2017, there are concerns that the NGT is waning and 'losing its bite'.[141] For example, limited availability of scientific expertise has resulted in reduced access to regional benches. To build legitimacy both in the NGT and environmental rule of law, a robust feedback loop would improve judicial accountability and good-quality services.

4.2. Efficiency

Efficiency relates to managing inputs, outputs and processes to achieve the best results for the communities and value for money. It includes factors such as quick disposal, costs, reasonable information, clearance rate, pending cases and average length of proceedings.[142] Both the Land and Environment Court and the NGT are *multi-door courthouses*. A 'just, quick and cheap resolution of real issues in proceedings'[143] increases confidence in the ECTs and the environmental rule of law. Streamlined processes 'ensure expedited proceedings consistent with a full and fair determination'.[144]

The Court's commitment to ADR illustrates a 'multi-door courthouse' approach that results in swifter dispute resolution.[145] The court offers in-house and external dispute resolution processes. These include conciliation, mediation, neutral evaluation and order mediation to a referee.[146] For instance, in 2019, 74 per cent of Class 1 appeals were

[139] Visser, Schouteten and Dikkers (n 11) 40–41.
[140] BJ Preston, 'Achieving Court Excellence: The Need for a Collaborative Approach' (2017) 8 *International Consortium for Court Excellence Newsletter* 4.
[141] Ramesh (n 96).
[142] European Commission (n 64).
[143] UNEP (n 1) 184.
[144] ibid, 211.
[145] Preston (n 57); BJ Preston, 'The Use of Alternative Dispute Resolution in Administrative Disputes' (2011) 22 *Alternative Dispute Resolution Journal* 144, 151–53; BJ Preston, 'The Land and Environment Court of New South Wales: Moving Towards a Multi-door Courthouse – Part I' (2008) 19 *Alternative Dispute Resolution Journal* 72.
[146] NSWLEC Act s 34; Civil Procedure Act 2005 (NSW), s 26. NSWLEC Rules 2007 (NSW), pt 6 r 6.2.

finalised by ADR processes and negotiated settlement.[147] To that extent, the Court's inbuilt efficient process improves accountability in environmental decision-making and ensures public legitimacy.

ADR is not included within the NGT's statutory mandate. The tribunal is a 'creation of a statute and its jurisdiction will have to be construed with reference to the language of its provisions'.[148] This omission is a missed opportunity especially within an Asian context because ADR reflects 'cultural acceptance of the resolution of community disputes'.[149]

Nevertheless, there is also the danger of a pressured compromise within this process, especially if inequality of arms exists between the parties. To promote the environmental rule of law, ADR should be a problem-solving process informed by relevant expertise to achieve an appropriate environmental outcome to the satisfaction of all the parties.

In regard to *better court administration*, managing cases through efficient procedures determines 'whether parties have confidence in the environmental rule of law'.[150] Consequently, ECTs must be fair, cost-effective, thorough, timely and user-friendly. For example, the Court's 'reasoned and transparent judgments'[151] and their public availability helps inform the parties and the public how environmental law is interpreted and applied. At an institutional level, concurrent evidence, sometimes called the 'hot tub', is an efficient method that saves the Court time and costs.[152] Additionally, the Court makes available explanatory documentation and information for external stakeholders. The Practice Notes set out 'the case management practices for the just, quick and cheap resolution of the proceedings'.[153] Efficiency is also highlighted in the Court's 2019 Annual Report, which states that there is an improvement in the overall clearance rate (Class 1–8), an increase in the percentage of pre-hearing attendances conducted online and an increase in the percentage of reserved judgments delivered within the Court's time standards. However, the Court also identified its underperforming areas and its willingness to improve its administrative functioning.[154] The adoption of user-friendly approaches ensures the Court's services and facilities are efficient and publicly available.[155]

Likewise, the NGT Act mandates a low-cost fee (£13) to file an application or appeal[156] and a fast-track process requiring the decision of cases within six months of

[147] www.lec.nsw.gov.au/lec/types-of-cases/class-1---environmental-planning-and-protection-appeals.html (accessed 10 August 2020). In 2019, the Court was a Finalist in the 'ADR Group of the Year' category at the Australian Disputes Centre ADR Awards (NSWLEC Annual Report 2019, 21).

[148] *M P Pollution Control Board v Commissioner Bhopal* NGT Judgment 8 August 2013, [7].

[149] Asian Development Bank, *Asian Judges Symposium on Environmental Decision Making, the Rule of Law and Environmental Justice* (Asian Development Bank, 2010) 43.

[150] UNEP (n 1) 188.

[151] Justice Terry Sheahan AO, 'Use of ADR in the New South Wales and in the Land and Environment Court' (Australasian Conference of Planning and Environment Courts and Tribunals, September 2010).

[152] McClellan (n 111); Justice R Pepper, '"Hot-Tubbing": The Use of Concurrent Expert Evidence in the Land and Environment Court of New South Wales and Beyond' (Annual Alaskan Bar Association Conference, May 2015).

[153] NSWLEC Annual Report 2019, 16.

[154] Annual Report (n 147) 3.

[155] ibid, 40.

[156] NGT Rules 2011 r 12.

application or appeal.[157] Financial accessibility and speedy justice reflects the NGT's open-door commitment to environmental justice. To illustrate, the latest official figures between July 2011and July 2021 state there were 35,558 filed cases, out of which 33,168 were disposed and 2390 remain pending.[158] Thus, 93.3 per cent of the cases were decided whereas 6.7 per cent of cases remain pending. Further, from 2018 onwards the Tribunal mandates an advance service of notice for speedy disposal of cases. Although the official clearance rates appear impressive, of late the NGT reality is disturbing. There is now a

> new 4-D approach to dealing with cases – 'dismiss, dispose, delegate and de-reserve' … without providing due reasons … [and] since July 2018, the Tribunal has disposed of over 700 cases, all at different stages of hearing, with largely generic orders directing the concerned authorities 'to look into the matter and take appropriate action in accordance with law'.[159]

These systemic disposal changes undermine the environmental rule of law and public trust. Reasoned and transparent decisions help 'build predictability of law and confidence in legal process and institutions'.[160]

4.3. Transparency

Transparency opens a window into the inner workings of organisations. Factors such as judicial independence, including appointment and removal processes, are indicators related to promoting institutional independence, impartiality and integrity.[161] In regard to *independence from the executive*, the establishment of the Land and Environment Court with its judicial independence has 'served as a bulwark against political attack'.[162] This encourages independent and impartial decisions leading to transparent and effective environmental decision-making. Granting tenure to judges further enhances independence and ensures impartiality and accountability.[163]

For the NGT, as in the Court, the statutory provisions act as a benchmark for a rigorous appointment process, with tenure and removal provisions subject to public scrutiny.[164] In *Wilfred J v Ministry of Environment and Forests*[165] the Tribunal observed that its appointment and selection process remains free from executive influence and ensures parliamentary scrutiny. However, India has developed a patronage culture that provides sinecures in the form of post-retirement assignments for former judges, senior administrators and technocrats in judicial and quasi-judicial bodies at national and state levels. This has been questioned and accusations have been made regarding

[157] NGT Act s 18(3).
[158] NGT website, https://greentribunal.gov.in/ (accessed 27 August 2021).
[159] M Ramesh, 'Nearly a Decade Old, Is the NGT Losing Its Bite?' *The Wire* (India, 11 May 2019); *Hariram Singh v State of Bihar* NGT Order 14 January 2019; *R R Raja v State of Jharkhand* NGT Order 3 May 2019.
[160] UNEP (n 1) 212.
[161] ibid.
[162] Stein (n 65) 7.
[163] NSWLEC Act ss 8–9; see Justice DH Lloyd, 'Judicial Accountability' (Judicial Conference of Australia, November 1998).
[164] NGT Act ss 4–5.
[165] NGT Judgments 17 July 2014.

the appointment of NGT judges. For example, the appointment of the present NGT Chairperson within hours of his retirement as a Supreme Court judge was raised in the Indian Parliament, which questioned whether this new role was a 'reward' for supporting Modi government policy whilst sitting as a Supreme Court judge.[166] Additionally, the appointment of two serving expert members has been questioned. They were senior officials in the Ministry of Forests involved in deciding forest clearance issues and are now hearing appeals against their previous decisions.[167] These executive interventions cripple the independence of the NGT and raise questions about the Tribunal's ability to maintain the environmental rule of law.

5. Conclusion

The prototype environmental court, the Land and Environment Court, established in 1980, is badged as a 'Rolls Royce model'. Today it stands *primus inter pares*. The national and international status of the Court is such that this chapter has placed its jurisdiction, structure, composition, judgments, accessibility and impact under a forensic microscope. The current Chief Judge, Brian Preston, identified and catalogued twelve key characteristics of the Court: the 'desirable dozen'. These are the building blocks of a successful environmental court.

This chapter unpacks and tests these key characteristics through the NPM paradigm and places them for a comparative review alongside its younger Indian counterpart, the NGT. The commonality is striking especially when the Tribunal's genesis is considered. This comparative analysis is undertaken through the lens of functionality underpinned by the environmental rule of law. It examines the common problems that produce the same or similar outcomes resulting in better solutions. Judicial institutions founded on the environmental rule of law 'solidify its legitimacy and trust across society'.[168] Although India is a developing country of 1.3 billion people it also shares the common law, the English language and democratic values with Australia. They both experience the daily consequences of the environmental crisis. There exists a unifying platform upon which similar environmental institutions were built. The Land and Environment Court continues to employ best practices as demonstrated through the NPM paradigm. It simultaneously offers in common cause its model and experiences to those nations that seek to contribute through law a meaningful response to current environmental issues in order to maintain the environmental rule of law.

Influenced initially by the diffusionary adoption of the Court's structure, processes and principles, the NGT has garnered widespread praise and popular expectation. This recognition, both national and international, ultimately produced a political backlash as politicians, government policy-makers and bureaucrats were unexpectantly exposed

[166] www.newindianexpress.com/nation/2018/jul/26/congress-raises-issue-of-appointment-of-justice-adarsh-kumar-goel-as-ngt-chairman-in-lok-sabha-1848938.html (accessed 4 January 2021).

[167] Dutta (n 138); Gill (n 70) 206 states that between 2010 and 2015 the Ministry of Environment and Forests was the defendant in 25.1% of all NGT cases.

[168] UNEP (n 1) 19.

to critical examination by the Tribunal and often found wanting.[169] A Thucydides trap was set and is now triggered. Jairam Ramesh, the architect of the NGT Act who shepherded it through Parliament while serving as Minister of Environment and Forests, has described the Tribunal as 'emasculated' and 'decimated'.[170] Institutions are subject to change due to both internal and external forces. Today, the NGT displays structural cracks and deficiencies when subjected to the analysis of the NPM paradigm. The practices and performance of the NGT require reassessment through a process of reconstruction and re-energising in order to support the environmental rule of law, strengthening both its legitimacy and trust throughout Indian society.

[169] *Sudeip Shrivastava v State of Chhattisgarh* NGT Judgment 24 March 2014; *K K Singh v National Ganga River Basin Authority* NGT Judgment 16 October 2014; Economic Times, 'Why Contempt Should Not Be Initiated Against Delhi Govt, DJB: NGT' *Economic Times Politics* (Delhi, 23 October 2017).

[170] Ramesh (n 96); https://twitter.com/jairam_ramesh/status/1317657118183354368.

PART II

Doctrine

7

Biodiversity and the Land and Environment Court of New South Wales

PAUL ADAM

1. Introduction

This chapter is an exploration of the engagement of the Land and Environment Court of New South Wales (the Court) with the concept of biodiversity. Consideration of the environment is central to the Court's functions, and, as biodiversity is an integral part of the environment, it is inevitable that the Court's engagement with biodiversity is significant.

Biodiversity is multifaceted. While the term is of recent invention, the concept is one that has long been intuitively understood by humans. The body of traditional knowledge about biodiversity is vast although much has been lost. The study of biodiversity is part of what has long been known as natural history, although natural history covers more than modern biodiversity science, which is defined in terms of living organisms and their requirements. Furthermore, biodiversity is both part of, and influenced by, the environment.

While biodiversity is now a prominent topic in the media and political debate, our thinking is constrained by our lack of knowledge of many aspects of biodiversity, the newness of the concept and our cultural and social history. The political and legal system in Australia has roots extending back to Britain, but was imposed on a continent whose First Nations have been in continuous occupation longer than the peoples of any other part of the globe. Their understanding of the continent's biodiversity, essential for their very existence, was developed over at least 60,000 years.[1] The biota and environment of Australia are different from those of Britain: the new colonists arrived with interpretations of the environment and biota of northern Europe developed over a few thousand years, and some of the ideas they arrived with still, unconsciously, underlie the policies and practices of environmental management today. The Court's engagement with biodiversity is thus not simply about protecting genetic variation in nature,

[1] CJA Bradshaw et al, 'Stochastic Models Support Rapid Peopling of Late Pleistocene Sahul' (2021) 12 *Nature Communications* 2440; SA Crabtree et al, 'Landscape Rules Predict Optimal Superhighways for the First Peopling of Sahul' (2021) *Nature Human Behaviour*, doi.org/10/1038/s41562-021-01106-8.

but requires recognising the interrelationships between culture and nature both now and historically.

The structure of this chapter is as follows. First, an overview is given of the concept and language of biodiversity. Second, an overview is given of New South Wales (NSW) biodiversity legislation. Third, the Court's case law in relation to biodiversity-focused legislative obligations is examined. Finally, two different examples of how biodiversity has shaped the Court's more general jurisprudence and practice are provided.

One note before I start. This chapter does not provide a textbook account of the Court's case law on biodiversity. It is more akin to an essay in which the complexity of biodiversity and the issues it creates for the Court are explored. What becomes clear from this analysis are the dangers of having too static and narrow an understanding of biodiversity (or any related term), particularly in the legal context.

2. The Concept and Language of Biodiversity

In order to have a sensible discussion about biodiversity and its components we need to have an agreed language. Professions and disciplines develop their own terminology and jargon. In some cases, terminology is unique to its field, but, in other cases, words with a broad meaning in everyday speech may have a specific meaning when used in a technical sense. Terminology and jargon enable more precise definitions and economy (one jargon word might otherwise require a paragraph to explain the concept) but equally they can provide a barrier to communication and conversation. Mastery of technical language is essential for professional advancement but carries the danger that a lay audience may find it completely incomprehensible. This is a problem for a court adjudicating on an environmental law question given the range of specialist expertise that may be called upon. The language of one discipline may be impenetrable to experts in other fields and to the lay public.

In this section I provide an overview of the concept of biodiversity at both the international level and in New South Wales. It illustrates the point made in the introduction that biodiversity is entangled with culture and history.

2.1. Biodiversity at the International Level

The term biodiversity was first popularised (as BioDiversity) in the title of a forum held in 1986 in Washington DC, the proceedings of which were published (under the title Biodiversity) in 1988.[2] The publication did not define the term, although the focus was on species. From the early 1980s, the International Union for the Conservation of Nature (IUCN), recognising that, globally, biological diversity was declining rapidly, and biological diversity should be conserved, had been working to provide a framework for future action. This resulted in the United Nations Convention on Biological Diversity, adopted in Nairobi in May 1992, and opened for signature at the UN Conference

[2] EO Wilson and FM Peter (eds), *Biodiversity* (Washington, DC, National Academy Press, 1988).

on Environment and Development in Rio de Janeiro in July 1992.[3] The Convention came into force in December 1993. Australia was among the early signatories to the Convention.

The Convention on Biological Diversity (CBD) led to a new paradigm for environmental stewardship and conservation practice – one that embodies aspects of the much earlier appreciation of the relationship between human society and nature, involving recognition of the place of human communities in the broader ecosystem, our reliance on services provided by ecosystems, and human obligations for the conservation of nature.

Article 2 of the CBD defines biological diversity as 'the variability among living organisms from all sources including, *inter alia*, terrestrial, marine and other aquatic ecosystems and the ecological complexes of which they are part; this includes diversity within species[4] between species and of ecosystems', and defines an ecosystem as 'a dynamic complex of plants, animals and microorganism communities and their non-living environment interacting as a functional unit', and a habitat as 'the place or type of site where an organism or population naturally occurs'. Although the word community appears in the definition of ecosystem, it is not separately defined.

Article 8 of the CBD provides for measures to be taken for the in situ conservation of biological diversity. These include inter alia:

(a) Establish a system of protected areas or areas where special measures need to be taken to conserve biological diversity;
(d) Promote the protection of ecosystems, natural habitats and the maintenance of viable populations of species in natural surroundings;
(h) Prevent the introduction of, control or eradicate those alien species which threaten ecosystems, habitats or species;
(k) Develop or maintain necessary legislation and/or other regulatory provisions for the protection of threatened species and populations;
(l) Where a significant adverse effect on biological diversity has been determined pursuant to Article 7, regulate or manage the relevant processes and categories of activities.

Article 8 encourages governments to develop further traditional conservation measures, including the reserve system and management of introduced species and threatening processes. Article 8(d) is not limited to the protected area network but requires consideration of the need for biodiversity conservation much more broadly of species and ecosystems on land (and sea) regardless of tenure. Article 9 deals with ex situ conservation which is 'predominantly for the purpose of complementing *in situ* measures'.

Much of the focus is on species both in themselves and as forming communities. However, there is a requirement to consider habitat, which includes the physical environment in which species and communities occur. Thus, there is necessarily a requirement to conserve the physical environment.

The definition of biodiversity in the CBD is not closed – it includes three levels of organisation, but a higher level that could be considered is the distribution of communities at landscape level. In their natural state some landscapes may be homogeneous

[3] 1760 UNTS 79.

[4] Variation within species is essential for long-term evolution and will be important if species are to adapt to changing environmental conditions.

across large areas. Other landscapes may, because of geological and geomorphological variation, support complexes of distinct ecological assemblages in small patches. In highly modified landscapes, the natural vegetation cover is fragmented and altered in composition. Conservation of landscape components will be essential for the conservation of species and communities.

The visual component of landscape is important for humans, but the landscape is also the context in which biodiversity occurs. The landscape is perceived differently by other species. What we imagine as a 'bird's-eye' view will be different to a bird, and the visual spectrum detectable by many species differs from that of humans, so the landscape to a dog or a bee will be in different colours to those we see. We know that plant species composition and vegetation structure of landscapes are important to fauna. Various planning instruments and policies require the maintenance of connectivity of habitat across landscapes – but different species will have different requirements, so no one prescription will suit all species.[5] Landscapes are appreciated using all our senses – and the scents, sounds and feel of particular landscapes are important aspects of the environment, although not regularly given consideration.[6] Protection and management of geological and geomorphological features of landscapes is practised in many countries.[7] In recent years there has been growing international interest in the concepts of geoheritage and geodiversity, the geological equivalent of biodiversity.[8]

2.2. Biodiversity in Australia: What's in a Name?

Most discussions involving biodiversity involve reference to particular species and communities. What names are to be used for these entities? This has been an issue ever since legislation needed lists of species either for the conservation of native species or the control of introduced noxious species. Long before the age of biodiversity, the earliest lists of species in legislation in New South Wales (the Game Protection Act 1866) contained relatively few species, which were listed under 'English' names. As the protection offered by legislation applied, initially, mainly to introduced species familiar to early colonists, this did not cause problems – but as the lists of species expanded to include more native species it became necessary to use scientific (binomial) names in the absence of agreed 'English' names. Even today, scientific names are seen as off-putting by many of the public. The first time I appeared as an expert witness in the NSW Court, in one of its earliest cases, the applicant's counsel during cross-examination, in a loud aside to the judge, asked: 'Why do we have to hear all this Latin?' The judge's

[5] See discussion in *Bottomline Group Pty Ltd v Snowy Monaro Regional Council* [2020] NSWLEC 1115, [190]–[202].

[6] E Brady, *Aesthetics of the Natural Environment* (Tuscaloosa, Alabama University Press, 2003) ch 6.

[7] The foundation document for central government involvement in conservation in England and Wales is Wildlife Conservation Special Committee, *Conservation of Nature in England and Wales* (Cmd 7122, 1947). It devoted considerable discussion to geology and geomorphology, and in Appendix 8 identified sites of particular geological interest.

[8] M Brocx, *Geoheritage from Global Perspective to Local Principles for Conservation Planning* (Perth, Western Australian Museum, 2008); I Creswell, 'Geoheritage and Geoconservation in Australia' (2019) 66 *Australian Journal of Earth Sciences* 75.

response was that lawyers tended to use a lot of Latin. Even now it is not uncommon for legal representatives or experts in other fields to indicate that they do not know how to pronounce species names. The phobia about Latin names is curious given that many five-year-olds know, and use, the scientific names of dinosaur species.

Although one of the aims of taxonomy (that branch of science which deals with the naming of organisms) is to provide nomenclatural stability, this is an unobtainable goal. Many species, probably the majority, are yet to be discovered and described, but for named taxa nomenclatural change still occurs. Some nomenclatural changes are corrections of previous procedural errors; others arise from new biological discoveries. Some nomenclatural changes are mandatory, but many are matters of opinion.

Given all of this, the Court, or any court for that matter, cannot be expected to be up to date with the current taxonomy and nomenclature of the whole of the biological world and must, for the most part, take species lists at face value. Just as the Court cannot keep track of all the taxonomic literature, neither can consultants, so occasionally the reports of experts differ between the parties in the nomenclature adopted. It is also the case that whereas legislation identifies species to be protected, our imperfect knowledge of biodiversity means that a large number of species are not yet named. Of the unnamed species, a proportion, varying between higher taxa, is likely to meet criteria so as to be regarded as threatened.[9]

In Australia, there is no requirement for a species to be formally named for it to be recognised as threatened. Specimens may have been collected and retained in herbaria and museum collections which have been recognised as being new species but are yet to be described and so do not have formal names. The Endangered Species Protection Act 1992 (Cth) (ESPA) included, in its schedules, entities identified to generic level, not assigned to species but categorised by some combination of the name of a collector, collecting number and locality. This practice was followed in NSW in the Threatened Species Conservation Act 1995 (NSW) (TSCA) and the Biodiversity Conservation Act 2016 (NSW) (BCA).

If an entity has been recognised as being a new taxon, sufficient information may exist for conservation status to be allocated as it may have been re-found only at the original site, and searches of other apparently suitable locations may not have resulted in new finds. Some of these unnamed specimens were first collected many decades ago. The failure to finalise their formal naming reflects both the need in some cases to carry out full taxonomic revisions of the entire genus before individual species can be properly assessed, and the paucity of taxonomists to carry out the necessary studies. Some, but not all, of these informal names appear in relevant flora accounts, so that it is possible to identify specimens to 'known but unnamed' entities.

The inclusion of known but unnamed species in schedules provides an indication to consultants to look out for these species when assessing sites, and, because earlier collections are available in institutions, specimens can be compared to confirm whether or not they are from the same entity. However, it is difficult for members of the public to carry out such investigations, such that a landholder might be unaware of the possibility of the

[9] Relatively few new species of birds or mammals would be expected, but there are many species of insect yet to be named, and in some invertebrate phyla possibly only a minority of species have been described.

presence of threatened species on their land. There are also specimens not assigned to genera, or, in some cases, even family, whose conservation status cannot be considered. It is also impossible to take into account the unknown unknowns – the many species of insects, for example, yet to be collected.

However, some of these species occur in ecological communities recognised as threatened. Only some of the species occurring in a community are included in its diagnosis in the determination of the Scientific Committee (the body responsible for making changes to schedules under the BCA), but the protection that the listing of a community brings to an area applies to all of the species within the community, including those known to exist but not yet named and those yet to be discovered.[10] Further difficulties arise in determining the extent of a community – although sharp boundaries may occur between communities on a site, in many cases there is a transitional zone (an ecotone); in some cases ecotones have themselves been recognised as endangered ecological communities in their own right (eg Shale Sandstone Transition Forest), but otherwise it is a matter of judgement where to draw an arbitrary line.

Western language is not the only source of biodiversity language and meaning. There is a rich indigenous vocabulary as well. Recognition of indigenous names for organisms is included within Article 8(j) of the CBD, but there is no legislative requirement to use indigenous names in schedules or reports. Indigenous names have not been consistently recorded, and many languages have been lost. Given the diversity of languages, widespread species may have had different names in different regions, whereas binomials are universal in application. But use of indigenous names where appropriate can help keep language alive and enhance awareness of traditional knowledge.[11]

It is also worth noting the role of vernacular language. The majority of English vernacular names for endemic Australian organisms are of recent origin (within the last 250 years) or are transplanted names because of a perceived similarity to northern European species. It is unlikely that many species, particularly those which are small and apparently insignificant, will have vernacular names. However, larger and more charismatic species have been given vernacular names. These form part of the rich tapestry of language but there are problems with using vernacular names in formal documents. Many different vernacular names may have been given to a single species in different parts of its geographic range, and the same vernacular name may have been given to several species (eg Blackwood and Blackbutt both cover several species). For some taxa there have been attempts to formalise vernacular names in official lists of species, but this exercise has been subject to as much instability as scientific nomenclature. Even minor changes to standard vernacular lists can attract surprising opposition.

The discussion so far has focused on species. It is also worth considering the language that applies in relation to ecological communities. Few Australian ecological communities have English vernacular names – except at the broadest level. This absence reflects that recognition of ecological communities at the level required for listings only

[10] The determinations provide lists of species, normally of vascular plants, which characterise the community and enable its identification, but these lists rarely include fauna.

[11] PM Wehi et al, 'Enhancing Awareness and Adoption of Cultural Values Through the Use of Maori Bird Names in Science Communication and Environmental Reporting' (2019) 43 *New Zealand Journal of Ecology* 387; L Maffi, 'Linguistic, Cultural and Biological Diversity' (2005) 34 *Annual Review of Anthropology* 599.

arose with the introduction of biodiversity legislation. A few indigenous terms such as mallee and wallum have been adopted into Australian English but our understanding of how indigenous peoples perceive and describe vegetation is very limited. Given this, when lay evidence (or evidence of experts in disciplines other than ecology) is given, references to vegetation communities may employ a confusing diversity of names. For example, 'wood' and 'forest' are used differently in Australia than in England. A wood in England usually refers to a discrete, fairly small stand of vegetation dominated by trees, whereas a forest, technically, was an area to which Forest Law applied, and which was often a mosaic of wooded areas and heath or grasslands. In Australia the difference between wood and forest is the spacing of the trees – woods are more open than forests, so a small stand with a canopy made up of closely spaced trees can be referred to as a forest. Overseas readers of Australian scientific literature do not always understand the nature of Australian vegetation described as forest or woodland.[12]

3. An Overview of Biodiversity Legislation in NSW

The discussion in the last section makes clear that, for the NSW Court, to engage with biodiversity is to engage with many different cultural and disciplinary ideas. The Court is not acting on a blank legal sheet. Throughout the Court's history there has also been an evolution of biodiversity legislation in both NSW and Australia.

The early litigation involving what we would now call biodiversity was not under biodiversity legislation, but under planning legislation – the Environmental Planning and Assessment Act 1979 (NSW) (the EPA Act). The 1980s saw a series of high-profile cases brought by conservationists and conservation groups challenging government decisions allowing logging of rainforests and old-growth eucalypt forests, causing significant harm to species and ecosystems. These cases focused on the inadequacy of the environmental impact assessment undertaken for those activities.[13] Moving closer to the concept of biodiversity, a case of particular significance brought under the National Parks and Wildlife Act 1974 (NSW) (NPWA), challenging the legality of logging activities and prompting subsequent biodiversity legislation, was *Corkill v Forestry Commission of New South Wales (No 2)*.[14]

The case involved proposals for logging moist hardwood forest in Chaelundi State Forest in northern NSW. Corkill argued that the proposed logging would breach the NPWA as it would involve taking and killing protected (section 98) and endangered (section 99) fauna. Chaelundi State Forest was exceptional in the richness and diversity of its vertebrate fauna. 'Take' was defined in section 5 NPWA to include 'disturb' and 'injure'. The removal of habitat through logging would result in the death of fauna.

[12] The names applied to broadscale vegetation in Australia are often distinctly Australian usages of terms that have long histories in English. The divergence between usage in England and in Australia in regard to terms such as scrub, brush and forest developed very early in colonial history. See J Atkinson, *An Account of the State of Agriculture & Grazing in New South Wales* (J Cross, 1826) chs 1, 2.

[13] *Prineas v Forestry Commission (NSW)* (1983) 49 LGRA 402; *Kivi v Forestry Commission of New South Wales* (1982) 47 LGRA 38; *Jarasius v Forestry Commission of NSW (No 1)* (1988) 71 LGRA 79; *Bailey v Forestry Commission of New South Wales* (1989) 67 LGRA 200.

[14] *Corkill v Forestry Commission of New South Wales (No 2)* (1991) 73 LGRA 126.

The offence claimed was not new. Stein J noted that it occurred in section 3 of the Birds and Animals Protection Act 1918 and in section 4 of the Fauna Protection Act 1948. Despite the references to 'take and kill' including disturbance, the legislation had not been interpreted as applying to clearing of forests or logging. Stein J considered that causing death or injury to an animal as a consequence of disturbance and loss of habitat[15] or food resource came within the prohibited 'take and kill'. Stein J's interpretation was clearly one that had been available in legislation for many years. The surprising thing about the judgment was not that it involved a novel interpretation of simple words, but that the point had not arisen previously.

Chaelundi State Forest was not the only state forest with protected and endangered fauna. The implication of the decision was that logging in all state forests could be in breach of the NPWA. This created serious problems for the industry and the government of the day. To address them, the Endangered Fauna (Interim Protection) Act 1991 (NSW) (EF(IP)A) was introduced to provide, on a temporary basis, for continued logging under conditions. The EF(IP)A contained a sunset clause expiring on 31 December 1995. The government was under notice that new legislation was required to commence on or before 1 January 1996 to provide a regime for fauna protection which would permit continuation of the forest industry.

While the state government was developing the required legislation, the Commonwealth became a signatory to the CBD. The High Court in the *Tasmanian Dam* case[16] had determined that the external affairs power of the Constitution (section 51(xxix)) permitted the Commonwealth to pass legislation to give effect to international treaties, and in that circumstance, Commonwealth legislation prevailed over state legislation. Signing a treaty did not in itself cause the treaty to have effect – legislation was required. This was achieved by the passage of the Environment Protection and Biodiversity Conservation Act 1999 (Cth) (the EPBC Act).[17]

However, the state government, in anticipation, expanded the scope of its legislation to replace the EF(IP)A so as to encompass biodiversity. The Threatened Species Conservation Act 1995 (NSW) (TSCA) was the result. Although the objects of the TSCA included conservation of biodiversity, the specific provisions related to conservation of threatened biodiversity. The TSCA provided for schedules of threatened species, populations and ecological communities. The initial schedules for vertebrate fauna were an expanded version of those in the EF(IP)A, and built on more than a century of legislation relating to animals, but added additional schedules to cover plants.

[15] Recognition of the importance of habitat of species in *Corkill* foreshadowed the acknowledgement of the link between habitat and ecological communities in the CBD and in legislation consequent on Australia being party to the CBD passed nationally and by states.

[16] *Commonwealth v Tasmania* (1983) 158 CLR 1.

[17] The EPBC Act applies throughout Australia, and species and ecological communities listed in the Act's Schedules are Matters of National Environmental Significance (MNES), the presence of which on sites where development and other activity is proposed may trigger a requirement for the matter to be referred to the Commonwealth, with subsequent assessment potentially leading to refusal of the proposal, or approval with conditions. There is similarity between the Commonwealth listings and those under state legislation, but not complete concordance. Although submissions in matters in the Land and Environment Court frequently draw attention to listings under the EPBC Act, the Act does not fall within the Court's jurisdiction (*Newcastle and Hunter Valley Speleological Society Inc v Upper Hunter Shire Council & Stoneco Pty Limited* (*NHVSS*) (2010) 210 LGERA 126, [77]).

What was new, but required by the CBD, was recognition of ecological communities which necessarily applied to areas outside the formal conservation estate. The TSCA was repealed and replaced by the Biodiversity Conservation Act 2016 which, despite having a more inclusive title, remains operationally focused on threatened entities. The schedules of the TSCA were transferred to the BCA. The category of endangered population does not exist in the BCA, but the TSCA schedule of existing endangered populations continues to have effect.

The listing of threatened species and communities on the schedules of the TSCA – now the BCA – makes it an offence for entities on the list to be damaged or destroyed without authorisation. Decisions to change the schedules lie with the Scientific Committee created under the Act (TSCA sections 127–36, BCA sections 4.30–4.41). Not all experts agree with Scientific Committee determinations, but those who disagree have a right to make a nomination to the Scientific Committee seeking either an amendment to the listing or its removal from the relevant schedule. In the context of a Class 1 merits appeal there is no avenue for a judge (or a commissioner) to reject or amend a determination of the Scientific Committee, or to add species or communities to the schedules. That said, rights to judicial review of Scientific Committee decisions exist, as they do with other legislation. Despite much public commentary on perceived errors by the Scientific Committee, since 1996 only one challenge has come to the Court. This was in relation to the listing of an endangered ecological community, Kurri Kurri Sand Swamp Woodland in the Hunter Valley. The applicant questioned the decision-making process conducted by the Scientific Committee and whether the description of the community was sufficiently certain so as to enable a landowner to decide whether the community was present on their land.[18] On appeal, the Court of Appeal unanimously upheld the original decision in three separate judgments. The judgments of Spigelman CJ[19] and Hodgson JA[20] provided important discussion of the uncertainty associated with the natural world. Their Honours recognised that landowners and managers need to be able to determine whether their land supported endangered species and/or endangered ecological communities, but considered that this did not require the distribution of communities to have been mapped, or that a minimum number of species needed to be present to constitute a community. Some degree of indeterminateness would be associated with the definition and recognition of communities, but this was inevitable given the nature of the environment and of legislation.

4. Biodiversity Issues before the Court

In the last two sections I have explored the complexity of biodiversity and legislation relating to it. In doing so, I have referred to some cases that have explained the legislation.

[18] *VAW (Kurri Kurri) Pty Ltd v Scientific Committee* (2002) 122 LGERA 231; *VAW (Kurri Kurri) Pty Ltd v Scientific Committee (Established under s127 of the Threatened Species Conservation Act 1995)* (2003) 58 NSWLR 631.

[19] *VAW (Kurri Kurri)* (CA) (n 18) [7]–[9].

[20] ibid, [236]–[238].

I now turn to examine the Court's case law on some other issues. A compendium of important biodiversity cases heard in the Court is available on its website.[21] Every case is different in terms of the location, species and communities involved and the nature and scale of the proposed development. However, two questions have arisen frequently over the years: (i) is a Species Impact Statement (SIS) required? (ii) Are the strategies to manage the development's impact on biological diversity appropriate and sufficient?

4.1. Is an SIS or a BDAR Required?

Under the TSCA an SIS was required if the proposed development or activity was likely to significantly affect threatened species or ecological communities or their habitats. Threatened species and communities are those included in the schedules of the TSCA and now the BCA. The word 'likely' means a 'real chance' or 'possibility', and 'significantly' means 'important', 'notable', 'weighty' or more than 'ordinary'. Both words are used in a general lay sense, and do not carry statistical connotations.[22]

Requirements to prepare SISs were first introduced in 1996 when the TSCA (and consequent changes to the EPA Act) came into force. The factors to be considered in order to determine whether a proposed development might have an impact on threatened species or endangered ecological communities were included in the EPA Act, initially in what was referred to as the eight-part test, which subsequently became the seven-part test. In the BCA the equivalent test appears in section 7.3, and is now a five-part test.

The BCA contains provisions for the preparation of SISs and the issuing of Environment Agency Head's requirements in sections 7.20 and 7.21. However, the circumstances under which an SIS might now be required are unclear. Under the BCA if a proposed development is likely to significantly affect threatened species and their habitats the application for development consent must be accompanied by a Biodiversity Development Assessment Report (section 7.7(2)) (BDAR). A BDAR must be prepared using the Biodiversity Assessment Method (BAM) by an accredited person (section 6.10). The questions within the five-part test do not necessarily apply in all circumstances – some apply only to species and others to communities (although it is possible for a site to contain both threatened species and communities). Although the essence of the questions covered by the various versions of the test remained the same, the five-part test in the BCA includes at section 7.3(1)(d):

> Whether the proposed development or activity is likely to have an adverse effect on any declared area of outstanding biodiversity value (either directly or indirectly).

[21] https://lec.nsw.gov.au/lec/publications-and-resources/issues-in-focus/biodiversi ty/biodiver sity-cases.html (accessed 15 July 2021).

[22] *NHVSS* (n 17) [82] and cases cited therein. The criteria for assessment of impacts on threatened entities that are 'likely' and 'significant' apply to all assessments of impacts on the environment under s 5.5 and s 5.7 of the EPA Act. Preston CJ has recently provided a comprehensive analysis of the requirements and citations of relevant cases in *Palm Beach Group Incorporated v Northern Beaches Council* (2020) 250 LGERA 212; [2020] NSWLEC 156, [160]–[161].

To date there are only four declared areas of outstanding biodiversity value (all of which were Critical Habitats under the TSCA). As yet there has been no litigation relating to any of the areas. However, recognition of direct and indirect effects has arisen in many matters. What constitutes 'indirectly'? How distant from the subject site might an 'indirect' effect be generated?

The need to consider effects distant from the focus of development arises in two ways. The first is from the proper description of the development proposed. An application may be for a development on a particular site, but the practical completion of the project necessarily requires completion of other physical works (eg road construction or drainage works outside the site). The judgment in *Hoxton Park Residents Action Group Inc v Liverpool City Council*[23] established that the project for which impacts were to be assessed was not only the building works for the school, but construction of the road to the school.

The judgment was followed in *Ballina Shire Council v Palm Lakes Works Pty Ltd*[24] by Preston CJ; development consent for a seniors' housing development could not be given without consideration of impacts of roads, drainage and civil infrastructure works – works that had not been included in the development application.

Indirect effects may also arise distantly from a development without additional construction being required. Two judgments in the Federal Court, the *Flying Fox* case[25] and the *Nathan Dam* case,[26] concerning matters under the EPBC Act, provide guidance as to how indirect effects might be identified and considered. In both matters the Federal Court found that activities outside World Heritage sites – Wet Tropics in the *Flying Fox* case and the Great Barrier Reef in the *Nathan Dam* case – could have impacts within the sites. In the *Flying Fox* case, the electrocution of flying foxes at an orchard could impact on the population of flying foxes in the Wet Tropics World Heritage Area. The flying foxes were important pollinators and fruit dispersers and were essential for maintaining the ecosystem. In the *Nathan Dam* case, agricultural development which would be facilitated by the Nathan Dam could have downstream effects including affecting water quality in the Great Barrier Reef.

The consent authority (including the Court on appeal) is not limited to consideration of the factors in the five-part test – 'there may be facts and circumstances relevant to the inquiry which are not specifically contained in any of the factors'.[27] A positive answer to one or more of the five questions need not result in an affirmative response to the overall question posed in section 7.3(1), but does not preclude a negative answer.[28]

The description of the development proposed is not restricted to the development itself 'but can also include remediation measures to prevent, mitigate, remedy or offset impacts' although these 'measures must have been proposed as part of the development

[23] *Hoxton Park Residents Action Group Inc v Liverpool City Council* (2011) 81 NSWLR 638.
[24] *Ballina Shire Council v Palm Lake Works Pty Ltd* [2020] NSWLEC 41, [6]–[8].
[25] *Booth v Bosworth* (2001) 114 FCR 39.
[26] *Minister for the Environment & Heritage v Queensland Conservation Council Inc* (2004) 134 LGERA 272.
[27] *NHVSS* (n 17) [85] and cases cited therein.
[28] ibid, [86] and cases cited therein.

application in the form before the Court at the end of the hearing'.[29] Measures first proposed as conditions of consent or restrictions on construction certificates are not able to be considered in answering the inquiry as to the likely impact.

If an applicant considers that the requirement for an SIS is triggered, then they must seek provision of requirements for the form and content of the SIS;[30] these will specify inter alia those species that must be considered (the list of species may be larger than those identified by the proponent when triggering the request).

Whether an SIS is required is a 'jurisdictional fact', and on appeal the Court must decide for itself whether the consideration required by section 7.3 of the BCA and other relevant factors results in a requirement to provide an SIS.[31] A requirement to produce an SIS does not predetermine the outcome. Production of an SIS requires a more detailed and focused investigation, but could result in an outcome that the impact would be acceptable, particularly if ameliorative measures are proposed as part of the SIS. Even when an applicant is of the view that an SIS is not required they may nevertheless, for an abundance of caution, prepare an SIS.[32]

4.2. Managing Impacts on Biodiversity

Unlike requirements for the production of SISs which are triggered by the presence of threatened species or ecological communities, requirements to manage impacts apply to biodiversity as a whole (although, in practice, proponents and consent authorities may give greater weight to threatened items, and amongst them, listed vertebrates).

Examples of strategies to manage impacts on biodiversity were listed in *Bulga Milbrodale Progress Association Inc v Minister for Planning and Infrastructure and Warkworth Mining Ltd* as, in order of priority, avoidance, mitigation and offsets.[33] The hierarchy is sometimes worded as avoidance, management and mitigation (where management includes minimise and mitigation includes offsetting).

Avoidance and mitigation (management/minimisation) have the highest priority, but frequently discussion leaps straight to offsetting. From a proponent's perspective the avoidance option may not be practicable. For a major infrastructure project such as a road there may be alternative routes that can be considered. For a residential development on a single small block, the proponent's options will be limited. If the block includes biodiversity values, the do-nothing option, with no management of environmental degradation, may be less desirable than approval, but proponents and consent authorities may agree to conditions requiring long-term protection of at least some biodiversity elements on the lot. In *Bulga*, Preston CJ provided a detailed guide to the

[29] ibid, [83].
[30] BCA s 7.3.
[31] *NHVSS* (n 17) [81].
[32] *Statewide Planning Pty Ltd v Blacktown City Council* [2019] NSWLEC 1397, [59].
[33] *Bulga Milbrodale Progress Association Inc v Minister for Planning and Infrastructure and Warkworth Mining Ltd* (2013) 194 LGERA 347.

mitigation hierarchy and explained how it was applied in the context of a large coal mine proposal,[34] producing a detailed critique of the proposed offsets package.[35]

New South Wales has been at the forefront internationally in the development and application of offsets policies. A biodiversity offset scheme is provided for in Part 6 of the BCA. Section 6.4(1) makes clear that offsetting is only to occur after avoidance and minimisation options have been exhausted. Offsetting is intended to be a last resort. There is a very extensive literature on biodiversity offsetting, much of it critical of the concept.[36] Nevertheless, ability to offset is part of government policy and is specifically provided for in the BCA. The Court must consider all stages of the hierarchy and make findings on the adequacy of the analysis of avoidance and minimisation. However, if reasonable attempts at addressing these goals have been made, then it is not open to the Court to reject offsetting on the basis that numerous sources doubt its feasibility and effectiveness.

Offsetting proposals may specify restoration/rehabilitation of degraded sites – either damaged as a result of previous activities or sites which will become available at the end of (for example) a major mining project. There is great interest in ecological restoration and 2021–2030 has been declared by the United Nations to be the Decade on Ecosystem Restoration.[37] The scale of the challenge is enormous and for many ecosystems the knowledge required to achieve success is not yet developed. In the context of approvals for major mining projects, if the majority of restoration will occur at the end of a project rather than sequentially, then there will inevitably be a hiatus in the provision of ecosystem services at the site.

4.3. Cumulative Impacts

Submissions by objectors, and contentions of consent authorities, frequently raise cumulative impacts as a reason why development consent should be refused. The threatened status of many species and ecological communities is a consequence of the cumulative impacts of numerous past decisions. The question for consent authorities is: when does any further loss result in crossing a critical threshold such that extinction is likely to be inevitable? The Court must make an assessment based on the impacts of the proposal under consideration, mindful of the effects of past development. It cannot assume future development proposals, the details of which are currently unknown.

Pain J observed in *BT Goldsmith Planning Services Pty Limited v Blacktown City Council*:

> The difficulty with assessing cumulative impact is often that no single event, be it clearing or another threatening process, can be said to have such a significant impact that it will irretrievably or significantly harm a particular habitat or endangered ecological

[34] ibid, [147]–[201].

[35] ibid, [202]–[255].

[36] See BJ Preston 'Biodiversity Offsets: Adequacy and Efficacy in Theory and Practice' (2016) 33 *Environmental and Planning Law* Journal 93; KL Miller et al, 'The Development of the Australian Environmental Offsets Policy: From Theory to Practice' (2015) 42 *Environmental Conservation* 306.

[37] J Aronson et al, 'A World of Possibilities: Six Restoration Strategies to Support the United Nation's Decade on Ecosystem Restoration' (2020) 28 *Restoration Ecology* 730.

> community. ... I consider the broad discretion I have under s 78A(8)(b) of the [EPA Act] in light of the objects of the [TSCA] does mean that taking into account cumulative impact is a relevant matter.[38]

An argument that the impacted area resulting from a proposal is only a fraction of the total area of the community, and de minimus, was rejected by Pain J: 'Arguing that a single site is a tiny percentage of what remains is really an argument which fails to acknowledge cumulative impacts.'[39] In *BT Goldsmith*, the area of the endangered ecological community which would have been impacted was about 3.9 ha, against a total area of the community (in numerous patches, varying considerably in condition) of 28,175 ha. The process of attrition leading to the decline of species and communities has been referred to as death by a thousand cuts or the tyranny of small decisions.[40]

4.4. Conditions and Adaptive Management

To reduce uncertainty, consent for development that will impact biodiversity may be granted on conditions requiring adaptive management. The appropriateness of an adaptive management approach was discussed in *Newcastle and Hunter Valley Speleological Society Inc v Upper Hunter Shire Council & Stoneco Pty Limited* (*NHVSS*).[41] In *NHVSS* the conditions provided for monitoring and feedback, to identify when it became necessary to modify the management regime.[42]

Although the goal set by particular conditions may be clear, it may be unattainable. In setting conditions there has been an implicit assumption that the environment will remain constant. However, we know that environments change and that, in the future, because of climate change and other pressures, changes are likely to be faster, more extensive and greater than in the recent past.[43] How long should an adaptive management regime imposed by conditions continue if the objective is no longer feasible? What mechanisms are required to enable new objectives to be set (this is an issue that has not yet been explored in NSW)?

Adoption of an adaptive management approach provides flexibility and reduces or eliminates any need to seek amendment of conditions subsequent to consent being granted. The measures provided for by conditions should be both practical and enforceable, and the Court's powers must be kept in mind. The Court, in a Class I matter, standing in the shoes of the Council, slips off those shoes immediately after judgment has been delivered and has no further role. It is up to the Council to enforce conditions.

[38] *BT Goldsmith Planning Services Pty Limited v Blacktown City Council* [2005] NSWLEC 210, [90].
[39] ibid, [90], see also [80]–[82].
[40] See *Bazzi v Sutherland Shire Council* [2017] NSWLEC 1662, [200].
[41] *NHVSS* (n 17) [183]–[189].
[42] ibid, [183], [216]–[224].
[43] While every attempt should be made to mitigate future climate change impacts, these may reduce the magnitude of change but changes underway will be inevitable. RK Craig, '"Stationarity Is Dead" – Long Live Transformation: Five Principles for Climate Change Adaptation Law' (2010) 34 *Harvard Environmental Law Review* 9 argues that current environmental law and policy (he stresses the United States, but the problem is global) pursues goals of preservation and restoration – but the future world will be different and adaptation should be given priority.

The Court does not have any responsibility to monitor outcomes of consents, nor would it be practicable to do so. This means there is no feedback to the Court that might influence conditions set in future matters. Licensing requirements may require reporting of monitoring data but there is no agency that oversees outcomes.

5. Biodiversity and Legal Doctrine

The discussion in the last section illustrated the important role the Court plays in interpreting, applying and enforcing legislation. Through its role in developing conditions attached to approvals the Court provides guidance to prospective proponents and the respondent council as to appropriate measures to be included in future proposals. The Court has not just developed legal doctrines concerning biodiversity legislation, however. Biodiversity has also led to a development of the Court's environmental law jurisprudence more generally. Here I provide two examples: the precautionary principle and expert evidence.

5.1. An Opportunity for Application of the Precautionary Principle?

As discussed in Section 1, there is much about biodiversity we do not know. In any ecosystem, at any location in the world, if it were possible to detect every species present, including invertebrates and microorganisms, there would be undescribed species. Does this mean that we should apply the precautionary principle to every biodiversity assessment?[44] While we should be aware that assessments are based on incomplete data, it would be disproportionate to impose onerous conditions without any idea of whether they would be relevant to the unknown unknowns. However, there are some circumstances where application of the precautionary principle is appropriate. In *NHVSS*, for example, a proposed limestone quarry involved removal of limestone from strata which might contain voids.[45] If there were voids, then, on the basis of international scientific literature, there was a likelihood that they contained organisms (stygofauna). There have been few studies of stygofauna in eastern Australia and no individual or communities of stygofauna are currently listed as threatened in NSW. As invertebrates in an aquatic habitat they would fall within the ambit of the Fisheries Management Act 1994, but they would also be a component of the total biodiversity of the site.

The quarry company pointed out that there was no statutory requirement in NSW identifying troglofauna or stygofauna as fauna to be considered – this is still the case. Nevertheless, if there is biota within the limestone it becomes a biodiversity consideration. NHVSS's fauna expert had very briefly raised the potential for biota to be present. The Court, exercising the functions of the consent authority in Class 1 of its jurisdiction, can seek to inform itself further about relevant matters. The Court provided the

[44] For a discussion of the precautionary principle, see Scotford, this volume.
[45] *NHVSS* (n 17).

parties with some recent scientific papers dealing with stygofauna and invited them to make submissions. The Court concluded that, absent site-specific information on biota, it was

> scientifically likely that some form of biota will be found in limestone on the site. Without being able to predict particular species which would be present it is beyond a mere possibility that biota would be present. The scientific likelihood is sufficient to engage the precautionary principle. … The precautionary principle is therefore activated. The Court should assume that there will be a serious or irreversible threat of environmental damage and take this into account, notwithstanding there is a degree of scientific uncertainty about whether the threat really exists: *Telstra Corporation Ltd v Hornsby Shire Council* at [150], [152]. Lack of full scientific uncertainly is not to be used as a reason to postpone taking measures to prevent environmental damage.[46]

Engagement of the precautionary principle did not translate into refusal of the quarry proposal, which would have been a disproportionate response. Rather the Court imposed conditions requiring monitoring to detect stygofauna and an adaptive management regime to respond to any findings of fauna within voids.[47]

In *NHVSS* the concern was the potential occurrence of biota in a habitat type that had rarely been investigated in the region. There are other habitats which have been similarly understudied and where the precautionary principle might arise in assessment. One such habitat is the sandy beach. There is sufficient data globally to be certain that any sandy beach will have infauna – but beaches are frequently managed as social environments and for operations such as regular beach grooming no attention is given to beaches as ecosystems. On many beaches off-road vehicles have unrestricted access between the tide lines. If any consideration is given to impacts on biodiversity, it addresses birds that nest (such as the little tern) or roost on beaches. The existence within the sand of a fauna is rarely considered. Interstitial beach faunas have been little studied in Australia although there are studies from South Africa and elsewhere which suggest that similar faunas exist on Australian shores.[48] Another perhaps unexpected example is soil. The presence of fauna in soil has been known and studied for hundreds of years, but impacts have mostly been studied in agricultural contexts, and in development impact assessment soils and their biota are rarely given attention. What these different examples make clear is that the complexities and uncertainties of biodiversity charted in the first section are not just of academic interest. They catalyse legal thinking and legal developments.

5.2. Experts and their Evidence in Biodiversity Cases

Another example of this can be seen in the way that in the last forty years the nature of the evidence received by the Court has changed – most particularly in relation to ecology.

[46] ibid, [177], [179].
[47] ibid, [183]–[189].
[48] See A McLachlan and O Defeo, *The Ecology of Sandy Shores*, 3rd edn (London, Academic Press, 2017); for NSW, see DM Dexter, 'Temporal and Spatial Variability in the Community Structure of the Fauna of Four Sandy Beaches in South-Eastern New South Wales' (1984) 35 *Australian Journal of Marine and Freshwater Research* 663.

Some landowners may be skilful natural historians, but many are likely to need to engage a consultant to advise them as to the biodiversity present at particular sites. In early matters the ecology experts would have visited the site and recorded the presence of vertebrates (for which detection may have required trapping) and vascular plants. The intensity of sampling varied, and the timing was not always optimal for recording particular species. In addition, searches of the literature and collections would be undertaken, but the ability to search large databases electronically was in its infancy, and even when locality data existed, the associated georeferencing may have been generalised and of no help in predicting likely occurrence at particular sites.

Tracks and scats observed have long been recorded for vertebrates; today a great range of non-visual techniques is used in compiling species lists. Insectivorous bats are largely detected acoustically, and over recent decades this technique has led to a great increase in knowledge of the distribution and abundance of bats, not just in Australia but worldwide. A new frontier is also provided by environmental DNA (eDNA) – sampling for molecular evidence of the presence of species. Modern molecular techniques are extremely sensitive and DNA present in very tiny amounts can be detected, and the costs of analysis are falling. The diversity of sequences recorded is related to the diversity of organisms present. Sampling of soils for eDNA allows an estimate of the total diversity of microorganisms without necessarily being able to identify to species level. The diversity present in the total assemblage provides an estimate of ecosystem health,[49] and thus the extent of pre-existing degradation. However, prediction of impacts of proposed development on microorganisms is in its infancy.

To identify target species requires a reference set of sequences to which comparisons can be made. The technique is likely to be particularly useful in aquatic ecosystems, as shown, for example, in the detection of the presence of platypus in waterways in the suburban fringes of both Melbourne and Sydney.[50] The sensitivity of eDNA analysis raises concerns about the accidental contamination of samples. In criminal matters, full documentation of the chain of custody of evidence is required, and evidence must be retained so as to permit independent reanalysis. In civil matters this does not always occur, but there may be a need to require secure retention of evidence rather than simply reporting findings. This is not a simple matter because some types of material may require storage facilities that consultants are unlikely to possess.

Although ecologists think that fraud and scientific misconduct is rare in their discipline, we cannot be complacent. There have been cases around the world where basic data on the distribution of species are either known, or are suspected, to have

[49] Evidence is emerging of a relationship between human health and the nature of the local soil biota: see JG Mills et al, 'Relating Urban Biodiversity to Human Health with the "Holobiont" Concept' [2019] *Frontiers in Microbiology* 10.3389/fmicb.2019.00550; EC Brevik et al, 'Soil and Human Health: Current Status and Future Needs' (2020) 13 *Air, Soil and Water Research* 10.1177/1178622120934441; and M Delgado-Baquerizo et al, 'Global Homogenization of the Structure and Function in the Soil Microbiome of Urban Greenspaces' (2021) 7 *Science Advances* eabg5809.

[50] Sampling for DNA avoids the need to trap and handle animals, and a single sample can be investigated for the presence of a large number of species. eDNA sampling can be much less time-consuming than many other survey methods and eliminates much of the disturbance which would otherwise occur. See E McColl-Gausden et al, 'On the DNA Trail of the Platypus' *Science Matters*, 26 October 2018, https://pursuit.unimelb.edu.au/articles/on-the-dna-trail-of-the-platypus (accessed 15 July 2021).

been falsified.[51] Even putting misconduct to one side, no investigation of species and communities at a site will ever list all the species present and we will never know what was there but not detected. Failure to record everything is unlikely to represent fraud, but if the sampling was inadequate in intensity or timing it may indicate incompetence. Even the most skilled and experienced consultants will not record everything. 'Observer error' has been reported in numerous papers in the plant ecology literature.[52] Observer error has been widely reported for plants and I have no reason to doubt that it will not occur in the record for other taxa. All this means is that the Court needs to be mindful of assessing the veracity of the material put before it – a challenge given the complexities of biodiversity.

Advances in computing and statistical techniques occur with increasing frequency, and it is difficult for experts in particular fields to keep up to date, let alone for generalists to easily digest complex reports. Mathematical modelling has long been important for the physical science aspects of proposals before the Court, and while there may be differences between parties over which proprietary model should be used, there is no dispute that models are needed. Differences between parties arising in the preparation of joint reports may concentrate on the appropriateness and adequacy of the data, and of the interpretation of output. However, these can normally be expressed in ways that do not require advanced-level mathematical knowledge by the Court in order to adjudicate. Although the issue of climate change is frequently raised when it comes to impacts on biodiversity, modelling is still limited by our understanding of the biology of species and the spatial and temporal imprecision of current model outputs. In the future there will be improvements in the scientific certainty of predictions, but at present, application of the precautionary principle to the assessment of impacts will be required. This will not necessarily result in projects being rejected, but may require the application of conditions requiring regular reporting, and mechanisms for adaptive management.

It is important to remember that consultants responsible for collection of site-specific data are not performing experiments. However, their sampling design should be appropriate and scientifically rigorous. The analysis of the data collected requires statistical or numerical techniques. Interpretation of analyses will be informed by published experimental studies, so that consultants need to be aware of recent literature, and justify their conclusions by reference to it. Consultants' reports may propose continuing monitoring and, where this goes beyond an anodyne statement that monitoring is required to specify how monitoring should be done, elements of experimental design may be required. In some circumstances, conditions of consent may specify details of monitoring methodology and the reporting required, so as to permit adaptive management. While the evaluation of these issues is challenging, the Court brings to its evaluation of evidence

[51] For a botanical example, see K Sabbagh, *A Rum Affair: A True Story of Botanical Fraud* (London, Allen Lane, 1999). There are a number of examples from ornithology: P Olsen and P Menkhorst, 'A Recent Investigation Highlights the Importance of Honesty in Ornithology and Conservation' (2020) 120 *Emu-Austral Ornithology* 178. There is no evidence of falsification being widespread across ecology, either in academia or the consulting industry. However, the doubt about some of the records of the night parrot, for example, makes assessing the distribution and ecology of this species difficult.

[52] LW Morrison, 'Observer Error in Vegetation Surveys: A Review' (2016) 9 *Journal of Plant Ecology* 367.

extensive experience and its own professional training. Occasionally this may permit it to raise issues that were not in contention or discussed in any detail by the experts (as occurred in *NHVSS*). Procedural fairness requires that the parties are given the opportunity to make submissions, and if they require, to give further evidence. If the parties had discussed an issue, but the Court, on the basis of its own knowledge and experience, disagreed with the position agreed by the parties' experts, the alternative view would be provided to the parties and submissions sought.

6. Prospects

This chapter has explored biodiversity and some examples of the NSW Court's engagement with it. Biodiversity is a complex and dynamic concept. Over the last forty years our understanding of the environment has evolved and, in important respects, aspects of the environment have undergone significant change. Future change is inevitable and will result in changes to legislation and planning instruments, and therefore the range of matters before the Court will change. Scientific advances will enable more data to be considered in assessment. That in turn will lead to legal submissions before the Court grounded on and utilising those insights and data. Whatever the case, given past history, the Court is likely to be a leader in responding to the growing breadth of submissions about biodiversity, and its decisions will have a major educative role for society and government.

8

Environmental Principles and the Construction of a New Body of Legal Reasoning

ELOISE SCOTFORD

1. Introduction

The Land and Environment Court of New South Wales (the Court or NSWLEC) has developed a highly evolved body of reasoning around principles of 'ecologically sustainable development' (ESD principles) over the last three decades. This body of legal reasoning has come about partly due to specific features of the Court – notably its history and distinctive jurisdictional identity – and developments that have flowed from this, including the Court adopting new lines and modes of reasoning, its transnational borrowing of legal ideas, and the evolving culture of the Court itself. Beyond these specific institutional features, the legislation that empowers the Court and shapes its reasoning has constructed an environment in which ESD principles have flourished as legal norms, through reasoning that might be seen as relatively routine in terms of the common law tradition of incremental reasoning. In combination, institutional, cultural and legislative features of the Court have cultivated a body of highly novel legal doctrine around ESD principles, making it a powerful seat for judicial 'strengthening [of] national efforts to realize the goals of environmentally-friendly development'.[1]

In light of this doctrinal innovation, it is fair to say that the Court is a global legal leader in reasoning involving environmental principles. However, this description – or accolade – brings with it potential preconceptions about what environmental principles are as legal concepts and how they might inform legal doctrine. This is because environmental principles are often framed as foundations for a global 'environmental

[1] D Kaniaru et al, *UNEP Judicial Symposia on the Role of the Judiciary in Promoting Sustainable Development* (no 22, 1998), as cited in BJ Preston, 'Benefits of Judicial Specialization in Environmental Law: The Land and Environment Court of New South Wales as a Case Study' (2012) 29(2) *Pace Environmental Law Review* 396, 398.

rule of law',[2] forging an international narrative around environmental principles as universal, transnational global norms that embed environmental protection within legal systems.[3] And although environmental principles are indeed symbolic and transformative concepts in environmental law globally,[4] they are evolving as legal norms, and driving legal developments, in many and varied ways across different jurisdictions.[5] The Court provides a particularly rich example of such jurisdictional developments, providing a fertile legal setting for environmental principles to embed systematically within a body of domestic environmental law. Its example also shows that, despite challenges in translating policy principles into legal norms, legal institutions can foster and develop environmental principles as legally relevant concepts within bodies of carefully crafted legal reasoning.

This chapter is a study of the legal context and developments involved in constructing a dense and specific body of legal reasoning involving environmental principles. Investigating the specific legal features of the NSWLEC's ESD reasoning, it shows how environmental principles have co-evolved with the legal culture of the Court and how these developments illustrate a highly evolved, but contingent, example of environmental principles in environmental law. The first section of the chapter examines how this legal reality lines up with the legal rhetoric around environmental principles, outlining narratives and emergent theories relating to the nature of environmental principles in environmental law, and demonstrating why framing these principles as legal concepts is fraught with complexity as well as potential. The potential of environmental principles derives from the fact that they are politically amplified and amorphous policy objectives, which lend themselves to multiple meanings and functions, including legal ones. Wresting these ideas onto the legal plane is a jurisprudentially complex exercise, not least because questions arise about the proper role of courts in developing or implementing policy ideas. The increasing roles played by environmental principles in judicial reasoning across diverse jurisdictions thus raises questions about how this legal translation happens and whether it is done justifiably.

The second section examines how environmental principles have become a legal reality in the specific context of New South Wales (NSW) law through the development of a dense body of the Court's case law on ESD principles. This body of legal reasoning is path-breaking in both its depth (it has built from modest steps first taken in the early 1990s), in its breadth (now covering a wide jurisdiction of environmental cases), and in the sheer intricacy of legal reasoning building on the unique statutory and institutional

[2] IUCN, *World Declaration on the Environmental Rule of Law* (2017) www.iucn.org/sites/dev/files/content/documents/world_declaration_on_the_environmental_rule_of_law_final_2017-3-17.pdf.

[3] L Krämer and E Orlando (eds), *Principles of Environmental Law* (Cheltenham, Edward Elgar, 2018); T Yang and RV Percival, 'The Emergence of Global Environmental Law' (2009) 36 *Ecology Law Quarterly* 615.

[4] N de Sadeleer, *Environmental Principles: From Political Slogans to Legal Rules*, 2nd edn (Oxford, Oxford University Press, 2020); E Scotford, 'Environmental Principles Across Jurisdictions: Legal Connectors and Catalysts' in E Lees and J Vinuales (eds), *Oxford Handbook of Comparative Environmental Law* (Oxford, Oxford University Press, 2019).

[5] E Scotford, *Environmental Principles and the Evolution of Environmental Law* (Oxford, Hart Publishing, 2017); LJ Kotzé and CB Soyapi, 'African Courts and Principles of International Environmental Law: A Kenyan and South African Case Study' (2021) 33(2) *Journal of Environmental Law* 257.

foundations of the Court. Over thirty years, an established body of environmental jurisprudence around ESD principles has been developed. There are now many examples of how legislative incorporation of ESD principles has sparked doctrinal developments in the Court's reasoning, from constituting mandatory requirements in environmental impact statements,[6] to elaborating the nature of regulatory offences,[7] to informing a breach of duty in negligence.[8] The concluding section reflects on this picture and asks some questions about the legitimacy of ESD reasoning in the Court, and how this reasoning should be understood and critiqued.

In considering the legal character and evolution of environmental principles – in general discussion and in the context of the NSWLEC – this chapter's analysis is confined to principles expressing substantive environmental policy. Globally, environmental principles of this kind remain an amorphous and open-ended group – ranging from the precautionary principle and polluter-pays principle to the principles of inter- and intragenerational equity and the principle of non-regression.[9] In the context of the NSWLEC, a more specific group of such 'ESD principles' are defined in NSW legislation – outlined in section 3.1 – giving environmental principles concrete identities in NSW law.

2. The Promise and Perils of Environmental Principles in Environmental Law

To understand the significance of reasoning involving environmental principles in the NSWLEC, it is important to understand environmental principles writ large. Environmental principles offer a lot of promise, as both policy and legal ideas. In policy terms, they express simple, powerful messages about environmental ambition in relation to multidimensional, interdisciplinary, often transnational environmental problems. They act as policy beacons that both raise the profile of environmental policy and set a policy direction, transcending the sociopolitical complexity that characterises many environmental problems.[10] They also speak to multiple audiences – policymakers, activists, citizens, legislators, courts – in different countries and different legal systems, which makes them easier to champion as universal ideas.[11] At the same time, the

[6] *Gloucester Resources Limited v Minister for Planning* [2019] NSWLEC 7, (2019) 234 LGERA 257.

[7] *Harrison v Perdikaris* [2015] NSWLEC 99.

[8] *JK Williams Staff Pty Limited v Sydney Water Corporation* (2021) 249 LGERA 109; [2021] NSWLEC 23.

[9] There is no definitive catalogue of environmental principles globally. There are some key international, soft law instruments that list environmental principles – notably the Brundtland Report 1987 (World Commission on Environment and Development, *Our Common Future* (Oxford, Oxford University Press, 1987) Annex 1); the Rio Declaration 1992 (United Nations Conference on Environment and Development, 'Rio Declaration on Environment and Development' (14 June 1992) UN Doc A/CONF.151/26 (vol I) 31 ILM 874 (1992)), the World Declaration on the Environmental Rule of Law 2016 (n 2), and the Draft Global Pact for the Environmental 2017 (https://globalpactenvironment.org/en/document/draft-global-pact-for-the-environment-by-the-igep/, accessed 11 July 2021). Each of these international instruments contains a different categorical list of principles, reflecting different contexts in which these agreements were made, and also different perspectives on what constitutes an environmental 'principle' and which principles are valuable to recognise.

[10] E Fisher, B Lange and E Scotford, *Environmental Law: Text, Cases and Materials*, 2nd edn (Oxford, Oxford University Press, 2019) ch 2.

[11] Scotford, *Environmental Principles and the Evolution of Environmental Law* (n 5) ch 2.

linguistically open-textured character of environmental principles also makes them vulnerable to different policy interpretations. The precautionary principle is perhaps most notorious in this respect, with fierce intellectual and trade policy debates over the merits of the principle often expressing different visions of what the principle means.[12]

All of this policy promise is compounded by – and sometimes conflated with – their legal promise.[13] The cataloguing of environmental principles in international agreements indicates that they have an international normative character, and there is much academic discussion of whether they constitute principles of international environmental law,[14] as well as serious efforts to formalise them in treaty form.[15] They are also advocated as foundations of new forms of law – such as 'global environmental law',[16] 'post-modern law',[17] or in reframing law based on a 'principle of sustainability'.[18] The legal reality is more complex. Their international normative character is hard to pin down partly because they are interstitial – they occupy a space between policy rhetoric and firm legal rules,[19] between international and domestic legal orders, between general international law and international environment law,[20] between science, law and politics[21] – but also because they can take on a variety of legal roles within domestic legal systems, and because their legal roles can be controversial.

Within specific domestic jurisdictions and legal cultures, environmental principles are living up to their potential as legal norms.[22] Environmental principles are being

[12] Ranging from a prohibitive, protectionist version of the principle (no action must be taken where there is any risk of environmental harm) to a more administrative version of the principle based on rigorous risk assessment and management processes: eg C Sunstein, *Laws of Fear: Beyond the Precautionary Principle* (Cambridge, Cambridge University Press, 2005); cf Commission of the European Communities, 'Communication from the Commission on the Precautionary Principle' COM (2000) 1.

[13] For more on the policy and legal reasons for the high profile of environmental principles, including the legal scholarly appetite for these principles in legitimizing environmental law as a discipline, see Scotford (n 5) ch 2.

[14] Kotzé and Soyapi (n 5) 3 note that environmental principles, as principles of international environmental law are 'famously abstract and have a uniquely amorphous nature that ranges between binding and non-binding normativity'.

[15] Draft Pact on Environmental Principles (n 9).

[16] Yang and Percival (n 3).

[17] de Sadeleer (n 4).

[18] K Bosselmann, *The Principle of Sustainability: Transforming Law and Governance* (Farnham, Ashgate 2008).

[19] They are 'twilight' norms in international law (Beyerlin, 'Different Types of Norms in International Environmental Law: Policies, Principles and Rules' in D Bodansky, J Brunee and E Hey (eds), *The Oxford Handbook of International Environmental Law* (Oxford, Oxford University Press, 2007) 426); they are an 'ideal *bridge* between ideals and duties, between values and rules' (L Krämer and E Orlando, 'Introduction' in Krämer and Orlando (n 3) 2). This conceptual ladder from policy ideal, through to principle, then legal rule invites jurisprudential comparison with 'legal principles' as framed by Ronald Dworkin, although his theory for common law reasoning based on principles explicitly distinguishes legal principles from collective expressions of policy, which are best left to political institutions to debate and implement: see Scotford (n 5) 41–44, 59–60.

[20] Teresa Fajardo del Castillo describes environmental principles as 'connecting vessels of domestic law and international law, and … also in the relations between international environmental law and general international law, or other specialist fields of international law': TF del Castillo, 'Environmental Law Principles and General Principles of International Law' in Krämer and Orlando (n 3).

[21] Scotford (n 5) 65 and ch 2 generally.

[22] Krämer and Orlando (n 3); Scotford (n 5).

adopted in legislative form,[23] informing constitutional norms[24] and infusing judicial reasoning.[25] In taking on these legal roles, environmental principles are fitting established doctrinal paths within domestic legal systems, such as informing the interpretation of legal rules through teleological reasoning or informing existing legal tests in EU law.[26] They are also catalysing new legal reasoning, and connecting developments between jurisdictions, as in the NSWLEC.[27] Connections between jurisdictions are often made through transnational judicial dialogue, where judges appeal to developments in other jurisdictions to support their reasoning involving similarly named environmental principles.[28] This, in combination with the sheer weight of global developments concerning environmental principles, confirms the scholarly view that environmental principles are central concepts in environmental law globally. However, rather than representing an emergence of international or global legal norms, this legal picture is best understood as 'global legal pluralism'[29] or 'globalised localisms',[30] whereby environmental principles are evolving as legal norms through specific legal cultures, and which spread transnationally.[31]

This global legal pluralism demonstrates that, encouraged by international soft law agreements headlining environmental principles,[32] environmental principles open up meaningful spaces for legal development in environmental law. These normative spaces are exploited extensively in the reasoning of the NSWLEC. At the same time, the evolving role of environmental principles in domestic legal systems can also be controversial. This is for at least two reasons. First, the indeterminate nature of environmental principles as policy ideas can also make them indeterminate or uncertain legal ideas. When employed to inform a legal test, interpret a legal norm or even establish a legal norm, a significant amount of interpretive or analytical work is required to flesh out what legal role that environmental principle is playing, and what conclusion it leads to. Thus, for example, some courts undertake extensive analysis in employing the precautionary principle to inform administrative decision-making,[33] or to inform the review of administrative decision-making.[34] Environmental principles provide space for courts to be 'norm entrepreneurs'.[35] This can be seen as a positive

[23] See section 3.1 below.

[24] eg *Vellore Citizens' Welfare Forum v Union of India* AIR 1996 SC 2715; *AP Pollution Control Board v Nayudu* AIR 1999 SC 812 (India).

[25] eg in EU law: Scotford (n 5) ch 4.

[26] ibid.

[27] Scotford (n 4).

[28] These kinds of appeals differ in 'form, function and degree of reciprocal engagement' but they all demonstrate a reliance on persuasive authority to legitimise new reasoning and reflect 'a common sense of judicial identity and enterprise': A-M Slaughter, 'A Typology of Transjudicial Communication' (1994) 29(1) *University of Richmond Law Review* 99, 101–02. See also Scotford (n 4).

[29] PS Berman, 'The Evolution of Global Legal Pluralism' in R Cotterrell and M Del Mar (eds), *Authority in Transnational Legal Theory: Theorising Across Disciplines* (Cheltenham, Edward Elgar, 2016).

[30] B de Sousa Santos, *Toward a New Common Sense: Law, Science, and Politics in the Paradigmatic Transition* (London, Routledge, 1995).

[31] See Scotford (n 5) ch 6 and generally.

[32] See n 9.

[33] *Telstra Corporation v Hornsby Shire Council* (2006) 67 NSWLR 256; [2006] NSWLEC 133.

[34] Case T-13/99 *Pfizer Animal Health SA v Council* [2002] ECR II-3305.

[35] Kotze and Soyapi (n 5) 5.

development with courts strengthening environmental protection through law,[36] or as worrying licence for courts to engage in reasoning about policy issues where no clear legal structures or rationales exist,[37] or where specific environmental problems might demand fine-grained policy debate.

The second reason for controversy around the legal roles of environmental principles relates to their essential character as policy-directing ideas. Policy and law are uncomfortable bedfellows in Anglo-American jurisprudence,[38] and, whilst policy is a firm feature of environmental law,[39] environmental principles inject collective policy ideas directly into environmental law regimes in ways that can test the balance of functions between judicial and political branches of the state. The heated debate around the merits of 'retaining' in UK law environmental principles – which are firmly embedded in EU law – after the United Kingdom's withdrawal from the European Union demonstrated this tension.[40] This is not to say that environmental principles are illegitimate as legal norms, or that mature bodies of law concerning environmental law cannot develop – the NSWLEC's example shows that this is possible – but that a finely tuned dance between environmental principles as policy concepts and legal norms plays out in many jurisdictions.

When environmental principles become constitutionalized or embedded as legal norms through a thick web of legal structures within specific jurisdictions, this is not a surprise. Their legal potential paves the way for such legal evolution. But this kind of legal development is complex to analyse and theorise, and raises questions about how this kind of legal development unfolds, and whether it is justifiable, which can only be addressed by exploring the relevant jurisdictional context. The NSW context demonstrates that highly evolved environmental principles in environmental law can develop within a legislative environment and body of jurisprudence constructed over decades, in which environmental principles co-evolve with a legal culture to orient its norms and reasoning around a core thread of environmental protection. The following section examines how this distinctive legal evolution has occurred in NSW law, and the features of the Court's legal culture that construct and explain the normative character of its environmental principles.

3. Making Environmental Principles a Legal Reality: The Pioneering Case of the NSW Land and Environment Court

The NSWLEC has developed a highly evolved body of reasoning around ESD principles over the last three decades. This reasoning has developed partly due to the specific

[36] B Preston, 'The Role of the Judiciary in Promoting Sustainable Development: The Experience of Asia and the Pacific' (2005) 9(2) *Asia Pacific Journal of Environmental Law* 109.

[37] eg criticism of Indian constitutional jurisprudence involving environmental principles: G Sahu, 'Implications of Indian Supreme Court's Innovations for Environmental Jurisprudence' (2008) 4(1) *Law, Environment and Development Journal* 375.

[38] R Dworkin, *Taking Rights Seriously*, 2nd edn (London, Duckworth, 1978) ch 2.

[39] Fisher, Lange and Scotford (n 10) ch 8.

[40] M Lee and E Scotford, 'Environmental Principles After Brexit: The Draft Environment (Principles and Governance) Bill' (2019 working paper), available at https://papers.ssrn.com/sol3/papers.cfm?abstract_id=3322341.

jurisdiction of the Court and also due to contingent developments, including political fortunes, new lines and modes of reasoning, transnational borrowing of legal ideas, and the evolving culture of the Court itself. Notably, this jurisprudence has also evolved through routine processes of law – the drafting of legislation and its interpretation, and incremental reasoning in judicial review and administrative appeals. The Court has thus developed a mature body of reasoning involving environmental principles through a combination of legal innovation and stabilising processes of legal development, all embedded within a specific jurisdictional context.

3.1. The Legislative Foundation of the NSWLEC's ESD Reasoning

The role of legislation in the development of the NSWLEC's ESD reasoning has been central. The initial emergence of ESD principles in Australia was through a national ESD policymaking process that responded to the international sustainable development agenda and developed a vision of how to make sustainable development operational in Australia.[41] This vision was articulated in the 1992 Intergovernmental Agreement on the Environment (IGAE) – a quasi-constitutional but non-legal agreement – which was drawn up to manage Australian federal–state governance arrangements over environmental matters as much as to pursue sustainable development.[42] Subsequent legislation embedded the IGAE's ESD principles into NSW law. This legislative incorporation process unfolded over the late 1990s and early 2000s,[43] and was not inevitable – scholarly and extra-judicial pressure[44] and political fortune played a part.[45] This legalising of ESD principles through legislation began mainly through including ESD in the 'objects' clauses of Acts relating to environmental protection and land use planning. A key amendment was the inclusion in 1998 of the object 'to encourage ecologically sustainable development' into the list of objects in section 5(a)(vii) (now section 1.3(b)) of the Environmental Planning and Assessment Act 1979 (the EPA Act).[46] This legislative prompt sparked the first 'planning principle' case on ESD principles – fleshing out what regard planning consent authorities should give to ESD principles.[47] This was not the first ESD case decided by the NSWLEC – the Court had previously relied on other aspects of its legislative framework to introduce ESD reasoning (see section 3.3 below) – but it represented a major doctrinal statement by the Court about the importance of its reasoning involving ESD principles.

[41] See Scotford (n 5) 99–106.

[42] ibid, 99–106.

[43] ibid, 110–13.

[44] eg R Harding (ed), 'Sustainability: Principles to Practice' (Fenner Conference on the Environment 1994) 6, 8; Paul Stein, 'Turning Soft Law into Hard – An Australian Experience with ESD Principles in Practice' (1997) 3(2) *Judicial Review* 91, 95.

[45] cf UK experience in reforming environmental law post-EU exit: E Scotford, 'Legislation and the Stress of Environmental Problems' (2021) 74(1) *Current Legal Problems* 299.

[46] Environmental Planning and Assessment Amendment Act 1997.

[47] *BGP Properties v Lake Macquarie City Council* [2004] NSWLEC 399, (2004) 138 LGERA 237. McClellan J's purposive interpretation of s 5(a)(vii) was also rationalising the increasing use of ESD principles in planning merits appeals: see nn 98, 99.

A next major legislative development was the introduction of a definition of 'ecologically sustainable development' through its elaboration as a set of ESD principles – this essentially adopted the list and explanation of ESD principles in clauses 3.2 and 3.5 IGAE, first incorporating these to define the ESD object of the NSW Environmental Protection Authority in section 6(2) of the Protection of Environment Administration Act 1991 (the POEA Act):

> (2) [E]cologically sustainable development requires the effective *integration* of social, economic and environmental considerations in decision-making processes. Ecologically sustainable development can be achieved through the implementation of the following *principles and programs*:
>
> (a) the *precautionary principle* – namely, that if there are threats of serious or irreversible environmental damage, lack of full scientific certainty should not be used as a reason for postponing measures to prevent environmental degradation.
>
> In the application of the precautionary principle, public and private decisions should be guided by:
>
> careful evaluation to avoid, wherever practicable, serious or irreversible damage to the environment, and an assessment of the risk-weighted consequences of various options,
>
> (b) *inter-generational equity* – namely, that the present generation should ensure that the health, diversity and productivity of the environment are maintained or enhanced for the benefit of future generations,
>
> (c) *conservation of biological diversity and ecological integrity* – namely, that conservation of biological diversity and ecological integrity should be a fundamental consideration,
>
> (d) improved valuation, pricing and incentive mechanisms – namely, that environmental factors should be included in the valuation of assets and services, such as:
>
> (i) *polluter pays* – that is, those who generate pollution and waste should bear the cost of containment, avoidance or abatement,
>
> (ii) the users of goods and services should pay prices based on the full life cycle of costs of providing goods and services, including the use of natural resources and assets and the ultimate disposal of any waste,
>
> (iii) environmental goals, having been established, should be pursued in the most cost effective way, by establishing incentive structures, including market mechanisms, that enable those best placed to maximise benefits or minimise costs to develop their own solutions and responses to environmental problems.

This legislative articulation of ESD principles is not a simple catalogue listing environmental policy 'principles' for achieving ecologically sustainable development – 'programmes' are also included, which is how the 'improved valuation, pricing and incentive mechanisms' in section 6(2)(d) might be best described. Furthermore, identifying the 'ESD principles' in this provision – precautionary principle, intergenerational equity, conservation of biological integrity, polluter pays, integration – is partly a matter of recognising these principles as familiar from global developments articulating environmental principles,[48] and also a process of their evolution as a group of 'ESD principles' in the reasoning of the Court over time.[49] This group has also been

[48] See eg nn 22–25.
[49] eg *BGP Properties* (n 47).

expanded in the reasoning of the Court, with the principles of 'intragenerational equity' and 'sustainable use of natural resources' included as complementary ESD principles.[50]

Other environmental and planning legislation subsequently defined statutory requirements and objects of ESD and ESD principles by referring back to the section 6(2) POEA Act definition, or by similarly incorporating the IGAE exposition of ESD and its principles.[51] This phase of legislative articulation and rationalisation of ESD principles embedded ESD principles widely across the dense network of NSW environmental and planning legislation and provided an opportunity for the Court to respond to and build on. As Stein J put it, the Court had an obligation 'to turn soft law [as he saw the ESD principles, deriving from international environmental law and the IGAE] into hard law' and to flesh out the ESD concept, thus providing a 'lead for the common law world'.[52] And the Court has special institutional foundations that allowed it to embrace and fulfil this obligation, as the following section outlines.

3.2. The Institutional Foundations of the NSWLEC's ESD Reasoning

The distinctive institutional design of the Court has also allowed an innovative body of ESD reasoning to flourish. Its construction as a 'superior court of record' in NSW[53] imbued the Court with authority and tradition, establishing it with seniority within a hierarchy of Australian common law courts. At the same time, the Court has a wide-ranging, legally heterogeneous jurisdiction relating to environmental problems. This hybrid identity created a setting where legal innovation has been balanced by legal stability, and deeply rooted legal developments concerning complex environmental disputes and challenges have been possible. At its very inception, the Minister for Planning and Environment envisaged that the Court would develop its own precedents on major planning issues[54] – it had a mandate to develop new environmental jurisprudence across the wide-ranging jurisdiction of the Court. The Court has taken this opportunity to develop a distinctive and intricately reasoned body of environmental jurisprudence, including ESD principles as core concepts.

The Court's special institutional identity is partly due to its history and the reasons for its establishment, and is also constructed by its distinctive jurisdiction as a 'one-stop shop' for all matters related to land use and protection of the environment in NSW.[55]

[50] *Bulga Milbrodale Progress Association Inc v Minister for Planning and Infrastructure and Warkworth Mining Limited*; [2013] NSWLEC 48, (2013) 194 LGERA 347, [492]; *Hub Action Group Incorporated v Minister for Planning* [2008] NSWLEC 116, (2008) 161 LGERA 136.

[51] eg Local Government Act 1993 (NSW), ss 3, 7(e), as amended by the Local Government Amendment (Ecologically Sustainable Development) Act 1997 (NSW) (effective 1999); Environmental Planning and Assessment Regulation 2000 (NSW) sch 2, cl 7; Environmental Planning and Assessment Amendment (Infrastructure and Other Planning Reform) Act 2005 (NSW).

[52] P Stein, 'Are Decision-Makers Too Cautious with the Precautionary Principle?' (2000) 17(6) *Environmental and Planning Law Journal* 33.

[53] Land and Environment Court Act (NSW) (LEC Act) s 5(1).

[54] DP Landa, New South Wales Legislative Council, *Parliamentary Debates (Hansard)*, 21 November 1979, 3355, cited in A Edgar, 'Managing Non-Compliance: The Land and Environment Court and Flexible Rules of Development Assessment' (PhD thesis, University of Sydney, 2003) 22.

[55] Preston (n 1) 402.

The Court was created in 1980 to take on the dual role of a tribunal (involved in administrative review)[56] and a court (exercising judicial power), which was a constitutionally ambiguous design.[57] One reason for this amalgamated jurisdiction was the need to reform a fragmented system of land use appeals, where the separation of legal and non-legal issues in planning appeals had been found to be counterproductive and unworkable[58] in an era of wider tribunal creation in Australia.[59] In taking on this rationalising role, its core identity as a superior court reinforced its function of acting 'independently and according to law',[60] and the Court's role in articulating and applying environmental law doctrine is central to its purpose. At the same time, a spate of new environmental protection legislation was introduced at the time of the Court's creation,[61] some of which contained ESD principles as discussed above, but also enlarging its jurisdiction and caseload and thus its scope for judicial activity. The Court's jurisdiction is now split over eight classes – ranging from merits review and judicial review to valuation and Aboriginal land claim cases, and criminal proceedings and appeals[62] – which comprise a wide range of judicial and review functions, but which all relate to land use or environmental protection.[63] Its role as a superior court also gives it the status to establish relevant legal principles across this composite jurisdiction.[64] In particular, this has allowed 'innovative decision-making in both substance and procedure by cross-fertilization between different classes of jurisdiction'.[65] This has been important for managing and expediting claims, and harnessing specialist expertise in environmental matters, but also for consistency and certainty in environmental decision-making, and '[facilitating] the development of environmental laws, policies and principles',[66] including ESD principles.

The inclusion of 'non-judicial' decision-making through the Court's merits review powers is a notable aspect of its broad jurisdiction. Merits review was introduced

[56] See Stein, this volume.

[57] E Fisher, 'Administrative Law, Pluralism and the Legal Construction of Merits Review in Australian Environmental Law' in L Pearson, C Harlow and M Taggart (eds), *Administrative Law in a Changing State* (Oxford, Hart Publishing, 2008) 330; C Warnock, 'Reconceptualising Specialist Environmental Courts and Tribunals' (2017) 37 *LS* 391.

[58] P Ryan, 'Court of Hope and False Expectations: Land and Environment Court 21 Years On' (2002) 14(3) *Journal of Environmental Law* 301.

[59] E Fisher, *Risk Regulation and Administrative Constitutionalism* (Oxford, Hart Publishing, 2007) 133–4.

[60] M Pearlman, 'The Land and Environment Court of New South Wales a Model for Environmental Protection' (2000) 123 *Water, Air and Soil Pollution* 395 ('One of the most important features of the Land and Environment Court is that it is a court').

[61] The Court's creation corresponded with a growing body of specialised legislation in the area of environmental protection as well as planning, which confer jurisdiction on the Court, eg National Parks and Wildlife Act 1974 (NSW); Protection of the Environment Administration Act 1991 (NSW); Threatened Species Conservation Act 1995 (NSW).

[62] See Preston, this volume.

[63] Some criticised the development of a court that could decide issues beyond those that were strictly 'legal' in the Diceyan tradition: see Z Lipman, 'The NSW Land and Environment Court: Reforms to the Merit Review Process' (2004) 21 *Environmental and Planning Law Journal* 415, 416. See also P Cane, 'Understanding Administrative Adjudication' in Pearson, Harlow and Taggart (n 57) 32.

[64] Preston (n 1) 434 ('The Court has shown that an environmental court of the requisite status has more specialized knowledge, has an increased number of cases and hence more opportunity to – and is more likely to – develop environmental jurisprudence').

[65] ibid, 425; Warnock (n 57) (environmental courts as 'highly innovative bodies, creatively responding to the demands of environmental conflict resolution and illustrative of a new, dynamic form of adjudication').

[66] ibid, 403.

through the tribunal system to fill a gap in Australian administrative law review, moving beyond public law doctrines of judicial review traditionally exercised by courts:[67]

> [In a merits appeal, a tribunal] sits in the place of the original administrative decision-maker and re-exercises the administrative decision-making functions. The decision of the [tribunal] is final and binding and becomes that of the original decision-maker.

A court having this merits review jurisdiction was unusual – and the Court has specialist Commissioners (sitting alongside Judges) to assist in these merits review cases. The Court's merits review jurisdiction occupies much of its caseload[68] and has provided opportunities for the Court to apply ESD principles in administrative decision-making (albeit on review), and thus to demonstrate the concrete implications of ESD principles for complex environmental and planning decisions (eg an open-cut coal mine should not be permitted,[69] a new wind energy development should be allowed).[70]

Indeed, the merits review jurisdiction of the Court has provided a significant space in which new lines and modes of reasoning about environmental principles have been possible. At common law, courts, in undertaking judicial review, are not meant to stray into evaluating or deciding the merits of a decision.[71] However, the NSWLEC is a court that undertakes both judicial review and merits review, and its ESD reasoning has developed in both kinds of cases, particularly in merits appeals. Merits review cases allow the full application – and thus definition – of environmental principles, as mentioned above, and they also fuel the development of legal doctrine. This occurs through the cross-fertilisation of legal reasoning concerning ESD principles from merits review to judicial review and then to other cases,[72] as well through express effort to develop the precedent-setting quality of merits appeals, including through formulation of 'planning principles' to promote consistency in decision-making.[73] The Court has designated two major merits appeals concerning ESD principles as planning principle cases: one on ESD principles generally, as mentioned above (*BGP Properties v Lake Macquarie City Council*),[74] and one concerning the precautionary principle (*Telstra Corp Ltd v Hornsby Shire Council*).[75]

Furthermore, merits appeals concerning the application of ESD principles beyond these explicit precedent-setting cases are not a 'wilderness' of fact-specific cases.[76]

[67] NSWLEC, *Land and Environment Court of NSW Annual Review 2019* (2020), 15.

[68] In 2021, Class 1 Environmental planning and protection appeals made up almost 70% of the Court's caseload: www.lec.nsw.gov.au/lec/types-of-cases/class-1---environmental-planning-and-protection-appeals.html (accessed 7 July 2021).

[69] *Bulga Milbrodale* (n 50).

[70] *Taralga Landscape Guardians Inc v Minister for Planning* [2007] NSWLEC 59, (2007) 161 LGERA 1.

[71] *Attorney-General (NSW) v Quin* (1990) 170 CLR 1, 38.

[72] eg *Gray v The Minister for Planning and Ors* [2006] NSWLEC 720, (2006) 152 LGERA 258 (judicial review), citing *BGP Properties* (n 47) (merits review), as one of '[n]umerous decisions of this Court [that] have confirmed the importance of ESD principles for decision makers making decisions under legislation which adopts ESD principles' [109].

[73] The Court defines a 'planning principle' as a 'a statement of a desirable outcome from a chain of reasoning aimed at reaching, or a list of appropriate matters to be considered in making, a planning decision': www.lec.nsw.gov.au/lec/practice-and-procedure/principles/planning-principals.html (accessed 7 July 2021).

[74] *BGP Properties* (n 47).

[75] *Hornsby* (n 33).

[76] M Kirby, 'Introduction' in Pearson, Harlow and Taggart (n 57) 7 (referring to Elizabeth Fisher's chapter in the same volume (see n 57), elaborating this very point).

Rather, they involve the development of legal doctrine. They build on previous reasoning to develop new lines of reasoning concerning ESD principles.[77] The Court's ESD merits appeals also reveal an overlap in doctrine between merits review and judicial review cases, particularly in relation to the doctrine of mandatory relevant considerations (a central administrative law doctrine). This is because, in both types of action (merits and judicial review), the Court needs to determine which considerations – in particular, which ESD principles – are legally required and relevant, either to review whether they have been properly taken into account (judicial review) or to apply them directly (merits review). This is particularly apparent in cases where a judicial review action is brought where no merits appeal is available, as in *Gray v The Minister for Planning and others*.[78] In this case, Pain J used ESD principles to conclude that the planning approval process for a coal mine project had been flawed. She found that, as a matter of law, the broad discretion of the relevant planning decision-maker (the Director-General) was to be exercised in accordance with ESD principles.[79] Pain J reached this conclusion by looking to the 'substantial judicial pronouncement' of *Telstra Corp Ltd v Hornsby Shire Council* (a merits appeal, and 'planning principle' case, discussed further below) as well as the considerable NSWLEC case law confirming the importance of ESD principles for decision-makers under Acts that adopt the principles (mainly merits appeals), including the planning legislation at issue in this case.[80] Pain J then determined that the principles of intergenerational equity and precautionary principle were relevant on the facts of this case, and that there had been a failure of the 'legal requirement' to consider the principles by the Director-General. This doctrinal reasoning was founded on ESD reasoning in merits appeals, showing that merits review is not just about 'resolving disputes, but … in doing so it [defines] categories and the boundaries of action' of environmental decision-makers.[81] New lines of administrative law reasoning have thus been shaped by the unique legal jurisdiction and culture of the Court, representing a particular form of environmental law, in which merits appeals concerning ESD principles play an important role.[82]

3.3. Developing ESD Reasoning through Localising Global Legal Ideas

A further distinctive feature of the Court's reasoning around ESD principles is its appeal to international instruments and transnational borrowing of legal ideas, allowing its

[77] eg *Newcastle & Hunter Valley Speleological Society Inc v Upper Hunter Shire Council and Stoneco Pty Limited* (2010) 210 LGERA 126; [2010] NSWLEC 48 (developing the Court's reasoning on the precautionary principle in the context of a series of factual uncertainties on which the enlivening of the principle depended).

[78] *Gray* (n 72). See also *Walker v Minister for Planning* [2007] NSWLEC 741, (2007) 157 LGERA 124.

[79] *Gray* (n 72) [115].

[80] See section 3.2.

[81] E Fisher, '"Jurisdictional" Facts and "Hot" Facts' (2015) 38 *Melbourne University Law Review* 968, 982 (merits appeals are thus a form of administrative law in that they are 'part of the day-to-day operation of the accountability of environmental decision-making').

[82] Australian environmental law scholars have treated merits appeals as part of 'environmental law' for some time: eg J Peel, 'Ecologically Sustainable Development: More Than Mere Lip Service?' (2008) 12(1) *Australasian Journal of Natural Resources Law and Policy* 1. See also Fisher (n 57).

ESD doctrine to develop with support from international regimes and developments in other courts, and contributing to a transnational judicial dialogue on environmental principles. The very beginnings of the Court's ESD case law were in early merits appeals where the Court drew inspiration from international developments such as the Rio Declaration, as well as national ESD policy developments, to find that ESD principles were relevant considerations in planning decisions.[83] Subsequently, as the Court's ESD case law become more sophisticated, so did its transnational reasoning, localising the global legal phenomenon of environmental principles.

This is well demonstrated in a case such as *Telstra Corp Ltd v Hornsby Shire Council*[84] – a 'planning principle' merits review case concerning the precautionary principle and its application by decision-makers in the planning context. In *Telstra*, Preston CJ maps out a lengthy multi-stage process of how the precautionary principle should be applied by decision-makers, seeking to provide some clarity amongst a growing body of case law that had firmly established the principle as a relevant planning consideration under section 79C (now section 4.15) of the EPA Act. Preston CJ considers a wide range of scholarly and legal articulations of the principle, including different applications of the principle in other jurisdictions, and its articulation in international sustainable development instruments.[85] Preston CJ uses these sources to give authority and legitimacy to his reasoning,[86] whilst also demonstrating a willingness 'to "domesticate" [the international norm of the precautionary principle] in order to further develop, enrich, and ultimately strengthen [this] domestic environmental law [regime]'.[87] Preston CJ sees this judgment as an important step in applying ESD principles internationally, as part of a 'paradigm shift [to a world] where a culture of sustainability extends to institutions, private development interests, communities and individuals'.[88] Within the Court, new doctrine on ESD principles consciously contributes to a broader project of developing a 'global jurisprudence' in relation to environmental principles and sustainability.[89] This outward-looking attitude to environmental law globally is part of the Court's legal culture that shapes its ESD doctrine.

3.4. Routine Legal Processes: Interpreting Legislation and Case Law Development

In addition to the special jurisdictional and institutional features of the NSWLEC outlined in sections 3.2 and 3.3, there are also more routine aspects of the Court and

[83] eg *Leatch v Director General of National Parks and Wildlife Service* (1993) 81 LGERA 270; *Northcompass Inc v Hornsby Shire Council* [1996] 130 LGERA 248.

[84] *Hornsby* (n 33).

[85] ibid, eg [108]–[112], [130]–[138], [144]–[149].

[86] cf Andrew Edgar, 'Institutions and Sustainability: Merits Review Tribunals and the Precautionary Principle' (2013) 16 *Australasia Journal of Natural Resources Law and Policy* 61.

[87] Kotze and Soyapi (n 5) 23.

[88] *Telstra* (n 108) [120].

[89] P Biscoe, 'Ecologically Sustainable Development in New South Wales' (5th Worldwide Colloquium of the IUCN Academy of Environmental Law, Brazil, 2 June 2007) [76]. See also Kotze and Soyapi (n 5); B Preston 'Leadership by the Courts in Achieving Sustainability' (2010) 27 *Environmental and Planning Law Journal* 321.

the law it applies that have been central to the development of a body of ESD jurisprudence. The Court's ESD reasoning is framed by the legislation that the Court must interpret and apply, and this has been elaborated through incremental case law reasoning, developed over decades. In combination with the special features of the Court and the open-textured nature of environmental principles, these more familiar aspects of lawmaking and common law adjudication have created a substantial and remarkable body of legal doctrine around ESD principles.

As detailed in section 3.1, legislation provided a firm legal foothold for the development of ESD jurisprudence. Unsurprisingly, significant ESD reasoning in the Court's case law is based on the direct incorporation of ESD principles in legislation. A prime example is seen in *Bushfire Survivors for Climate Action Incorporated v Environment Protection Authority*,[90] where the Court construed the duty on the NSW Environmental Protection Authority under section 9(1) of the POEA Act 'to develop environmental quality objectives, guidelines and policies to ensure environment protection' in light of the EPA's objective (in section 6(1) of the Act), by which it must have regard to the 'need to maintain ecologically sustainable development', as expressed through its constituent ESD principles (elaborated in section 6(2) – see section 3.1 above). This was a foundational step in a detailed exercise of legislative interpretation by the Court, leading to the conclusion that the EPA was under a duty to develop environmental quality objectives, guidelines and policies to ensure environment protection from climate change specifically, which duty it had not yet fulfilled.[91]

The strong legislative basis for the Court's ESD jurisprudence has also arisen through other statutory provisions that have been interpreted by the Court to reflect ESD the principles. As Ceri Warnock points out, a 'critical element with environmental legislation [is] that it tends to guide rather than prescribe', giving the Court an important interpretive role.[92] In the landmark 1993 case that first embraced the precautionary principle as a legally relevant consideration in a merits appeal – *Leatch v Director General of National Parks and Wildlife Service*[93] – Stein J drew on two statutory provisions to support his endorsement of the precautionary principle as being legally relevant: the NSWLEC's requirement to take into account the 'public interest' in all LEC merits appeals,[94] and the requirement of the National Parks and Wildlife Act, directly at issue in this case, that 'any matter [considered to be] relevant' should be taken into account in decisions regarding fauna destruction licence applications.[95] Both statutory considerations were broad enough to include a reference to the precautionary principle through the Court's interpretation of them, including by reference to international sustainable development developments.

[90] *Bushfire Survivors for Climate Action Incorporated v Environment Protection Authority* (2021) 250 LGERA 1; [2021] NSWLEC 92.

[91] ibid, [61] ('Protection of the environment from climate change implements the principles of ecologically sustainable development, including the precautionary principle, intergenerational equity, conservation of biological diversity and ecological integrity, and the polluter pays principle, thereby enabling the achievement and maintenance of ecologically sustainable development').

[92] C Warnock, *Environmental Courts and Tribunals: Powers, Integrity and the Search for Legitimacy* (Oxford, Hart Publishing, 2020) 164.

[93] *Leatch* (n 82).

[94] Land and Environment Court Act 1979 (NSW). Section 39(4) requires that in making a decision in a relevant 'appeal', the Court 'shall have regard to this or any other relevant Act, any instrument made under any such Act, the circumstances of the case and the public interest'.

[95] National Parks and Wildlife Act 1974 (NSW) s 92A (now repealed).

By 2004, the Court was confident in finding that ESD principles were relevant to a wide range of statutes granting it jurisdiction. Thus, in the judicial review decision in *Murrumbidgee Ground-Water Preservation Association v Minister for Natural Resources*,[96] which concerned powers exercised under the Water Management Act 2000 (NSW), McClellan J held that ESD principles are to be applied 'when decisions are being made under … any … Act which adopts the principles'.[97] In McClellan J's view, the common ESD purpose across NSW environmental and planning law – with ESD and ESD principles included across a wide range of statutes – was of such significance that ESD principles were relevant considerations in decisions made under any such Act, in the common law administrative law sense.

The legal relevance of ESD principles as expressing the 'public interest' has been particularly important in the evolution of NSWLEC ESD reasoning. A longstanding line of the Court's case law has established that ESD principles are legally relevant considerations in determining planning consent decisions, since the decision-maker must take into account the 'public interest',[98] and this includes giving effect to ESD principles.[99] The fundamental role of the 'public interest' importing ESD principles into planning decisions is seen particularly in relation to approval of major projects and infrastructure under the EPA Act. These are often very controversial decisions – many concerning approval of coal mines[100] or major residential developments[101] – which are regulated by bespoke planning legislation designed to give decision-making discretion to Ministers or planning commission bodies with minimal intervention by the Court. The now repealed Part 3A regime for major projects[102] showed that, despite more limited statutory scope for imputing the relevance of ESD principles, ESD principles were nonetheless relevant in approving such projects in a series of judicial review and merits appeals cases.[103] Some of the reasoning in these cases is very intricate, particularly since it needs to engage with complex statutory frameworks,[104] but this succession of cases showed a determination by the court to interpret all planning decision-making as implicating the public interest, particularly where environmentally sensitive issues arose. Thus, in *Bulga Milbrodale*, Preston CJ did not find it necessary to determine that ESD principles were mandatory relevant considerations in this Part 3A major development, since it was sufficient to conclude that 'as an aspect of the public

[96] *Murrumbidgee Ground-Water Preservation Association v Minister for Natural Resources* [2004] NSWLEC 122.

[97] ibid, [178]. McClellan J explicitly rejected the view that the precautionary principle was a 'merely a political aspiration'. See also *BT Goldsmith Planning Services v Blacktown City Council* [2005] NSWLEC 210 (Pain J adopting similar reasoning to widen the application of the precautionary principle to all decisions under the EPA Act).

[98] EPA Act, s 4.15 (previously s 79C).

[99] *Carstens v Pittwater Council* (1999) 111 LGERA 1; [1999] NSWLEC 249; *BGP Properties* (n 7).

[100] *Gray* (n 72); *Bulga Milbrodale* (n 50); *Gloucester Resources* (n 6).

[101] *Drake-Brockman v Minister for Planning* (2007) 158 LGERA 349; [2007] NSWLEC 490; *Walker v Minister for Planning* (2007) 157 LGERA 124; [2007] NSWLEC 741.

[102] Environmental Planning and Assessment Amendment (Infrastructure and Other Planning Reform) Act 2005 (NSW); Environmental Planning and Assessment Amendment (Part 3A Repeal) Act 2011.

[103] See Scotford (n 5) 240–50 (including on the complexity of applying judicial review doctrine in these cases).

[104] See eg Gray (n 72) [105]–[115].

interest they may be taken into account in cases where issues relevant to the principles of ESD arise'.[105] This was supported as matter of law by the NSW Court of Appeal in *Walker*:

> [T]he principles of ESD are likely to come to be seen as so plainly an element of the public interest, in relation to most if not all decisions, that failure to consider them will become strong evidence of failure to consider the public interest and/or to act bona fide in the exercise of powers granted to the Minister, and thus become capable of avoiding decisions.[106]

The NSW Court of Appeal subsequently interpreted Hodgson JA's reasoning in *Walker* as 'authority for the proposition that where it is necessary to consider the environmental impact of a project, the public interest [embraces ESD]'.[107] With the introduction of a new NSW regime for major projects – with specific regimes for approving State Significant Development (SSD) and State Significant Infrastructure (SSI) under the EPA Act, and limiting even further the review oversight of the Court[108] – the statutory scheme retains a role for ESD principles. This is most clearly seen for SSD,[109] where the 'public interest' (informed by ESD principles) is reintroduced as a mandatory relevant planning consideration, alongside a requirement to conduct an environmental impact statement,[110] which must include 'the reasons justifying the carrying out of the development, activity or infrastructure in the manner proposed, having regard to biophysical, economic and social considerations, including the principles of ecologically sustainable development'.[111] A high-profile 2019 merits appeal in an SSD case – *Gloucester Resources Limited v Minister for Planning*[112] – contains important reasoning outlining how the principle of intergenerational equity is applied, reinforcing the ongoing centrality of ESD principles across the Court's reasoning despite complexities in its evolving legislative environment for large-scale infrastructure development.

This outline of NSW legislative developments also highlights the Court's progressive ESD reasoning in applying and interpreting this legislation. After decades of development, the Court's ESD jurisprudence is notable due to its sheer reach. The Court's doctrinal reasoning around ESD principles has cross-fertilised into all classes of its jurisdiction,[113] and now freely extends beyond legislative frameworks.[114]

[105] *Bulga Milbrodale* (n 50) [59].

[106] *Minister for Planning v Walker* [2008] NSWCA 224, (2008) 161 LGERA 423.

[107] *Warkworth Mining Limited v Bulga Milbrodale Progress Association Inc* (2014) 86 NSWLR 527; [2014] NSWCA 105 [296]. In the Law and Environment Court decision under challenge, *Bulga Milbrodale* (n 50), Preston CJ had relied on the ESD objects of the act and the *implicit* duty of the Minister to consider the public interest, citing *Minister for Planning v Walker* (ibid): 'Although that requirement is not explicitly stated in the Act, it is so central to the task of a Minister fulfilling functions under the Act that it goes without saying' [56].

[108] EPA Act, ss 5.26, 5.27, 8.6(3)(a).

[109] For SSI, there is a requirement to prepare an environmental impact statement, which, on the Court's previous case law, would import a requirement to consider ESD principles: n 107.

[110] EPA Act, ss 4.12(8) and 5.16.

[111] Environmental Assessment Regulation 2000, sch 2, para 7(1)(f).

[112] *Gloucester Resources Limited v Minister for Planning* (n 6).

[113] eg *Bentley v BGP Properties* [2006] NSWLEC 34, (2006) 145 LGERA 234 (criminal proceedings), citing *Murrumbidgee* (n 96), a judicial review action, to find that ESD principles were central to informing common law sentencing principles. See Scotford (n 5) ch 5.

[114] eg *Taralga* (n 70).

There are major precedent-setting judgments on the precautionary principle,[115] the principle of intergenerational equity,[116] the principle of intragenerational equity[117] and the principle of the sustainable use of natural resources.[118] This reasoning is not strictly common law reasoning by analogy[119] – there is a 'top-down' element with ESD principles framing developments, and there are dense thickets of legislation and administrative decision-making to navigate – however, the reasoning is doctrinal and incremental, building on previous cases applying the same legislation, interpreting new legislation as importing the ESD principles into decision-making, drawing doctrinal threads across related legal cases. These incremental steps are familiar features of common law reasoning,[120] and have provided deep legal foundations for the Court to apply the principles in cases where issues relevant to the principles of ESD arise.[121] As a result of this steady, progressive reasoning, ESD and its principles now extend across the jurisdiction and reasoning of the Court as a 'touchstone, a central element in decision-making relating to planning for and development of the environment and the natural resources that are the bounty of this environment'.[122] Within a complex body of environmental law – driven by the complexity of environmental problems (our developing knowledge about them, society's changing political views in addressing them, their intersecting and interdisciplinary dimensions)[123] – the common thread of ESD principles through NSW environmental and planning law provides valuable stability and coherence.

4. Final Reflections: Questions of Legitimacy and Critique

Before the creation of the NSWLEC, '[t]here was no [NSW] environmental law as we now know it'.[124] A key feature of this body of law is the central role played by ESD principles in its evolving jurisprudence. As shown in the sections above, this jurisprudence has evolved through a combination of political developments, institutional reform, unique jurisdictional design, new lines and modes of legal reasoning, openness to international soft law developments and transnational judicial dialogue, as well as applying and interpreting an intricate body of environmental and planning legislation through an expansive and cross-fertilising case law, reasoned over time to generate ESD doctrine, all expressing and coevolving with the legal culture of the Court. This is not an easily replicable legal example.

[115] *Hornsby* (n 33).
[116] *Bulga Milbrodale* (n 50).
[117] ibid.
[118] *Hub Action Group* (n 50); *Gloucester Resources* (n 6).
[119] A Young, 'Public Law Cases and the Common Law: A Unique Relationship?' in E Fisher, J King and A Young (eds), *The Foundations and Future of Public Law* (Oxford, Oxford University Press, 2020).
[120] Sir John Laws, 'Lecture One – The Common Law and State Power', in *The Common Law Constitution* (Cambridge, Cambridge University Press, 2014) 3.
[121] See n 107.
[122] *Bentley v BGP* (n 275) [57].
[123] Fisher, Lange and Scotford (n 10) ch 2.
[124] Preston (n 1) 402.

This body of law shows that, despite the controversial features of environmental principles outlined in section 2, it is possible to develop a mature body of legal reasoning based on environmental principles. Legally entrenching environmental principles through legislative incorporation and carefully reasoned case law in some respects looks like familiar legal reasoning in the common law tradition. However, it is a distinctive body of law in which policy ideas are being fleshed out and determined by courts rather than administrative or political decision-makers. As indicated above, one might respond to this state of affairs with a political response – it is either a good thing that a court is pursuing an agenda of ecological sustainability through law, or it is inappropriate for courts to engage in such reasoning. Both reactions might mistakenly assume that the Court's decisions are all 'anti-development'; they are not.[125] Moreover, they fundamentally misunderstand the legal work of the Court. As with any court, it has a duty to adjudicate the disputes that come before it[126] and it is empowered with a specific and valuable jurisdiction, which frames legal actions around environmental problems and not vice versa.[127] The central subject matter of its jurisdiction – environmental problems[128] – necessitates complex reasoning, and ESD principles facilitate this. This is because ESD principles not only pursue an agenda of environmental protection but they recognise the uncertainty (precautionary principle), interdisciplinarity (conservation of biological diversity), economic and social implications (polluter pays, integration) and temporal dimensions (intergenerational equity) of environmental problems. As legally relevant considerations in many environmental regimes, they provide the normative space for these aspects of environmental problems to be examined with careful reasoning. Thus, for example, taking into account scientific uncertainty in an environmental dispute is not a simple calculation of right versus wrong that can be determined along a bright line of common law principle (or even rights-based reasoning); it requires painstaking assessment of facts against a careful set of decision-making steps that can be tested for their rigour, as the Court's precedent-setting articulation of the precautionary principle has demonstrated.[129] As Warnock argues, the legitimacy of the Court's reasoning is both questioned and answered by its approach to reasoning that is both judicial and appropriate for the nature of the complex environmental disputes before it,[130] taking seriously their polycentricity,[131] scientific uncertainty and their impact on diverse communities and complex ecologies.

Recognising this specific and important jurisdiction of the Court raises questions about how its ESD reasoning should be critiqued. ESD principles remain open-textured and there are many different fact-specific articulations of the principles even as the

[125] The Court has approved many contentious developments after weighing the relevant considerations, including ESD principles: *Greenpeace Australia v Redbank Power* (1994) 86 LGERA 143; *Telstra* (n 33); *Hunter Environment Lobby Inc v Minister for Planning* [2011] NSWLEC 221.

[126] Preston (n 1).

[127] Environmental law is notoriously fragmented due to the wide range of legal issues implicated by environmental problems: Fisher, Lange and Scotford (n 10) ch 1.

[128] Including land use problems.

[129] *Hornsby* (n 33).

[130] Warnock (n 92) ch 6 and generally.

[131] The reasoning in *Bulga Milbrodale* (n 50) expressly confronts and addresses the polycentricity of environmental problems.

Court develops more and more leading precedents articulating what the principles mean and how to apply them in specific contexts. In this respect, the incremental, methodical nature of the Court's reasoning provides legal stability and authority for its reasoning. But just as the principles are not purely legal, and environmental problems display multiple dimensions, so the evaluation of the Court's ESD case law raises extra-legal questions. We are in newly charted jurisprudential territory in the Court's ESD case law, as is justified by the nature of environmental problems, and critiques of its case law must at once respect the Court's jurisdiction whilst also taking seriously the contestable dimensions of environmental problems and environmental policy. Overall, the NSWLEC's jurisprudential gift to environmental law is a huge body of dedicated judicial work and enterprise putting environmental problems and principles at the heart of a body of legal reasoning and doctrine; it is a pioneering body of law.

9

The Land and Environment Court of New South Wales and the Recognition of Indigenous Peoples' Environmental Rights

MEGAN DAVIS

The way in which the self-determination of indigenous peoples is recognized by the State plays a significant role in its realization, and such recognition differs greatly between States, regions and indigenous peoples. Mechanisms that support the domestic implementation of the right to self-determination, including constitutional recognition, treaties, legislation on political participation, consultation and free, prior and informed consent are crucial indicators of the stage of indigenous peoples' self-determination. (United Nations Expert Mechanism on the Rights of Indigenous Peoples)[1]

1. Introduction

This chapter examines how the Land and Environment Court of New South Wales (the Court) has developed the law in relation to the environmental rights of Indigenous peoples.[2] The Court has adapted the law and its institutional processes to demonstrate an appropriate and highly developed sensitivity that allows for a recognition, acknowledgement and respect for Indigenous peoples and their cultural heritage that may otherwise not be given as much weight in other non-specialised superior courts. This chapter provides some examples of this. It uses the United Nations Declaration on the Rights of Indigenous Peoples (UNDRIP)[3] as a framework for examining the Court's unique and pioneering jurisdiction. While not legally binding in the dualist legal order of Australia, as the quote that opens this chapter underscores, it provides a template and set of indicators for understanding the significance of what the Court has done.

[1] Efforts to Implement the United Nations Declaration on the Rights of Indigenous Peoples: Indigenous Peoples and the Right to Self-determination Report of the Expert Mechanism on the Rights of Indigenous Peoples, A/HRC/48/75, [43].

[2] 'Indigenous' and 'Aboriginal' are used interchangeably throughout. 'Indigenous' is the term used in international law and the UNDRIP. 'Aboriginal' is the term used in the NSW jurisdiction.

[3] Declaration on the Rights of Indigenous Peoples, GA Res 61/295, UN GAOR, 61st session, UN Doc A/RES/47/1 (2007).

I write this chapter both as a practitioner and a scholar. In regard to the former, I write this as an Aboriginal lawyer and expert in Indigenous peoples and the law. My experience, as a legal counsel for the United Nations and then the statutory Aboriginal and Torres Strait Islander Commission – drafting the UNDRIP from 1998 to 2006 – is germane to asserting the Court's contribution to Indigenous recognition; as is my statutory role as an Acting Commissioner of the Land and Environment Court of New South Wales. Section 12(2)(g) of the Land and Environment Court Act 1979 (NSW) states that Aboriginal land claims assigned to Class 3 are heard by a Judge, assisted by one or more Commissioners appointed with suitable qualifications.

But I am also a scholar. In this chapter I revert to my academic practice; I provide my own legal assessment and consider the scholarly analysis of the Land and Environment Court, which is sparse – not uncommon in subject matter areas relating to Indigenous peoples and the law in Australia. The scant literature remains useful in terms of scholarly observation, especially Aboriginal authors who are assessing the decisions from a cultural perspective.

As an Acting Commissioner, I understand the relevant case law in a functional sense apropos the relevant provisions in specific legislation and the incremental ways significant decisions have moved the law forward, fenced it in, or where a superior court has decided the application or interpretation of a legislative provision. The value of scholarly literature, however, is for its broader sociocultural observations and commentary.

This chapter is structured as follows. In section 2, I provide an overview of the Court's jurisdiction in relation to Indigenous people's environmental rights. In section 3, I turn to UNDRIP to provide a framework for structuring an analysis of the Court's case law in this area. Based on this, section 4 runs a ruler across some of the activity of the Court examining: (1) the interpretation of the Aboriginal Land Rights Act 1983 (NSW) (ALRA); (2) judicial assessment of cultural heritage; (3) penalties for damage or destruction of Aboriginal cultural heritage: (4) use of restorative justice by the Court; and (4) intergenerational equity. In section 5 I consider some of the ways in which the Court has evolved as an institution to ensure it properly adjudicates in relation to Indigenous matters.

2. The Court's Jurisdiction in Relation to Indigenous Peoples' Environmental Rights

As an Aboriginal Acting Commissioner of the Court's jurisdiction, I am acutely aware of the critical importance of 'Country' for Aboriginal peoples. It involves land rights recognition as well as the many manifestations of being Aboriginal including Aboriginal connection to land and community. From that, flows language, culture, belonging and identity. To talk of Indigenous environmental rights is to talk of a set of complex legal ideas.

The Court has five main areas of legal activity in relation to the rights of Indigenous people. These areas of jurisdiction arise under different legislative regimes. They primarily engage legal questions particularly to do with administrative law and criminal law.

The first area concerns appeals and references relating to Aboriginal land claims made pursuant to the ALRA.[4] This Act has its genesis in Aboriginal activism for land rights. Originating from a parliamentary inquiry in the late 1970s and early 1980s and a Green Paper on Aboriginal Land Rights in New South Wales,[5] the passage of the Act by the NSW Parliament was a significant act of recognition decades before the United Nations General Assembly adopted the UNDRIP that recognised the pre-existing and continuing rights of Aboriginal people to land. As will be seen in section 4.1, much of this case law in relation to the Act focuses on the statutory construction of the Act and thus the legal logic of that regime.[6]

The second relevant area of the Court's work concerns matters relating specifically to Aboriginal cultural heritage, including applications for judicial review challenging permits to destroy Aboriginal objects granted under the National Parks and Wildlife Act 1974 (NSW) (NPWA).[7] In these cases the Court is often dealing with administrative law questions concerning the grant of consent to destroy Aboriginal relics, including relevant and irrelevant considerations and procedural fairness.[8] There are also applications for judicial review or civil enforcement of development consents that are argued to be relevant to Aboriginal objects or places under the Environmental Planning and Assessment Act 1979 (NSW) (the EPA Act).[9] As with the above, these cases raise mainly administrative law questions about what is legally valid under the Act; for example, what needs to be taken into account and considered in relation to Aboriginal heritage.[10]

The third area of the Court's work concerns merits review of determinations of development applications under the EPA Act to carry out development that might impact Aboriginal cultural heritage. One example of this is Justice Preston's decision in *Gloucester Resources Limited v Minister for Planning*[11] which involved a merits review challenge to a coal mine. Government guidelines do require an assessment of the impact on Aboriginal culture to be considered as part of a social impact assessment.[12] The Court found in this case that the social impact assessment for the project had failed to assess the social impacts of the Rocky Hill Coal Project on Aboriginal people[13] and

[4] This is under Class 3 jurisdiction, see s 19(g2) and (g3) Land and Environment Court Act 1979 (NSW).

[5] Ministry of Aboriginal Affairs, Green Paper on Aboriginal Land Rights in New South Wales (NSW Government, 1982).

[6] eg *Minister Administering the Crown Lands Act 1989 v New South Wales Aboriginal Land Council* (2018) 231 LGERA 145; *Minister Administering the Crown Lands Act v NSW Aboriginal Land Council* (2008) 237 CLR 285 and *New South Wales Aboriginal Land Council v Minister Administering the Crown Lands Act* (2016) 260 CLR 232.

[7] eg *Williams v Homestake Australia* (2002) 122 LGERA 319.

[8] eg *Kennedy v Director-General of the Department of Environment and Conservation and Another* [2006] NSWLEC 456.

[9] eg *Anderson v Ballina Shire Council* [2006] NSWLEC 76; *Anderson v Minister for Infrastructure Planning and Natural Resources* (2006) 151 LGERA 229; *Warren v Electricity Commission of New South Wales* (1990) 130 LGERA 565; *Dates v NSW Minister for Planning* [2009] NSWLEC 38; and *Tenodi v Blue Mountains City Council* [2011] NSWLEC 1183.

[10] *Anderson v Minister for Infrastructure Planning and Natural Resources* (n 8) [63].

[11] *Gloucester Resources Limited v Minister for Planning* (2019) 234 LGERA 257.

[12] ibid [270]. See also Department of Planning and Environment, *The Social Impact Assessment Guideline* (2017).

[13] *Gloucester Resources* (n 11) [342]. See also S Aravind, 'Gloucester Resources and its Radical Implications for Indigenous Environmental Justice' *Oxford Human Rights Hub Blog* (18 March 2019), https://ohrh.law.ox.ac.uk/gloucester-resources-and-its-radical-implications-for-indigenous-environmental-justice; and J Watts et al, 'What You Didn't Know about the Landmark Rocky Hill Judgment' (2019) 57 *Law Society Journal* 72.

had failed to adequately assess the importance of Country and landscape that would have been affected by the Project to the Aboriginal people and, as a consequence, to assess the social impact of the Project on Aboriginal people.[14] The area of the project had been inadequately surveyed for Aboriginal sites.[15] There had also been an inadequate acknowledgement of the importance of Country and landscape to the Aboriginal people. The Court emphasised a 'whole of landscape' approach, stating that: 'Heritage value lies not merely in particular Aboriginal sites but in the landscape as a whole.'[16]

The fourth area of the Court's work involving Indigenous issues concerns civil enforcement proceedings relating to acts affecting Aboriginal relics and objects under the NPWA.[17] These cases largely focus on whether there has been a breach of the Act. For example, in *Williams v Barrick Australia Ltd* declaratory and injunctive relief was sought against a mining company for breaching both the NPWA and the permit issued to them under the Act.[18] The final area in which the Court hears cases concerns the prosecution of offences relating to the destruction of Aboriginal objects or places under the NPWA. This has given rise to a rich body of doctrine and practice concerning sentencing and restorative justice.[19]

3. UNDRIP

As will be seen in the next two sections, the Court has been innovative in developing the law and its processes in relation to the different Indigenous issues that have come before it. But before going forward, it needs to be noted that any assessment of the Court's jurisprudence faces an immediate challenge. While the Court has contributed much to the recognition of Indigenous rights, there is little literature or discourse that specifically examines the way in which the jurisprudence of the Court affects Indigenous peoples.

Rather, issues of Indigenous rights are often addressed through other areas of debate. For example, Butterly and Lixinski argue that heritage law reform processes are a 'microcosm of broader recognition' in Australia and are used 'as opportunities for Indigenous peoples to seek "recognition" and control of governance mechanisms that relate to their heritage'.[20] The lack of this explicit literature on the Court and Indigenous rights is a deficiency.

All this means that there is little by way of a framework to understand and assess what the Land and Environment Court is doing in this legal space. In this chapter I use the UNDRIP to provide that frame. The UNDRIP is the primary normative framework in international law relating to the rights of Indigenous peoples. The UNDRIP was a declaration that was advocated for, and debated on, for thirty years by UN member

[14] *Gloucester Resources* (n 11) [343].
[15] ibid [345].
[16] ibid [346].
[17] eg *Henry and Ors v Shellharbour City Council and Ors* [2005] NSWLEC 600.
[18] *Williams v Barrick Australia Ltd* (2003) 128 LGERA 80.
[19] See section 4.4.
[20] L Butterly and L Lixinski, 'Aboriginal Cultural Heritage Reform in Australia and the Dilemmas of Power' (2020) 27 *International Journal of Cultural Property* 125, 126.

states and the global Indigenous peoples' caucus and movement.[21] It was adopted as a non-binding declaration of the UN General Assembly in 2007.[22] It sets out minimum standards agreed to by the global community for states to meet in the accommodation of Indigenous peoples within the framework of the democratic state.

Each article in the Declaration derives from already recognised rights in international human rights law that applies to individuals, the difference being that the UNDRIP is a collective rights framework. The rights contained therein are clustered in themes, including the right to self-determination; life, integrity and security; cultural, religious, spiritual and linguistic identity; education and public information; political participatory rights; lands, territories and resources; and the exercise of self-determination. Not all these rights are relevant to the work of the Land and Environment Court.

Australia has a dualist model of international law and therefore enabling legislation is required for international law to be incorporated into the domestic legal system. The UNDRIP is 'non-binding' in the sense that it lacks the bindingness of an international treaty incorporated into statute. It might nevertheless influence how courts construe the meaning of a statute that refers to it.[23]

There are two key principles to understand about the UNDRIP. The first is that the Declaration contains remedial rights and constitutive rights. On remedial rights, this means that it recognises rights that are intended to arrest, mitigate and redress historical and contemporary injustice. The UNDRIP also contains substantive or constitutive rights. These are intrinsic to being Indigenous. The second key principle is that the UNDRIP is a group rights framework. The fact that it enumerates collective rights is novel in the international human rights law system. However, there is much baggage that comes along with collective rights and that is the attendant concern of states about secession.

Indeed, the UNDRIP as a declaration took so long to draft because it invoked self-determination as a collective right, and this was viewed as a threat to some UN member states. Either way, the UNDRIP rights are conventional human rights expressed collectively and as applying within the borders of the state. Article 3 of UNDRIP reads:

> Indigenous peoples have the right of self-determination. By virtue of that right they freely determine their political status and freely pursue their economic, social and cultural development.

The right to self-determination is operationalised in Articles 4, 5, 18, 19, 20 and 33 of the Declaration. These articles explain how a state should implement the rights at a domestic level. It is Article 3 that informs the entirety of the Declaration's articles meaning. It imbues every subject matter of the UNDRIP, including lands, territories and resources clusters, political participation, cultural heritage, media, languages, labour force rights, intellectual property, free, prior and informed consent, etc, as collective and within the framework of the state. Without Article 3, no other articles can be properly realised.

[21] M Davis, 'United Nations Declaration on the Rights of Indigenous Peoples' (2008) 9 *Melbourne Journal of International Law* 439.

[22] S James Anaya, 'Situation of Human Rights and Fundamental Freedoms of Indigenous People', UN Doc A/65/264 (9 August 2010) 17, [59]–[61].

[23] Acts Interpretation Act 1901 (Cth) s 15AB; Interpretation Act 1987 (NSW) s 34.

There are two ways that the right to self-determination is implemented in terms of the Indigenous collective – one internally and the other externally.

Article 4 adds nuance to Article 3 by affording recognition in terms of self-determination, practised as self-government or autonomy and obligating the state to provide financing for their autonomous functions. Article 5 provides that while Indigenous peoples have the right to their own institutions, they have a right to participate fully in state affairs. Article 5 also invokes a concept of choice, the right of Indigenous peoples to choose to participate in the democratic life of the state. If not, they can opt out.

Turning to the right to self-determination within the state, Articles 18–20 set out the institutional framework for the realisation of the right to self-determination within the political structures of the state. This is the architecture of political participation, which begins with Indigenous peoples' right to participate in decision-making affecting their rights through representatives chosen by themselves in accordance with their own procedures, as well as to maintain and develop their own indigenous decision-making institutions. These articles set out for states the way in which Indigenous peoples should be recognised institutionally by way of legislation or administratively and the processes the states undertake before doing so. They are also relevant to the recognition of Indigenous peoples' rights in relation to the land and the environment. The UN Expert Mechanism on the Rights of Indigenous Peoples (EMRIP) states:

> For indigenous peoples, land is not only, or even primarily, an economic asset. It is the defining element of their identity and culture and their relationship to their ancestors and future generations. Access to lands, territories and resources is obtained through community membership, not the free market. For indigenous peoples, land rights are often intergenerational and thus carry an obligation of stewardship for the benefit of present and future members and as the basis for their continued existence as a people.[24]

The EMRIP emphasises the relationship Indigenous peoples have with the land as one that is not driven by free-market aspirations but cultural values. Rather, the land has an intergenerational dimension to it. As will be discussed in section 4.5, the Court has adjudicated on these issues of intergenerational rights and the obligation of stewardship of 'Country' for Aboriginal people in NSW. It has also had to grapple with the intersection of the more internal and autonomous aspects of self-determination such as governance and membership.

The right to self-determination and cultural rights traverses wide-ranging issues from language, ceremonial and cultural heritage, spirituality and sports rights, and its meaning is expanded upon throughout the Declaration (Articles 11–16, 31 and 34). According to the UN Expert Mechanism study on the 'Promotion and Protection of the rights of Indigenous Peoples with Respect to their Cultural Heritage', Indigenous peoples' culture includes

> tangible and intangible manifestations of their ways of life, world views, achievements and creativity, and should be considered an expression of their self-determination and their

[24] Expert Mechanism on the Rights of Indigenous Peoples, 'Right to Land under the United Nations Declaration on the Rights of Indigenous Peoples: A Human Rights Focus, Study of the Expert Mechanism on the Rights of Indigenous Peoples (15 July 2020) A/HRC/45/38, [5].

> spiritual and physical relationships with their lands, territories and resources. While the notion of heritage encompasses traditional practices in a broad sense, including language, art, music, dance, song, stories, sports and traditional games, sacred sites, and ancestral human remains, for indigenous peoples the preservation of heritage is deeply embedded and linked to the protection of traditional territories. Indigenous cultural heritage is a holistic and inter-generational concept based on common material and spiritual values influenced by the environment. It also includes biocultural heritage and traditional food production systems such as rotational farming, pastoralism, artisanal fisheries and other forms of access to natural sources.[25]

The EMRIP definition of Indigenous peoples' culture is useful in understanding the notion of contemporary manifestations of culture – that they are not static but evolve – and that there is an intergenerational dimension to Indigenous culture and spirituality. The UNDRIP states that self-determination insofar as cultural heritage includes the rights to practice and revitalise cultural traditions and customs, to maintain, protect and develop the past, present and future manifestations of their cultures such as archaeological and historical sites, artefacts, designs, ceremonies, technologies, and visual and performing arts and literature (Article 11). The UNDRIP also provides that states shall provide redress including restitution for cultural, intellectual, religious and spiritual property. This includes the right to maintain, protect and have access in privacy to their religious and cultural sites (Article 12).

Future generations feature in the UNDRIP: Indigenous peoples have the right to revitalise, use, develop and transmit to future generations their histories, languages, oral traditions, philosophies, writing systems and literatures, and to designate and retain their own names for communities, places and persons (Article 13). The obligation on states is to take effective measures to ensure this right is protected and that Indigenous peoples can understand and be understood in political, legal and administrative proceedings, where necessary through the provision of interpretation or by other appropriate means.

In relation to the right to recognition to uphold 'future generations', Article 25 is relevant. It states:

> Indigenous peoples have the right to maintain and strengthen their distinctive spiritual relationship with their traditionally owned or otherwise occupied and used lands, territories, waters and coastal seas and other resources and to uphold their responsibilities to future generations in this regard.

The other cluster of articles related to the work of the Court concerns lands, territories and resources (Articles 26 and 27). Article 26 sets out the right to lands, territories and resources, 'which they have traditionally owned, occupied or otherwise used or acquired'. Article 26(3) provides that: 'States shall give legal recognition and protection to these lands, territories and resources. Such recognition shall be conducted with due respect to the customs, traditions and land tenure systems of the indigenous peoples concerned.' Furthermore Article 27 sets up the obligation of states to create

[25] Promotion and Protection of the Rights of Indigenous Peoples with Respect to their Cultural Heritage, A/HRC/30/53 (19 August 2015).

infrastructure, in consultation with Indigenous peoples to give due 'recognition' to Indigenous peoples involving

> a fair, independent, impartial, open and transparent process, giving due recognition to indigenous peoples' laws, traditions, customs and land tenure systems, to recognize and adjudicate the rights of indigenous peoples pertaining to their lands, territories and resources, including those which were traditionally owned or otherwise occupied or used. Indigenous peoples shall have the right to participate in this process.

This analysis of UNDRIP is not exhaustive. What it highlights, however, is that the rights of Indigenous people are interwoven with environment and culture. That is not just in the present, but also in the future. Clearly how those rights are adjudicated upon is crucial to whether they are realised or not. It is to the work of the Land and Environment Court to which I now turn.

4. Examining the Court's Recognition of Indigenous Peoples' Rights

As seen in section 2, the work of the Land and Environment Court relates to Indigenous issues in a variety of ways. In this section I take a deeper dive into some of the case law to examine the ways in which the Court realises the types of rights that are expressed in the UNDRIP. My approach in this section is to provide my own observations as a specialist in Indigenous peoples and the law. This section also has regard to the legal and scholarly commentary that has focused on the Court's work and how it has contributed to the recognition of Indigenous peoples' rights.

4.1. The Aboriginal Land Rights Act 1983

The jurisprudence of the Court, insofar as ALRA Class 3 appeals, has traversed many of the well-trodden issues globally that arise in relation to Indigenous recognition, most specifically the conduct of the state in litigation. The starting point is ALRA itself.

Under ALRA if the minister refuses a land claim, the Aboriginal Land Council can appeal to the Court. This type of appeal process is important, as seen by Article 27 of the UNDRIP as discussed above. The Act places the burden of proof on the state insofar as establishing the use and likely use of claimable land.[26] This is interesting to note. The United Nations Permanent Forum on Indigenous Issues (UNPFII) and the EMRIP have, for some time, been advocating the use of dispute resolution between Indigenous peoples and the state. A UNPFII report on implementing the UNDRIP also states that: 'The Declaration could also help to shift the dynamics of disputes so that the burden of proof was not always placed on indigenous peoples, but rather on States.'[27]

[26] *Deerubbin Local Aboriginal Land Council v Minister Administering the Crown Lands Act* (1997) 95 LGERA 353.

[27] M Davis, 'Adding a New Dimension: Native Title and the UN Declaration on the Rights of Indigenous Peoples' [2009] *Australian Law Reform Commission Reform Journal* 17.

The focus of most of the jurisprudence is section 36(1) and the definition of 'claimable Crown land'. This has given rise to a rich body of Land and Environment Court,[28] NSW Court of Appeal[29] and High Court of Australia[30] case law. The ALRA is understood as 'beneficial and remedial legislation'. As stated early on by the NSW Court of Appeal:

> The Aboriginal Land Rights Act 1983 is beneficial and remedial legislation. Clearly, it was enacted to give important rights in Crown land to the representatives of the Aboriginal people. By common acknowledgement, such people have suffered substantial injustice and loss consequent upon the deprivation of their land following the settlement of Australia.[31]

As such the courts tend towards a liberal interpretation, albeit not for all interpretations as the 'focus is on the meaning of specific words'.[32] Likewise, the exception clauses to 'claimable Crown land' in section 36(1) are 'narrowly construed'.[33]

This intent of the ALRA to be remedial, and the beneficial interpretation it is given, in order to acknowledge the substantial injustice and loss caused to Aboriginal people as a consequence of dispossession, resonates with the UNDRIP. The UNDRIP also has a remedial function to make redress for gross violations of human rights. One of the preambular provisions of the UNDRIP states:

> *Concerned* that indigenous peoples have suffered from historic injustices because of, inter alia, their colonization and dispossession of their lands, territories, and resources, thus preventing them from exercising, in particular, their right to development in accordance with their own needs and interests.

That said, the ALRA is by no means perfect. For example, under the Act the minister also has the statutory power to block a claim by issuing a certificate under section 36(8), which is a final and conclusive certificate, and unable to be called into question in any proceedings, nor liable to be appealed or reviewed on any grounds. Overall, it is an illustration of a spectrum of state conduct – with resistance at one end and recognition at the other. States do create statutes of recognition in many contexts and then actively resist in terms of the implementation of those rights.[34] This is known as regulatory ritualism.

[28] eg *NSW Aboriginal Land Council v Minister Administering the Crown Land Management Act 2016 – Helensburgh Police Station* [2020] NSWLEC 133; *Minister Administering the Crown Lands Act 1989 v New South Wales Aboriginal Land Council* (n 6); and *La Perouse Local Aboriginal Land Council v Minister Administering the Crown Lands Act (No 2)* (2016) 220 LGERA 1.

[29] *Minister Administering the Crown Lands Act v Bathurst Local Aboriginal Land Council* (2009) 166 LGERA 379; and *New South Wales Aboriginal Land Council v Minister Administering the Crown Lands Act (the Nelson Bay Claim)* (2014) 205 LGERA 219.

[30] *New South Wales Aboriginal Land Council v Minister Administering the Crown Lands Act* (n 6) and *Minister Administering the Crown Lands Act v NSW Aboriginal Land Council* (n 6).

[31] *Minister for Natural Resources v New South Wales Aboriginal Land Council* (1987) 9 NSWLR 154, 157.

[32] *New South Wales Aboriginal Land Council v Minister Administering the Crown Lands Act* (n 6) [33].

[33] *Minister Administering the Crown Lands Act v NSW Aboriginal Land Council* (n 6) [19] per Kirby J; *Minister Administering the Crown Lands Act v Deerubbin Local Aboriginal Land Council [No 2]* (2001) 113 LGERA 148; and *NSW Aboriginal Land Council v Minister Administering the Crown Land Management Act 2016 – Helensburgh Police Station* (n 28) [125].

[34] J Braithwaite, T Makkai and V Braithwaite, *Regulating Aged Care: Ritualism and the New Pyramid* (Cheltenham, Edward Elgar, 2007).

The scale of that oscillation between recognition and non-recognition is demonstrated in the bottleneck of claims; in 2021 there were 39,000 outstanding claims that will take over 100 years to resolve at current rates of clearance.[35] It demonstrates the ritualism of departments who are subject to regulatory frameworks and publicly recognise and promote the recognition of Indigenous rights by means of statute but also internally reject or display routine behaviour in defiance of the statute's intent. As Stein J noted in *Darkingung Local Aboriginal Land Council v Minister for Natural Resources (No 2)*, 'the legislation resembles the act of giving food with one hand and taking it away with the other, before the food has reached the mouth'.[36]

4.2. Judicial Assessment of Cultural Significance in Court Cases

As seen in the discussion of the UNDRIP in section 3, the recognition of cultural significance is fundamental to the recognition of Indigenous rights. It therefore follows that the cases the Court hears in relation to issues to do with cultural significance to Indigenous peoples are particularly important. These issues can arise in the different contexts discussed in section 2.

Before looking at some examples of those cases, it is useful to note that there is a general body of literature dealing with Aboriginal cultural heritage laws in NSW that discusses the Court in passing.[37] Much of that literature focuses on the long-awaited overhaul of NSW's outdated and inadequate Aboriginal cultural heritage system, with scholars analysing the adequacy of various iterations of reform proposed by the NSW government over the last twenty years.[38] Other literature relating to Aboriginal cultural heritage laws generally focuses on discrete issues, such as the issue of who 'speaks for Country' when it comes to Aboriginal cultural heritage,[39] and deficiencies in existing consultation practices about Aboriginal cultural heritage.[40] The work of the Court must be seen against this backdrop and, generally speaking, it is recognised that the Court has had a significant impact in assessing the cultural significance of a site in a way that recognises unique Indigenous cultural value of land and cultural heritage. It has done so in cases concerning Class 1 appeals.[41]

[35] C Ronalds, 'A Review of the Land Negotiation Program, A Review Conducted for the Department of Planning, Industry and the Environment' (Frederick Gordon Chambers, Sydney, 2020).

[36] *Darkingung Local Aboriginal Land Council v Minister for Natural Resources (No 2)* (1987) 61 LGRA 218, 203.

[37] See, for example, J Hunt and S Ellsmore, 'Navigating a Path through Delays and Destruction: Aboriginal Cultural Heritage Protection in New South Wales Using Native Title and Land Rights' in PF McGrath (ed), *The Right to Protect Sites: Indigenous Heritage Management in the Era of Native Title* (Canberra, Australian Institute of Aboriginal and Torres Strait Islander Studies, 2016); and L Butterly and R Pepper, 'Are Courts Colour-blind to Country: Indigenous Cultural Heritage, Environmental Law and the Australian Judicial System (2017) 40 *University of New South Wales Law Journal* 1313.

[38] eg K Lingard et al, 'Are We There Yet? A Review of the Proposed Aboriginal Cultural Heritage Laws in New South Wales, Australia' (2021) 28 *International Journal of Cultural Property* 107.

[39] N Laing and K Stanford, 'Who "Speaks for Country" in NSW?' (2015) 18 *Law Society of New South Wales Journal* 88.

[40] K Lingard, 'The Impact of the Law on Consultation Practices and Purpose: A Case Study of Aboriginal Cultural Heritage consultations in NSW' (2012) 1 *International Journal of Rural Law and Policy* ID 2712.

[41] *Kirkness v Gosford City Council* [2012] NSWLEC 1060.

For example, commentators have expressed approval of the wider 'landscape perspective' of Aboriginal cultural heritage that was taken in the Court's judgment in *Darkinjung Local Aboriginal Land Council v Minister for Planning and Infrastructure* (*Darkinjung*).[42] In *Darkinjung*, Commissioner Dixon and Acting Commissioner Sullivan upheld objector Class 1 appeals under the EPA Act on the basis that the proposed expansion of a sand quarry would, inter alia, have a negative impact on Aboriginal cultural heritage. In arriving at this conclusion, the Court applied the Burra Charter principles – a set of Australian guidelines for heritage conservation practice in Australia.[43] The Burra Charter principles include the difference between tangible and intangible elements, and the principles of ecologically sustainable development (ESD), including the precautionary principle. They also include recognition of the dynamic nature of cultural significance. The Court used the guidelines to both structure and guide its analysis to determine the connectedness and relationship between sites and their location in the broader landscape.

There is consensus that this judgment reflects a more enlightened approach to the conceptualisation of Aboriginal cultural heritage, revealing that judicial understandings have moved beyond the older archaeological focus on 'relics' to embrace a more holistic view of the complex, living and often intangible nature of Aboriginal cultural heritage. This approach can be seen in other Court cases, although this does not necessarily result in an area being found to have cultural significance.[44] That said, the approach in *Darkinjung* marks a progression in the recognition of Aboriginal law by courts as envisaged by the UNDRIP in relation to the notion that Aboriginal culture is static and unchanging. Across several articles including Articles 11, 12 and 31, the language of 'maintain, control, protect and develop their cultural heritage' is repeated. It reveals a more sophisticated understanding of cultural heritage that is beyond artefacts.[45] Similarly, Sack and others argue that *Darkinjung* demonstrates that the Court 'is moving with contemporary practice in cultural heritage assessment and management'.[46] The Court has also contributed to greater public education and understanding of the unique nature of Aboriginal culture, which would more indirectly contribute to the achievement of the rights in these articles. The decision in *Darkinjung* especially is an exemplary example of the way the Court has developed process to bring to the fore recognition of Indigenous culture, for example the Court's use of the Burra Charter.

If *Darkinjung* is a high watermark, then *Chief Executive of the Office of Environment and Heritage v Ausgrid*[47] (*Ausgrid*) may be a low-watermark decision in terms of recognition of Aboriginal cultural heritage. The case concerned sentencing after Ausgrid had pleaded guilty to an offence under section 86(2) of the NPWA due to it harming an Aboriginal object. As Alison Packham notes, the rock engraving

> was particularly significant because of the high rate of destruction of Aboriginal cultural heritage and that it was a rare example of an intact engraving that could not be replaced.

[42] *Darkinjung Local Aboriginal Land Council v Minister for Planning and Infrastructure* [2015] NSWLEC 1465.
[43] Australia International Council on Monuments and Sites, *Burra Charter and Practice Notes* (2017).
[44] *Hunter Environment Lobby Inc v Minister for Planning and Infrastructure (No 2)* [2014] NSWLEC 129.
[45] Butterly and Pepper (n 37), 1330.
[46] B Sack et al, 'Determining the Adequacy of Aboriginal Cultural Heritage Assessments: Amber Lights and Red Lights (2016) 33(3) *Environmental and Planning Law Journal* 264, 269.
[47] *Chief Executive of the Office of Environment and Heritage v Ausgrid* (2013) 199 LGERA 1.

> Further, it was a marker of the cultural route between the site of the engraving and Narrabeen Lake. It was part of the story of the landscape as a whole and its significance could not be viewed in isolation.[48]

Justice Pepper, however, held that the prosecution failed to adequately prove the significance of the rock engraving, and as a result held that for the purposes of sentencing the environmental harm was 'moderate' instead of 'substantial'.

Packham, who worked on the case, has been critical of this finding, arguing that the significance of Aboriginal cultural heritage should be a matter for Aboriginal people and that current legal approaches that require proof of the significance of Aboriginal culture, including reliance on the values in the Burra Charter, demand that Aboriginal values 'be explained and dissected in a manner that fits a traditional Western analysis'.[49] She further argues that Pepper J's observations about the lack of maintenance, care and attention of the rock engraving in question 'imposed Western values of how significant sites should be maintained'.[50] In this respect, she writes:

> The danger in this approach is that the intricacies of the connection between culture and landscape and how individual objects and places relate to this story are lost. Issues such as rarity, research potential, representativeness and educational potential are relevant to a Western notion of significance; however, they do not necessarily transfer to the Aboriginal value system. As Sullivan argues, Aboriginal concepts of value include the additional *Burra Charter* value of spiritual value. Further, and as Taubman argues, the problem of expressing significance in terms of the categories of the *Burra Charter* is that it can emphasise certain values over others and a rock engraving with outstanding aesthetic value may attract greater protection than a sacred site that lacks obvious signs of human activity.[51]

The Burra Charter criticism is a valid one. The UNDRIP is a declaration that responds to the imposition of Western frameworks upon Indigenous culture. Hunt and Ellsmore also criticise Pepper J's comments on the fact that the site was covered in leaf matter and dirt and was not protected by a fence,[52] arguing that this would be the case 'for all but a tiny majority of known sites in New South Wales'.[53]

Packham also notes that Pepper J's finding about the significance of the rock engraving showed that she had viewed the incident in isolation and failed to take into account the cumulative effect of the destruction of Aboriginal cultural heritage.[54] Packham argues that '[m]easuring degrees of strength of significance is "counterintuitive and perhaps counterproductive"' and 'a more integrated approach that protects cultural landscapes, or "Country" is required'.[55]

That said, there are other judgments in which the importance of cultural heritage and Country have been recognised. *Gloucester Resources* discussed in section 2 is one

[48] A Packham, 'Between a Rock and a Hard Place: Legislative Shortcomings Hindering Aboriginal Cultural Heritage Protection' (2014) 31 *Environmental and Planning Law Journal* 75, 81.
[49] ibid 82.
[50] ibid, 83.
[51] ibid, 83.
[52] Hunt and Ellsmore (n 37) 86.
[53] ibid, 86.
[54] Packham (n 48) 83.
[55] ibid, 83.

example,[56] but there are also other examples.[57] What these judgments highlight is not just the importance of giving recognition to Aboriginal cultural heritage but also to developing a body of reasoning and legal practice concerning recognition as well as the legal consequences of such recognition.[58] I now turn to some examples of how the Court has developed a body of law concerning those consequences.

4.3. Damage or Destruction of Aboriginal Cultural Heritage: Penalties Imposed by the Court

One obvious example of the Court needing to develop legal reasoning relates to sentencing. *Ausgrid* is one illustration of the Court's role in prosecutions and sentencing under the NPWA in relation to the protection of Aboriginal cultural heritage.[59] As will be seen in section 4.4, in exercising its Class 5 jurisdiction, the Court has developed a set of restorative justice practices. The focus here is on sentencing – an exercise of Court power that recognises Indigenous rights both practically and symbolically. The Court's case law in this area is part and parcel of a larger case law on sentencing for environmental crime.[60] As White has noted, in developing this case law the Court has been mindful of its role as a 'problem solving court'.[61] It is also circumscribed by what legislation allows as a maximum penalty, an issue I will return to below.

To harm an Aboriginal object or place without an Aboriginal Heritage Impact Permit is a strict liability offence.[62] To date, there have been few prosecutions for the strict liability offences of harming Aboriginal objects and places under the Act, with only five such prosecutions occurring prior to 2018.[63] While the penalties that may be imposed by the Court are determined by statute and the decision to investigate and prosecute lies outside of the powers of the Court,[64] the Court retains the ability to deter offenders and denounce the offending in its sentencing jurisprudence.

Penalties imposed by the Court for offences relating to Aboriginal cultural heritage are significant in terms of protection of Aboriginal cultural heritage and play a role in future deterrence. The low fine imposed in *Ausgrid* did not recognise the damage caused to Aboriginal cultural heritage. The NSW Aboriginal Land Council expressed extreme

[56] *Gloucester Resources* (n 11). For discussion, see Watts et al (n 13).

[57] *Anderson v Ballina Shire Council* (n 8) and *Milne v Minister for Planning (No 2)* [2007] NSWLEC 66. See also the discussion below.

[58] A Sneddon, 'Dynamic Heritage and Static Maps: A Comment on the Critical Distinction Between Identifying and Assessing "Re-inscribed" Indigenous Heritage Places in Australian Heritage Practice' (2021) 87 *Australian Archaeology* 144.

[59] Lingard et al (38), 22.

[60] See White, this volume.

[61] R White, 'Reparative Justice, Environmental Crime and Penalties for the Powerful' (2017) 67 *Crime, Law and Social Change* 117, 122.

[62] NPWA, ss 86–87.

[63] *Garrett v Williams* (2007) 151 LGERA 92; *Plath v O'Neill* (2007) 174 A Crim R 336; *Director of National Parks and Wildlife Service v Histollo Pty Ltd* [1995] 88 LGERA 214; *Chief Executive of the Office of Environment and Heritage v Ausgrid* (n 55); *Chief Executive, Office of Environment and Heritage v. Clarence Valley Council*, (2018) 236 LGERA 291.

[64] For criticism of the monitoring and enforcement of offences relating to Aboriginal cultural heritage, see Lingard et al (n 38).

disappointment about the sentence.[65] The Metropolitan Local Aboriginal Land Council also expressed the view that the sentence sent a message to developers that they would only receive a 'slap on the wrist' for destroying Aboriginal heritage.[66]

In other cases, fines have been more significant. In *Chief Executive, Office of Environment and Heritage v Clarence Valley Council* (*Clarence Valley River*) a $300,000 fine was imposed on the Clarence River Council for destruction of a scar tree,[67] which is a tree that has bark removed for cultural purposes such as the construction of a canoe. This was a small but fleeting victory and was 'at least a heftier fine that the $4,690 fine energy company Ausgrid was given for destroying a known urban heritage site in Cromer just three years earlier'.[68] It is also important to note that only to focus on fines is to miss the bigger picture. Restorative justice practices are discussed in the next section, but it is also the case that legal costs and loss of property values can be significant in these cases even if the fines are relatively small.[69] More significantly, what can be seen in these cases is a structured and reasoned approach to sentencing in which the Court is considering both the objective circumstances of the offence and the subjective circumstances of the defendant.[70]

In understanding these decisions, it is also important to see the role that legislative change plays. As Justice Preston noted in *Clarence Valley Council*, there was in 2010 a fifty-fold increase in the maximum penalty for 'knowingly harming or desecrating an Aboriginal object' 'from 200 penalty units ($22,000) to 10,000 penalty units ($1,100,000)'.[71] As he then went on to note, that change

> reflects the increased seriousness with which the legislature (and the community) views the protection and conservation of Aboriginal cultural heritage and the offences of harming Aboriginal cultural heritage. This increased level of concern about the offences, as reflected in the increased maximum penalty, is to be reflected in the sentences which the Court impose: *R v Howland* (1999) 104 A Crim R 273; [1999] NSWCCA 10 at [17].[72]

4.4. Restorative Justice Conferences in the Court

One of the most significant practices that the Court has developed in relation to offences of destruction and harming objects of Aboriginal significance is restorative justice. Restorative justice has been important to Indigenous communities as it has developed in Australia.[73] This is because restorative justice adopts a less punitive approach to wrongdoing and adopts one of mediation and agreement. It seeks to restore, as much as possible, a sense of dignity to the victim. Restorative justice has been adopted in the

[65] Hunt and Ellsmore (n 37) 86.
[66] Packham (n 48) 84.
[67] See *Chief Executive, Office of Environment and Heritage v Clarence Valley Council* (n 63).
[68] J Hunt, 'Cultural Vandalism: Regulated Destruction of Aboriginal Cultural Heritage in New South Wales' (Centre for Aboriginal Economic Policy Research, ANY College of Arts & Social Sciences, 2020).
[69] *Plath v O'Neill* (n 63) [95], [105].
[70] ibid and *Garrett v Williams* (n 63).
[71] *Clarence Valley Council* (n 63) [38].
[72] ibid, [39].
[73] R White, 'Indigenous Communities, Environmental Protection, and Restorative Justice' (2014) 18 *Australian Indigenous Law Review* 43.

criminal justice sector particularly in sentencing circles involving Indigenous elders and in youth and family conferencing. The development of restorative justice processes by the Court has been identified by several scholars who have noted in passing or examined in some detail the use of restorative justice processes in the Court in matters involving Aboriginal litigants.[74] Such developments have been possible because the Court operates within a relatively flexible legislative framework.[75] Accordingly, the Court has over time developed practices, and restorative justice is accommodated in its practice notes.[76]

The first restorative justice conference in the Court's criminal jurisdiction occurred in *Garrett v Williams*.[77] In this matter, the defendant (a director of a mining company) entered a plea of guilty to a series of offences under the NPWA in relation to destroying Aboriginal objects. At the time, the maximum penalty for each of the offences was, for an individual such as the defendant, $5,500 or imprisonment for six months or both.[78]

Prior to sentencing, Preston CJ asked the parties if they wished to participate in a restorative justice conference. The parties agreed, and the conference was attended by the parties, as well as representatives of the Broken Hill Aboriginal Land Council. The role of restorative justice is to allow voices and positions to be ventilated in a manner that adversarial litigation cannot achieve. It enables perspectives to come to the fore that normally would not be heard by either party, as the defendant stated in evidence to the Court:

> During the course of these proceedings [ie as a result of the restorative justice conference] I have learnt a significant amount about Aboriginal archaeology and the importance of the Aboriginal place. I have also realised how both Aboriginal objects and the Aboriginal place are more important to Aboriginal people than I had previously appreciated. … I believe that I can confidently say that a situation such as the present will not arise again.[79]

The Court took into account the defendant's participation in the restorative justice conference and the significant costs that the defendant has incurred in, and as a result of, that conference; as well as the defendant's offers to meet further costs.[80] The contrition and the remorse of the defendant was also recognised.[81]

In terms of outcome, the defendant offered to pay the fees and disbursements of the facilitator for the restorative justice conference (which were estimated to be around $11,000 for four days' preparation and conferencing). The defendant and representatives of the Broken Hill Local Aboriginal Land Council also reached preliminary agreement for ongoing collaboration.[82] Further progress resulted in agreement in how to 'discuss moving forward in a cooperative manner'. These included: fostering indigenous

[74] J McDonald, 'Restorative Justice Process in Case Law' (2008) 33(1) *Alternative Law Journal* 41; BJ Preston, 'The Use of Restorative Justice for Environmental Crime (2011) 35 *Criminal Law Journal* 136; and M Hamilton, 'Restorative Justice Intervention in an Aboriginal Cultural Heritage Protection Context: Chief Executive, Office of Environment and Heritage v Clarence Valley Council' (2019) 36 *Environmental and Planning Law Journal* 197.

[75] White (n 73).

[76] Land and Environment Court of New South Wales, *Practice Note: Class 5 Proceedings* (2020) [28].

[77] *Garrett v Williams* (n 63).

[78] NPWA, s 90(1).

[79] ibid, [110].

[80] ibid, [117].

[81] ibid, [133].

[82] ibid, [62].

employment opportunities; establishing a Wilykali Pinnacles Heritage Trust to which the defendant would donate; donation of equipment; and the preparation of a Cultural Heritage Archaeological Management Plan to be used as a preliminary basis in their work towards the development of a Voluntary Conservation Agreement.[83]

In 2019 another restorative justice conference was utilised in the Court in *Clarence Valley Council*,[84] discussed above. The case involved a prosecution for an offence of destroying an Aboriginal object under section 86(1) of the NPWA. In this matter, a scar tree was lopped and removed. The parties agreed to a restorative justice conference, which was held at the Gurehlgam Indigenous Healing Centre and attended by the mayor, the deputy mayor, the general manager of the council, council field officers and members of the local Aboriginal community. As Justice Preston said of the conference:

> The restorative justice conference in this case recognised and gave primary voice to the Aboriginal people whose cultural heritage had been harmed by the commission of the offence. The conference allowed the Aboriginal people to express their views on the significance of the Aboriginal object that had been harmed and how that in turn had harmed both them individually and the Aboriginal community generally. The conference provided a forum for the Aboriginal people to express their views on the matters that the Court is required to take into consideration in sentencing for an offence under the NPW Act s 194(1)(a), (b) and (f).[85]

The Council paid to facilitate the restorative conference ($13,000) as well as paying the prosecutors' costs ($48,000). More importantly, the restorative justice conference informed the amount to be paid ($300,000) in order to facilitate a programme devised and agreed to at the conference which included funding a series of initiatives for supporting the protection and fostering of Aboriginal heritage in the area.[86]

The use of restorative justice initiatives in sentencing in the Court advances the principle of participation in decision-making as set out in the UNDRIP. In particular these examples can be seen as giving meaning to the adjudicative and participatory rights in Article 27. Restorative justice is a series of fair and impartial participatory processes.

5. Intergenerational Equity

The final issue to raise in relation to the Land and Environment Court and the UNDRIP is the concept of intergenerational equity. As stated above, the corpus of Indigenous peoples' rights is one predicated on land. The importance of land is fundamental to Indigenous cultures. Indigenous peoples do not view land as an economic asset but view it as relational, connecting Indigenous peoples to ancestors and to future generations. For this reason, the intergenerational equity of land decisions is critical to the survival of culture.[87] The jurisprudence of the Court has contributed to a more nuanced understanding of Indigenous peoples' obligation of stewardship for the benefit of present and

[83] ibid, [63].
[84] *Clarence Valley Council* (n 63).
[85] ibid, [105].
[86] ibid, [121].
[87] *Darkinjung Local Aboriginal Land Council v Minister for Planning and Infrastructure* (n 42) [142]–[190].

future members for the culture to survive. Intergenerational equity is also a principle of ESD.[88] Thus, this case law has seen a symbiosis between these two different areas of legal thought, Aboriginal and Western. Ideas of intergenerational equity can be seen to animate much of the reasoning discussed above, but here it is useful to provide a few more examples. *Anderson v Director General, Department of Environment and Conservation* involved a challenge to the giving of consent for the destruction of objects under the NPWA.[89] One of the arguments before the Court was the legal relevance of intergenerational equity. Justice Pain stated:

> [The decision-maker] is not literally required by the NPW Act to refer to [ESD principles] but in the circumstances of this case it is striking that he has not referred to issues relevant to an assessment of significance from an inter-generational perspective. This is particularly so in light of the Applicants' claim that the reason this site was so important to them was because of the destruction on the other half of Angels Beach of Aboriginal objects significant to the Bandjalung people. … A key matter attested to in the Applicants' affidavits and evidence in the case is the importance to Aboriginal people of sites where their ancestors have been present demonstrated by, inter alia, the presence of objects which they consider significant by virtue of that association. Obviously the fewer of these sites that remain the less opportunity there will be for future generations of Aboriginal people to enjoy the cultural benefits of those sites.[90]

Another example, *Gloucester Resources*, discussed in section 2, found that distributive injustice or inequity would result from approval of the Rocky Hill Coal Project, and that this distributive inequity would disproportionately impact Aboriginal people.[91] The Court held that:

> The social impacts on culture and community, especially for the Aboriginal people whose Country has been mined, will persist. A sacred cultural land created by the Ancestors of the Aboriginal people cannot be recreated by mine rehabilitation. As discussed below, the Project will emit greenhouse gases and contribute to climate change, the consequences of which will burden future generations.[92]

In *Clarence Valley Council*,[93] the Court also recognised that destruction of the culturally significant scar tree caused intergenerational inequity. The Court observed:

> The protection and conservation of places, objects and features of cultural significance to Aboriginal people implements inter-generational equity by ensuring that the present generation, who have inherited cultural heritage from previous generations, maintains, enhances and bequeaths that cultural heritage for the benefit of future generations.[94]

[88] BJ Preston, 'What's Equity Got to Do with the Environment?' (2018) 92 *Australian Law Journal* 257.

[89] *Anderson v Director-General, Department of Environment and Conservation* (2006) 144 LGERA 43. On appeal, the NSW Court of Appeal also recognised the intergenerational equity in conservation of Aboriginal cultural heritage: *Anderson v Director General, Department of Environment and Climate Change* (2008) 163 LGERA 400 [85]–[92].

[90] *Anderson v Director-General, Department of Environment and Conservation* (n 89) [199].

[91] *Gloucester Resources* (n 11) [398], [407].

[92] ibid, [415].

[93] *Clarence Valley Council* (n 63).

[94] ibid, [27]. See also at [35], [105].

6. Process

The above is not an exhaustive analysis, but it highlights how the Land and Environment Court has evolved doctrines in relation to Indigenous rights. This is not just a story of law on the page, however. It is also a story of law in action. The Court as an institution has developed by necessity processes and practices to facilitate proper recognition of Indigenous issues, and this heightened sensitivity has allowed it to develop as an adjudicative forum. In particular it has attempted to manifest the principle expressed in Article 19 of the UNDRIP of ensuring 'free, prior and informed consent [of Indigenous peoples] before adopting and implementing legislative or administrative measures'.

It can be seen to do so in two ways. First, the Court allocates people with applicable expertise to hear and determine matters, matching the skill set of the decision-maker to the matter. Thus, Aboriginal Commissioners are allocated to hear and adjudicate matters concerning Aboriginal land rights. Aboriginal Commissioners, and those with expertise in Aboriginal cultural heritage, are allocated to hear and adjudicate matters concerning items and places of Aboriginal cultural significance. In *Darkinjung*, Acting Commissioner Sharon Sullivan, who had expertise in Aboriginal cultural heritage, was allocated to sit with Commissioner Dixon (as she then was).

Second, the subject matter of proceedings also informs the Court's process for allocations, and the hearing itself, to be respectful and sensitive to Aboriginal cultural beliefs that may be associated with an item or place of cultural significance. For example, smoking ceremonies have been held at the beginning of site views in several matters.

In *Darkinjung*,[95] as the proceedings related to a 'women's dreaming site' of significant cultural importance, not only were the Commissioners of the Court female, but the Court also facilitated a hearing which reflected a sensitivity and respect for this. This included: all parties briefed female counsel to appear on their behalf; a female member of the Planning Assessment Commission met on the site with Aboriginal women and elders to inspect places of Aboriginal cultural heritage significance;[96] a female Aboriginal Cultural Heritage Officer was the representative for the Guringai Tribal Link Aboriginal Corporation;[97] the majority of experts were female; males did not attend the women's site on the site view; and sensitive information about the women's site was redacted from the judgment.

7. Conclusion

This chapter has set out the framework of the UNDRIP – as a universally accepted normative framework for the recognition of Indigenous peoples' rights – as a template to assess the Land and Environment Court's contribution to the recognition of Indigenous environmental rights. As the UN says of recognition:

> Recognition of indigenous peoples as such is critical in and of itself but also paves the way for the fulfilment of the entire array of collective and individual rights enshrined in the

[95] *Darkinjung* (n 48).
[96] ibid, [109].
[97] ibid, [150].

> Declaration and other sources of international law, including self-determination, rights to lands, territories and resources, and cultural rights. Recognition of the rights under the Declaration should involve constitutional and statutory forms in addition to concrete actions, including measures of reparation for past wrongs.[98]

The work of the Court in relation to Indigenous peoples' rights is an important example of the way legal systems put 'meat on the bones' of those rights. A study of the work of the Court is thus critical internationally and domestically to an understanding of the effective operationalising of Indigenous rights.

This chapter has set out five ways in which the Court is having a meaningful influence in promoting Indigenous justice: hearing appeals under the ALRA; developing legal reasoning in relation to 'cultural significance'; sentencing practices; restorative justice practices; and intergenerational equity reasoning. This not only develops the law but also develops legal processes. These examples show the way the Court is giving voice and recognition to Aboriginal people.

[98] 'Efforts to Implement the United Nations Declaration on the Rights of Indigenous Peoples: Recognition, Reparation and Reconciliation', Report of the Expert Mechanism on the Rights of Indigenous Peoples A/HRC/EMRIP/2019/3/Rev.1, [17].

10

The Administrative Law Expertise of the Land and Environment Court of New South Wales

ELIZABETH FISHER*

1. Introduction

Administrative law is the law of public administration.[1] Much of the adjudicative work of the Land and Environment Court of New South Wales (the Court) concerns public administration – both local and state government institutions. Ergo, much of the legal work of the Court is administrative law work.[2] Given the nature of environmental/planning problems and environmental/planning law, that legal work has required judges to be 'active'. By this I mean judges have had to apply and develop administrative law doctrine in a manner responsive to the complexity of environmental and planning law and the problems these areas of law apply to.[3] The end result is that over its forty-year history the Court has developed considerable administrative law expertise. Highlighting that expertise highlights the importance of having a 'thicker' legal understanding of the Court and of environmental courts more generally.

The chapter is structured as follows. An overview of the administrative law jurisdictions of the Court is examined in section 2. In sections 3–5 I explore three examples of the active administrative law work of the Court: in interpreting 'legislation'; in the judicial review of factual evaluation; and in the judicial review of the exercise of judgement. In the last section I reflect on what this survey of case law reveals about the expertise of the Court and the implications of this for thinking about the role and nature of environmental courts.

* I am grateful to Katie Allan, Mark Aronson, Joanna Bell, Navya Jannu, Brian Preston, Samuel Ruiz-Tagle and Ceri Warnock for comments on an earlier draft of this chapter. Any errors or omissions remain my own.

[1] E Fisher and S Shapiro, *Administrative Competence: Rethinking Administrative Law* (Cambridge, Cambridge University Press, 2020).

[2] I am grateful to Katie Allan for the concept of 'administrative law work'.

[3] See also D Fisher, this volume, and Ceri Warnock, *Environmental Courts and Tribunals: Powers, Integrity and the Search for Legitimacy* (Oxford, Hart Publishing, 2020).

Three points should be made before starting. First, I proceed on the basis that the reader has a nodding acquaintance with administrative law.[4] Second, my analysis focuses on judicial review doctrine. The role of merits review should not be discounted, however.[5] Third, given space, my analysis is illustrative not exhaustive. In this chapter it is only possible to glimpse the legal richness of the Court's administrative law work. I have weighted my analysis towards a study of a 'mine-run'[6] of recent cases to show that the administrative law expertise of the Court is not a historic relic.[7]

2. The 'Active' Administrative Law Work of the Land and Environment Court

Much of environmental and planning law is administrative law. It consists of legislative regimes that vest powers, duties and other legal obligations in local and state administrative decision-makers in relation to environmental problems and planning governance.[8] While many of these statutes create legally conventional powers for administrative action, particularly in relation to authorising activities, this legislation is also often legally novel. It introduces new types of legal obligations and powers into the law.[9] Alongside legislation are swathes of delegated legislation and policy.[10] These regimes create structures for administrative decision-making processes and may require different forms of factual assessment and deliberative processes. These may include (but are not limited to): general duties to consider environmental impact;[11] specific obligations to consider types of environment impact statement;[12] third party appeal processes;[13] and multi-step decision processes.[14]

All this means that a significant part of the Court's workload relates to administrative law. The Court has powers of merits review in Classes 1–3 of its jurisdiction regarding

[4] For those wanting an overview of Australian judicial review doctrine, see M Aronson, M Groves and G Weeks, *Judicial Review of Administrative Action and Government Liability*, 7th edn (London, Thomson Reuters, 2021).

[5] E Fisher, 'Administrative Law, Pluralism and the Legal Construction of Merits Review in Australian Environmental Courts and Tribunals' in L Pearson, C Harlow and M Taggart (eds), *Administrative Law in a Changing State: Essays in Honour of Mark Aronson* (Oxford, Hart Publishing, 2008) and Elizabeth Fisher, 'Administrative Tribunals: An Essay about the Legal Imagination of Administrative Law Scholars' in J Goudkamp, L McDonald and M Lunney, (eds) *Taking Law Seriously: Essays in Honour of Peter Cane* (Oxford, Hart Publishing, 2022).

[6] K Llewellyn, *The Common Law Tradition: Deciding Appeals* (Boston, MA, Little Brown, 1960) ch 1.

[7] That case law also builds on the previous decisions of the Court. For a discussion of this, see Preston, this volume.

[8] eg Environmental Planning and Assessment Act 1979 (NSW) (EPA Act); Local Government Act 1983 (NSW); and Biodiversity Conservation Act 2016 (NSW). See also s 20(3) of the Land and Environment Court Act 1979 (NSW) (LEC Act) listing legislation which are 'planning and environmental law'.

[9] Douglas Fisher, this volume.

[10] On the legal significance of policy, see G Weeks and L Pearson, 'Planning and Soft Law' (2018) 24 *Australian Journal of Administrative Law* 252, 257–65.

[11] eg s 5.5 EPA Act.

[12] eg s 5.7 EPA Act.

[13] eg 8.8 EPA Act.

[14] eg ss 4.11–4.20 EPA Act.

a range of administrative decisions made under different pieces of legislation.[15] Not all appeals in these classes will raise administrative law issues, but many will. In its Class 4 jurisdiction, the Court hears judicial review cases.[16] The Court also has powers to hear appeals on questions of law against a decision or an order of a Commissioner made in appeals in Classes 1–3 and 8 of its jurisdictions.[17] Administrative actions (eg enforcement or information notices) may also be collaterally challenged.[18]

The Court is not carrying out this administrative law adjudicative work in a vacuum; its judges have the status of, and can serve as, judges of the Supreme Court.[19] Much of the administrative law doctrine relating to the Court comes from the NSW Court of Appeal,[20] due to the legislated routes of appeal to that court from the Land and Environment Court.[21] As a superior court of record, the Court is applying its own precedents and those of higher courts.[22] Likewise, in practice the jurisdictions of the Land and Environment Court cannot always be easily cleaved from that of the Supreme Court.[23]

The Court is kept busy with its administrative law work.[24] Environmental and planning legislation has a broad reach. Planning and environmental decision-making is contentious. Collective decisions are required to be made which will result in winners and losers: 'One person's perceived potential development bonanza may be another person's consequential construction curse.'[25] The polycentric impact of decision-making also means that there are often legal disputes over what exactly a decision-maker should take into account.[26] This is made more complicated due to the exact nature of ecological impacts often being difficult to ascertain.[27] Parties to a case are also often putting forward competing visions of what is good administrative decision-making.[28]

Referring to the socio-political and scientific complexity of environmental and planning controversies may give the impression that the administrative law work of the Court is not particularly legal. That is far from being the case. That complexity is embedded in the legislative regimes discussed above. In carrying out administrative law adjudication, the Court must make legal sense of these legislative frameworks and

[15] Appeals in Classes 1, 2, 3 ss 17–19 LEC Act.

[16] Class 4, s 20(2) LEC Act 1979. Also note Class 8, mining matters, s 21B LEC Act.

[17] s 56A LEC Act.

[18] *Environment Protection Authority v Eastern Creek Operations Pty Limited* [2020] NSWLEC 182.

[19] The converse is also true. LEC Act, s 11A and Supreme Court Act 1970 (NSW), s 37B.

[20] For this reason in this chapter I cite the relevant case law from the Court of Appeal.

[21] ss 57–58 LEC Act.

[22] BJ Preston, 'Administrative Law in an Environmental Context: An Update' (2007) 15 *Australian Journal of Administrative Law* 11.

[23] eg consider the issue of injunctive relief: *Minister for Local Government v Blue Mountains City Council* [2018] NSWCA 133; (2018) 97 NSWLR 1132; (2018) 229 LGERA 197, [59]–[90].

[24] For statistics, see Land and Environment Court of New South Wales, *Annual Review 2020* (State of New South Wales, 2021) 33–34.

[25] *Manning v Bathurst Regional Council (No 2)* [2013] NSWLEC 186; (2013) 199 LGERA 147, [74].

[26] On the legal significance of polycentricity in environmental decision-making, see *Bulga Milbrodale Progress Association Inc v Minister for Planning and Infrastructure and Warkworth Mining Limited* [2013] NSWLEC 48, (2013) 194 LGERA 347, [31]–[43], upheld by *Warkworth Mining Limited v Bulga Milbrodale Progress Association Inc* [2014] NSWCA 105; (2014) 86 NSWLR 527; (2014) 200 LGERA 375.

[27] *Newcastle & Hunter Valley Speleological Society Inc v Upper Hunter Shire Council and Stoneco Pty Limited* [2010] NSWLEC 48; (2010) 210 LGERA 126.

[28] E Fisher, *Risk Regulation and Administrative Constitutionalism* (Oxford, Hart Publishing, 2007) ch 4.

the powers that those frameworks grant to administrative law decision-makers. Even in merits review, the Court needs to ask a series of legal questions, particularly around its jurisdiction.[29] A single judicial review case may require analysis of doctrine, primary legislation, regulations, state environmental planning policies (SEPPs), local environmental plans, consent conditions, expert reports, and impact statements.[30]

But the Court must also relate those frameworks to more generic administrative law doctrines that operate in Australian administrative law. Mark Aronson has described this as requiring relating 'horizontal principles' as expressed in the grounds of judicial review, to the 'vertical rules' of a governing statute.[31] As he notes:

> Any application for judicial review of an administrative exercise of statutory power requires a consideration of both the generic and the specific. The most difficult task in many cases lies in fixing the meeting point of the horizontal and vertical axes – more specifically, how best to fit the particular with the generic.[32]

While the Land and Environment Court is a specialist Court, it is not exempt from this process of finding the 'best fit' between these two axes. Indeed, as we will see in sections 2–5, it is this process that is often animating legal reasoning.

Finding that 'best fit' often involves the Court having to reconcile two different 'elements' of law. As Preston has noted:

> [Roscoe Pound] identifies in the legal system two elements: a traditional or habitual element and an enacted or imperative element. The latter is usually the modern element, exemplified by statute, and is becoming more predominant. The former is the older or historical element upon which juristic development proceeds by analogy. Pound posits that we must bring about the infusion of social ideas into the traditional element of the law. In this way there will be a body of law which will satisfy the demands of the society of today.[33]

The vertical and the horizontal will not always map onto the imperative and habitual – Preston is careful to use the word 'usually' – but what this makes clear is that there is more to the vertical and horizontal than them *just* being specific and general.

Thus, for example, Australian judicial review doctrine tends to display a formalistic reasoning style. There is a commitment to

> the employment of formal, conceptual and logical analysis, often related to literalism and sometimes originalism; a belief that law is an inductive science of principles drawn from the cases, rather than the application of broad, overarching principles to particular disputes; a downplaying of the role of principle, policy, values and justice.[34]

A prime example of legal formalism in Australian administrative law thought is the ongoing judicial commitment to ideas of jurisdictional error.[35] At the same time, as

[29] *Planners North v Ballina Shire Council* [2021] NSWLEC 120.

[30] Eg *Denoci Pty Ltd v Liverpool City Council* [2020] NSWLEC 102 (local environmental plan and species impact statement) and *KEPCO Bylong Australia Pty Ltd v Bylong Valley Protection Alliance Inc* (2021) 250 LGERA 39; [2021] NSWCA 216.

[31] M Aronson, 'Judicial Review of Administrative Action: Between Grand Theory and Muddling Through' (2021) 28 *Australian Journal of Administrative Law* 6, 9.

[32] ibid.

[33] B Preston, 'The Art of Judging Environmental Law Disputes' (2008) 12 *Southern Cross Law Review* 103, 104.

[34] M Taggart, '"Australian Exceptionalism' in Judicial Review' (2008) 36 *Federal Law Review* 1, 7.

[35] *Kirk v Industrial Court (NSW)* (2010) 239 CLR 531, 571. See LB Crawford and J Boughey, 'The Centrality of Jurisdictional Error: Rationale and Consequences' (2018) 30 *Public Law Review* 18.

noted above, environmental legislation tends to be novel, and reflects 'policy, values and justice'. The principles of ecologically sustainable development as included in several NSW statutes are a case in point.[36]

The Court's judicial review jurisdictions sit alongside its merits review jurisdictions. This requires the Court to be self-conscious and explicit about how it is exercising its legal powers as the mixture of classes of jurisdictions creates an awareness about the relationship between jurisdiction and doctrinal method. Thus, the Court continually demarcates the line between merits and judicial review and the different legal tasks involved.[37] The diversity of the Court's jurisdictions creates an acute 'fidelity' to any legal task being undertaken – a fidelity enforced by the appellate system.[38] Case law concerning the powers of Commissioners in merits review is a case in point.[39]

Furthermore, the structural complexity of environmental problems noted above will also affect the application of the vertical and horizontal and the imperative and habitual. Much of the case law of the Court thus involves decisions incorporating some form of expert analysis and/or gives rise to considerable community conflict.[40] This is because this structural complexity is often legally novel and thus legal imagination needs to evolve to ensure robust application of the law.[41] For example, while the Court is applying mainstream grounds of judicial review in its Class 4 jurisdiction, that doctrine has often evolved with less polycentric and less scientifically embedded decision-making in mind than that involved in the Court's workload.[42]

Overall, the Court is engaging in *active* administrative law work. I do not mean that the Court is activist.[43] What I mean is that the Court cannot be passive.[44] It must sort through arguments and keenly and conscientiously apply and develop administrative law doctrine in a deliberate and responsive manner to environmental and

[36] For a discussion of this, see Scotford, this volume, and E Scotford, *Environmental Principles and the Evolution of Environmental Law* (Oxford, Hart Publishing, 2017) ch 5.

[37] *Drake-Brockman v Minister for Planning & Anor* [2007] NSWLEC 490, (2007) 158 LGERA 349, [123]–[124]; *Walsh v Parramatta City Council* [2007] NSWLEC 255, (2007) 161 LGERA 118; [56]; *Fullerton Cove Residents Action Group Incorporated v Dart Energy Ltd (No 2)* [2013] NSWLEC 38; (2013) 193 LGERA 222 [154]; *KEPCO Bylong Australia Pty Ltd v Independent Planning Commission (No 2)* [2020] NSWLEC 179 [158].

[38] BJ Preston, 'The Enduring Importance of the Rule of Law in Times of Change' (2012) 86 *Australian Law Journal* 175, 184.

[39] *Ku-ring-gai Council v Bunnings Properties Pty Ltd* (2019) 236 LGERA 35, [2019] NSWCA 28. See Fisher (n 5) for a discussion.

[40] These are features of many different types of development and activity. Consider the cases cited in the footnotes and *Gray v Minister for Planning* [2006] NSWLEC 720; (2006) 152 LGERA 258 (natural resource development); *Friends of Tumblebee Incorporated v ATB Morton Pty Limited (No 2)* [2016] NSWLEC 16; (2016) 215 LGERA 157 (steel fabrication workshop and distribution facility); and *Oshlack v Rous Water* [2013] NSWCA 169; (2013) 194 LGERA 39 (water fluoridation).

[41] E Fisher, 'Environmental Law as "Hot" Law' (2013) 25 *Journal of Environmental Law* 347; E Fisher, 'EU Environmental Law and Legal Imagination' in P Craig and G de Búrca (eds), *The Evolution of EU Law*, 3rd edn (Oxford, Oxford University Press, 2021); and C Warnock, 'Environment and the Law: The Normative Force of Context and Constitutional Challenges' (2020) 32 *Journal of Environmental Law* 365.

[42] E Fisher, *Environmental Law: A Very Short Introduction* (Oxford, Oxford University Press, 2017) chs 5 and 10.

[43] A term that suffers from a lack of serious of analytical precision. See T Josev, *The Campaign Against the Courts: A History of the Judicial Activism Debate* (Alexandria, Federation Press, 2017).

[44] Although too often tribunals are thought of in such terms. See Fisher, 'Administrative Tribunals': (n 5).

planning law.[45] A single administrative decision can give rise to many different legal questions in relation to a range of issues and legislation.[46] In judicial review cases, the Court is regularly hearing overlapping arguments along the full spectrum of grounds of judicial review, including jurisdictional error;[47] jurisdictional fact;[48] procedural fairness;[49] improper purpose;[50] improper delegation;[51] public consultation obligations;[52] *Wednesbury* unreasonableness;[53] and not taking into account material considerations.[54] These legal arguments in section 56A appeals can also apply to the decisions of Commissioners.[55] Parties in these cases are putting forward a range of different administrative law arguments about why a decision is legally invalid.[56] Parties may also present 'distinctly contrasting decision-making matrices' in describing how decisions are made.[57] The Court must work through this legal material both to resolve disputes and to provide an authoritative and legitimate understanding of the law.[58] A rather obvious consequence of these arguments, and the legal and other material that the Court is working with, is that the Court's judgments are often quite long.

Detailed examples of this active administrative law expertise could easily fill a book. Trying to capture the legal complexity of this sort of legal work in the space of a chapter is a challenge. In the next three sections I sketch three aspects of the administrative law work the Land and Environment Court engages in: statutory construction; judicial review of factual assessment; and judicial review of the exercise of administrative judgement. Each of these aspects of the Court's work interlink and reinforce each other.

3. Statutory Construction

A focus on legislation is fundamental to Australian administrative law doctrinal method. In part this reflects the legal reality that statutes dominate administrative law. Environmental law is no exception. Delve into cases cited in the footnotes in this chapter and you will find that the Land and Environment Court is considering legal disputes in relation to a vast array of different legislative regimes that relate to environmental protection, planning, and local government. Legislation governs not only primary

[45] See also Douglas Fisher, this volume, and Warnock (n 3).

[46] *Hunter Industrial Rental Equipment Pty Ltd v Dungog Shire Council* [2019] NSWCA 147; (2019) 241 LGERA 321, [295].

[47] eg *Wirrabara Village Pty Limited v The Secretary of the Department of Planning and Environment* [2018] NSWLEC 138.

[48] eg *Ryan v Northern Regional Planning Panel (No 4)* [2020] NSWLEC 55.

[49] eg *Armidale Regional Council v O'Connor* [2020] NSWLEC 77, (2020) 245 LGERA 56.

[50] eg *Agricultural Equity Investments Pty Limited v The Hon Chris Hatcher MP, Minister for Resources and Energy, Special Minister* [2015] NSWLEC 23.

[51] eg *Kinloch v Newcastle City Council* [2016] NSWLEC 109.

[52] eg *Friends of Turramurra Inc v Minister for Planning* [2011] NSWLEC 128.

[53] eg *Boomerang & Blueys Residents Group Inc v New South Wales Minister for the Environment, Heritage and Local Government and MidCoast Council (No 2)* [2019] NSWLEC 202, [262]–[273].

[54] eg *Wollongong Coal Pty Ltd v Minister for Planning and Environment* [2016] NSWLEC 154.

[55] *278 Palmer St Pty Ltd v The Council of the City of Sydney* [2020] NSWLEC 165.

[56] eg see the ten grounds in *Australian Coal Alliance Incorporated v Wyong Coal Pty Ltd* [2019] NSWLEC 31.

[57] *Pittking Properties Pty Ltd v Waverley Council* [2020] NSWLEC 21, [82].

[58] On legitimacy and its relationship to environmental problems, see Warnock, this volume.

decision-makers but also the jurisdictions of the Court.[59] That legislation, delegated legislation and policy are not fixed. They are subject to ongoing reform. The Court is thus adjudicating in a crowded and dynamic legislative space.

This is not the only reason why legislation is a focus of administrative law method, however. The formalism of Australian judicial review doctrine places significant legal emphasis on statutory construction.[60] It is the starting point for determining what is a jurisdictional error[61] as well as other grounds of review.[62] It is also crucial in determining whether an error is so material as to warrant judicial intervention.[63] As Bateman and McDonald note, the High Court of Australia's judgment in *Project Blue Sky v Australian Broadcasting Authority*[64] has a 'centripetal' force that 'further draws administrative law analysis inward towards statutory specifics and statutory purpose'.[65]

In doing so, the Court is drawn into finding the 'best fit' between the vertical and the horizontal aspects of judicial review doctrine. A significant aspect of the legal method of the Court relates to legislation and involves an active process of statutory construction. These principles also apply to regulations, SEPPs, and local environmental plans.[66] Legal disputes may also arise in relation to interpreting consent conditions.[67]

Statutory construction is an exercise in working with text to determine meaning.[68] It requires 'intelligent reading' that encompasses a consideration of context and purpose.[69] That legal work exists in a 'symbiotic' relationship with the common law.[70] Some statutory language will have well-established legal 'connotations'.[71] Other language will not.[72] Overall, '[c]ourts try to avoid uncertainty by adopting a construction which gives statutory instruments and decisions practical effect'.[73]

[59] See the legal analysis in *Minister for Local Government* (n 23); *Ku-ring-gai Council* (n 39) and *Al Maha Pty Ltd v Huajun Investments Pty Ltd* [2018] NSWCA 245; (2018) 365 ALR 86; (2018) 233 LGERA 170.

[60] eg *Loder v Narrabri Shire Council* [2020] NSWLEC 109, [60]. For a general discussion of this in administrative law, see S Young, 'The Blue Sky Effect: A Repatriation of Judicial Review or a Search for Flexibility?' (2020) 27 *Australian Journal of Administrative Law* 165.

[61] eg *Brown v Randwick City Council* [2011] NSWLEC 172, (2011) 183 LGERA 382, [30]–[40].

[62] eg *Walsh* (n 37) [59].

[63] *Project Blue Sky v Australian Broadcasting Authority* (1998) 194 CLR 355.

[64] ibid.

[65] W Bateman and L McDonald, 'The Normative Structure of Australian Administrative Law' (2018) 45 *Federal Law Review* 153, 169.

[66] eg *JK Williams Staff Pty Limited v Sydney Water Corporation* (2021) 249 LGERA 109; [2021] NSWLEC 23, [61] and *Environment Protection Authority v Grafil Pty Ltd* (2019) 238 LGERA 147; [2019] NSWCCA 174 at [257]–[261], [272].

[67] *Muswellbrook Shire Council v Hunter Valley Energy Coal Pty Ltd* [2019] NSWCA 216; (2019) 238 LGERA 295 and *KEPCO Bylong Australia Pty Ltd* (n 30).

[68] K Hayne, 'Statutes, Intentions and the Courts: What Place Does the Notion of Intention (Legislative or Parliamentary) Have in Statutory Construction?' (2013) 13 *Oxford University Commonwealth Law Journal* 271, 272.

[69] ibid, 277. On how context is important to consider initially, see *SZTAL v Minister for Immigration and Border Protection* (2017) 262 CLR 362, [14].

[70] M Leeming, 'Theories and Principles Underlying the Development of the Common Law – The Statutory Elephant in the Room' (2013) 36 *University of New South Wales Law Journal* 1002, 1014 quoting Gleeson CJ in *Brodie v Singleton Shire Council* (2001) 206 CLR 512, 532 [31].

[71] ibid, 1015. One example of this is the idea of 'use of land' (see below) which is a long-established feature of planning legislation. See the discussion in *Chamwell Pty Ltd v Strathfield Council* [2007] NSWLEC 114; (2007) 151 LGERA 400 [27]–[28], [34]–[36].

[72] eg 'being land which displays the hydrological and floristic characteristics of coastal wetlands or littoral rainforests'. See *Reysson Pty Ltd v Minister Administering the Environmental Planning and Assessment Act 1979* [2020] NSWCA 281, (2020) 247 LGERA 277.

[73] *Ulan Coal Mines Limited v Minister for Planning and Moolarben Coal Mines Pty Limited* [2008] NSWLEC 185, (2008) 160 LGERA 20, [66].

This exercise in statutory construction may be about providing authoritative interpretations of legislative terms. What is a valid 'complying development certificate'[74] or the nature of 'development consent'[75] are two simple examples. Another is that the phrase '"use of land" is repeatedly deployed in the language of the [Environmental Planning and Assessment Act 1979] but is not defined by the Act'.[76] For example, whether something is a 'use of land' will determine whether it is an 'activity' and thus may be subject to the general environmental impact assessment obligation in section 5.5 of the EPA Act.[77] Given the wording of section 5.5 (see below), that requires also consideration of other legislation.[78] The Court has thus had to develop over time an authoritative understanding of what is 'use of land'.[79]

Given that different statutory terms will have different legal implications it is very quickly the case that statutory construction is not just a narrow exercise in interpreting specific terms. As a form of legal analysis, it must also encompass the legal context and framework any statutory term appears in. Take, for example, the issue of what is a legally valid development consent.[80] That has required development of a body of doctrine concerning its relationship to a development application; what legal material can be used to construe a development consent; and what are legally valid conditions to impose.[81] The consents for different types of development applications will also have different requirements in relation to conditions.[82] Overall, the Court, by providing an authoritative understanding of the legal nature of 'development consent', is making the planning system work properly and legitimately by creating stable understandings of a key term.

Statutory construction can also concern the duties of public bodies. Consider the question of statutory construction in *Bushfire Survivors for Climate Action Incorporated [BSCA] v Environment Protection Authority*.[83] The case concerned the duty placed on the Environment Protection Authority by section 9(1)(a) of the Protection of the Environment Administration Act 1991 (NSW). That subsection states that 'The Authority is required to – (a) develop environmental quality objectives, guidelines and policies to ensure environment protection.' The question before the Court concerned how this related to the Authority developing such instruments in relation to climate change. The Court concluded:

> [I]n the current circumstances, [it] includes a duty to develop instruments of the kind described to ensure the protection of the environment in New South Wales from climate

[74] *The Owners Strata Plan 83556 trading as Aspect Apartments v Dehsabzi* [2020] NSWLEC 175, [78]–[102].

[75] *Ku-ring-gai Council v Buyozo Pty Ltd* [2021] NSWCA 177, (2021) 248 LGERA 300.

[76] *Snowy Mountains Brumby Sustainability & Management Group Incorporated v State of New South Wales* [2020] NSWLEC 92, [25].

[77] s 5.1(1)(a) EPA Act.

[78] *Palm Beach Protection Group Incorporated v Northern Beaches Council* (2020) 250 LGERA 212; [2020] NSWLEC 156, [130]–[203].

[79] See the discussion of authorities in *Snowy Mountains Brumby Sustainability & Management Group Incorporated* (n 76) [19]–[28] (finding wild horse management in a national park a 'use of land').

[80] *Winn v Director General of National Parks and Wildlife and Ors* [2001] NSWCA 17, 130 LGERA 508, [4], [199].

[81] eg *Mison v Randwick Municipal Council* (1991) 23 NSWLR 734 and *Hunter Industrial Rental Equipment Pty Ltd* (n 46), [46]–[80], [295]–[311].

[82] eg *Ulan Coal Mines Limited* (n 73) [80] and *Pittwater Council v Minister for Planning* [2011] NSWLEC 162, (2011) 184 LGERA 419, [69].

[83] *Bushfire Survivors for Climate Action Incorporated v Environment Protection Authority* (2021) 250 LGERA 1; [2021] NSWLEC 92.

> change, although this does not demand that such instruments contain the level of specificity contended for by BSCA, such as regulating sources of greenhouse gas emissions in a way consistent with limiting global temperature rise to 1.5°C above pre-industrial levels. The EPA has a discretion as to the specific content of the instruments it develops under s 9(1)(a) to ensure the protection of the environment from climate change.[84]

As the Court found that the Authority had not performed its duties, it made an order of mandamus to compel it to do so.[85]

The Court's conclusions did not come out of nowhere. The Court's legal analysis of section 9(1)(a) and what it compels was grounded in an analysis of the statutory text, its purpose, administrative law doctrine (both general and specific), the institutional nature of the Authority, and the environmental logic of the powers and duties vested in it.[86] In providing an authoritative interpretation of section 9(1)(a) the Court was engaging with a rich and varied body of law.

Much statutory construction work is thus about stabilising the frameworks for administrative law action.[87] On the one hand, this might be seen as quite mundane work – what is 'consent' doesn't get the environmental law heart racing in the way environmental principles do – but it is crucial. Given the polycentricity and contestation that is involved in environmental and planning decisions,[88] these basic statutory terms are often subject to conflicting interpretations. As are the legislated processes for how appeals are heard;[89] what is reasonable relief;[90] and what are the fundamental steps in the consideration of a development application.[91] Much of the administrative law work is thus working through these competing interpretations to make clear what the law actually is. Given the diversity of legal argument put before it, the Court cannot be passive in its legal analysis.

4. Factual Assessment

Statutory construction is often thought of as a quintessentially legal enterprise. But environmental and planning statutes are often imposing a duty on decision-makers to assess complex facts and material.[92] The centrality of factual assessment to administrative decision-making in this area is one of the purposes behind the structure of the Land

[84] ibid, [16].
[85] ibid, [144]–[149].
[86] ibid, [20]–[59].
[87] See also E Fisher, 'Law and Energy Transitions: Wind Turbines and Planning Law in the UK' (2018) 38 *OJLS* 528.
[88] *Bulga Milbrodale Progress Association Inc* (n 26) and *Randren House Pty Ltd v Water Administration Ministerial Corporation* [2020] NSWCA 14, (2020) 246 LGERA 1, [11]–[16].
[89] eg *278 Palmer St Pty Ltd v The Council of the City of Sydney* [2020] NSWLEC 165 (dealing with appeals of issues to do with procedural fairness) *Segal & Anor v Waverley Council* [2005] NSWCA 310, (2005) 64 NSWLR 177, (2005) 64 LGERA 177.
[90] *Warringah Shire Council v Sedevcic* (1987) 10 NSWLR 335, 339–41 and *ACR Trading Pty Ltd v Fat-Sel Pty Ltd* (1987) 11 NSWLR 67, 82.
[91] *Manning* (n 25), [76].
[92] eg s 4.15 EPA Act.

and Environment Court and other environmental and planning courts.[93] The Court's merits review jurisdiction allows a form of external review of factual assessment and thus contributes to the legitimacy of decision-making.[94] This is also one of the reasons why merits review decisions have informal precedential value – they create authoritative frameworks that guide decision-makers in the complex assessment of environmental and planning issues.[95] But review of factual assessment is not the sole province of merits review. Not only is the possibility of a merits review appeal not available for all decisions[96] and all parties,[97] but given the assessment duties that are laid out in legislation, those duties inevitably give rise to legal questions.

Two classic examples of how factual assessment figures in judicial review concern the statutory construction and application of sections 5.5 and 5.7 of the EPA Act. Section 5.5 states:

> For the purpose of attaining the objects of this Act relating to the protection and enhancement of the environment, a determining authority in its consideration of an activity shall, notwithstanding any other provisions of this Act or the provisions of any other Act or of any instrument made under this or any other Act, examine and take into account to the fullest extent possible all matters affecting or likely to affect the environment by reason of that activity.

This creates an 'overarching duty'[98] that operates in relation to activity not caught by the main development control regimes of the EPA Act, and thus not subject to merits review appeals. Section 5.7 relates to a more specific set of circumstances. It states:

> A determining authority shall not carry out an activity, or grant an approval in relation to an activity, being an activity that is a prescribed activity, an activity of a prescribed kind or an activity that is likely to significantly affect the environment, unless –
>
> (a) the determining authority has obtained or been furnished with and has examined and considered an environmental impact statement in respect of the activity –
>
> (i) prepared in the prescribed form and manner by or on behalf of the proponent, and
> (ii) except where the proponent is the determining authority, submitted to the determining authority in the prescribed manner.

These are classic types of environmental impact assessment obligations that can be found in environmental legislation across the world.[99] In NSW they are complemented,

[93] E Fisher, '"Jurisdictional" Facts and "Hot" Facts: Legal Formalism, Legal Pluralism, and the Nature of Australian Administrative Law' (2015) 38 *Melbourne University Law Review* 968.

[94] Warnock, this volume, particularly her discussion of The Hon J S Cripps QC and others, Report of the Land and Environment Court Working Party (2001).

[95] See n 5; *Gloucester Resources Limited v Minister for Planning* [2019] NSWLEC 7; (2019) 234 LGERA 257; and Peel, this volume.

[96] eg where the decision has been made by the Independent Planning Commission with a public hearing. See s 8.6(3) EPA Act. An example of the type of judicial review action it begets is *KEPCO Bylong Australia Pty Ltd* (n 30).

[97] Compare the respective appeal right for applicants and objectors in s 8.7 and s 8.8 EPA Act. See *Stannards Marine Pty Ltd v North Sydney Council* (2021) 250 LGERA 318; [2021] NSWLEC 66 for a discussion of the history of objector rights to appeal.

[98] *Palm Beach Protection Group Incorporated* (n 78) [260].

[99] See also s 5.16 EPA Act. For another example of Australian jurisdictions, see the different assessment processes under the Environment Protection and Biodiversity Conservation Act 1999 (Cth). For discussion,

and expanded on, by delegated legislation and other legislation.[100] From the early days of the Court, sections 5.5 and 5.7 (and their predecessors) have given rise to a rich seam of case law on how they should be properly construed and what grounds of judicial review are possible in relation to them.[101]

In terms of judicial review, provisions such as these require careful consideration of the grounds of judicial review and how they should be applied. A defining feature of judicial review is its focus on legal validity.[102] That has meant that administrative lawyers commonly understand the fact/law distinction as an important boundary.[103] Policing it is understood as shorthand for policing the line between judicial review and merits review. But in the operation of judicial review that boundary is blurred, and in environmental law it is particularly blurred.[104] On the other hand, given that legislative provisions such as sections 5.5 and 5.7 require decision-makers to engage in factual evaluation, it is also the case that not only is the boundary blurred, but that factual assessment does give rise to legal questions.

One example of this is the 'jurisdictional fact' doctrine.[105] The doctrine was reinvigorated in Australian administrative law in the late 1990s and early 2000s, some of this case law being Land and Environment Court judgments on appeal.[106] A jurisdictional fact is understood to be a fact that is so 'essential' to the power of an administrative decision-maker that that decision-maker can only exercise that power if that fact exists.[107] This is because the existence of the fact 'enlivens' the power of the decision-maker.[108] For a fact to take on this role it needs to be clearly identifiable, 'essential' and 'objective'.[109] Finding that a legislative obligation incorporates a 'jurisdictional fact' allows the Court to hear evidence on that fact.[110] Whether a fact is jurisdictional or not is a matter of statutory construction that considers the structure of the legislation and the nature of the task that the legislation requires to be undertaken.[111] Given how much the determination and assessment of facts is a feature of environmental legislation it is inevitable that the issue of whether a particular

see BJ Preston, 'Contemporary Issues in Environmental Impact Assessment' (2020) 37 *Environmental and Planning Law Journal* 423.

[100] eg cl 228 Environmental Planning and Assessment Regulation 2000 (NSW) and s 7.8 Biodiversity Conservation Act 2016 (NSW).

[101] eg *F Hannan Pty Ltd v Electricity Commission of NSW* (1983) 51 LGRA 353, 365–66. For an excellent summary, see *Palm Beach Protection Group Incorporated* (n 78) [260]-[261]. For another recent example, see *Pittking Properties Pty Ltd* (n 57).

[102] *Attorney-General (NSW) v Quin* (1990) 170 CLR 1, [17].

[103] Aronson, Groves and Weeks (n 4) ch 4.

[104] ibid.

[105] Fisher (n 93) 978.

[106] *Timbarra Protection Coalition Inc v Ross Mining NL* (1999) 46 NSWLR 55; *Corporation of the City of Enfield v Development Assessment Commission* (2000) 199 CLR 135; and *Woolworths v Pallas Newco* (2004) 61 NSWLR 707.

[107] *Timbarra Protection Coalition* (n 106) 63–64.

[108] *Corporation of the City of Enfield* (n 106) 148.

[109] *Woolworths v Pallas Newco* (n 105) 713 [19] (Spigelman CJ); *Anvil Hill Project Watch Association Inc v Minister for the Environment and Water Resources* (2008) 166 FCR 54, 58 [16] (Tamberlin, Finn and Mansfield JJ).

[110] eg *Ryan* (n 48) [144]–[148] explaining the approach.

[111] *Reysson Pty Ltd* (n 72) [55].

provision gives rise to a 'jurisdictional fact' is often argued before the Court.[112] It is also a question regularly appealed to the NSW Court of Appeal.[113]

For example, it has been argued that 'jurisdictional facts' arise in relation to sections 5.5 and 5.7 of the EPA Act. In *Fullerton Cove Residents Action Group Incorporated v Dart Energy Ltd (No 2)* Pepper J found that section 5.5 (then section 111), did not give rise to a jurisdictional fact although limited evidence 'may be admissible' to show whether obligations had not been discharged.[114] In contrast, she concluded section 5.7 (the old section 112) did.[115] She only came to this conclusion after significant legal analysis of legislation, case law concerning other provisions, and mainstream administrative law principles. As Pain J noted in a later case about the analysis:

> [A]lleged breaches of s 111 and s 112 are different in nature, reflecting the different drafting in these two sections. A breach of section 111 of failing to consider to the fullest extent possible environmental impacts gives rise to injunctive relief restraining the potentially environmentally harmful activity. Section 112 is directed to whether, determined objectively, an activity is likely to significantly affect the environment and therefore whether an EIS is required under subsection (1). The most recent case for several years to fully consider s 112 is *Fullerton Cove Residents Action Group Inc v Dart Energy Ltd* [2013] NSWLEC 38; (2013) 195 LGERA 329. Pepper J concluded at [300] after an exhaustive analysis of authorities and from her own application of first principles that s 112(1) of the EPA Act gives rise to a jurisdictional fact that the Court must determine for itself on all the available evidence whether an activity is likely to significantly affect the environment.[116]

These cases are not isolated examples.[117]

The important point is that, while raising issues of what sort of evidence should be submitted in a judicial review hearing,[118] this is a process of legal analysis that is very distinct from merits review and requires engagement with mainstream judicial review doctrine, albeit reconciling it with environmental legislation. As I have argued elsewhere, that reconciliation is not always straightforward.[119] This is another example of where the Court needs to exercise its administrative law expertise in an active way. It is a form of legal analysis that is not only paying careful attention to legal text and legal doctrine but also institutional context.[120]

[112] eg ibid; *Trives v Hornsby Shire Council*; [2015] NSWCA 158, (2015) 208 LGERA 361; and *Muswellbrook Shire Council* (n 67).

[113] *Timbarra Protection Coalition Inc* (n 106); *Woolworths* (n 106); *Trives* (n 112); and *Reysson Pty Ltd* (n 72).

[114] *Fullerton Cove Residents Action Group Incorporated* (n 37), [142]–[145].

[115] ibid, [300].

[116] *Gold and Copper Resources Pty Limited v Hon Chris Hartcher MP, Minister for Resources and Energy, Special Minister (No 2)* [2014] NSWLEC 30, [92].

[117] For a summary of this case law, see *Pittking Properties Pty Ltd* (n 57).

[118] eg *Help Save Mt Gilead Inc v Mount Gilead Pty Limited* [2018] NSWLEC 88, [42] and *Muswellbrook Shire Council* (n 67) [43]–[45].

[119] See Fisher (n 93).

[120] A point made in by Hon Mr Justice Derrington, 'Migrating Towards a Principled Approach to Reviewing Jurisdictional Facts' 84 (2020) 27 *Australian Journal of Administrative Law* 70, 84.

5. Judgement

Administrative decision-makers in planning and environmental law are not just law-appliers and fact-finders. They must exercise their administrative judgement.[121] Such 'judgement' is distinct from the judgment of a Court – hence the different spelling. Take section 5.5 of the EPA Act. It requires a decision-maker to 'examine and take into account to the fullest extent possible' environmental impacts. This obliges a decision-maker to exercise its institutional capacity and discretion. Many of the legal arguments before the Court concern exactly what such legislative obligations legally require of decision-makers in terms of considering a particular issue or matter.[122]

The starting point for the Court is 'the level of particularity with which a matter is identified in the statute'.[123] In adjudicating on arguments about adequate consideration the Court is ever vigilant to ensure judicial review does not collapse into merits review.[124] In doing this it tethers reasoning to mainstream administrative law doctrine.[125] The Court also needs to think of the implications of arguments for making decision-making process workable.[126] Furthermore, it also must consider what should be expected of a decision-maker in terms of their knowledge and expertise.[127]

In considering arguments about these types of legal errors, the Court's task is an exercise in statutory construction that is grounded in the approach discussed in section 3. One example of this is the case law interpreting section 4.15 of the EPA Act (and its earlier versions).[128] That section now lists 'matters for consideration' that a consent authority is to 'take into consideration'. A body of precedent has developed. Some of this, building on core administrative law doctrine, is directed at what sort of exercise of judgement is generally required by the section.[129] Other precedents concern specific provisions.[130]

Or take the statutory construction of section 5.5 of the EPA Act. Over its history, the Court and the NSW Court of Appeal has developed a body of precedent about what that section requires. In *Palm Beach Protection Group Incorporated v Northern Beaches Council* Preston CJ summarised much of that case law. The starting point for his analysis

[121] On the nature of such judgement, see Fisher and Shapiro (n 1) ch 2.

[122] Besides the examples below, there are many others, eg *Anderson v Director General of the Department of Environment and Climate Change* [2008] NSWCA 337; (2008) 163 LGERA 400; and *Minister for Planning v Walker* [2008] NSWCA 224; (2008) 161 LGERA 423, [28]–[56].

[123] *Walsh* (n 37), [59]–[60].

[124] *Kindimindi Investments Pty Ltd v Lane Cove Council* [2006] NSWCA 23, (2006) 143 LGERA 27 [79] and cases at n 37.

[125] eg *Minister for Aboriginal Affairs v Peko-Wallsend Limited* (1986) 162 CLR 24 and *Minister for Immigration and Citizenship v Li* (2013) 249 CLR 332.

[126] *KEPCO Bylong Australia Pty Ltd* (n 30), [23].

[127] eg *City of Ryde Council v State of New South Wales* [2019] NSWLEC 47; (2019) 242 LGERA 211, [98].

[128] Some of the Court's earliest case law was on this issue. See *Parramatta City Council v Hale* (1982) 47 LGRA 319, 339 (the NSWCA upholding the Land and Environment Court's decision).

[129] *Kindimindi Investments Pty Ltd* (n 124), [74]–[75] discussing *Khan v Minister for Immigration and Ethnic Affairs* (1987) 14 ALD 291 and *Bruce v Cole* (1998) 45 NSWLR 163.

[130] eg *Teys Australia Southern Pty Limited v Burns* [2015] NSWLEC 1, (2015) 206 LGERA 186, [68]–[71] (s 4.15(1)(a)(ii)) and *BGP Properties Pty Limited v Lake Macquarie City Council* [2004] NSWLEC 399, (2004) 138 LGERA 237, [113] (4.15(1)(e)).

was the consideration of the doctrine concerning part 5 of the EPA Act.[131] He then considered at length the case law concerning section 5.5. For example, he stated:

> The duty is to 'examine and take into account' the environmental impact of an activity. Both verbs require positive action by the determining authority. Examination of the environmental impact of an activity involves inspection, inquiry or investigation of the environmental impact (see Macquarie Dictionary definition). Taking into account involves not merely consideration of the environmental impact but also some responsiveness and reflectiveness to the environmental impact in the determining authority's decision-making. In *Willoughby City Council v Minister administering the National Parks and Wildlife Act* (1992) 78 LGERA 19 at 29, Stein J observed: 'The obligation imposed on a determining authority under s 111, to examine and take into account to the fullest extent reasonably practicable all matters likely to affect the environment, imposes a positive obligation to conduct a proper examination. It requires more than merely adverting to a relevant matter and this would be regarded as paying no more than "lip service" to the obligation'.[132]

This was only one of a number of points about the legal obligations imposed by section 5.5 that Preston CJ made. His legal analysis was built on precedent, logic, an analysis of context, and the legislative scheme.

6. Reflecting on the Administrative Law Expertise of the Court

This brief survey of the Land and Environment Court's administrative law is incomplete. The analysis of the case law could be deeper and broader. But even though not comprehensive, it does underscore the Court's *legal* expertise, specifically its administrative law expertise.[133] What can be seen is that the Court has developed a body of knowledge, skills, and experience in relation to adjudicating on administrative law issues that relate to environmental and planning issues. This is not to discount other forms of expertise, legal or otherwise, that the Court has in relation to other areas of law and environmental and planning problems.[134] Nor is it to argue that the Court's administrative law expertise is independent of these. It is not. For example, the Court's interactional expertise in relation to environmental problems[135] begets its administrative law expertise because the Court is relating the complexity of environmental problems to mainstream legal thinking.[136]

To highlight the administrative law expertise of the Court is to draw attention to one aspect of what makes the Court a 'specialist' court. That is not just a matter of passing intellectual interest. As Pain has noted:

> [A] great deal is expected of [environmental courts and tribunals]. Substantively, they must undertake complex decision-making across a number of disciplines, apply appropriate

[131] *Palm Beach Protection Group Incorporated* (n 78) [254]–[255].

[132] ibid, [260].

[133] On the different forms of the Court's expertise, see Preston, this volume.

[134] eg its criminal law expertise (see White, this volume) and its Indigenous law expertise (see Davis, see this volume). On the different forms of expertise, see Preston, this volume.

[135] Preston, this volume.

[136] Warnock, this volume.

> processes to achieve desirable outcomes and be expert across a range of complex disciplines in doing so. Their decisions matter for wider society, not just the parties. They also operate in a results-driven environment and must deliver decisions quickly and grapple with the allocation of limited judicial and other resources.[137]

Understanding what makes the Court 'expert' in such circumstances is important. Specifically, it ensures that false expectations are not placed on the Court and/or its work is assessed against the wrong yardsticks.

For anyone with experience of the Court, drawing attention to the administrative law expertise of the Court is an exercise in pointing out an obvious legal reality. But in wider policy and intellectual debates about environmental courts, that expertise is often overlooked.[138] Attention is often only given to distinctive 'environmental' cases. More significantly, the expertise of an environmental court is often understood to be its expertise with environmental problems not its expertise with legal reasoning.[139] As Pain's comment also highlights, environmental courts are often understood in instrumental terms in which the emphasis is on the outcomes of their decisions rather than how such courts are legal actors that are part of the wider argumentative discipline of law.[140] Besides the fact that these assumptions do not accord with what the Court is actually doing, it also means that there is a greater risk that the Court's more high-profile cases are misunderstood as forms of political activism. This is because without seeing those cases in the context of the Court's administrative law work these judgments are untethered from the body of legal reasoning they have developed out of.

As I have argued elsewhere, the Court's case law on the precautionary principle flows from its understanding of administrative law.[141] Scotford has also shown how its environmental principles case law can only be understood by understanding the legal nature of the Court.[142] Similar comments could also be made about some of the Court's decisions concerning how climate change should be factored into environmental assessment.[143] To put the matter slightly differently, the case law on 'ecologically sustainable development'[144] is part and parcel of a body of doctrine that is concerned with questions about what is 'use of land' and what does it mean to consider a document or issue.

Conversely, the Court is also a contributor to more general administrative law doctrine.[145] In working with the vertical and the horizontal, the habitual and the imperative, it is part of the wider administrative law community. Indeed, the Court's administrative law presence in Australian law has arguably been more significant than would be expected given its place in the judicial hierarchy. The Court's case law, including its merit review decisions, are cited by other courts, especially in environmental

[137] N Pain, 'Book Review: Ceri Warnock, Environmental Courts and Tribunals' (2021) 5 *Chinese Journal of International Law* 109, 116.
[138] For an excellent overview of those types of debates see Warnock (n 3) ch 3.
[139] Fisher, 'Afterword', this volume.
[140] ibid.
[141] Fisher (n 28) ch 4.
[142] Scotford (n 36) ch 5.
[143] eg *Gloucester Resources Limited* (n 95).
[144] Scotford, this volume.
[145] Fisher, 'Administrative Tribunals' (n 5).

courts and in environmental cases.[146] More interestingly, much of the Court's administrative law presence is evidenced in the appeals to the NSW Court of Appeal and the precedents those appeals create. Thus, for example, there are cases where the Court of Appeal has upheld the reasoning of the Land and Environment Court, thus creating a more general administrative law precedent.[147] But there are also cases where the Court of Appeal has created important precedents by overturning the reasoning of the Land and Environment Court.[148] Furthermore, there are examples where the Court's judgments have catalysed doctrinal development around particular concepts such as 'polycentricity'.[149] Returning to the language I used in section 2, the Court in having to legally engage with the 'vertical' and the 'imperative' is influencing the 'horizontal' and 'habitual' across administrative law.

Overall, drawing attention to the administrative law expertise of the Court points to the need to understand it in 'thicker' terms.[150] This requires engagement with the 'complex conceptual structures' of law and administration.[151] Thus, as seen above, in carrying out judicial review, the Court needs to develop a robust body of doctrine in light of complex environmental problems, a range of legal materials and different modes of legal thought. Furthermore, what makes the Court 'expert' in administrative law is not just that it is dealing with administrative law questions, but that it has developed knowledge and skills in relation to these questions and that a community of lawyers doing administrative law work has developed around the Court.[152]

Carrying out a 'thick' analysis of the work of the Court also makes clear the Court is in many ways a product of its legal culture. As discussed in section 2, the Court's administrative law work needs to be understood against the backdrop of its legal structure. The Court's jurisdictions are a mixture of merits review and judicial review jurisdictions – a combination that makes it both an administrative tribunal and a superior court of record.[153] While the same institution having this combination is relatively rare, the ensuing mixture of state-sponsored legal pluralism and legal formalism is a defining feature of Australian administrative law.[154] As noted in section 2, that mixture has meant that the Court has to be constantly mindful of questions of jurisdiction.

[146] See www.austlii.edu.au/cgi-bin/viewdb/au/cases/nsw/NSWLEC/?view=most_cited for a list of the Court's most cited decisions; although note that much of this is recording citations of the Court citing its own decisions – a good example of the Court developing a body of precedent.

[147] eg *Parramatta City Council* (n 128) and *Kindimindi Investments Pty Ltd* (n 124).

[148] eg *Timbarra Protection Coalition Inc* (n 106). I have argued that this is an example of tensions between legal pluralism and legal formalism in action. See Fisher (n 93).

[149] eg *Tubbo Pty Ltd v Minister Administering the Water Management Act 2000* [2008] NSWCA 356; (2008) 302 ALR 299; *Bulga Milbrodale Progress Association Inc* (n 26); *Warkworth Mining Limited* (n 26); and *Randren House Pty Ltd* (n 88).

[150] E Fisher, 'Through "Thick" and "Thin": Comparison in Administrative Law and Regulatory Studies Scholarship' in P Cane et al (eds), *The Oxford Handbook of Comparative Administrative Law* (Oxford, Oxford University Press, 2020) and Preston, this volume.

[151] Fisher (n 150) 625, quoting Clifford Geertz.

[152] Smith and Higginson, this volume.

[153] B Preston, 'The Land and Environment Court of New South Wales: A Very Short History of an Environmental Court in Action' (2020) 94 *Australian Law Journal* 631, 633.

[154] On how these different ideas pervade Australian legal culture, see Fisher (n 93). Also see P Cane, 'The Making of Australian Administrative Law' in P Cane (ed), *Centenary Essays for the High Court of Australia* (LexisNexis Butterworths, 2004) 314.

Seeing the legal work of the Court in 'thicker' terms also holds insights for how to approach the study of environmental adjudication. The Land and Environment Court is unique, but its administrative law work is similar to that of generalist and specialist courts in other jurisdictions.[155] Those courts are needing to answer the same type of legal questions in relation to the same type of problems as the Land and Environment Court.[156] While courts are operating in different legal cultures and with different legal powers, there is a commonality in the legal work they are doing. Seeing that commonality aids in understanding what is it that environmental courts do, and what should be expected of them.

In regard to the former, like all courts and tribunals engaged with administrative law,[157] at the core of the Court's legal expertise is the authoritative adjudication and resolution of disputes about administrative power.[158] In resolving disputes authoritatively in its Class 4 jurisdiction, the Court is expositing the law by applying judicial review doctrine.[159] In regard to what can be expected of such courts, the Court is making the law more 'calculable' and thus contributing to the rule of law.[160] As can be seen from sections 3–5, that is about developing a robust body of reasoning. As Jeremy Waldron has noted: 'We want to be ruled thoughtfully. Or to put it in a more democratic idiom, we want our engagement in governance to be thoughtful and reasoned, rather than rigid and mechanical.'[161] Thoughtfulness for Waldron is 'the capacity to reflect and deliberate, to ponder complexity and confront new and unexpected circumstances with an open mind'.[162] This aspect of the rule of law stems from the fact that 'law is an argumentative discipline'.[163] All administrative law is concerned with begetting thoughtfulness,[164] but in environmental law this is particularly significant given the features of it discussed above.

What we can see from the analysis above is that the Court is developing authoritative and relatively stable yardsticks for determining what is legally valid and legally reasonable. As Waldron has noted: 'A conception of the reasonable in some sphere fills out [a] schema, by indicating the interests that are to be particularly taken into account, the weight to be accorded to them, and the idea of a fair balance among them.'[165] As he also notes: 'Standards [such as reasonableness] often help to sponsor thoughtfulness and reflection in the law, on the part of those who are called on to apply it

[155] Warnock (n 3) and H Leventhal, 'Environmental Decision-Making and the Role of the Courts' (1974) 122 *University of Pennsylvania Law Review* 509.

[156] Fisher, 'Afterword', this volume.

[157] L Jaffe, *Judicial Control of Administrative Action* (Boston, MA, Little, Brown, 1965), 323. Indeed, Llewellyn argued that that was a feature of all law: K Llewellyn, *The Bramble Bush* (Oxford, Oxford University Press, 2008) ch 1.

[158] See the discussion in Stein, this volume concerning the importance of the legal authority of the Court.

[159] Preston, this volume.

[160] J Waldron, *The Rule of Law and Measure of Property* (Cambridge, Cambridge University Press, 2012) 53 and Preston (n 38).

[161] J Waldron, 'Thoughtfulness and the Rule of Law' (2011) 18 *British Academy Review* 1, 1. On the importance of the rule of law in the Court's doctrine, see Preston, this volume.

[162] Waldron (n 161) 1.

[163] ibid, 8 citing McCormick.

[164] Fisher and Shapiro (n 1) 217.

[165] J Waldron, 'Clarity, Thoughtfulness, and the Rule of Law' in G Keil and R Poscher (eds), *Vagueness and Law: Philosophical and Legal Perspectives* (Oxford, Oxford University Press, 2017) 320–21.

(including its primary addressees).'[166] As can be seen above, in developing those standards the Court is not operating in a vacuum. It is working with the vertical and the horizontal, the habitual and the imperative, and is doing so as part of a wider administrative law community.

7. Conclusion

This chapter has surveyed some examples of the active administrative law work of the Land and Environment Court when it is exercising its judicial review jurisdiction. The administrative law expertise of environmental courts is often overlooked. The Court's significant legal work of statutory construction and judicially reviewing factual assessment and administrative judgement has not had the attention it has deserved. Casting a spotlight on it reveals much. It reveals the type of legal materials and questions the Court is working with, the ways in which the decisions of the Court relate to general administrative law, and the attention given to developing robust legal reasoning. Drawing attention to the legal expertise of the Land and Environment Court illuminates the nature of what the Court does and what its expertise is. It is also essential in developing a model of what should be expected of it and other environmental courts.

[166] ibid, 327.

11

Ecocentrism and Criminal Proceedings for Offences against Environmental Laws

ROB WHITE

1. Introduction

This chapter examines the Land and Environment Court of New South Wales (the Court) from the point of view of ecocentrism and criminal proceedings. The concern of the chapter is how the Court adjudicates criminal cases by utilising a frame of analysis and action based on ecocentrism.

An ecocentric approach, based on the intrinsic value of nature, highlights the importance of ecological perspectives in assessing environmental harm, and in sensitivity to and expertise in understanding the changing dynamics of the natural environment.[1] How the Court deals with breaches of the law, particularly offences involving non-human environmental entities such as landscapes, trees and non-human animals, can be analysed in the light of this overarching approach.

From a green criminology perspective,[2] the Court is significant for several reasons. First, while much of the scholarly comment and empirical research of green criminology provides critical exposure of environmental harms and crimes, less attention has been devoted to how positive environmental measures – especially those guided by

[1] See eg J Koons, 'Earth Jurisprudence: The Moral Value of Nature' (2008) *Pace Environmental Law Review* 263; V De Lucia, 'Competing Narratives and Complex Genealogies: The Ecosystem Approach in International Environmental Law' (2015) 27 *Journal of Environmental Law* 91; C Williams 'Wild Law in Australia: Practice and Possibilities' (2013) 30 *Environmental and Planning Law Journal* 259.

[2] Green criminology refers to criminological research and scholarship that focuses on environmental crimes, with particular attention given to crime prevention, law enforcement and the use of criminal justice sanctions. As a whole, green criminology focuses on the nature and dynamics of *environmental crimes and harms* (which may incorporate wider definitions of crime than that provided in strictly legal definitions), *environmental laws* (including enforcement, prosecution and sentencing practices), *environmental regulation* (systems of administrative, civil and criminal law that are designed to manage, protect and preserve specified environments and species, and to manage the negative consequences of particular industrial processes) and *eco-justice* (the valuing of and respect for humans, ecosystems, non-human animals, and plants). See R White and D Heckenberg, *Green Criminology: An Introduction to the Study of Environmental Harm* (London, Routledge, 2014).

ecocentric considerations – might be institutionalised within criminal justice processes and practices. The approach of the Court to criminal cases involving environmental offences provides a valuable illustration of how ecocentric principles can be incorporated into judicial decision-making. It thus provides concrete evidence of developments within the criminal justice domain which can be pointed to, and built upon, in other jurisdictions and indeed other areas of criminal justice practice such as policing and corrections.

Second, claims are frequently made in criminological, legal and sociolegal research that courts (in a generic sense, but generally referring to magistrate-level courts) deal with environmental issues in a trivialising and/or uninformed way, and that the penalties imposed by courts tend to be lenient and thereby inconsequential in terms of deterrence or reprobation.[3] These issues have been acknowledged in a number of jurisdictions including Sweden, Canada, the United States, the United Kingdom and Europe more generally.[4] They have also been noted in Australia but have not been empirically tested.[5] From a green criminology viewpoint it is essential not only to evaluate the accuracy of this belief about leniency but also to investigate how courts, in responding to environmental harm, can foster good environmental outcomes more generally. As a specialist environment court with a broadly ecocentric orientation, the Land and Environment Court provides an exemplar of how criminal proceedings for offences against environmental laws might be approached.

For present purposes, the focus is on the concept of ecocentrism, assessments of environmental harm and the sentencing of environmental offenders. Specifically, the chapter explores the manner in which environmental harms are conceptualised, determined and quantified by the Court – that is, the criteria utilised by the Court to ascertain the nature and scale of environmental harms – and the penalties imposed by the Court in regard to criminal offences involving environmental harm. Green criminology favours criminal justice responses to environmental offences that focus on repairing the harms as well as prosecuting offenders.[6] These considerations are likewise relevant

[3] See C Fogel and J Lipovsek, 'Green Crime in the Canadian Courts' (2013) 6(2) *Journal of Politics and Law* 48; S Chin, W Veening and C Gerstetter, *Policy Brief 1: Limitations and Challenges of the Criminal Justice System in Addressing Environmental Crime* (European Union Action To Fight Environmental Crime, November 2014); M Lynch et al, 'The Weak Probability of Punishment for Environmental Offences and Deterrence of Environmental Offenders: A Discussion Based on USEPA Criminal Cases, 1983–2013' (2016) 37 *Deviant Behavior* 1095.

[4] See also S Bell and D McGillivray, *Environmental Law*, 7th edn (Oxford, Oxford University Press, 2008); M O'Hear, 'Sentencing the Green-Collar Offender: Punishment, Culpability, and Environmental Crime' (2004) 95 *Journal of Criminal Law and Criminology* 133; and Environmental Audit Committee, *Environmental Crime and the Courts* (HC 126, 2004).

[5] Bates observes that in the past environmental crime has tended to not be regarded as 'real crime' particularly in lower courts in Australia, and there are illustrative examples where penalties have been manifestly low: G Bates, *Environmental Law in Australia*, 10th edn (LexisNexis Butterworths, 2019) 823. Recent research on sentencing by the Land and Environment Court has also examined the questions of consistency and proportionality; that is, how consistent the Court has been in applying additional maximum penalties in cases where they appear to be warranted. While not focused on the issue of leniency per se the study has demonstrated that a substantial number of cases involved sentences that are well below the expected penalty threshold. See A Burke, 'Threatened Species, Endangered Justice: How Additional Maximum Penalties for Harming Threatened Species Have Failed in Practice' (2016) 33 *Environmental and Planning Law Journal* 451.

[6] White and Heckenberg (n 2).

when considering the broad functions and responses of the Court in regard to criminal matters. The chapter draws upon judgments involving the sentencing of offenders for environmental offences against non-human environmental entities such as trees and non-human animals. Its aim is to determine the nature and scope of specialist knowledge used in sentencing, and the unique sentencing regimes and rationale construed and implemented by this Court, with a view to determining how ecocentrism influences the Court's reasoning.

The chapter refers to research that examines judicial reasoning by the Court relating to the Native Vegetation Act 2003 (NSW) (NVA) and the National Parks and Wildlife Act 1974 (NSW) (NPWA) within the temporal scope of decisions published between the years 2000 and 2013.[7] These Acts include provisions that refer specifically to harm directed at flora and fauna.

Following this introduction, section 2 provides an overview of the conceptual elements typically associated with ecocentric approaches to law. The purpose of this section is to discuss indicators that can be drawn on in assessing ecocentrism in the processes and outcomes of the Court. Section 3 outlines the indicia utilised by the Court in determining the seriousness of environmental harm in relation to the NVA and the NPWA. Section 4 considers the way in which the Court determines the seriousness of the offence and assigns penalties and remedies. Section 5, the conclusion, highlights that best practice is made possible by specialist expertise and the availability of wide-ranging sentencing options.

2. Ecocentrism and Environmental Harm

The environment and its resources are what sustains humanity and non-human living entities. These are diminishing rapidly, putting all into peril.[8] Existential threats arising from natural resource exploitation also put into question the dominant worldview of *anthropocentrism* (or human-centredness) which justifies and perpetuates such exploitation.[9]

By contrast, *ecocentrism* refers to valuing nature for its own sake. This ecophilosophical orientation asserts that social practices should incorporate ecological sensitivities and heightened awareness of the intrinsic value of flora, fauna, ecosystems and non-living entities such as rivers and mountains. Within the domain of green criminology this sentiment translates into an *eco-justice* framework, one that is comprised of three key elements: *environment justice* (involving humans), *ecological justice* (involving specific environments) and *species justice* (involving non-human animals and plants).[10]

[7] R White, 'The Sentencing of Environmental Offences Involving Non-Human Environmental Entities in the NSW Land and Environment Court' (Master of Laws (LLM) thesis, University of Tasmania, 2017).

[8] Intergovernmental Science-Policy Platform on Biodiversity and Ecosystem Services (IPBES), *The IPBES Global Assessment Report on Biodiversity and Ecosystem Services* (IPBES, 2019).

[9] The defining characteristic of anthropocentrism is that humans are ends-in-themselves, while other entities are only means to attain the goals of humans. See Du Lucia (n 1).

[10] R White, *Environmental Harm: An Eco-Justice Perspective* (Bristol, Policy Press, 2013).

Crimes against the environment affect the living and the non-living (eg rivers) and, ultimately, are destroying and degrading planet Earth. Environmental harm is ubiquitous even though there are important qualitative differences in regard to the nature, dynamics and seriousness of the harm as these pertain to non-human animals, ecosystems, plant species and human populations.[11] Understanding and acknowledging these differences is vital to the work of the Court in regard to criminal proceedings for offences against environmental laws.

The term 'natural object' has been used to describe non-living entities such as rivers, mountains and oceans.[12] Fauna, or animal life, is ordinarily dealt with through use of the term 'animal' (which can be subdivided into, among other categories, 'native wildlife' and 'threatened species'), while flora (plant life) is ordinarily referred to under the broad category of 'vegetation'.[13] Ecosystems have been defined in key international conventions as 'a dynamic complex of plant, animal and micro-organism communities and their non-living environment interacting as a functional unit'.[14] Together these entities comprise what is described herein as *non-human environmental entities*.

Consideration of the non-human environmental entity incorporates discussion of individual landscape features and specific living entities, through to particular ecosystems. Any ecosystem is made up of both abiotic components (air, water, soil, atoms and molecules) and biotic components (plants, animals, bacteria and fungi).[15] When destruction, degradation or diminishment of these occurs in a manner deemed in environmental law to be criminal, then harm can be said to have occurred. Thus, the concern of the present chapter is directed to instances in which flora and fauna, and the habitats and landscapes of which they are a part, are legally determined to be harmed by particular acts and omissions, as expressed in specific legislation.

Protection of the environment may be based on either one of or a combination of conceptions of the *rights of* nature (both as subject with rights, or object worthy of protection) and *duties to* nature (its intrinsic worth which therefore imposes a moral obligation and duty of care).[16] A fundamental aspect of ecocentrism is to see entities such as non-human animals, plants and rivers as potential rights-holders and/or as objects warranting a duty of care on the part of humans, since their interests are seen to be philosophically significant (ie deserving greater respect and formal recognition).[17]

[11] See IPBES (n 8); World Meteorological Organization, *WMO Provisional Statement on the State of the Global Climate in 2019* (WMO, 2020).

[12] C Stone, 'Should Trees Have Standing? Toward Legal Rights for Natural Objects' (1972) 45 *Southern California Law Review* 450.

[13] See specifically, for example, P Sankoff and S White (eds), *Animal Law in Australasia: A New Dialogue* (Alexandria, Federation Press, 2009); and more generally, Bates (n 5).

[14] Convention on Biological Diversity (adopted 5 June 1992, entered into force 29 December 1993) 1760 UNTS 76, Art 2.

[15] C Merchant, *Radical Ecology: The Search for a Liveable World*, 2nd edn (London, Routledge, 2005).

[16] D Fisher, 'Jurisprudential Challenges to the Protection of the Natural Environment' in M Maloney and P Burdon (eds), *Wild Law – In Practice* (London, Routledge, 2010). For extended discussion of rights and recognition as these pertain to issues of justice and/or for nonhuman entities, see D Schlosberg, *Defining Environmental Justice: Theories, Movements, and Nature* (Oxford, Oxford University Press, 2007). See also P Burdon (ed), *Wild Law: Essays in Earth Jurisprudence* (Kent Town Wakefield Press, 2010); and P Higgins, *Earth Is Our Business: Changing the Rules of the Game* (London, Shepheard-Walwyn, 2012).

[17] See T Berry, *The Great Work: Our Way into the Future* (Harmony/Bell Tower, 1999); and De Lucia (n 1).

The notion of Earth jurisprudence refers to a philosophy of law that asserts that humans are just one part of a wider community of subjects and that the well-being of each member of the community is reliant on the well-being of the Earth as a whole.[18] The Earth ('the environment') ought to be seen as having certain intrinsic value, and Earth rights should extend to all species and ecosystems on the planet.[19] There is a distinction between a moral and ethical argument that nature has rights, and the legal rights of nature as such.[20] Philosophically, Earth jurisprudence is an expression of ecocentrism in that it places moral weight on the worth of non-human environmental entities.

Regimes of environmental protection incorporate both anthropocentric and ecocentric approaches. The history of environmental law is a history of evolving gradations of anthropocentrism and ecocentrism.[21] Anthropocentrism, while privileging the human over the non-human, nonetheless can express a moral concern for nature. This can involve an ethic of responsibility *to* nature as well as responsibility *for* nature, albeit framed in terms of human interests.[22] Protecting the environment for human benefit, for example, is evident in international agreements such as the Rio Declaration (1992) that explicitly acknowledges the environmental rights of humans, not intrinsic environmental rights as such.[23] However, nature's intrinsic value has also been recognised in recent decades; for example, in the Convention on Biological Diversity (1992).[24] The non-human is increasingly recognised for its intrinsic, as well as instrumental, value.[25]

Acknowledgement of the intrinsic worth and value of nature is vital from the point of view of an ecocentric approach, but this does not mean that instrumental uses of nature by humans are thereby rendered unimportant. Indeed, it is possible and logical to view humans *in* nature as necessarily using nature for their own ends. To argue otherwise, as implied in some Earth law commentaries, has been described as at best a paradox and at worst meaningless.[26] However, the instrumental use of nature can nonetheless be guided by ecocentric considerations, such as doing the least amount of harm in the process of its use.[27]

From an ecocentric perspective, the activities of the Court can be gauged by assessing the manner in which determinations of environmental harm and the penalties

[18] Williams (n 1).

[19] See eg UNESC, *Study on the Need to Recognize and Respect the Rights of Mother Earth*, 9th session, Permanent Forum on Indigenous Issues (19–30 April 2010).

[20] Williams (n 1).

[21] See A Pelizzon and A Ricketts, 'Beyond Anthropocentrism and Back Again: From Ontological to Normative Anthropocentrism' (2015) 18(2) *Australasian Journal of Natural Resources Law and Policy* 105; Fisher (n 16).

[22] Fisher (n 16); B Donelly and P Bishop, 'Natural Law and Ecocentrism' (2007) 19 *Journal of Environmental Law* 89.

[23] For example, Principle 1 of the 1992 Rio Declaration states that: 'Human beings are at the centre of concerns for sustainable development.' UN Doc.A/CONF.151/26 (vol 1); 31 ILM 874 (1992) (Rio Declaration).

[24] The Preamble to the Convention on Biodiversity (n 14) begins with the statements: 'Conscious of the intrinsic value of biological diversity and of the ecological, genetic, social, economic, scientific, educational, cultural, recreational and aesthetic values of biological diversity and its components.' See also Fisher (n 16).

[25] Pelizzon and Rickets (n 21); but also see De Lucia (n 1).

[26] Donnelly and Bishop (n 22) 96.

[27] R Eckersley, *Environmentalism and Political Theory: Toward an Ecocentric Approach* (New York, State University of New York Press, 1992) 57.

assigned in relation to this harm reflect certain principles and values. Detailed study of case law involving offences against non-human environmental entities (in this instance clear-felling of forests and threats to endangered animals and plants) has established that the Court makes reference to five key indicators of ecocentrism (see Table 1).[28] Examination of the Court in relation to these indicators takes into account the statutory frameworks within which the Court operates and the development of the culture, expertise and experience of the Court since its establishment.

Table 1 Indicators of ecocentrism

Indicator	Example
The extent to which the intrinsic value or worth of the non-human environmental entity is taken into consideration	Laws and judgments which acknowledge the rights of nature
The use of ecological perspectives to estimate the degree of harm to non-human environmental entities	References to ecological criteria by courts in assessing the degree and nature of environmental harm
The kinds of expertise mobilised within and demonstrated by a court to capture adequately the nature and complexities of the environmental harm	Expert knowledge of judicial officers in regard to ecological integrity, environmental health and sustainability
The gravity of the offence against the non-human environmental entity as reflected in the penalties given	The quantum and type of penalty, and the judicial rationales for the penalty given
The measures taken to ensure the maintenance, restoration or preservation of ecological integrity	The imposition of orders that involve remediation activities

Source: R White, 'Ecocentrism and Criminal Justice' (2018) 22(3) *Theoretical Criminology* 342, 349.

Harm perpetrated against non-human animals, plants and ecosystems is reflected in specific provisions dealing with offences against environmental laws. Dealing with non-human environmental entities is, however, complicated by the specific knowledge needed to ascertain the nature and extent of the harm, as well as by the intricacies of legislation and classificatory schemes that attempt to capture the essence of such harms at particular moments in time. At the heart of Table 1 is ecology, involving a holistic understanding of the natural world. For judicial officers this requires a modicum of specialist expertise on environmental matters and an appreciation of the importance of ecological integrity. Fundamentally, it requires the elevation of the intrinsic worth of nature (and its various component parts) to the level of first principles.

Determining whether harm has occurred, and the seriousness of the harm, is a vital task of the Court. It is also a precursor to assigning penalties and choosing the most appropriate sanction. One of the tasks of the Court, therefore, is to ascertain the nature and quantum of environmental harm. To do this well, a court must be ecologically

[28] White (n 7).

literate, since the subject matter – harm and sanctions pertaining to non-human environmental entities – is immensely complicated and ever changing. The chapter now turns to describe how the Court undertakes this role in regard to determining the seriousness of environmental harm.

3. Determining Environmental Harm

This section examines the indicia used in determining the nature and extent of harm to non-human environmental entities under the NVA and NPWA. Ordinarily, it would be reasonable to expect that the higher the ecological value/vulnerability of the environment, the more substantial will be the harm caused to that environment.[29] How environmental harm is measured in specific circumstances forms the substantive content of this section.

The NVA came into force in 2005. It heralded in an era in which broadscale clearing of forests and woodlands was prohibited in New South Wales unless it could be demonstrated that such clearing would improve or maintain environmental outcomes.[30] The NPWA established protected areas whereby land may be reserved for a wide variety of purposes, including the creation of national parks, state conservation areas and nature reserves.[31]

The work of the Court occurs within the statutory context of legislation, which provides a modicum of support for an ecocentric approach. For example, both section 3 of the NVA and section 2A(2) of the NPWA include the direction that the objects of these Acts are to be achieved by applying the principles of ecologically sustainable development (ESD). These principles are described in section 6(2) of the Protection of the Environment Administration Act 1991 (NSW) and include the precautionary principle, intergenerational equity, the conservation of biological diversity and ecological integrity.

Determination of the harm caused by the offender goes to the heart of how best to conceptualise the nature of harm involving non-human environmental entities. Over time, the Court has drawn upon a wide range of general and specific indicia in determining the harm caused to the environment by commission of the offence. This has invariably involved reliance upon expert analysis and opinion. Judicial officers have developed ecological expertise over the course of the forty-year history of the Court in the weighing up of a range of variables relating to site analysis, as well as statutory prescriptions and case precedent, in determining matters of fact.[32] This means that the Court continually makes decisions over the veracity of the information before it,

[29] B Preston, 'Principled Sentencing for Environmental Offences – Part 2: Sentencing Considerations and Options' (2008) 31 *Criminal Law Journal* 142, 146.

[30] M Taylor and C Dickman, *NSW Native Vegetation Act Saves Australian Wildlife* (Sydney, WWF-Australia, 2014).

[31] Bates (n 5) 455.

[32] For in-depth discussion of issues pertaining to expert opinion in the NSWLEC in regards to environmental harm, see R White, 'Experts and Expertise in the Land and Environment Court' (2017) 49 *Australian Journal of Forensic Science* 392.

including challenging or dismissing expert evidence due to its speculative nature or poor methods and methodologies.[33] Likewise, persons who are not qualified to give expert opinion are identified by judicial officers and dismissed.[34]

Proscribed activity is set out in the NVA.[35] The seriousness of the harm arising from undertaking proscribed activity is determined through judicial decision-making in which the Court is required to develop indicia that best reflect the intent and purposes of the legislation.

Determination of the seriousness of harm and objective gravity requires the Court to consider the nature of the offence, the maximum penalty, the harm caused to the environment by the commission of the offence, the reason for committing the offence, the foreseeable risk of harm to the environment and the offender's control over the cause of harm to the environment.[36] It is then up to the Court to determine the 'harm done to the victim of the crime and the community' since there are no statutory prescribed criteria for assessing the objective seriousness of the offence.[37] The Court draws upon many factors to assess the seriousness of the harm in particular cases.

The analyses below provide a distillation of indicia that pertain to the type and magnitude of environmental harm involving non-human environmental entities. To determine the quantum of harm, the Court first describes the particular events and individuals involved, and then draws upon expert opinion and precedent to gauge the seriousness of the harm and the gravity of the offence.

In regard to offences related to the NVA, there are five broad categorisations that denote how the Court gauges environmental harm generally (see Table 2). These indicia were identified by the author through close examination of Court descriptions of specific instances of harm. In other words, the indicia are not derived from the Act but have been developed by the Court as the ecology-based knowledge of judicial officers has grown over time. The first indicium deals with land clearing and the technical and legal aspects of this (eg land clearing permits and issues pertaining to definitions of regrowth). The second examines vulnerability at a general systems level (eg ecosystems

[33] See eg *Chief Executive, Office of Environment and Heritage v Rummery* (2012) 192 LGERA 314, [108]–[111]; *Carmody v Brancourts Nominees Pty Limited; Carmody v Brancourt [No 2]* [2003] NSWLEC 84, [22]; and *Garrett v Freeman (No 5); Garrett v Port Macquarie Hastings Council; Carter v Port Macquarie Hastings Council* (2009) 164 LGERA 287, [113]–[116].

[34] *Corbyn v Walker Corporation Pty Ltd* (2012) 156 LGERA 442, [7].

[35] eg Part 3(1)(12) of the NVA stipulates that native vegetation must not be cleared except in accordance with: (a) a development consent granted in accordance with the Act, or (b) a property vegetation plan. A person who carries out or authorises the carrying out of clearing in contravention of this section is guilty of an offence and is liable to the maximum penalty provided for under s 126 of the Environmental Planning and Assessment Act 1979 (NSW) for a contravention of that Act. In regards offences under the NVA the seriousness of offence is indicated by the use of criminal law, its status as a strict liability offence and high maximum penalties.

[36] *Bentley v BGP Properties Pty Ltd* (2006) 145 LGERA 234, [163] and *Director-General of the Department of Environment and Climate Change v Rae* (2009) 197 A Crim R 31, [14].

[37] *Director-General, Department of Environment and Climate Change v Calman Australia Pty Ltd; Iroch Pty Ltd; GD & JA Williams Pty Ltd t-as Jerilderie Earthmoving* [2009] NSWLEC 182, [25].

and habitats); the third drills down to specific species (eg particular kinds of plants). The fourth indicium focuses on impact and effects and the temporal aspects of harm (eg short-term or long-term and cumulative effects). The final indicium refers to the possibility of remediation. The most frequently mentioned indicium across the NVA cases are 'possibilities of remediation', 'adverse impact at a systems level', 'extent of cleared area and type of clearing' and 'adverse impacts in relation to specific species'.[38]

Table 2 Indicia used by the Land and Environment Court to determine environmental harm in relation to the Native Vegetation Act 2003 (NSW)

Indicators of harm	**Specific examples**
Prior and present land clearing	• Extent of cleared area and type of clearing • Conditions under which land permitted to be cleared (eg routine agricultural management activities) • Prior use and regrowth
Vulnerability at general systems level	• Categories of vulnerability • Adverse impacts at systems level • Climate change
Vulnerability at specific levels	• Adverse impacts in relation to specific species • Scale
Temporal and proximity impacts and effects	• Primary and secondary impacts • Short-term and long-term impacts • Indirect effects • Cumulative effect • Harm to the environment need not only be considered in terms of actual harm
Possibilities of remediation	• Possibilities for remediation

With respect to the NPWA, there are six broad indicia that describe the nature of the harm (see Table 3). The first is direct damage. The second refers to likely impacts (eg effects of demise of habitat on birds). The third considers the status of the species damaged or destroyed (eg endangered or threatened). The fourth considers the complexity and totality of the damage. The fifth and sixth refer to re-establishment time and reparation strategy, respectively. Details of the top four indicia provide a more in-depth illustration of the Court's appreciation of ecological issues and the importance of ecological assessments of environmental harm.

[38] See eg *Director-General, Department of Environment and Climate Change v Calman Australia Pty Ltd; Chief Executive, Office of Environment and Heritage v Rummery* (n 33); *Director-General of the Department of Environment and Climate Change v Rae* (n 36).

Table 3 Indicia used by the Land and Environment Court to determine harm in relation to the National Parks and Wildlife Act 1974 (NSW)

Indicator of harm	Specific examples
Direct damage	• Changes in a landscape or particular biotic community • Size and content of area cleared
Immediate, potential and indirect impact	• In relation to specific threatened and vulnerable species • Likely harm, indirect impacts, likely indirect impacts • Habitat and movement corridors
Status of species damaged or destroyed	• Endangered and vulnerable species • Significance of population of threatened species • Reserved land
Complexity and totality of ecological damage	• Particular ecological communities • Connectivity • Specific strata of species
Re-establishment time	• Length of time before damage is redressed • Whether the damage can be redressed at all
Reparation strategy	• Environmental service order • Distribution of fines • Substantive measures to address the harm

The example *habitat and movement corridors* (under the indicium 'immediate, potential and indirect impact') acknowledges a continuum of harm in which immediate apparent harms also contain the possibility of potential future harm. In part, this is related to the impact of land clearance on the habitats of various threatened and vulnerable species. This affects the suitability of a site as a foraging habitat, the availability of available nest sites, exposure of vulnerable or threatened species to predators and so on.[39] There are also impacts on habitat connectivity at the local level that can affect fauna (eg their ability to move from one place to another place).[40] For plants, damage to vegetation can lead to susceptibility to 'edge effects', such as the susceptibility to the establishment of environmental weeds, and thereby to change in the flora habitat.[41]

Another example of harm relates to *endangered and vulnerable species*. Conservation as it applies to biodiversity is integral to determining the seriousness of harm, and particular attention is given by the Court to species vulnerability. Species are listed variously as vulnerable, endangered or protected, which acknowledges gradations of

[39] *Director General of National Parks and Wildlife v Wilkinson & Anor; Director General of the Department of Land and Water Conservation v Wilkinson & Anor* [2002] NSWLEC 171, [36]–[38].

[40] *Director-General, Department of Environment, Climate Change and Water v Forestry Commission of New South Wales* [2011] NSWLEC 102, [72]; and *Gordon Plath of the Department of Environment and Climate Change v Fish; Gordon Plath of the Department of Environment and Climate Change v Orogen Pty Ltd* (2010) 179 LGERA 386, [80]–[81].

[41] *Plath v Knox* [2007] NSWLEC 670, [3ix], [3xv].

threat and vulnerability. Damage or destruction to individual plants and animals are considered, as is the concept of endangered ecological community (EEC) and direct and indirect threats to the EEC.[42] The significance of the population of threatened species is assessed according to criteria such as conservation significance, total area of native vegetation cleared and potential genetic isolation.[43]

Where harm occurs is important, especially if it is on *reserved land*. The location of species is relevant because if they are located in a World Heritage area or nature reserve, then this compounds the gravity of the offence given that these areas are designed precisely to protect vulnerable species.[44] The purpose of establishing nature reserves places them in the upper levels of the hierarchy of reserved land and thus is a significant indicator of environmental harm.[45]

Another example of environmental harm are *changes in landscape or particular biotic community*. This refers to the direct damage as measured in accordance with the species or land in question. In regard to a forest plant community, for example, the damage might be described in terms of loss of prior species as well as an increase of new and/or invasive species due to illegal land clearing.[46] Harm can be measured in regard to the size of area as well as the content of the area that is cleared.[47] Gauging the extent of harm also may require reference to benchmark data that describes the situation prior to and arising from an offence (eg unauthorised taking of bird eggs in relation to the overall bird population).[48]

Other relevant factors utilised by the Court as indicia of harm include the size and content of the area cleared,[49] immediate, potential and indirect impact in relation to specific threatened and vulnerable species,[50] the likelihood or potential for harm,[51] significance of the population of species,[52] and the length of time it would take before the damage is redressed.[53]

It is important to view evaluation of discrete indicia as part of an overall assessment process relating to the totality of the environmental harm. For instance, in keeping with the mandate to engage in protection of biodiversity, the deliberations of the Court

[42] See *Department of Environment & Climate Change v Sommerville; Department of Environment and Climate Change v Ianna* [2009] NSWLEC 194.

[43] *Bentley v Gordon* [2005] NSWLEC 695, [75]–[93].

[44] *Plath v Chaffey* [2009] NSWLEC 196, [29].

[45] *Chief Executive, Office of Environment and Heritage v Leda Management Services Pty Ltd* [2013] NSWLEC 111, [28].

[46] *Director General of National Parks and Wildlife v Wilkinson & Anor* (n 39) [32].

[47] *Department of Environment & Climate Change v Sommerville* (n 42) [36].

[48] *Plath v Chaffey* (n 44) [44]–[48].

[49] See *Department of Environment & Climate Change v Sommerville* (n 42) [36].

[50] See for example, *Director General of National Parks and Wildlife v Wilkinson & Anor* (n 39) [36] in regards to the Little Bent-wing bat.

[51] *Bentley v Gordon* (n 43) [69].

[52] For example, harm is considered low in regards to some types of species in a national park environment. In *Plath v Glover*, for example, the environmental harm was considered low. '*Banksia integrifola* was a common plant in the Reserve. The number of cones collected, relative to their abundance, was not significant': *Plath v Glover* [2010] NSWLEC 119, [31].

[53] For example, in *Plath v Vaccount Pty Ltd t/as Tableland Timbers* it was noted that 503 trees were felled, pushed over or damaged and because of their maturity, the replacement of the 503 trees was estimated to take in excess of 100 years. *Plath v Vaccount Pty Ltd t/as Tableland Timbers* [2011] NSWLEC 202, [72].

require an integrated understanding of nature and, specifically, sensitivity to the interrelationship of habitat, biodiversity, landform and landscape. A good exemplar of this is provided in *Department of Environment & Climate Change v Sommerville; Department of Environment and Climate Change v Ianna*,[54] where environmental harm included the following elements (emphasis added):

- Permanent removal of a large area of an *EEC*
- *Severing of connectivity* between remnant vegetation and increasing the level of habitat fragmentation
- *Removal of threatened fauna and flora habitat*, including features that are limiting factors affecting distribution and abundance of fauna, for example tree hollows
- Loss of *biodiversity values*
- Loss of *ecosystem services*, including soil stabilisation, wind protection, carbon storage and fixation, sediment trapping and nutrient filtration, slowing and detention of floodwaters and groundwater recharge
- Loss of *regeneration potential* for a high conservation value vegetation community through loss of above ground reproductive function as well as loss of soil seed-bank
- Increased *prevalence of introduced species* including environmental weeds
- *Soil compaction*
- *Reduced resilience of ecosystem to withstand and adapt to impacts of climate change*
- Reduced capacity to maintain *genetic diversity of component species*, including a reduced opportunity for genetic exchange and reduction in gene pool.

While individual indicia were identified across the cases, it was the totality of indicia in any given case that ultimately shaped the determination of harm. This is why, for example, harmful activity at the local scale may be considered serious (eg because the vegetation contains a diversity of native plant species) but is discounted in the Court's judgment by the fact that it is less harmful at the landscape level (eg the vegetation communities on the land consist of vegetation communities that are well represented in the wider region including within conservation reserves).

As demonstrated by this example, the Court uses a wide range of indicia in determining harm in regard to native vegetation protected under the NVA, and landscapes, flora and fauna protected under the provisions of the NPWA. The sheer number of indicia invoked, and their strategic synthesis in determining the seriousness of environmental harm in each specific case, indicates that the Court mobilises considerable non-legal expertise in order to adequately capture the nature and complexities of the environmental harm. An ecological perspective is central to these determinations.

4. Sentencing Offenders

The seriousness of *offence*, as distinct from the seriousness of *harm*, takes into account subjective factors pertaining to the human offender as well as objective factors pertaining to the offence (ie harms to the environment). Sentencing is thus an inherently anthropocentric activity – it is the human perpetrator who is at the centre of the punishment process.

[54] *Department of Environment & Climate Change v Sommerville; Department of Environment and Climate Change v Ianna* (n 42).

The question is to what degree or in what ways ecocentric considerations also feature in sentencing decisions.

The sentencing practices of the Court are shaped by legislation that sets out the hierarchy of sanctions available within this jurisdiction.[55] Sentencing options available to the Court for enforcement and compliance purposes are provided under the Protection of the Environment Operations Act 1997 (NSW). Options include terms of imprisonment, fines, clean-up or preventative action orders, and orders for compensation to those who suffered damage to property as a result of the offence or who incurred costs in taking steps to clean up the harm caused by the offence.[56]

The NPWA was amended in 2010 to expand the range of measures that could be imposed.[57] These include additional orders that provide the Court may do any one or more of the following:

> (a) Order the offender to take specified action to publicise the offence (including the circumstances of the offence) and its environmental and other consequences and any other orders made against the person,
> (b) Order the offender to take specified action to notify specified persons or classes of persons of the offence (including the circumstances of the offence) and its consequences and of any orders made against the person (including, for example, the publication in an annual report or any other notice to shareholders or a company or the notification of persons aggrieved or affected by the offender's conduct),
> (c) Order the offender to carry out a specified project for the restoration or enhancement of the environment in a public place or for the public benefit,
> (d) Order the offender to pay a specified amount to the Environmental Trust established under the Environmental Trust Act 1998, or a specified organization, for the purposes of a specified project for the restoration or enhancement of the environment or for general environmental purposes,
> (e) Order the offender to attend, or to cause an employee or employees or a contractor or contractors of the offender to attend, a training or other course specified by the court,
> (f) Order the offender to establish, for employees or contractors of the offender, a training course of a kind specified by the court.[58]

The National Parks and Wildlife Amendment Act 2010 also includes general provisions pertaining to matters to be considered in imposing penalty.[59] Section 194(2) extends the purview of the Court beyond the specific factors laid out in section 194(1) by permitting the Court to 'take into consideration other matters that it considers relevant'. This gives the Court wide discretion in determining what factors to take into account in sentencing offenders.

For the criminal offences covered by NPWA, this meant the possibility of creative and innovative ways for dealing with offenders. This, too, is of great interest to this chapter because, as noted previously, courts have been criticised for both leniency in sentencing environmental offenders, and general ineffectiveness in either remedying or preventing harm.[60] A rough survey of various countries, for example, shows that most

[55] Such as, for example, the Crimes (Sentencing Procedure) Act 1999 (NSW).
[56] See ss 244–51 Protection of the Environment Operations Act 1997 (NSW).
[57] National Parks and Wildlife Amendment Act 2010 (NSW).
[58] ibid, s 205(1).
[59] ibid, s 19.
[60] See Chin, Veening and Gerstetter (n 3).

offences involving the environment are prosecuted in lower courts (or dealt with by civil and administrative penalties), and that most penalties are on the lower rather than higher end of the scale, usually involving fines, and that these are low level.[61]

However, a range of penalty types, approaches and mechanisms have emerged in Australia in recent years in regard to environmental sentencing options indicating a shift upwards in ordinal rankings of seriousness (ie these sorts of crimes compared to other crime types) and/or attempts to fashion responses that better match the nature and dynamics of environmental harm.[62] Altogether such measures appear to denote a change in the seriousness with which the community regards environmental offences, as reflected in legislative changes to offence classifications and sentence regimes.[63] How this burgeoning range of sentencing options translates into sentencing outcomes is of particular interest because prosecutorial and judicial interventions around environmental harm provide concrete evidence of the specific valuing of environmental harm in and by the criminal justice system at any point in time.

How a court responds to environmental harm depends upon the sanctions available. Where there is wide latitude to use penalties in combination with each other, the possibilities for appropriate sanctioning are increased. In this instance, the Court operates in a statutory context which provides for substantial penalties for environmental offences, and which provides a broad spectrum of sanctions that can be drawn upon in sentencing offenders. The cost to offenders therefore can be substantial and involve financial, reputational and resource consequences. The penalties imposed by the Court also include requirements that the defendant *do* something. That is, they are not simply passive recipients of penalties such as fines (or, indeed, of imprisonment). Rather, punishment is also, in some circumstances, something that must be accomplished *by* the offender.[64] This can be time, energy and resource consuming, especially if it involves relatively substantial remediation or rehabilitation works. Combining financial sanctions such as fines with activity-based sanctions (eg remediation) means that the Court imposes sentences of greater burden to the offender than otherwise might be the case.

It has been suggested that the effectiveness of combining different types of orders is that they put a spotlight on the fact that a crime has been committed, while simultaneously producing an environmental good.[65] If this is indeed the case, then such sentencing processes appear to address matters of the seriousness of environmental crime better than previous approaches. They also reflect key concerns of an ecocentric approach with respect to the appropriateness of the penalty and matters of ecological integrity, in particular repairing of harm. Not only does the Court determine the nature of the harm to non-human environmental entities by reference to ecological criteria, it imposes penalties that include measures designed to ensure the maintenance, restoration or preservation of the harmed plant and animal species, ecological community and ecosystem.

[61] For examples, see above nn 3 and 4.

[62] R White, 'Prosecution and Sentencing in Relation to Environmental Crime: Recent Socio-Legal Developments' (2010) 53 *Crime, Law and Social Change* 365.

[63] Preston (n 29); see also Bates (n 5).

[64] See C Boyd, 'Expanding the Arsenal for Sentencing Environmental Crimes: Would Therapeutic Jurisprudence and Restorative Justice Work?' (2008) 32 *William & Mary Environmental Law and Policy Review* 483.

[65] S Bricknell, *Environmental Crime in Australia*, AIC Reports Research and Public Policy Series 109 (Canberra, Australian Institute of Criminology, 2010).

The Court is thus also futures-oriented, not only in terms of the deterrent effect of combined penalties, but in regard to repairing the harm. This entails directing funds to suitable conservation organisations and for the purposes of direct remedial action. This highlights the value of the non-human environmental entity and positions it as having significant worth.

The matters to be included in sentencing include not only the statutory considerations but also general considerations such as the purposes and principles of sentencing, including proportionality, parity, totality, consistency, parsimony and so on.[66] Proportionality refers to the idea that punishment must be proportionate to the gravity of the offending behaviour.[67] The approach adopted by the Court in assessing proportionality includes the objective circumstances of the offence and the subjective circumstances of the offender. Consideration of objective circumstances involves the maximum penalty plus the seriousness of the environmental harm (eg the significance of population of endangered species, fragmentation, weed infestation, edge effects and direct damage). An ecocentric approach is central to consideration of the seriousness of environmental harm since it is ecological factors which are used in determining the nature and extent of such harm.

Consideration of aggravating features of the offence involves the state of mind of the offender at the time of the offence (eg knowledge of species, knowledge of obligation, knowledge of potential impact, reasons for commission of offence).[68] The focus on the offender is informed by anthropocentric considerations.[69] It is the offender as an actor that is assessed, including their behaviour subsequent to being charged with the offence.[70] Legislation sets out the broad categories denoting 'aggravating' and 'mitigating' factors.[71] It is the job of the Court, however, to interpret specific facts as particular factors in sentencing – that is, to use legislative guidelines for practical application. The types of mitigating factors identified by the Court include, for example, defendant poor health,[72] defendant of otherwise good character,[73] offender remorse,[74] the adverse effect of negative publicity on the offender,[75] adverse effect on professional reputation[76]

[66] See New South Wales Law Reform Commission, *Sentencing*, Discussion Paper No 33 (1996); New South Wales Law Reform Commission, *Role of Juries in Sentencing*, Report No 118 (2007); and M Bagaric and R Edney, *Sentencing in Australia* (Sydney, Law Book, 2014).

[67] *Director-General of the Department of Environment and Climate Change v Rae* (n 36).

[68] See *Bentley v Gordon* (n 43) [163]; *Garrett on behalf of the Director-General of the Department of Conservation and Environment v House* [2006] NSWLEC 492, [33]; and *Chief Executive, Office of Environment and Heritage v Leda Management Services Pty Ltd* (n 45), [62] and NPWA, s 194 sentencing matters and ss 200, 205 orders.

[69] This obtains for both individuals and corporations. The latter are prosecuted under s 175B of the NPWA, 'offences by corporations', and in some instances the manager is prosecuted as part of the proceeding. This is provided for in sections of the National Parks and Wildlife Amendment Act 2010 pertaining to offences by corporations under which each person who is a director of a corporation or who is concerned in the management of the corporation is taken to have contravened the same provision (subject to specific exceptions).

[70] For example, cooperating with authorities and facilitating the administration of justice. See ss 22A and 23 Crimes (Sentencing Procedure) Act 1999 (NSW).

[71] Specifically, Part 3 of the Crimes (Sentencing Procedure) Act 1999 (NSW).

[72] *Plath v Chaffey* (n 44).

[73] *Garrett on behalf of the Director-General of the Department of Conservation and Environment v House* (n 68).

[74] *Chief Executive, Office of Environment and Heritage v Rummery* (2012) 192 LGERA 314.

[75] *Garrett on behalf of the Director-General of the Department of Conservation and Environment v House* (n 68).

[76] *Gordon Plath of the Department of Environment and Climate Change v Fish; Gordon Plath of the Department of Environment and Climate Change v Orogen Pty Ltd* (2010) 179 LGERA 386.

and offsetting environmental benefit (such as eradication of noxious animals).[77] Aggravating factors include, for example, blatant disregard of expert advice,[78] no remorse,[79] prior convictions,[80] attempts at concealment,[81] public body ignoring regulatory environment and statutory obligation[82] and illegal activity continuing after departmental contact and expert advice.[83]

It has been noted that the Court's case law interprets the principle of proportionality to refer to how proportionality controls the upper and lower boundaries of a sentence.[84] Importantly, proportionality as applied to an environmental offence is measured by the degree of environmental harm, such that the more serious the harm, then ordinarily the higher the penalty.[85] This appears to establish a strong ecocentric dimension to assessments of proportionality. The substantive content of the penalty also reflects an ecocentric approach above and beyond the severity of penalty as such.

The Court uses a full repertoire of sentencing options as part of criminal proceedings for offences against environmental laws.[86] These range from community service and publication orders through to fines and restoration schemes (see Table 4).

Table 4 Types of penalties imposed by the Land and Environment Court

Type of penalty imposed	**Specific order**
Fines	• General consolidated revenue • Directed to environmental fund • Directed to specific environmental project
Costs[a]	• Prosecutor costs • Investigation costs
Community service order	• General community benefit
Reprobation (in relation to the defendant)	• Publication order • Public notice (in regard to a specific site) • Publicity related to fine order (so as not to benefit from financial contribution ordered as part of an offence resolution)
Rehabilitation (in relation to the environment)	• Environmental service order • Monitoring • Rehabilitation/remediation

[a]Strictly speaking awarding of costs is not a formal penalty, but it does increase the burden on the defendant and may be experienced as part of the sanction.

[77] *Chief Executive, Office of Environment and Heritage v Kennedy* [2012] NSWLEC 159.

[78] *Chief Executive, Officer of Environment and Heritage, Department of Premier and Cabinet v Powell* [2012] NSWLEC 129.

[79] *Chief Executive, of the Office of Environment and Heritage v Newbigging* [2013] NSWLEC 144.

[80] *Corbyn* (n 34).

[81] *Chief Executive, of the Office of Environment and Heritage v Newbigging* (n 79).

[82] *Garrett v Freeman (No.5)* (n 33).

[83] *Carmody v Brancourts Nominees Pty Limited* (n 33).

[84] Burke (n 5) 456.

[85] Compare, for example, *Director-General, Department of Environment and Climate Change v Jack & Bill Issa Pty Ltd (No. 6)* [2010] NSWLEC 43, and *Director General of National Parks and Wildlife v Wilkinson & Anor* (n 39).

[86] For specific examples, see R White, 'Reparative Justice, Environmental Crime and Penalties for the Powerful' (2016) 67 *Crime, Law and Social Change* 117.

The sanctions frequently involve elements of both punishment of the offender and reparation for the environment. For example, in *Plath v Vaccount Pty Ltd t/as Tableland Timbers*[87] the defendant was convicted for offences associated with the unlawful harvest of trees in a national park that involved the felling of 503 trees. The defendant was fined $73,000 and ordered to pay prosecutor's costs and disbursements of $47,100 and prosecutor's investigation costs to the amount of $2,900. The defendant was ordered to pay a specific recipient, the Northern Rivers Catchment Management Authority, the money to be used for general environmental purposes. Notably, the Court also ordered that all future public references by Vaccount Pty Ltd t/as Timberlands Timbers to the payment above shall be accompanied by the following passage:

> The contribution by Vaccount Pty Ltd, trading as Timberland Timbers, to the Northern Rivers Catchment Management Authority is part of a penalty imposed on it by the Land and Environment Court of NSW after it was convicted of damaging reserve land, being an offence against s 156A of the National Parks and Wildlife Act 1974.

This case features the payment to a specific agency for general environmental purposes. The additional reference to any publicity pertaining to the payment of the fine is important as well. It has been observed that compliance with regulations (or in this case, with a court order) is sometimes used by companies as part of a public relations exercise in which they claim to be environmentally virtuous because of the compliance or financial contribution.[88] The Court forestalled this by imposing the above order.

If the purpose of the Court is seen primarily in the repairing of harm and deterrence of future offending, then what counts is how sentencing can best contribute to these purposes. Fines, in this instance, are not simply a 'cost of business'.[89] They are intended to be large enough to have deterrent effect but, just as importantly, they are translated into meaningful projects and programmes that attempt to concretely remediate the damage and repair the harm. The linking of fines to specific environmental purposes thereby marks it off from more generic fine schemes in which the money is channelled into consolidated revenue.

5. Conclusion

The two interrelated factors that seem to facilitate an ecocentric approach are specialist expertise and having a wide range of sentencing options. The tailoring of sanctions and remedies by the Court, over time, including in the direction of remediation, is significant. When specific remedies are examined, they indicate evidence of specialist knowledge and expertise by the judiciary about the nature of environmental harm and sustained efforts to ensure that the sentence fits the crime. This requires sensitivity to the importance of ecological principles, including regeneration and reparation, as well as knowledge of what might be most suitable in given circumstances. The content of

[87] *Plath* (n 53).

[88] See S Beder, *Global Spin: The Corporate Assault on Environmentalism* (Totnes, Green Books, 2002); and G Pearse, *Greenwash: Big Brands and Carbon Scams* (Collingwood, Black, 2012).

[89] Bricknell (n 65).

extended environmental service orders also indicates reliance upon and/or awareness of scientific knowledge and methodological nous, as well as reflecting experience of likely offender behaviour post-hearing. With respect to this, the fact that the Land and Environment Court is a specialist court seems to be particularly important.

As indicated throughout this chapter, putting principles into practice in an effective manner requires a combination of informed decision-making, the ability to exercise judicial discretion and suitable legislatively provided sentencing regimes to be in place. Specialist expertise is vital to an ecocentric approach because assessing harm in instances involving non-human environmental entities demands an appreciation of and reliance upon ecological and other associated types of specialist knowledge (such as botany and zoology).

Specialist environment courts provide an ideal forum for the development and deployment of just such expertise.[90] For instance, an international survey and evaluation has found that specialist environment courts, that is, courts and tribunals established specifically for dealing with environmental matters and for which particular expertise among court officers is fostered, can and do have greater insight into the nature of environmental offences.[91]

Among the building blocks for an effective and appropriate response to environmental offences are the mobilisation of scientific and technical expertise and the competence of judges and decision-makers.[92] There need not be a separate court, as such, as long as specialist expertise can be acquired by the judiciary within the particular court that hears environmental crime cases. Even where specialist expertise is available, however, this is no guarantee that the penalty will be proportionate to the offence. Again, this depends in part upon the status of the court in question. For example, in South Australia the Environment, Resources and Development Court is comprised of district court judges and the court is constrained by its status to impose fines only within certain limits, which are well below the legislative maximum penalty for environmental offences.[93] By contrast, the Land and Environment Court of NSW has the status and powers of the Supreme Court, and thus is enabled to set harsher penalties than its South Australian counterpart, as well as draw upon a wide spectrum of penalty options.

Adopting an ecocentric approach in assessing and responding to harm is difficult because it requires extensive breadth and depth in the knowledge and expertise to be drawn upon. An informed and flexible perspective is needed precisely because of the intricacies of nature itself. For example, a crucial consideration is the uncertainty

[90] See eg R Walters and D Westerhuis, 'Green Crime and the Role of Environmental Courts' (2013) 59 *Crime, Law and Social Change* 279; D Westerhuis, 'A Harm Analysis of Environmental Crime' in R Walters, D Westerhuis and T Wyatt (eds), *Emerging Issues in Green Criminology* (Basingstoke, Palgrave Macmillan, 2013); R White, 'Environmental Crime and Problem-Solving Courts' (2013) 59 *Crime, Law and Social Change* 267.

[91] G Pring and C Pring, *Greening Justice: Creating and Improving Environmental Courts and Tribunals* (The Access Initiative, 2009). See also C Voigt and Z Makuch (eds), *Courts and the Environment* (Cheltenham, Edward Elgar, 2018); and Fogel and Lipovsek (n 3).

[92] See K Markowitz and J Geradu, 'The Importance of the Judiciary in Environmental Compliance and Enforcement' (2012) 29 *Pace Environmental Law Review* 538; Preston (n 29).

[93] Bates (n 5) 784.

surrounding knowledge about present species and future developments.[94] Nature is always in a constant state of flux, making the estimation of a suitable baseline or threshold by which to gauge harm complicated, and these also vary depending upon the species and ecosystems.

These considerations illustrate the complexities of trying to assess present conditions and future prospects in regard to non-human environmental entities. The Court has a significant role to play in evaluating the objects that have been harmed, and the ways in which they have been harmed. Adoption of an ecocentric approach is enhanced by the intersection of legislative frameworks supportive of ecological sustainability, the employment of assessment methods that categorise harm and facilitate determination of its seriousness according to ecological criteria, and the developing ecological expertise of the judiciary that is in part fostered by regular exposure to relevant experts (eg botanists, arborists and ecologists) in the course of court proceedings. Categorisations of harm based upon prior decisions and knowledge built up by the Court over time, as well as critical scrutiny of expert opinion (which likewise indirectly builds expertise), enable the Court to continue to develop specific indicia for evaluating environmental harm to non-human environmental entities. The success of the Court depends upon judges being knowledgeable and competent – they need to be 'environmentally literate'.[95]

In a similar vein, the Court utilises sanctions in ways that are innovative, progressive and productive. It is able to draw upon selected measures that best suit each particular situation and combine punitive as well as reparative elements. From the point of view of ecocentrism, this also provides for more supportive and nuanced responses to the harms against non-human environmental entities than application of fines as a punitive measure in its own right. There is a demonstrated concern on the part of the Court with remediation and reparation – both in ascertaining the scope and nature of environmental harm, and in responding with appropriate penalties where harm has occurred. In other words, the non-human environmental entity is treated as 'victim' insofar as it is deemed worthy and of enough value to warrant specific treatment intended to repair the harm. While violation of environmental law is a crime against the state, victim needs can nonetheless be acknowledged through such sentencing strategies.

The activities of specialist courts such as the Land and Environment Court are worthy of green criminological attention insofar as they embody many of the ideals and values underpinning an ecocentric approach. Not all courts do this, and, indeed, not all environment courts actually protect the environment (rather, they serve more as licencing and regulatory bodies for industry exploitation of the environment). However, the Court has, for forty years, developed expertise and jurisprudence that over time has consistently signalled a strong eco-justice message. For green criminology, the Court provides a shining example of how ecocentrism can be grounded in specific institutional practices and contexts. And for this, we are grateful.

[94] B Preston and P Adam, 'Describing and Listing Threatened Ecological Communities Under the Threatened Species Conservation Act 1995 (NSW): Part 1 – The Assemblage of Species and the Particular Area' (2004) 21 *Environmental and Planning Law Journal* 250; and B Preston and P Adam, 'Describing and Listing Threatened Ecological Communities Under the Threatened Species Conservation Act 1995 (NSW): Part 2 – the Role of Supplementary Descriptors and the Listing Process' (2004) 21 *Environmental and Planning Law Journal* 372.

[95] B Preston, 'Characteristics of Successful Environmental Courts and Tribunals' (2014) 26 *Journal of Environmental Law* 365, 377.

PART III

Process

12

You Can Only Keep Something by Giving it Away

TIM BONYHADY

1. Introduction

A new court has many firsts. One for the Land and Environment Court of New South Wales (the Court) was an appeal brought by one of Australia's greatest artists, Arthur Boyd. From the 1940s, working in and outside Melbourne, Boyd created his own distinctive iconography – often powerful, usually disturbing, but not easily interpreted. From the 1960s, he enjoyed great success not only in Australia but also in England where he lived. In the last decades of his life, he was best known as a landscape painter, above all for his pictures of the Shoalhaven River which rises from the Southern Tablelands of New South Wales and reaches the Pacific Ocean near Nowra on the Shoalhaven River on the South Coast of New South Wales.

Having recently acquired two properties inland from Nowra on the Shoalhaven, Boyd and his wife Yvonne instituted an appeal in the Court in 1981 to overturn a local council decision allowing a local company, Foster Emery, to dredge sand and gravel from the river. This case, which was heard by the Court in 1982 when it was less than two years old, has attracted some attention from art historians because of Arthur Boyd's significance as an artist and the importance for him of the Shoalhaven. But the case has been ignored by lawyers, despite it being the first third-party merits appeal heard by the Court.[1]

An obvious reason is that the case was heard by one of the Court's assessors, who delivered a brief, muddled judgment after the Shoalhaven Council conceded that it had no jurisdiction to approve the dredging. Yet the case is of great interest as an example of intense, immediate attachment to a particular landscape giving rise to a passion

[1] According to P Ryan, 'Environmental Court System' (1981) 4 *University of New South Wales Law Journal* 11, 23, 'there were very few third party appeals' in the Court's 'first months of operation' from 1 September 1980, implying that there were some, which would have preceded the Boyds' case. However, the Boyds' appeal was the first reported in the *Land and Environment Notes 1980–1982* and investigation of the Court's records by Elizabeth Orr reveals that the Boyds' case was the first.

to protect it. The proceedings also played a significant part in stopping the dredging, although the Emery family almost immediately proceeded with a related development on their own land so the Boyds' success in the Court was only a partial victory. The case is all the more interesting – and complex – because it was intertwined with the Boyds' ambition to persuade government to accept their newly acquired properties, Riversdale and Bundanon, as a gift, with Arthur Boyd articulating a radical critique of private landownership:

> There is something dramatically wrong with one man owning a landscape. You can't take it with you, and I cannot bear to think of Bundanon being chopped up and ruined. I wanted Bundanon made safe and secure, so all Australians can share this marvellous spot forever.[2]

The case is also of great interest because the surviving files kept for the Boyds provide an opportunity to consider not just the letter of the law but also the law in action. These files record how the Boyds exposed the environmental hazards of dredging, rebutting many of the arguments put forward by Foster Emery. They reveal how Foster Emery had more influence in Nowra but the Boyds had more influence in Sydney, triggering an extraordinary intervention in the case by the New South Wales premier, Neville Wran. These files also provide a window onto the initial distrust of the new court among conservationists. Far from welcoming the opportunity to have it consider the dredging on appeal, the Boyds' advisers saw the Court as a last, unfortunate resort and would have preferred a public inquiry into the dredging, in keeping with a larger enthusiasm at the time for this type of review.[3] Before long, this stance would be reversed, with environmentalists, for good reason, having scant confidence in inquiries and wanting more opportunities to appear before the Court.[4]

2. The Essence We've Been Thinking About

Bundanon's river flats had been used for many different purposes including dairy farming, a piggery, fattening cattle and cropping, but its forest of ironbark, messmate, bloodwood and stringybark on the rocky ground above the river was largely intact when one of Arthur Boyd's many art dealers, Frank McDonald, bought Bundanon along with the art writer Sandra McGrath and her stockbroker-banker husband Tony in 1968. Over the next few years, McDonald and the McGraths set about returning Bundanon to what they conceived as its nineteenth-century state. Their prime focus was Bundanon's two-storey Georgian homestead which had become a barn. But McDonald and the McGraths demolished most of Bundanon's nineteenth- and early twentieth-century work buildings and an old schoolhouse. They also erected a new barn and workshop,

[2] J Hawley, 'Boyd's Gift: A $20M Landscape for All to Share' *Sydney Morning Herald* (28 January 1993).

[3] J Cole, 'Environmental Law and Environmental Politics' (1981) 4 *University of New South Wales Law Journal* 55, 68–71.

[4] D Farrier, 'Environmental Assessment in Australia' (1984) 1 *Environmental and Planning Law Journal* 151, 166; N Pain, 'Third Party Rights: Public Participation Under the Environmental Planning and Assessment Act 1979 (NSW)' (1989) 6 *Environmental and Planning Law Journal* 26, 29–30, 32, 34.

established a cottage garden, planted American poplars and significantly modified the homestead's interior.[5]

The Boyds first visited at McDonald's invitation in the summer of 1971–72 as part of returning to Australia for their first extended visit in twelve years so Arthur could take up a three-month fellowship in Canberra at the Australian National University. After probably spending just a day or two at Bundanon with McDonald, they seemingly returned at least once more before returning to England at the end of February 1972. 'Congratulations on the vision you've made real', Yvonne wrote in a letter of thanks. For the Boyds, Bundanon was 'the essence we've been thinking about all these years'.[6]

Arthur's success as an artist was allowing the Boyds to acquire a multitude of properties, for themselves and their children, in Australia, England and Italy. After they asked McDonald to look for one on the Shoalhaven, he suggested Riversdale: '140 acres with a derelict wooden cottage' offering 'superb' river views, a short distance downstream from Bundanon.[7] On receiving McDonald's photographs, the Boyds telegrammed, 'Do not let it go. We love it. Please try to secure it' and bought Riversdale early in 1974 without having been there. Back in Australia later that year, they rented an adjoining property called Eearie Park which the McGraths also owned, then moved into Riversdale in 1975 after they had its house restored and extended and built a studio for Arthur. After another stint in England, they spent 1978 at Riversdale, then bought Bundanon in 1979 and built another studio there, while Boyd's brother-in-law, the artist Sidney Nolan, who had visited Riversdale with his wife Mary in 1977, acquired part of Eearie Park which the McGraths had begun subdividing.[8]

Boyd loved how Bundanon combined 'a desire to transport an English vision' to Australia, while preserving 'the original concept of a wild Australia or an Australia that was still untamed'.[9] On the one hand, there was the Georgian homestead and a century-and-a-half of European land use on the river flats. On the other hand, there were many areas – and vistas – unchanged by Europeans. Boyd would recount how, when he first climbed above the Shoalhaven between Bundanon and Riversdale, he delighted in how he could see the river on both sides 'so vast – not a hut or a house. It seemed absolutely untouched.' His experience of the power of the river in flood led him to identify the Shoalhaven as 'the only untamed landscape I have ever seen'.[10]

When Boyd began living at Bundanon in 1981, he found its immediate environment under threat. Where there had been 'not a sound on the river' when he first visited, water skiers had 'discovered the place', destroying much of the Shoalhaven's tranquillity on weekends.[11] The Emerys, who owned Wogamia on the other side of the river to

[5] Peter Freeman Ltd, *The Bundanon Trust Properties Heritage Management Plan*, vol 2 (2007) 3-20-22, 26–7.

[6] S McGrath, *The Artist and the River: Arthur Boyd and the Shoalhaven* (Bay Books, 1982) 92. Some sources date the Boyds' visit to December 1971, others to January 1972. Some sources also suggest, improbably, that Boyd spent a fortnight or even 'several weeks' at Bundanon over the summer of 1971–72. See D Bungey, *Arthur Boyd: A Life* (London, Allen & Unwin 2007) 470–72, 474–75; U Hoff, *The Art of Arthur Boyd* (London, André Deutsch, 1986) 64, 226; B Pearce, *Arthur Boyd: Landscape of the Soul* (Bundanon Trust Travelling Exhibition) 60.

[7] N Hellyer and J Potts, *Culturescape: An Ecology of Bundanon* (Bundanon Trust, 2019) 46.

[8] Bungey (n 6) 475, 481.

[9] J McKenzie, *Arthur Boyd at Bundanon* (London, Academy Editions, 1994) 14.

[10] McGrath (n 6) 50, 192, 206.

[11] J Hawley, 'Why Arthur Boyd Is Giving it Away' *Sydney Morning Herald, Good Weekend* (4 March 1989) 38, 43.

Riversdale and had been selling soil from there since 1974, were also looking to expand their operations. Through their family company, Foster Emery and Sons, they were seeking permission to dredge a sand bar on the Shoalhaven, which was visible at low tide. They wanted to extract up to 2000 cubic metres of sand and gravel from the river each week and build a plant on Wogamia where they would wash the sand and gravel before selling it, radically changing the immediate environment of Riversdale, Bundanon and Eearie Park.

Because the sand bar was Crown land, Foster Emery could only exploit it with state approval. The relevant approval was a 'permissive occupancy' – granted for decades without statutory basis until a judicial finding that this process was probably unlawful.[12] When the government duly legislated to authorise the Minister for Lands to grant such approvals, he was given an almost unfettered discretion. The new statutory provision empowered the minister to issue permissive occupancies 'for such purposes and upon such terms and conditions as to him may seem fit'.[13] It failed to identify how applications for these permissions should be made and gave members of the public, including adjoining landowners, no rights to be notified or to object or to appeal. As a matter of practice, applications to the local Land Board office could be 'quite informal', accompanied simply by 'a sketch of the desired area'.[14]

With the exception of residential flat buildings, legislation in New South Wales – alone in Australia – had also failed to provide members of the public with any rights to be notified of development applications, object against them or appeal against their approval.[15] The law assumed local councils would give effect to the public interest in considering these applications – or perhaps assumed that the public had no interest. As highlighted by Murray Wilcox, then the state's foremost barrister to specialise in the law of land development, the result was a flawed process in which developers typically served their self-interest by putting only the case for approval, leaving councils often unaware of the counter-arguments.[16]

When the Labor government of Neville Wran introduced new environmental planning legislation in 1979, one of the doyens of Australian administrative law, Harry Whitmore, argued that this legislation should allow all members of the public to object against development applications before local councils, then challenge their approvals on the merits in the Land and Environment Court. Whitmore dismissed the conventional fear that such a provision would trigger a flood of appeals as unfounded. Building on Murray Wilcox's earlier arguments, he declared a general right of objection necessary because it had been possible for applicants and councils 'to deliberately

[12] *Barrow v Brooksby* (1958) 37 LVR 14.

[13] Crown Lands Consolidation Act 1913 (NSW) s 136K.

[14] AG Lang, *Crown Land in New South Wales* (London, Butterworths, 1973) 17–18, 125–26.

[15] A Fogg, 'Third Party Objections and Appeal in Development Control Decisions under Town Planning Legislation' (1985) 2 *Environmental and Planning Law Journal* 4, 5–6.

[16] M Wilcox, *The Law of Land Development in New South Wales* (Sydney, Law Book, 1967) 431–32; M Wilcox, 'The Environmental Planning and Assessment Bill 1979: A Conceptual and Legal Framework' in *Environmental Planning and Assessment Bill: A New Era for Planning and Development in New South Wales* (Australian Seminar Service, 1979) 1, 2.

flout the public interest safe in the knowledge that there was no right of appeal against a consent once given'.[17]

Instead, Part IV of the 1979 Act confined the right of members of the public to object and appeal to a new class of 'designated development', to be specified by regulations,[18] which were subject to additional scrutiny because their proponents had to prepare an environmental impact statement. While the designated development categories were criticised almost immediately for being far too narrow, one was 'extractive industries'. When Foster Emery wanted to dredge the river, the Shoalhaven Council probably advised that the dredging would be covered by the interim development order which served as its planning scheme; hence Foster Emery would have to comply with the designated development provision and advertise its proposal in the press and notify adjoining landowners that they had four weeks to object in writing.[19]

3. You Have to *Do* Something

Arthur Boyd was in many ways an unlikely objector. While always left-leaning and committed to pacificism, he generally eschewed direct political involvement, unlike his wife Yvonne who was an active member of the Australian Communist Party for several years from 1945. Boyd's public stances on political issues from the late 1950s through the 1960s into the 1970s were episodic – and always involved him joining causes led by others. The Shoalhaven River and Boyd's aspirations for Riversdale and Bundanon set him on a new course aged sixty in May 1981 when he – or Yvonne, who was responsible for most of his correspondence – wrote a letter to the local council in Nowra, asking if he could attend its regular meetings. In response, most likely puzzled at this request from one of Australia's great artists, came an immediate letter from the mayor declaring it 'extremely heartening' that Boyd was interested in 'the council operation'.[20] When notified a couple of weeks later of Foster Emery's application, Boyd replied: 'I wish to protest very strongly.'[21]

Boyd's response was spurred by both his love for his new environment and his aspiration to give it away. In doing so, Boyd was building on his first major public benefaction – his gift in 1975 to the National Gallery of Australia in Canberra of several thousand of his works ranging from drawings, prints and paintings to sculptures and tapestries. He was also influenced by an earlier proposal of Frank McDonald and the McGraths that the New South Wales government buy Bundanon and transform it into a regional gallery. Above all, he was responding to the destruction of two family sites in Victoria – 'Open Country' at Murrumbeena in suburban Melbourne and The Grange outside Berwick – where members of his family, including Arthur himself, had lived,

[17] H Whitmore, 'Appeal Mechanisms and Administration of the New Planning Legislation' in *Environmental Planning and Assessment Bill: A New Era for Planning and Development in New South Wales* (Australian Seminar Service, 1979) 6.3.

[18] Environmental Planning and Assessment Act 1979 (NSW) s 158.

[19] Environmental Planning and Assessment Act 1979 (NSW) s 84(1); Farrier (n 4) 159–60.

[20] Letter from Shoalhaven Mayor to Arthur Boyd (12 May 1981).

[21] Letter from Arthur Boyd to Mayor, Shoalhaven Council (11 June 1981).

drawn, painted, sculpted, made pottery and written. Although his family had no prior connection with the Shoalhaven, Boyd wanted Bundanon to celebrate the exceptional creativity of his family over multiple generations. With quarrying for blue metal having led to the demolition of The Grange, he sought to do all he could to protect his new home. While pessimistic about the future of the planet, fearful 'of the environment being destroyed and everything being overwhelmed by technology', his credo was: 'You have to *do* something … make some positive move.'[22]

Sidney Nolan, who met Boyd in Melbourne in the 1940s and grew close to him in London in the 1960s, influenced his plans. As he led Boyd in giving away much of his own work out of a mix of generosity and eye for his enduring reputation, Nolan offered twenty-four of his greatest Ned Kelly, Burke and Wills, and Eliza Fraser paintings to the Australian government in 1974 on the condition that it find a suitable place to exhibit them. That was no simple task when the National Gallery of Australia was yet to open and the Canberra Museum and Art Gallery did not exist. The federal government proposed Lanyon, a 9,500-acre property on the Murrumbidgee River in the Australian Capital Territory, which it had recently acquired. The government wanted most of Lanyon's land for urban development but was looking for a use for Lanyon's Georgian homestead. When Nolan agreed, preservation of Australia's colonial heritage conjoined with display of some of its best twentieth-century art, which the *Australian* recognised in lauding how Nolan's work would 'be seen in a building which a few years ago, under a different environmental climate, might well have been bulldozed'.[23]

Here was a precedent: Boyd's greatest contemporary finding a rural, Georgian setting for some of his paintings as part of donating them to the Australian people. Yet here also was a warning about the complexity of making such a gift, as the placement of Nolan's work in the homestead was contested immediately by the Canberra chapter of the National Trust, which wanted Lanyon to become a period piece filled with mid-nineteenth-century furniture. 'Nolan does not do justice to Lanyon and Lanyon does not do justice Nolan', the Trust maintained, as it began campaigning to gain control of the homestead and its outbuildings, even before Nolan's paintings were first displayed there in 1975.[24] Others were more vehement. The reduction of Lanyon to 'a sterile art gallery' was a 'disaster' reckoned one contributor to the *Canberra Times*. How could it be, asked another, that such a 'serene and beautiful building' had become home to 'meaningless daubs possibly rescued from mediocrity by an admirable use of colour'?[25] In vain, the *Canberra Times*'s art critic, Geoffrey de Groen, declared it appropriate that 'Nolan's magnificent works' be seen in a 'gracious old homestead' of 'such beauty'.[26]

The federal government resolved this conflict by erecting a purpose-built gallery a few hundred metres from the Lanyon homestead, which opened in 1980. When Boyd

[22] McGrath (n 6) 20; Hoff (n 6) 67–68; Hawley (n 2) 44.

[23] B Adams, *Sidney Nolan: Such Is Life* (Hutchinson 1987) 223–25; N Underhill, *Sidney Nolan* (Sydney, UNSW Press, 2015) 340.

[24] *Canberra Times* (30 January 1975) 3.

[25] *Canberra Times* (31 January 1976) 2; *Canberra Times* (15 February 1978) 19; *Canberra Times* (7 June 1979) 2.

[26] *Canberra Times* (10 March 1975) 6.

began looking to give Bundanon to the people of New South Wales, Nolan suggested he talk to David Chalker, the officer in the federal Department of the Australian Capital Territory responsible for the new Nolan Gallery. After they met in March 1981 when Boyd visited Lanyon for the opening of an exhibition of Nolan drawings, Chalker visited Boyd at Bundanon at the start of May and began helping Boyd to develop his gift idea for his properties on the Shoalhaven which, among many other public benefits, provided a rare opportunity to bring river frontage back into public ownership. Through 1981, Chalker's role was personal and voluntary, then he took twelve months' leave to work for Boyd.

At the start of June 1981, Chalker sent Boyd a preliminary document outlining two possibilities. One was for a Boyd Trust. The other, which Boyd preferred, was for a Boyd Regional Art Museum. In return for Boyd donating Bundanon and a collection of several thousand art works made by five generations of his family, he looked to the New South Wales government and the Shoalhaven Council to establish and manage in perpetuity a regional art museum where the Boyd art gift would be housed. He also expected the state government and the local council to zone the surrounding area 'to prevent exploitation by further subdivision and uses inconsistent with its natural character' and manage the area to 'preserve and promote an appreciation of its natural and anthropological significance for the public benefit'.[27]

Environmental impact assessment was a new feature of Australian land-use decision-making – intended, according to the New South Wales Department of Environment and Planning, to ensure that projects which might significantly damage the environment would be the stuff of 'detailed analysis'.[28] Foster Emery's response to this requirement was to commission an environmental impact statement (EIS) from a consultant with an arts degree but no scientific qualifications, which ran to less than ten pages of original material. Despite there already being two dredging operations on the Shoalhaven, the EIS argued that there was local demand for more sand and gravel which the new plant would satisfy. The EIS also maintained that dredging would remedy 'large scale river erosion' and 'large scale river bank erosion' and prevent 'worse flooding due to siltation of the river channels'.[29] The EIS argued the plant would not be an eyesore as it would be small-scale and be screened from the river and nearby higher ground by plantings of fast-growing local wattles and eucalypts.[30]

Boyd responded by identifying Foster Emery's project as 'sand mining' which, in one sense, it was. But 'sand mining' at the time usually meant extracting rutile, zircon and ilmenite – three heavy minerals, sometimes found inland or underground, but usually found on beaches. Because the extraction of these mineral sands often involved great environmental damage, it had triggered a myriad of disputes and extensive litigation, most famously on Queensland's Fraser Island.[31] To describe the dredging at Bundanon

[27] D Chalker, 'The Boyd Regional Art Museum and the Boyd Trust: Two Alternative Proposals for Bundanon' (May 1981).

[28] New South Wales Department of Environment and Planning, *A Guide to the Environmental Planning Legislation* (1980) 9.

[29] Foster Emery & Sons, *Environmental Impact Statement* (5 April 1981) 1, 7–8, 10.

[30] ibid, 6, 9, app 5.

[31] *Sinclair v Mining Warden at Maryborough* (1975) 5 ALR 513; *Murphyores Inc P/L v Commonwealth* (1976) 126 CLR 1.

as 'sand mining' put it in this company – a sleight-of-hand identified by two contributors to the local press in Nowra.[32]

Otherwise Boyd addressed the dredging with much more rigour than Foster Emery, commissioning two hydrologists to respond to the company's EIS.[33] The hydrologists' report, which was more than twice the length of the EIS, argued that Foster Emery had failed to provide an adequate description of the project or its environmental and aesthetic impacts. The hydrologists contended that, just as the two existing operations on the Shoalhaven had not reduced siltation of the river, Foster Emery's operation would also fail to do so because the siltation was due to dams being built higher on the river and its tributaries and water being extracted from it for irrigation. If the dredging opened a channel, there was a risk of significant erosion downstream because of the increased speed of the water. The only effective way of stopping bank slump and erosion was to plant trees. Dredging would irreversibly change the river's ecology and create noise and dust. The existing plants on the river could supply local needs and, if more sand were required, state policy was to expand existing plants rather than create new ones. Because the washing plant was to be more than ten metres high, it would blight the appearance of the river when the New South Wales Planning and Environment Commission had recognised its lower reaches as an area of particular significance.[34]

Water skiing was one part of this debate, with a contributor to the local *Shoalhaven and Nowra News* challenging Boyd to oppose it along with the dredging. 'Does he enjoy the strident noise of power boats, some towing skiers up and down the peaceful river from before dawn until dark all day Saturday, Sunday and holidays?', this contributor asked. 'If not, when does he plan to mount a campaign against them, for they pollute the atmosphere with petrol fumes, waste fuel, cause wash damage to river banks and prevent the quiet, peaceful enjoyment of the river.' In keeping with Tony Emery's own enjoyment of water skiing, Foster Emery implicitly supported it. The company's EIS claimed its dredging would make the river 'much safer for water skiers'.[35] The Boyds' hydrologist consultants were scathing:

> Water skiing in a reach of the Shoalhaven River already experiencing 'fluvial problems' associated with river bank erosion *should not be permitted*. As is widely known, the wash generated by skiers actively attacks river banks – to suggest that Foster Emery want to encourage skiing and at the same time talk of the farmers' awareness of the bank erosion problem at Wogamia needing to be remedied are contradictory.[36]

Boyd's plans to give away Bundanon were still nascent, but he decided to announce them to transform how the dredging was viewed. It would not just impact an adjoining property which happened to be owned by a great artist; it would, Boyd wrote to the local mayor, also 'jeopardise' his gift. In another letter, sent among others to Neville Wran,

[32] *Shoalhaven and Nowra News* (15 July 1981). See further T Bonyhady, *Places Worth Keeping: Conservationists, Politics and Law* (London, Allen & Unwin, 1992) ch 1. A contemporary NSW case was *Hastings Municipal Council v Mineral Deposits Ltd* (1981) 1 NSWLR 310, [169].

[33] WJ Gregory, 'A Review of the Proposed Sand and Gravel Extraction on the Shoalhaven River at Wogamia by Foster, Emery and Sons Pty Ltd' (unpublished, 1981).

[34] NSW Planning and Environment Commission, *Draft Illawarra Regional Plan* (1979).

[35] Foster, Emery & Sons (n 29) 9.

[36] *Shoalhaven and Nowra News* (26 August 1981) 4; Gregory (n 33) s 8.

Boyd declared 'the proposal would be unrealisable if this area of the Shoalhaven River were to be given over to commercial interests of any sort. That would be the beginning of activity that would eventually destroy this unique environment.'[37]

By the end of June, Sidney Nolan had not only joined Boyd in opposing the dredging but was 'prepared to throw in art works and land' – his newly acquired portion of Eearie Park – increasing what the public might secure. But Boyd also appears to have realised that he may have overreached in suggesting he would only make his gift if there were no dredging. Instead, he stated that he would be 'extremely disappointed' were the dredging to be approved. In the first public document about his gift, written by David Chalker, Boyd revealed that his vision for Bundanon involved much more than preserving and displaying family material. Boyd also wanted to protect the natural environment, Aboriginal sites and colonial heritage, and bring young artists there, with one annual fellowship to be 'awarded to an Aboriginal Australian, and another to a non-Aboriginal Australian', and other artists and craftspeople to 'be encouraged to work at Bundanon as resources permit'.[38]

At the start of July, Tony Emery sought a rapprochement with Boyd, writing to allay his 'fears of potential pollution, both visual and physical' by showing that the dredging would not threaten Boyd's 'ideals for this area' because it would have 'the very minimum effect on you and the surrounding environment'. Emery argued that the dredging was necessary to protect his land. He also argued that it had become 'obvious' that, if Foster Emery did not proceed, 'other companies would do so and we would have no control over what they did, and we, like all our neighbours, did not want this river spoiled by another mine like Burrier', the big existing plant on the river upstream from Bundanon. 'Our family will always have complete control over the sand-mining operation', he declared in an attempt to demonstrate it would have a different ethic.[39]

The Emerys also issued a public statement, published by both the local *Shoalhaven and Nowra News* and the *South Coast Register*. In it, they not only restated their case that the dredging would be environmentally beneficial, not destructive, but also made much of how, as the fifth generation of his family to live there, Tony Emery had 'a closer affinity to the area than the objectors'. The public statement identified the Emerys as

> a locally known and highly respected family. They love the district. It is part of their family history, part of their children's future. They wish to emphasise that they will not be a party to any activity which will be detrimental to the amenity of the area in which they and their neighbours live.[40]

4. A No Man's Land of Environmental Planning

Law and legal advice – overseen by William Lasica, Boyd's long-standing Melbourne solicitor – were integral to Boyd's response. The prime focus was the new Environmental

[37] Letter from Arthur Boyd to Mayor, Shoalhaven Council (11 June 1981); letter from Arthur Boyd to Neville Wran (17 June 1981); letter from David Chalker to Michael Egan (23 July 1981).

[38] Record of discussion between Sidney Nolan and Arthur Boyd (29 June 1981); David Chalker, *Bundanon*, July 1981.

[39] Letter from Tony Emery to Arthur Boyd (3 July 1981).

[40] *South Coast Register* (15 July 1981); *Shoalhaven and Nowra News* (15 July 1981).

Planning and Assessment Act 1979 (NSW). In August 1981 Boyd received his first legal bill of $795 from Lasica's Sydney agents, Murphy & Moloney – most of it for an opinion from one of Sydney's leading planning barristers, Murray Tobias QC. The context was manifestly unfavourable with the mayor of the Shoalhaven Council, Greg Watson, declaring it better to get sand from the river than dunes near beaches, and dismissing the opposition as 'a storm of protest much of which is somewhat difficult to comprehend'.[41] One of Boyd's advisers predicted that the council would 'largely ignore' the detailed provisions in the Environmental Planning and Assessment Act specifying the matters to be taken into account in deciding development applications. He expected the council to 'approve the development on an unstated assumption that, even though there is no demand for more sand locally, free enterprise competition is inherently healthy and to be encouraged'.[42]

If so, Boyd could appeal on the merits to the Land and Environment Court,[43] which had already become the subject of detailed study by Patricia Ryan of Macquarie University. In the first major essay about the Court, published at the start of 1981, she argued that, because of its mix of personnel and its principal legislation, the Court had 'enormous' potential to 'add an environmental or public dimension to traditional narrowly focussed dispute settlements and prosecutions'. But she also recognised that the Court's 'unique qualities' and a 'general failure' by government 'to inform the community about the court' had made it the stuff of 'depressing ignorance' and 'a target for cynicism and criticism', including within legal circles.[44]

Boyd's advisers were among them. Far from looking forward to there being a complete rehearing of Foster Emery's application before the new court, they had no confidence in it. One thought it 'better to stop development as early as possible rather than relying on rights of appeal to the Land and Environment Court'. While recognising that it might consider environmental and social factors beyond those in Foster Emery's EIS, this adviser observed: 'whether judges and assessors of the court are very environmentally conscious is another matter altogether'.[45]

Because of their fears, Boyd's advisers looked for another forum where the dredging might be assessed. Since New South Wales had created significant legislative provision for environmental inquiries from the mid-1970s, they hoped for such an inquiry. But they did so in a context of negligible support from governmental agencies. A senior official with the federal government's Australian Heritage Commission observed that the 'moral issues' involved 'in this decision were solely whether Arthur Boyd had any right to an unspoilt view over his section of the river', expecting that if Boyd 'stopped the dredging someone else upstream or downstream would get it outside their home'.[46]

Bundanon was listed on the federal heritage list, the National Estate, but this listing only affected Commonwealth decisions.[47] Bundanon was also listed under the

[41] *South Coast Register* (15 July 1981).
[42] L Flynn, 'Legal Situation on the Sand Mining' (unpublished manuscript in Boyd case files) 15.
[43] Environmental Planning and Assessment Act 1979 (NSW) s 98(1).
[44] Ryan (n 1) 20, 28.
[45] Flynn (n 42) 19.
[46] Cole (n 3) 69–71; Flynn (n 42) 16.
[47] Australian Heritage Commission Act 1975 (Cth) s 30 (1).

New South Wales National Trust legislation,[48] but that was of no legal consequence. The Mining Act 1973 (NSW), which made provision for public objections to mining applications, a mechanism much used by conservationists in the 1970s, did not apply because sand was not a prescribed mineral under this legislation.[49] While the Boyds had set about having Bundanon declared a wildlife refuge under the National Parks and Wildlife Act 1974 (NSW),[50] that was yet to take effect and would apply only to the Boyds' own land.

Boyd's advisers hoped the state's Minister for Planning and Environment would exercise his power to 'call-in' Foster Emery's development application and replace the council as the decision-maker, entitling Boyd to demand a public inquiry.[51] Before its enactment, this section excited particular condemnation from Murray Wilcox who, as part of more generally identifying the Environmental Planning and Assessment Act's many provisions for state intervention as 'appalling', declared the call-in power 'worst of all'. Because the minister could 'pick a special tribunal for a particular case', he could shape if not determine its findings, and his decision was not open to appeal on the merits.[52]

The state government had already begun using this call-in power to provide favoured developers with a preferential pathway to approval. Boyd's advisers hoped that, unusually, the minister would exercise this power to stop a proposed development, demonstrating that the minister was 'less biased' than the Shoalhaven Council.[53] But for all Boyd's efforts, which saw him give newspaper, magazine and radio interviews, resulting in articles in the *Sydney Morning Herald*, the *Australian* and the *Australian Women's Weekly*, the state government advised that Boyd had failed to elevate the issue to 'the level of conflict necessary' to spur ministerial action.[54] As a result, according to one of Boyd's advisers, it remained in 'a no-man's land of environmental planning between a department only motivated by extreme public protest, and between local government bodies, whose unfamiliarity with environmental values is witnessed by the development littering the country'.[55]

The Shoalhaven Council's professional staff displayed much more rigour than that. Its planner recommended rejection of the application because of the impact of the dredging on 'views and intrusion into a quiet, particularly attractive section of the river valley and immediate effect of heavy truck traffic on some residents alongside the road'. Since there was 'no strong evidence' that the sand adjoining Wogamia was a 'vital' source, he concluded that 'the creation of a new extractive industry in this location, which is so highly regarded by residents and visitors alike, would not be warranted'. The council's engineer suggested that it negotiate with the company for a shared cost of road maintenance since, in the initial stages of the operation, there would be more than 100 trucks a day carrying sand and gravel from the site, not ten loads per day as Foster Emery had specified in its EIS.[56]

[48] National Trust of Australia (NSW) Act 1960 (NSW).
[49] Mining Act 1973 (NSW) ss 6(1), 112.
[50] National Parks and Wildlife Act 1974 (NSW) s 68.
[51] Environmental Planning and Assessment Act 1979 (NSW) ss 88(3), 89(1), 101(1), 119(1)(b).
[52] Wilcox, 'The Environmental Planning and Assessment Bill 1979' (n 16) 1.8–1.9.
[53] Flynn (n 42) 9.
[54] ibid.
[55] ibid, 10.
[56] *Shoalhaven and Nowra News* (undated).

The councillors on the Town Planning and Development Committee dismissed these arguments as 'technical' and recommended that the proposal be approved.[57] The council agreed in December 1981, having met with Foster Emery but not the objectors. It approved the application despite a noisy demonstration and a petition against dredging which attracted more than 700 signatories. The approval's twenty-seven conditions included limiting truck movements to twenty-five a day, requiring Foster Emery to seal a strip of an access road close to another house, which Foster Emery estimated would cost $10,000, and requiring it to contribute six cents per tonne to the maintenance of this road.[58]

Boyd's lawyers remained reluctant to appeal to the Land and Environment Court. A decision just reached by the Court may have been a factor. It involved another application to dredge sand which was also treated as a designated development, spurring the preparation of an EIS. While the Hawkesbury Shire Council rejected this application, one of the Court's assessors, Joan Domicelj, approved it in a merits appeal, deciding that an array of conditions would be sufficient to protect the 'fragile swamp ecology' and that, under the relevant planning instrument, the applicant did not have to demonstrate 'need or economic benefit' for the community.[59]

Murray Wilcox, who acted in many merits appeals in the Court's first few years, later observed: 'There were some assessors who rarely, if ever, upheld an appeal. There were some who rarely, if ever, dismissed an appeal. There were others where, beforehand, there was a serious question about what might happen.' Wilcox thought that was to be expected, given how, for all the technical requirements, determination of these cases involved 'different value judgments'.[60] Rather than cast their continued search for another forum in such terms, Boyd's lawyers identified it as a means 'to avoid confrontation with the council'.[61] But once again, they failed, despite John Hatton, the independent member for the South Coast, mentioning the dispute in state parliament.[62] With no other option, the Boyds appealed to the Court, while Foster Emery cross-appealed, seeking unrestricted use of the access road without having to seal any part of it.

The expense of the appeal was an issue. Having just submitted another invoice to Boyd for $1,426, Murphy & Molony estimated the likely costs of a one-day hearing.[63] They expected their fees would be $2,500. Expert witnesses – possibly a planner, hydrologist, heritage specialist and economist – would be $3,000. Junior counsel would be $1,500. Senior counsel, if required, would be $2,250. 'Extraordinary amount of money' someone annotated this document, appalled by a total of $9,250. Boyd responded by suggesting payment in kind: that Murphy & Molony select some of his paintings and, in January 1982, they agreed while still requiring Boyd to pay their costs

[57] *Shoalhaven and Nowra News* (undated).

[58] *Shoalhaven and Nowra News* (28 April 1982).

[59] *McInerney v Hawkesbury Shire Council* Land and Environment Notes 1980–1982 [387], decided 11 December 1981.

[60] M Wilcox, 'The Promise of the Environmental Legislative Scheme' in *Promise, Perception, Problems and Remedies: The Land and Environment Court and Environmental Law 1979–1999* (Chippendale, Nature Conservation Council of NSW, 1999) 14.

[61] Letter from Murphy & Molony to Arthur & Yvonne Boyd (8 February 1982).

[62] Parliament of New South Wales, Hansard, Legislative Assembly, 10 February 1982, 1743.

[63] 'Estimated expenses for appeal', undated memorandum.

and disbursements in the interim.[64] When the case first came before the Court for a compulsory conference, the parties expected the hearing of the appeal to last not one day but four.[65]

The Sydney barrister, Bill Davison, who acted for the Boyds, recognised there were possible points of law involving the inadequacy of Foster Emery's EIS but opted to focus on the merits of the council's decision. Davison advised that the Boyds had 'reasonable prospects of success' because Foster Emery's arguments about the need for a new sand and gravel plant on the Shoalhaven and its arguments about the benefits of dredging for the river's flow were both weak. Far from conceding any failing on its part when it came to these matters, the Shoalhaven Council relaxed the conditions it had imposed on Foster Emery, giving it little to cross-appeal about. In the wake of Foster Emery arguing that the requirement to strip seal part of the road to Wogamia was contrary to the council's own policies, the council abandoned this condition. It also reduced its limit of twenty-five truckloads per day from a daily maximum to a monthly average.[66]

5. A Most Generous Offer

All along, Boyd and his advisers looked directly for help from Neville Wran who, in 1976, had become the first premier of New South Wales to be also its Minister for Arts, with his Premier's Department including a Cultural Division. By 1981, Wran had not only enhanced the funding of the Art Gallery of New South Wales and the State Library but also supported the creation of the Sydney Theatre Company and the Powerhouse Museum and transformed the city's Macquarie Street by transferring both the Mint and the Hyde Park Barracks to the Museum of Applied Arts and Sciences. He also had done much for regional art galleries which had generally been in a parlous state, depending on poorly funded local councils for very limited financial support.

One consequence was a new gallery for western Sydney, although the experience of the Lewers family demonstrated the difficulties in establishing such a gallery. In 1973, Margo Lewers, one of Sydney's foremost abstract artists, offered to give the Penrith City Council the property on Emu Plains where she and her late husband, the sculptor Gerald Lewers, had lived since 1951. Lewers wanted it to become a community arts centre, maintaining its existing collection of the Lewers' own works and those of many of their contemporaries and preserving its garden, which included an array of sculptures, fountains, mosaics and murals. But the Penrith City Council repeatedly refused her offer, fearful of the costs of sustaining the centre.[67]

[64] Letter from Murphy & Moloney to William Lasica (28 January 1982).

[65] *Boyd v Foster Emery and Sons*, Land and Environment Court file 10643/1981, report of conference 19 January 1982.

[66] WR Davison, Advice (20 April 1982); letter from Morton and Harris, solicitors, Nowra, to Arthur Boyd (20 May 1982); *Shoalhaven and Nowra News* (28 April 1982). The legal requirements for an EIS would soon be considered in *Prineas v Forestry Commission of NSW* (1984) 53 LGERA 160. See BJ Preston, 'Adequacy of Environmental Impact Statements in New South Wales' (1986) 3 *Environmental and Planning Law Journal* 194.

[67] D Hickey, *Gerald and Margo Lewers: Their Lives and their Work* (Grasstree Press, 1982) 8; J Lewis, *A Bequest: The Friends, the Blossoming of a Gallery* (Mini-Publishing, 2008) 4–6.

After Margo Lewers died in 1978, the Lewers' daughters not only persisted but also made their offer more attractive by expanding it to include a house designed by one of Australia's foremost modernist architects, Sydney Ancher, and making their offer unconditional. Recognising the need for a regional gallery in western Sydney, Wran's cultural division funded a feasibility study and, in 1979, after extensive lobbying from members of the local community, the Penrith Council accepted the Lewers' gift on condition that the state government pay the salaries of the professional staff who would run the new gallery and fund half its capital costs. In 1981, Wran presided at the gallery's opening.[68]

In a letter to Arthur Boyd that June, David Chalker described the Lewers museum as 'an equivalent' to a Boyd Regional Art Museum, but there were significant differences. The Boyds' offer did not come from an artistic family with deep roots in the local community, it lacked substantial local support and was not sited in a major population centre. When Frank McDonald and the McGraths had proposed Bundanon's public acquisition as the site of a regional gallery, the state government had rejected this proposal despite Wran reputedly responding 'very positively' while visiting there.[69] Whether the Boyds might secure a different result turned partly on their gift, which stripped away the initial outlay for government, enhanced the cachet of the proposed gallery and included a fabulous conjunction of natural and cultural environments. It also turned on whether Boyd's cultural standing gave him political power.

After Boyd first wrote in June 1981, Wran's office responded that he would be in touch 'as soon as possible'. But further representations on Boyd's behalf by the Labor member of parliament, Mike Egan, failed to elicit a formal reply. Instead, Wran's most senior cultural officer, Evan Williams, informally advised Boyd that the government was unlikely to accept his gift, and another official reiterated this advice in September – most likely, because of the magnitude of the continuing operating costs and fears that the new gallery would attract few visitors.[70] Nevertheless Boyd persisted through another of his art dealers, Rudy Komon, who had been showing his work for almost twenty years.

Wran's wife, Jill Hickson, has recalled how, when he became premier, she complained to Komon about 'the rubbish' the Art Gallery of New South Wales had offered for Wran's office – 'small, undistinguished Victorian paintings, dredged up from the bowels of the gallery'.[71] Komon, who often lent paintings from his stockroom to the rich and powerful, invited Hickson to his store where she selected a group of paintings by some of Australia's foremost post-war artists – Jon Molvig, John Percival, John Olsen, Fred Williams and Brett Whiteley.[72] Before long, the Wrans were buying these paintings and going on many expeditions with Komon and his wife Ruth, including one when the

[68] Lewis (n 67) 6–7.

[69] Letter from David Chalker to Arthur Boyd (2 June 1981); letter from David Chalker to Michael Egan (23 July 1981); Peter Freeman Ltd (n 5) vol 1, 2.4.

[70] Letter from David Chalker to Edmund Capon (1 December 1981).

[71] R Raymond (ed), *52 Views of Rudy Komon* (Art Gallery of New South Wales 1999) 149–50.

[72] The Australian diplomat, Richard Woolcott, was another beneficiary of Komon's stockroom. While Australia's ambassador to Manila, Komon lent Woolcott one painting by Clifton Pugh and another by Jon Molvig. On shifting to Washington in 1982, Woolcott sought – and received from Komon – 'a Boyd Shoalhaven'. See letter from Rudy Komon to Richard Woolcott (29 June 1982); Komon papers, A 1981–84, folio 6, MS8327, NLA.

Komons helicoptered the Wrans to Bundanon for lunch in January 1982 with the Boyds, Sidney and Mary Nolan, and David and Margaret Chalker.

Hickson would remember this lunch as 'a relaxed, happy affair … a rare, soft unforgettable day' among 'all the hoo-ha of public life'.[73] But Wran made no commitment to supporting the project, leading the Boyds' solicitors to look again to Komon to 'assist in opening the lines of communication with the Premier'. The Boyds' lawyers sought 'some positive indication' from Wran of 'his support of the Bundanon proposal'. Eager as ever to avoid the Court, they hoped Wran would instigate an immediate public inquiry by the Land Board into the dredging.[74]

On 21 June 1982, the opening day of the Boyds' appeal in the Court, Wran responded in the form of a letter to David Chalker. 'Having several times visited the property and seen many of the items which would form a permanent collection', Wran declared himself 'delighted to learn of the proposed establishment of the Bundanon Trust', lauding Arthur Boyd for his 'most generous offer', and maintaining that Bundanon in its 'picturesque surroundings on the Shoalhaven River' would 'lend itself admirably to the formation of a regional art centre'. He also declared himself confident that the Bundanon Trust would 'attract the support of many lovers of art and other interested groups', resulting in 'a permanent and valuable addition to our cultural life'. He concluded: 'Future generations will honour the Boyd family for their generosity, and remember with gratitude all those who have assisted in realising the full scope of this project. I wish the venture every success.'[75] He did not mention that, beyond this letter, he did not want to assist it.

Wran's letter was produced at the start of the hearing before Ken Riding, one of the Court's assessors, who had been an engineer, town planner and member of the New South Wales Local Government Appeal Tribunal. When the Shoalhaven mayor testified, he surprised the parties by supporting Boyd's proposal to create a gallery at Bundanon, declaring it 'a wonderful gesture on Mr Boyd's part', which 'would be of great benefit to the area', with 'lack of adequate road access' being his 'only concern'.[76] But this – and other testimony – became of no account when Bill Davison sought 'strict proof of zoning' on the trial's second day.[77]

At issue was the reach of the local interim development order which, in accordance with the Environmental Planning and Assessment Act,[78] divided land in the Shoalhaven local government area into zones, then specified the development that could be carried out without consent, with consent, or was prohibited in those zones. Until then, everyone had assumed that Foster Emery's application fell within the council's domain, making it the proper body to consider the proposal. Belatedly it emerged that, as with many other local environmental plans, the council's jurisdiction stopped at the Shoalhaven's banks. The bed of the river was unzoned.[79]

[73] Raymond (n 71) 151.
[74] Letter from Murphy & Molony to Bill Lasica (28 April 1982).
[75] Letter from Neville Wran to David Chalker (21 June 1982).
[76] Memorandum, 28 June 1982, WR Davison, 2.
[77] ibid, 1.
[78] Environmental Planning and Assessment Act 1979 (NSW) s 76.
[79] *Land and Environment Notes 1980–1982* [647]; Farrier (n 4) 153.

In a very short judgment, Assessor Riding stated:

> During the course of the hearing it became clear, and was accepted by the parties, that the Shoalhaven River is not included in the Interim Development Order [IDO] and hence that the proposed activity is not a designated development. Accordingly the applicants have no standing as objectors and the appeal has been dismissed.[80]

Riding was correct that the river was not included in the IDO. However, the dredging was of a type declared to be a designated development. What mattered was that the river was outside the IDO which meant that the council could not validly approve it. Nor could the Court on appeal. Rather than focusing on how the Boyds had no standing as objectors or appellants, Riding might instead have said that Foster Emery had no standing as an applicant or cross-appellant.

While Riding cast the appeal as a loss for the Boyds, Bill Davison with much more reason cast it as a win for them, emphasising his own role in establishing that the bed of the river was outside the planning scheme. The local *Shoalhaven and Nowra News* concurred. 'Opponents of the sand mining in the Shoalhaven River near Wogamia have won the latest round in a legal battle', the *News* reported. 'The Court upheld the third party appeal against the proposed mining by Foster Emery and Sons.'[81]

Davison responded by raising the possibility of an award of costs in the Boyds' favour. But in keeping with what was already the Court's rule, Riding informed the parties that 'in the circumstances' he 'would make no order for costs even if an application was made'; 'all parties had an obligation to ascertain the basic facts and there were no exceptional circumstances to justify an award of costs'. Having paid the initial invoice from Murphy & Molony for $795, Boyd owed more than $21,000, including $9,000 to Bill Davison. When Boyd paid in kind by offering a selection of his paintings, Davison appropriately received one of Boyd's many versions of *Jinker with a Sandbank* – a scene set on the Shoalhaven with its sandbank intact, safe from mining, which he first painted in 1976 and then replicated many times with minor variations.[82]

To proceed, Foster Emery would have to reapply under a different part of the Environmental Planning and Assessment Act – Part V, which applied where the approval of a public authority such as the Land Board was required,[83] and provided for EISs where projects were likely to have a significant impact on the environment.[84] Boyd's lawyers advised that, rather than resubmit their existing EIS, Foster Emery would have to prepare a new one subject to 'much more stringent' requirements. They also wrote a barrage of letters requesting the Minister for Planning and Environment to order an inquiry into the proposal and seeking more rigorous scrutiny of Foster Emery's application for a permissive occupancy of part of the Shoalhaven. The lawyers' goal was to get Foster Emery to abandon 'their proposal having regard to the huge expense they have already incurred and the prospect of further expense'.[85]

[80] *Arthur Merric Bloomfield* Boyd *& Anor v Foster Emery & Sons Pty Ltd & Shoalhaven CC*, LEC No 10643/81.

[81] WR Davidson, Memorandum, 28 June 1982; *Shoalhaven and Nowra News* (30 June 1982).

[82] Ryan (n 1) 26–27; letter from Murphy & Molony to Arthur and Yvonne Boyd (2 July 1982); P Barry, 'Lawyer Sticks Head in the Sand, Receives $1.9 million' *Sydney Morning Herald* (27 February 1981).

[83] Environmental Planning and Assessment Act 1979 (NSW) s 110.

[84] ibid, ss 111, 112.

[85] WR Davison, Memorandum, 28 June 1982.

That left Foster Emery's application for a permissive occupancy on the Shoalhaven; it sought an 800-metre stretch of the river. The only legislative precondition was that the Land Board secure the approval of the Department of Mineral Resources, which did not object to this extraction of sand and gravel. As a matter of practice, the Land Board also sought approval from the Department of Public Works, which advised that it would respond when Foster Emery's EIS was 'properly defined and substantiated, especially in relation to the effects on flooding and erosion'.[86]

This process typically favoured applicants. In this case, it benefited the Boyds because Neville Wran made a personal representation to the Land Board. In October 1982, having 'considered the proposal in the light of replies received from other affected authorities and information arising from the Shoalhaven City Council's processing of the applicant's Environmental Impact Study', the Board refused to grant the permissive occupancy on the basis 'that the public interest would best be served by not disposing of the Crown Estates'. Even if Foster Emery submitted a new environmental impact statement under Part V of the Environmental Planning and Assessment Act, it would not be able to dredge the Shoalhaven.[87]

The Emerys responded by changing tack. In 1982, they established a new family partnership, Shoalhaven Sand Soil and Gravel (SSSG), which began operating from Wogamia without securing development approval. In 1985, SSSG began composting and waste recycling operations to minimise its use of soil and improve its quality, again without seeking development approval. In the wake of the New South Wales government introducing a state environmental planning policy in 1993 directed at many unregulated extractive plants,[88] SSSG applied for development approval. While the Shoalhaven Council could have classified this application as a designated development, which would have required SSSG to prepare an EIS and given all members of the public a right to object and appeal, the Council's Development Committee opted not to do so. In 1996, when the Emerys had transferred the business of SSSG to a new corporate entity Soilco, it secured approval to extract, compost and manufacture soil products at Wogamia.[89]

Meanwhile, in 1982, the Boyds secured the proclamation of more than 300 hectares as a wildlife refuge and committed to maintaining more than 200 hectares of open eucalypt forest in its natural state, creating wetlands and attempting a biological control

[86] Crown Lands Consolidation Act 1913 (NSW) s 136K (2); letter from Murphy & Molony to Arthur and Yvonne Boyd (21 January 1982); letter from Lands Board Office, Nowra, to Murphy & Molony (29 January 1982).

[87] Letter from ARL Gordon, Minister for Local Government and Lands to Neville Wran (October 1982).

[88] State Environmental Planning Policy 37 – Continued Mines and Extractive Industries (1993/210) (SEPP 37).

[89] See Soilco's website at www.soilco.com.au/about/ (accessed 22 November 2020); SEPP 37 (n 88) reg 20; Soilco, *Environmental Impact Statement Wogamia Quarry and Composting Facilities* (2000) 45; Peter Freeman Ltd (n 5) vol 1, 2:2.4, provides a different account, suggesting that 'only days' after the Land and Environment Court's decision, the Shoalhaven Council 'approved development of a sand extraction and soil based business on the Emery's land at Wogamia'. In 2009, Tony Emery of Wogamia, the managing director of Soilco, became a member of the board of the Bundanon Trust. In July 2020, Soilco sought approval to triple the size of its operations. Its EIS made no mention of the potential impacts on the Bundanon Trust properties. The responses of the Council's internal Natural Resources and Floodplain section, 20 August 2020, and the NSW EPA, 26 August 2020, raise questions about the adequacy of the EIS in considering the vulnerability of the expanded operation in the event of a 1-in-a-100-year flood and the odours that will emanate from the proposed plant.

of the property's infestation with lantana as well as preserving its historical buildings. In 1985, when Sandra McGrath decided to subdivide her remaining part of Eearie Park if she could not sell it as one lot, the Boyds and Nolan jointly bought Eearie Park II as they called it, linking their individual holdings, and had Eearie Park and Riversdale proclaimed as wildlife reserves. Arthur Boyd also renewed his efforts to have the government take Bundanon. 'You can only keep something by giving it away', he declared, sure that 'no one could really own a landscape', and by implication no individual should. In 1993, the federal Labor government of Paul Keating accepted the Boyds' great gift.[90]

[90] Letter from Eric Bedford, Minister for Planning and Environment, to Arthur and Yvonne Boyd (24 August 1982); Janet Hawley, 'Boyd Pleads for His Gift to Be Accepted Soon' *Sydney Morning Herald* (9 October 1989); M Goldrick, 'Ramsholt Revisited', *Eureka Street* (July/August 1999) 30; Bungey (n 6) 518–19.

13

'Please Come In': Access to Justice and the Development of Jurisprudence in the Land and Environment Court of New South Wales

JEFF SMITH AND SUE HIGGINSON

1. Introduction

At a conference to reflect on the promise and performance of the Land and Environment Court of New South Wales (the Court) over its first twenty years, a leading barrister and a fledgling solicitor in the field of environmental law concluded:

> [O]ne finding stands above them all: that is, by seemingly adopting a wait-and-see approach to the interpretation of sustainable development, the Court is arguably undermining its own claims to be a specialist Court. Whilst it has developed a strong public interest jurisprudence and some discrete environmental principles, it has failed to actively engage in the development of the central principle (or set of principles) in environmental law today. This amounts to a serious deficiency in the Court as it approaches its twentieth anniversary.[1]

One of the presenters would be awarded silk later that year and go on to lead the Court from 2005 to the present day; the other would go on to head up the Environmental Defenders Office (EDO) NSW, the leading public interest environmental law centre in Australia, from 2002 to 2016.

This chapter updates and revises this twenty-year-old evaluation of the Court in the light of what has happened since. It argues that the approach of the Court over the past forty years can be understood as falling into two distinct periods: a first generational focus on process followed by a second generational focus on both process and outcomes.

This chapter is structured as follows. Section 2 demonstrates that the first period spawned a public interest jurisprudence within the Court without a concomitant

[1] BJ Preston and JO Smith, 'Legislation Needed for an Effective Court', in *Promise, Perception, Problems and Remedies: The Land and Environment Court and Environmental Law 1999 Conference Proceedings* (Nature Conservation Council of NSW, 1999) 114, 121.

jurisprudence on ecologically sustainable development (ESD). Section 3 shows that the second period has seen the Court both consolidate and extend its public interest jurisprudence as well as develop a cogent environmental jurisprudence through its interpretation and application of the principles of ESD. Section 4 seeks to explain this generational divide, and the factors that have underpinned the jurisprudential leap that has taken place during the second period of the Court.

2. The First Period of Public Interest Environmental Law (1979–1999)

The first period of the Court was characterized by two ostensibly contrary developments. On the one hand, the Court carefully crafted a public interest jurisprudence. On the other hand, an unapologetic cautiousness on ESD held sway, stifling the development of an environmental jurisprudence.

The Court's development of a public interest jurisprudence from the outset was significantly influenced by its clear remit. First, the Court was introduced as part of far-reaching reforms to the planning system alongside the Environmental Planning and Assessment Act 1979 (NSW) (the EPA Act) and the Heritage Act 1977 (NSW), all of which reflected fulsome notions of community participation and the public interest. Second, the advent of the Court arose in response to an extended period of entrenched corruption and politicised decision-making.[2] The Court – established as a superior court of record – was a victory for the rule of law in the field of environment and planning. Third, the Court was designed from the outset to be different.[3]

All this would profoundly affect the Court's approach to access to justice, a fundamental tenet of the rule of law. For example, the Court resisted early and ongoing attempts to read down the 'trail blazing' open standing provision introduced under the EPA Act.[4] Nearly fifteen years after the Court began, Justice Stein was minded to restate the historical evidence in relation to open standing:

> [T]he fact is that fourteen years' experience of open standing provisions in the Land and Environment Court has produced little more than a modest flow barely wetting the wellies.[5]

[2] See H Lewi et al, 'Regenerating Communities: The 1970s and Beyond' in H Lewi and D Nichols (eds), *Building Modern Australia* (Sydney, UNSW Press, 2010); D Nichols, '"Boiling in Anger": Activist Local Newspapers of the 1960s and 1970s' (2005) 2 *History Australia* 1; Z Nittim, 'The Coalition of Resident Action Groups' in J Roe (ed), *Twentieth Century Sydney: Studies in Urban and Social History* (Chippendale, Hale & Ironmonger, 1980); J Cole, 'Environmental Law and Politics' (1981) 4 UNSWLJ 55; A Saffron, *Gentle Satan: Growing up with Australia's Most Notorious Crime Boss* (Penguin, 2008).

[3] The Honourable Paul Landa, Minister for Planning & Environment, in *Hansard (NSW)* Cognate Environmental Planning Bills, Second Reading Speech, 21 November 1979, 3355.

[4] See *Rowley v New South Wales Leather and Trading Co Pty Ltd and Woollahra Municipal Council* (1980) 46 LGRA 250; *Building Owners & Management Association (Aust) (Ltd) v Sydney City Council* (1984) 53 LGRA 54 and (1985) 54 LGERA 444; and P Stein 'New Directions in the Prevention and Resolution of Environmental Disputes – Specialist Environmental Courts', South-East Asian Regional Symposium on the Judiciary and the Law of Sustainable Development (Manila, 6 March 1999) [30].

[5] *Oshlack v Richmond River Shire Council* (1994) 82 LGERA 236, 245.

More crucially, the Court took seriously the dictum from Justice Toohey that open standing – without more – would be of limited use:

> Relaxing the traditional requirements for standing may be of little significance unless other procedural reforms are made. Particularly is this so in the area of funding of environmental litigation and the awarding of costs. There is little point in opening the doors to the courts if litigants cannot afford to come in.[6]

During this time, the Court advanced and fine-tuned a number of procedural changes to complement the formal right to institute proceedings.

First, absent a discrete joinder power,[7] the Court initially permitted third parties to participate in proceedings where the Court considered that those third parties wished to raise issues that would not otherwise be raised by the respondent council.[8] In this regard, the Court used its 'inquisitorial' powers under section 38 of the Land and Environment Court Act 1979 (NSW) (the LEC Act) to ensure a full consideration of the issues.[9] These powers included where the Court may 'inform itself on any matter in such manner as it thinks appropriate and as the proper consideration of the matters before the Court permits' and the Court may 'obtain the assistance of any person having professional or other qualifications relevant to any issue arising for determination in the proceedings and may receive in evidence the certificate of any such person'.

Second, the Court promoted the notion of public interest litigation in *Oshlack v Richmond River Council*, which went to the High Court on the issue of costs. In this key case, the High Court agreed with Stein J at first instance in the Land and Environment Court that Al Oshlack, the unsuccessful public interest litigant, did not need to pay the costs of the victorious party. The High Court agreed that the litigation could be characterised as having been brought in the public interest and that there were 'sufficient special circumstances' to depart from the ordinary rule as to costs including: the need to uphold environmental law and the preservation of endangered fauna; the significant number of members of the public who were interested in the outcome of the proceedings; and the 'significant issues' regarding the interpretation and future administration of the relevant statutory provisions that were raised and resolved.[10] This signalled a departure from the usual rule and affirmed the width of the discretion of that Court in awarding costs, including the relevance of public interest litigation.[11]

[6] Justice Toohey and Anthony D'Arcy, 'Environmental Law – Its Place in the System', *Proceedings of the First NELA/LAWASIA International Conference on Environmental Law* (June 1989) 79.

[7] Joinder is a legal process where parties (or claims) are added to a matter before the Court. A discrete joinder power was not introduced into the Land and Environment Court Act 1979 (NSW) (LEC Act) until 2002.

[8] See *Double Bay Marina Pty Ltd v Woollahra Municipal Council* (1985) 54 LGRA 313; *Geoform Design Pty Ltd v Randwick City Council* (1995) 87 LGERA 140 (Land and Environment Court of NSW, Pearlman CJ, 19 May 1995); *Monaldo v Baulkham Hills Council* (1995) 87 LGERA 165; *Humphrey & Edwards Pty Ltd v Woollahra Municipal Council* [1998] NSWLEC 285; *Ziatabari v Ku-ring-gai Council* [1999] NSWLEC 139.

[9] LEC Act s 38(2)–(3). Based on the approach taken in these cases and the issues arising from resident groups not being parties, EDO NSW proposed an amendment to the LEC Act in 2002 to allow for joinder of parties where, amongst other things, it is in the public interest. This amendment was accepted: see s 39A. Joinder now falls under s 8.15 of the (NSW) EPA Act.

[10] *Oshlack v Richmond River Council* (1998) 193 CLR 72, 116.

[11] See *Oshlack v Richmond River Shire Council & Anor* (n 5); and *Oshlack* (n 10). Cases where this was followed in the Land and Environment Court include *Jacobs v Hurstville City Council* [2011] NSWLEC 15, [16];

Third, the Court amended its Rules regarding security for costs in 1996 to remove the requirement for security for costs, except in exceptional circumstances.[12]

Fourth, from early on the Court in its history did not follow the practice of automatically requiring an undertaking as a condition of grant of an interlocutory injunction;[13] rather, the failure to give an undertaking was a factor to be considered in whether to grant the injunction.[14]

Running contrary to its active engagement in developing a public interest jurisprudence, the Court adopted a cautious, 'wait and see' approach in relation to ESD. This cautiousness was signified by the approach taken by the Chief Judge, Justice Mahla Pearlman, in *Greenpeace v Redbank Power Co Pty Ltd*.[15] In this merits review case, Greenpeace argued that the Court should refuse to allow a power station to go ahead on the basis of the precautionary principle. The Chief Judge said:

> [I]t is not for the court to impose such a prohibition … a cautious approach should be adopted in evaluating the various relevant factors in determining whether or not to grant consent; it does not require that the greenhouse issue should outweigh all other issues.[16]

The Chief Judge amplified and extended these thoughts when speaking extra-curially:

> The most obvious function of the Court is therefore to apply the law, and so in applying the law there is often little scope to achieve the advancements in environmental law that some people may wish to see. … In my opinion the successful application of ESD requires the principles themselves to be made more workable and tangible. It is for the legislature to provide more guidance to the Court as to how it wishes this objective to be achieved, and particularly how it relates to other provisions. The Court has a limited role in that it must act according to law. It cannot be expected to fill gaps in policy, or to stretch the law where it does not go.[17]

Martin v NSW Minister for Mineral and Forest Resources [2011] NSWLEC 38, [43]–[48]; *McGinn v Ashfield Council* (2011) 185 LGERA 230, [17]–[24]; *Friends of Turramurra Inc v Minister for Planning (No 2)* [2011] NSWLEC 170, [31]; *McCallum v Sandercock (No 2)* [2011] NSWLEC 203, [25]–[30]; *Oshlack v Rous Water (No 3)* [2012] NSWLEC 132, [6]–[14] and *Lester v Ashton Coal Pty Ltd (No 2)* (2012) 193 LGERA 293.

[12] Land and Environment Court Rules 1996 (NSW) (LEC Rules), Part 13, rule 40. It is instructive to remember that parties regularly sought security for costs in the first half of the Court's operation: see *Levensrath Community Association Inc v J & J Toms and anor* (Unreported, NSWLEC, Bignold J, 26 November 1998, 40057/98); *Razorback Environment Protection Society Inc v Wollondilly Council and anor* [1999] NSWLEC 8; *Donnelly & anor v Capricornia Prospecting Ltd and ors* (1999) 102 LGERA 310; *Donnelly and anor v Ross Mining NL and ors* [1999] NSWLEC 76; *Ryde Pool Action Group Inc v Ryde City Council* [1999] NSWLEC 96 as noted in L Ogle, 'The Court Process and the Public Interest Litigant', *Promise, Perception, Problems and Remedies: Conference on the Land and Environment Court and Environmental Law 1979–99* (27–28 August 1999) 33–34.

[13] Ogle (n 12) 35.

[14] However, as Ogle (n 12) noted, the Court only granted injunctions without such an undertaking on rare occasions (35): see *Ross v State Rail Authority of NSW* (1987) 70 LGRA 91 and *Residents of Blacktown and Seven Hills Against Further Traffic v RTA* (Land and Environment Court of NSW, Stein J, 40106/1996).

[15] (1994) 86 LGERA 143.

[16] ibid, 153.

[17] M Pearlman, 'Managing Environmental Impacts – The Role of the Land and Environment Court of New South Wales', New Zealand Planning Congress (9 April 2002).

In contrast to his fellow judges, Justice Stein was troubled by this cautious approach:

> [M]y thesis is that there is the opportunity, if not the obligation, in the absence of clear legislative guidance, to apply the common law and assist in the development and fleshing out of the principles. Our task is to turn soft law into hard law. This is an opportunity to be bold spirits rather than timorous souls and provide a lead for the common law world. It will make a contribution to the ongoing development of environmental law.[18]

At the time, other commentators also criticised the Court for its reluctance to deal with the principles of ESD. As Pearson commented in 1996, 'the experience in the NSW Land and Environment Court has so far not been encouraging'.[19] Cases such as *Leatch v National Parks and Wildlife Service*[20] and *Northcompass Inc v Hornsby Shire Council*[21] notwithstanding, the Court had clearly taken a cautious approach to ESD in the first phase of its history.

The criticisms of the Court regarding ESD during this first period were essentially threefold. First, the Court showed a disinclination to engage in the debate about ESD (in contrast to its strong judicial and extra-curial position on the public interest and its importance within environmental law). Second, and relatedly, the Court failed to use the language of ESD wherever possible. Third, and crucially, the Court had declined to play a lead role in the interpretation of ESD.[22]

At the same time, it is clear that the Court sought to develop environmental law in NSW. In the field of nature conservation, the Court placed species conservation on a firm ecological footing in *Corkill v Forestry Commission of NSW (No 2)*[23] and underpinned its decision in *Willoughby City Council v Minister Administering the National Parks and Wildlife Act*[24] with the public trust doctrine (much developed in the United States). Likewise, in the field of pollution, the Court defined the liability of officers and corporations, stressing the obligations and limits pertaining to a right to pollute,[25] and was vocal in its preference for civil remedies over criminal prosecutions in pollution matters.[26]

[18] PL Stein, 'Are Decision-Makers Too Cautious with the Precautionary Principle?' (2000) 17 *Environmental and Planning Law Journal* 3, 3.

[19] L Pearson 'Incorporating ESD Principles in Land-Use Decision-Making: Some Issues after Teoh' (1996) 13 *Environmental and Planning Law Journal* 47, 53.

[20] *Leatch v National Parks and Wildlife Service* (1993) 81 LGERA 270.

[21] *Northcompass Inc v Hornsby Shire Council* (1996) 130 LGERA 248.

[22] See Preston and Smith (n 1) 114–15; D Robinson, 'Public Interest Environmental Law – Commentary and Analysis' in D Robinson and J Dunkley (eds), *Public Interest Perspectives in Environmental Law* (Chichester, Wiley Chancery, 1995) 314–15.

[23] *Corkill v Forestry Commission of NSW (No 2)* (1991) 73 LGRA 126.

[24] *Willoughby City Council v Minister Administering the National Parks and Wildlife Act* (1992) 78 LGERA 19. For discussion of this case, see T Bonyhady 'A Usable Past: The Public Trust in Australia' (1995) 12 *Environmental and Planning Law Journal* 329, 330–31.

[25] See *SPCC v CSR Ltd* (unreported, Land and Environment Court, Cripps J, July 1989) and also the Court's dismissal of a submission that licences imposed targets not limits in *SPCC v BHP Pty Co Ltd (No 1)* (1991) 74 LGRA 351.

[26] See *Farrell v Dayban Pty Ltd* (unreported, Land and Environment Court, Cripps J, 7 June 1989) and Justice Hemmings, 'The Role of the Land and Environment Court in Pollution Control', National Environmental Law Conference (15 June 1990).

3. The Second Period of Public Interest Environmental Law (2000–2020)

The second period of the Court has seen the consolidation and expansion of its public interest jurisprudence together with the clear development of an environmental jurisprudence on ESD.

Over the past twenty years, the Court has 'thickened' its public interest jurisprudence, continuing to consolidate and expand the foundations already pegged out. A number of examples highlight this point.

First, and importantly, the Court has had to be vigilant to ensure access to justice. Respondents in public interest proceedings continue to challenge the right and legitimacy of community groups to hold decision-makers accountable and/or participate in environmental decision-making. For example, in *Kepco Bylong Australia Pty Ltd v Independent Planning Commission*[27] the Bylong Valley Protection Alliance Incorporated (the Alliance) sought to be joined to judicial review proceedings commenced by Kepco following the refusal of development consent for its Bylong coal mine project by the Independent Planning Commission.[28] The Commission was the only original respondent to the proceedings, and duly filed a submitting appearance. This essentially left no contradictor to Kepco's contentions.

Kepco sought to limit the Alliance's role to an amicus, meaning the Alliance would be able to cross-examine and adduce evidence, but only by discretion and not as a right.[29] In seeking to deny the Alliance access as a party, Kepco argued that part of the test for joinder requires the rights and liabilities of a party to be directly affected by the orders sought and that an interest in the outcome of the litigation is not sufficient to maintain an action.[30] It also argued that the Alliance had no interest that was special for the purposes of joinder, being in the same position as the other 1,200 persons who made submissions.[31] This argument inevitably included the 'floodgates' component – that is, Kepco argued that, if the Alliance was permitted to join as a party, then the some thousand other objectors to the development would likewise need to be joined.[32]

The Court gave short shrift to these arguments, finding that the basis for the Alliance to be joined as a party to the proceedings 'is the desirability, in the public interest, of having a contradictor able to participate fully and respond to several of the grounds pleaded'.[33] Nevertheless, the case demonstrates the perseverance of myths such as the

[27] *Kepco Bylong Australia Pty Ltd v Independent Planning Commission* [2020] NSWLEC 38.

[28] Kepco sought a declaration that the Commission's decision to refuse consent to the Bylong coal mine was invalid and of no effect, and an order remitting the development application to the Commission for redetermination in accordance with law: ibid, [4].

[29] ibid, [48].

[30] ibid, [52].

[31] ibid, [54].

[32] ibid, [55]. In making an order to join the Alliance as a party to the proceedings, the Court swiftly disposed of the 'floodgates' argument: 'although the floodgates might be opened, there is no evidence that the consequence of doing so is even a minute trickle flowing through them as a result' [79].

[33] ibid, [82]. The Court also found that the substantive proceedings raised significant matters of broad public interest and that based on the Alliance's participation in the Commission's processes it was well-placed

'floodgates' and the ever-present resolve of parties to seek to limit the role of public interest litigants.

Similarly, in *Fullerton Cove Residents Action Group Incorporated v Dart Energy Ltd*[34] the Court affirmed its commitment to access to justice in public interest matters. This case involved a challenge to the drilling of coal seam gas exploration wells at Fullerton Cove near Newcastle until a challenge to the proposal by the Fullerton Cove Residents Action Group (FCRAG) had been decided. In preliminary injunction proceedings, Justice Sheahan found that this was a public interest case, and, as such, the FCRAG was not required to provide any undertaking as to damages.[35] The FCRAG, however, lost the substantive hearing. Subsequently, the Department pursued its costs of the case from the FCRAG, claiming that the case was not brought in the public interest. This claim was resisted by the FCRAG. The Court refused to award costs to the Department, saying that the FCRAG's case 'epitomises the very concept of litigation properly brought in the public interest'.[36] The Court also ordered the Department to pay the FCRAG's legal costs in relation to the Department#s cost application. In reaching this conclusion, Justice Pepper, cautioned against 'rendering nugatory open standing provisions by the stultifying spectre of adverse costs orders'[37] and went on the say:

> It is for this reason that jurisprudence has been developed in this Court, as the repository of much of the exclusive jurisdiction to hear and determine environmental disputes in New South Wales, to provide for a principled framework within which proceedings may be characterised as having been properly brought in the public interest.[38]

Second, a discrete joinder power was introduced into the Land and Environment Court Act 1979 (NSW) in 2002.[39] This reform meant that, once joined, a party has all the rights of other parties to the proceedings. This includes the capacity to raise other and additional grounds than those identified in the joinder application, subject to leave of the Court.[40] Previously, the Court had had to rely on its inquisitorial powers and

as a party to the proceedings, which would better serve the Court than as an amicus. The Court found that it was appropriate that the Alliance be joined as a party to the proceedings because its participation as a party is necessary to the determination of all matters in dispute in these proceedings [88]. The Court subsequently dismissed the judicial review challenge in *KEPCO Bylong Australia Pty Ltd v Independent Planning Commission (No 2)* (2020) 247 LGERA 130.

[34] *Fullerton Cove Residents Action Group Incorporated v Dart Energy Ltd (No 3)* [2013] NSWLEC 152.

[35] *Fullerton Cove Residents Action Group Incorporated v Dart Energy Ltd* [2012] NSWLEC 207, [39].

[36] *Fullerton Cove Residents Action Group Incorporated v Dart Energy Ltd (No 3)* (n 34) [16].

[37] ibid, [24].

[38] ibid, [24].

[39] Joinder has since been moved into the EPA Act s 8.15 for certain planning matters and more generally is provided for in the Uniform Civil Procedure Rules 2005 (NSW) (UCP Rules), Part 6 Division 5, in particular rule 6.24 and 6.27.

[40] The success of an application is ultimately a discretionary matter for the Court's determination: *Morrison Design Partnership Pty Limited v North Sydney Council and Director-General of the Department of Planning* (2007) 159 LGERA 361, [43]. Once joined, a party has all the rights of other parties to the proceedings. This includes the capacity to raise other and additional grounds than those identified in the joinder application, subject to leave of the Court: *Morrison Design Partnership Pty Limited v North Sydney Council and Director-General of the Department of Planning* [36]. See also *Avalon Beach Property Pty Limited ACN 609856224 as Trustee for the Avalon Beach Property Trust v Northern Beaches Council* (2017) 227 LGERA 393 [24] per Preston CJ. For example, as was the case in *Manderrah Pty Ltd v Woollahra Municipal Council (No 2)* [2013] NSWLEC 115.

Double Bay Marina orders.[41] However, that participation did not amount to joinder and, accordingly, those third parties had no right of appeal. Third parties who were not objectors to designated development were also not necessarily permitted to call expert evidence.

Third, the Court strengthened its rules in relation to proceedings in the public interest in 2007, giving the Court broad discretion not to require costs, security for costs, or an undertaking for damages if satisfied that the proceedings have been brought in the public interest.[42]

Fourth, *Caroona Coal Action Group Inc v Coal Mines Australia Pty Ltd (No 3)*[43] provided further guidance under which the discretion to depart from the usual costs rule is to be exercised in public interest litigation.[44] Importantly also, the current Chief Judge highlighted the need for the courts to ensure access to justice in environmental matters[45] and noted the disparity of interests that come before the Court:

> One consequence of costs acting as a barrier to access for justice for citizens seeking to enforce environmental law is that this aspect of the public interest risks being unrepresented or, at least, underrepresented, in the courts.
>
> In contrast, costs typically do not operate to deter other aspects of the public interest, such as promotion of social development or economic development, from being represented in the courts. These aspects are upheld by other parties to litigation, such as the government and persons with private proprietary, business or financial interests, such as developers. Relative to applicants who seek to enforce public law to ensure environmental protection, costs usually are not as critical to these parties because of their greater access to financial resources and ability to pass on the costs to other persons (such as taxpayers or consumers of goods and services) or to spread the costs over a larger revenue and expenditure base and over time.[46]

Fifth, the Court has continued to innovate in the name of ensuring access to justice. For example, a protective costs order[47] was first used in NSW in *Blue Mountains*

[41] These orders are named after the case where they were developed, *Double Bay Marina Pty Ltd v Woollahra Municipal Council* (n 8), and may include a right, granted to an objector, to cross-examine expert witnesses and make submissions. Under such orders, the involvement of third parties is usually limited in scope to defined issues which will be specifically relevant to them.

[42] LEC Rules, rule 4.2(1)–(3). See also s 98 of the Civil Procedure Act 2005 (NSW); the LEC Rules prevail over the UCP Rules to the extent of any inconsistency.

[43] *Caroona Coal Action Group Inc v Coal Mines Australia Pty Ltd (No 3)* (2010) 173 LGERA 280.

[44] The Chief Judge set out a three-step approach, as well as guidance as to how this approach should be applied: ibid, [13]–[20], [60]. See also *Local Democracy Matters Incorporated v Infrastructure NSW; Waverley Council v Infrastructure NSW (No 4)* [2019] NSWLEC 140.

[45] *Caroona Coal Action Group Inc* (n 43) [27].

[46] ibid, [34]–[35].

[47] Protective costs orders are orders that limit or cap the costs of proceedings at the outset: for a more detailed discussion of protective costs orders, see R Pepper and N Pain 'Legal Costs Considerations in Public Interest Climate Change Litigation' (2019) 30 *King's Law Journal*, 211, 214–18 and N Pain, 'Protective Costs Orders in Australia: Increasing Access to Justice by Capping Costs' (2014) 31 *Environmental and Planning Law Journal* 450. Such orders further promote the purpose of open standing provisions: see *Delta Electricity v Blue Mountains Conservation Society Inc* (2010) 176 LGERA 424 [197] per Basten JA (Macfarlan JA agreeing). They are available in NSW under the UCP Rules and they may be varied if the interests of justice require it: rule 42.4(1) and (3).

Conservation Society v Delta Electricity.[48] In this case, the plaintiff sought, and was granted, an order that limited costs to $20,000. The plaintiff had indicated that it would not be able to proceed if costs went beyond this amount and the Court held that it would not be in the public interest for the case to fold. Subsequently, the respondent sought security for costs over and above $20,000 but the Court dismissed this application.[49] The Court refined its approach in *Nerringillah Community Association Inc v Laundry Number Pty Ltd*,[50] making a unidirectional costs order whereby if the applicant was unsuccessful in the proceedings the respondent could only recover a maximum amount of $40,000 in costs (but not vice versa). This approach recognised the possible structural and inequitable effects of ordering a protective costs order covering all parties.[51]

However, the most profound change during this second period has been the development of a clear and abiding jurisprudence on ESD. To paraphrase Justice Stein on standing, the floodgates have opened over the past twenty years regarding an environmental jurisprudence on ESD,[52] as compared to 'barely wetting the wellies' in the first period of the Court.[53] The development of an environmental jurisprudence per se is discussed in more detail elsewhere.[54]

[48] *Blue Mountains Conservation Society v Delta Electricity* (2009) 170 LGERA 1. See also *Olofsson v Minister for Primary Industries* (2011) 210 LGERA 375 and *Nerringillah Community Association Inc v Laundry Number Pty Ltd* (2018) 236 LGERA 102 (where a unilateral protective costs order was granted).

[49] *Blue Mountains Conservation Society v Delta Electricity (No 2)* [2009] NSWLEC 193. The Court of Appeal summarily dismissed an application for leave to appeal on the issue of security for costs and dismissed an appeal against the protective costs order: *Delta Electricity v Blue Mountains Conservation Society Inc* (2010) 176 LGERA 424.

[50] *Nerringillah Community Association Inc v Laundry Number Pty Ltd* (n 47).

[51] ibid, [187].

[52] See eg *BGP Properties Pty Ltd v Lake Macquarie City Council* (2004) 138 LGERA 237; [2004] NSWLEC 399; *BT Goldsmith Planning Services Pty Ltd v Blacktown City Council* [2005] NSWLEC 210; *Port Stephens Pearls Pty Ltd v Minister for Infrastructure & Planning* [2005] NSWLEC 426; *Gales Holdings Pty Ltd v Tweed Shire Council* (2006) 146 LGERA 236; *Gray v Minister for Planning* (2006) 152 LGERA 258; *Telstra Corp Ltd v Hornsby Shire Council* (2006) 148 LGERA 124; *Taralga Landscape Guardians Inc v Minister for Planning* (2007) 161 LGERA 1; *Walker v Minister for Planning* (2007) 157 LGERA 124; *Anderson v Director General, Department of Environment and Climate Change* (2008) 163 LGERA 400; *Hub Action Group Inc v Minister for Planning* (2008) 161 LGERA 136; *Ulan Coal Mines Ltd v Minister for Planning* (2008) 160 LGERA 20; *Rivers SOS Inc v Minister for Planning* (2009) 178 LGERA 347; *Newcastle and Hunter Valley Speleological Society Inc v Upper Hunter Shire Council and Stoneco Pty Ltd* (2010) 210 LGERA 126; *Hunter Environment Lobby Inc v Minister for Planning* [2011] NSWLEC 221; *Bulga Milbrodale Progress Association Inc v Minister for Planning and Infrastructure and Warkworth Mining Limited* (2013) 194 LGERA 347; *Wollar Progress Association Incorporated v Wilpinjong Coal Pty Ltd* [2018] NSWLEC 92; *Gloucester Resources Limited v Minister for Planning* (2019) 234 LGERA 257 (the *Rocky Hill* decision).

[53] The cases of *Leatch v National Parks and Wildlife Service and Shoalhaven City Council* (1993) 81 LGERA 270 and *Northcompass Inc v Hornsby Shire Council* (1996) 130 LGERA 248 stand as obvious exceptions.

[54] See n 47 and a host of other papers by Judges of the Court including N Pain, 'Recent Developments in Climate Change Litigation in Australia and Beyond', Law Society of NSW Young Lawyers Environment Committee Annual Conference (Sydney, 23 March 2019) 3–6; B Preston 'The Judicial Development of Ecologically Sustainable Development' in D Fisher (ed), *Research Handbook on Fundamental Concepts of Environmental Law* (Cheltenham, Edward Elgar, 2016); R Pepper 'Climate Change Litigation: A Comparison Between Current Australian And International Jurisprudence', Sixth ASEAN Chief Justices' Roundtable on Environment (12 November 2016) 3–5; P Biscoe, 'Ecologically Sustainable Development in NSW', 5th Worldwide Colloquium of the IUCN Academy of Environmental Law (June 2007); BJ Preston, 'The Role of the Judicial in Promoting Sustainable Development: The Experience of Asia and the Pacific' (2005) 9 *Asia Pacific Journal of Environmental Law* 109.

It is clear, however, that the Court's resolute support for access to justice has had a profound impact on the development of ESD in NSW. As the present Chief Judge has stated simply: 'open standing provisions have facilitated environmental public interest litigation'.[55] Likewise, the accessibility of the Court in its merits jurisdiction has greatly increased the ability of the Court to develop an environmental jurisprudence on ESD. As Justice Biscoe noted, this function has, in large part, been performed and enhanced through the merits review process:

> [D]ecisions on ecologically sustainable development (ESD) by the Land and Environment Court … mostly have been in its merits review jurisdiction. It is because the Court has an unusual merits review jurisdiction that it has been able to deliver a significant number of judgments on ESD in which, standing in the shoes of the administrative decision-maker, it has determined the dispute on the merits.[56]

The case of *Bulga Milbrodale Progress Association Inc v Minister for Planning and Infrastructure and Warkworth Mining Limited*[57] demonstrates this point. In this case, a community group appealed an approval to extend an open-cut coal mine in the Hunter Valley owned by Rio Tinto. The approval would extend the life of the mine for ten years, allow the extraction of an additional eighteen million tonnes of coal from the mine every year, allow open-cut mining in an area that had been originally set aside for protection as a biodiversity offset area and bring the mine closer to the village of Bulga.

The Association sought refusal of the mine extension on the basis that the mining of the biodiversity offset is contrary to the public interest and ESD, and that the expansion would result in detrimental economic and social impacts on the Bulga community that are contrary to the principles of ESD. In a landmark decision, the Court overturned the approval. The Court concluded that the project would have significant and unacceptable impacts on biodiversity, as well as unacceptable noise and social impacts. The Court considered that the proposed conditions of approval were inadequate and would not allow the project to achieve satisfactory levels of impact on the environment, including the residents and community of Bulga. The Court highlighted the polycentric nature of environmental legal decision-making, finding that these matters outweighed the substantial economic benefits and positive social impacts of the project on the region, and that the extension project should not go ahead.[58]

Similarly, the Court's continued attention to ensuring access to justice has facilitated substantive outcomes. For example, in *Blue Mountains Conservation*

[55] BJ Preston, 'Environmental Public Interest Litigation: Conditions for Success', International Symposium Towards an Effective Guarantee of the Green Access: Japan's Achievements and Critical Points from a Global Perspective (30–31 March 2013) 16.

[56] Biscoe (n 54) 27–28.

[57] *Bulga Milbrodale Progress Association Inc* (n 52).

[58] *Bulga Milbrodale Progress Association Inc v Minister for Planning and Infrastructure and Warkworth Mining Limited* (n 52). The mining company's appeal was dismissed by the NSW Court of Appeal: *Warkworth Mining Limited v Bulga Milbrodale Progress Association Inc* (2014) 86 NSWLR 527. Following this decision, the mining company submitted a further application, which was approved by the Planning Assessment Commission in late 2015.

Society Inc v Director-General of National Parks and Wildlife & Ors[59] a local community group was seeking an injunction to prevent filming of a war movie in the Grose Wilderness area of the Blue Mountains National Park in May 2004. The application for an injunction was filed on Tuesday 27 April 2004 following the Anzac Day long weekend with filming due to begin on Friday 30 April 2004. The film company said that any disruption to the filming schedule would cost them $500,000 per day.[60] The Court agreed to expedite the matter rather than deal with the interlocutory matter. This approach balanced the interests of the parties – avoiding both an undertaking that the community group could not afford and a delay that the film company could ill afford – while still ensuring that the matter was heard. A hearing was held the next day, and judgment given the day after. The Court ruled in favour of the community group, holding that 'wilderness is sacrosanct'.[61]

Furthermore, the landmark *Rocky Hill* case[62] has been heralded as a watershed for climate action in Australia[63] and remains a significant decision in the pursuit of climate justice globally. It was the first time a coal mining project had been refused by the Court on climate grounds, amongst others. The result may well have been different, however, if the Court had determined that Groundswell Gloucester could not be a party to the proceedings.[64] Groundswell Gloucester only filed an application for joinder after the minister's case was revealed, seeking to raise two issues in the substantive proceedings which were not pressed by the minister – namely, the unacceptable social impacts on the residents and community of Gloucester and the impact of the development on greenhouse gases.[65]

The mining company strongly opposed the joinder application, arguing that the climate change issue is 'really a complaint about global geo-political relations, the resolution of which this merits appeal is a most singularly inappropriate vehicle'.[66] Further, the company submitted that the climate change issue was beyond the jurisdiction of the Court and framed the issue as a 'hopeless issue',[67] which at its core was 'misconceived'[68] and raised an 'absurdity'.[69] On this basis, it contended that allowing the climate change issue would represent a time-consuming and unhelpful addition to the proceedings, that it would be a 'side show and a distraction'[70] and therefore there would be little

[59] *Blue Mountains Conservation Society Inc v Director-General of National Parks and Wildlife & Ors* (2004) 133 LGERA 406.

[60] ibid, [3].

[61] ibid, [59].

[62] *Gloucester Resources Limited v Minister for Planning* (n 52).

[63] Lesley Hughes, 'The Rocky Hill Decision: A Watershed for Climate Change Action' (2019) 37 *Journal of Energy & Natural Resources Law* 341.

[64] *Gloucester Resources Limited v Minister for Planning and Environment (No 2)* [2018] NSWLEC 1200.

[65] This latter ground included a quantitative assessment of potential Scope 1, 2 and 3 greenhouse gas emissions; a qualitative assessment of the potential impacts of these emissions on the environment; and an assessment of reasonable and feasible measures to minimise greenhouse gas emissions and ensure energy efficiency: ibid, [9].

[66] ibid, [20].

[67] ibid, [25].

[68] ibid, [28].

[69] ibid, [26].

[70] ibid, [31].

point in joining Groundswell Gloucester to the proceedings.[71] The Court did not agree, exercising its discretion to join Groundswell Gloucester as a respondent.[72] The decision to allow Gloucester Groundswell to join the proceedings opened the doors to the Court, allowing for the ventilation of important issues around greenhouse gas emissions, carbon budgets, market substitution and the social impact of mining.

4. Towards an Explanation

How, then, do we explain this bifurcation – or this cleaving – of the Court into two distinct jurisprudential periods? A number of overlapping explanations suggest themselves.

First, it is certainly possible to see the Court in evolutionary terms – that is, it is arguable that the Court's environmental jurisprudence on ESD could not have emerged so emphatically without being sustained and reinforced by the bedrock of public interest jurisprudence that both went before it, and continues alongside it. By dismantling the barriers to justice and opening up the Court, the Court has given space for the public and lawyers to advocate innovatively and daringly, and to demand accountability and transparency from decision-makers. As Sax has argued, this is a vital arm in the struggle for environmental protection:

> Litigation, then, provides an additional source of leverage in making environmental decision-making operate rationally, thoughtfully, and with a sense of responsiveness to the entire range of citizen concerns.[73]

Second, it is argued that the Court has benefited from greater legislative and administrative attention – albeit episodic and inconsistent – to the concept of ESD. References to ESD are now commonplace in second- or third-generation NSW laws on pollution control, waste management, natural resource management and biodiversity conservation.[74] This has enlivened a jurisprudence around, and discussion of, the principles of ESD both in and outside the Court.[75]

[71] ibid, [28].

[72] ibid, [31]. In doing so, the Court took into account the objective under planning legislation of providing opportunities for community participation and its concomitant relationship with improved decision-making. The Court found that the criteria for joinder under planning law was made out, namely that Groundswell Gloucester would raise an issue that should be considered, and which would not likely be sufficiently addressed if it were not joined as a party [34]. Separately, the Court also found that it was in the interests of justice and the public interest to grant joinder, given the significant public interest in the proceedings [35].

[73] J Sax, *Defending the Environment* (New York, Vintage Books, 1971) 115.

[74] See eg Native Vegetation Conservation Act 1997 (NSW) s 3(g) (now repealed); Protection of the Environment Operations Act 1997 (NSW) s 3(a); Water Management Act 2000 (NSW) s 3(a); Waste Avoidance and Resource Recovery Act 2001 (NSW) s 3(a) and (h); National Parks and Wildlife Act 1974 (NSW) s 2A92 (commenced on 4 October 2002); Native Vegetation Act 2003 (NSW) s 3 (now repealed); and Biodiversity Conservation Act 2016 (NSW) s 1.3.

[75] Cases include *Anderson v Director-General, Department of Environment and Climate Change* (2006) 144 LGERA 43; *Gray v Minister for Planning* (n 52); *Taralga Landscape Guardians Inc v Minister for Planning* (n 52); *Hub Action Group Inc v Minister for Planning* (n 52); *Hill Top Residents Action Group Inc v Minister for Planning* (2009) 171 LGERA 247; *Caroona Coal Action Group Inc v Coal Mines Australia Pty Ltd (No 3)* (n 43); *Bulga Milbrodale Progress Association Inc v Minister for Planning and Infrastructure and Warkworth*

Third, it is clear that the Court abandoned its cautiousness around ESD in this second period. A decision early in the tenure of the Chief Judge who succeeded Justice Pearlman, Justice McClellan, in *BGP Properties Pty Ltd v Lake Macquarie City Council*[76] essentially required consideration of ESD and the precautionary principle, where relevant. A decision of the next Chief Judge, Justice Preston, in *Bentley v BGP Properties* soon followed, affirming the centrality of ESD; a 'touchstone' for meeting the needs of present and future generations.[77] The case of *Telstra v Corporation Ltd v Hornsby Shire Council* evolved the law even more, giving 'serious judicial attention'[78] to the precautionary principle with meticulous legal reasoning.[79] A raft of other cases have followed, further explicating the principles of ESD and applying them in practice.[80] The Court has complemented this with an ongoing commitment to extra-curial writings on ESD, amplifying and contextualising the decisions and thus facilitating access to justice.[81]

However, in any analysis of the Court it is crucial to avoid a largely top-down analysis. As one branch of the government, there are very real limits to what the Court can achieve on its own. The Court cannot devise principles around ESD, let alone rule on procedural issues such as standing and justiciability, without appropriate advocates, experts, clients and matters coming before it; at best, the Court often only has an enabling function. As Sax has said:

> Courts alone cannot and will not do the job that is needed. But courts can help to open the doors to a far more limber governmental process. The more leverage citizens have, the more responsive and responsible their officials and fellow citizens will be.[82]

Finally, it is submitted that it is precisely this element – that is, the changing nature of public participation or what Sax calls 'the leverage that citizens have' – that helps to explain the development of an environmental jurisprudence on ESD in NSW over the past twenty years. As Justice Stein has long argued, public participation can help to spawn the development of an environmental jurisprudence itself:

> Citizen participation in environmental decision-making, the ability to restrain breaches of the law by civil enforcement and to judicially review decisions, have the proven capacity to develop a new body of environmental law.[83]

Mining Limited (n 52); *Save Little Manly Beach Foreshore Incorporated v Manly Council* (2013) 198 LGERA 304; *Fullerton Cove Residents Action Group Incorporated v Dart Energy Ltd* (n 34); and *Gloucester Resources Limited v Minister for Planning* (n 52).

[76] *BGP Properties Pty Ltd* (n 52) 262.

[77] *Bentley v BGP Properties* (2006) 145 LGERA 234, 243.

[78] K Woolaston and E Hamman, 'The Operation of the Precautionary Principle in Australian Environmental Law: An Examination of the Western Australian White Shark Drum Line Program' (2015) 32 *Environmental and Planning Law Journal* 327, 331.

[79] *Telstra v Corporation Ltd v Hornsby Shire Council* (2006) 67 NSWLR 256, 107–24 (on ESD), 125–83 (on the precautionary principle).

[80] See *Gloucester Resources Limited v Minister for Planning and Environment (No 2)* (n 70).

[81] At the time of wiring, the current members of the Court had over 150 speeches and papers on the Court website, many of these on ESD: see www.lec.nsw.gov.au/lec/publications-and-resources/judicial-speeches-and-papers.html#Current1.

[82] Sax (n 73) 115.

[83] P Stein 'An Antipodean Perspective on Environmental Rights' (1995) 12 *Environmental and Planning Law Journal* 50, 53.

But Justice Stein's astute observation begs the question as to what has changed and what sets the two periods of the Court apart? It is submitted that there are four related factors.

First, the accessibility of the Court has enabled the development of a cohort of informed, resolute and sophisticated clients who – in a very real sense – have helped to forge a cogent environmental jurisprudence in NSW, including Groundswell Gloucester, the Bulga Milbrodale Progress Association, the Northern Inland Council for the Environment, Maules Creek Community Council, the Southern Highlands Coal Action Group, the Fullerton Cove Residents Action Group and the Hunter Environment Lobby. These clients have shaped the formative environmental cases on ESD over the past twenty years.[84]

Second, enhanced funding support for EDO NSW – the largest public interest environmental law firm in Australia – from 2003[85] enabled it to better and more fully assist the community to protect the environment through law. Public interest environmental litigation is difficult, and requires careful calibration and sufficient resources to both work well and contribute to the development of an environmental jurisprudence. Enhanced funding support allowed the office to both attract and retain lawyers during this period, as well as ensuring that it could continue to represent clients in long-running and complicated matters such as *Bulga Milbrodale*,[86] *Rocky Hill*[87] and *Blue Mountains Conservation Society v Delta*.[88]

Third, as cases such as *Gray*,[89] *Telstra*,[90] and *Taralga*[91] highlight, it has not only been public interest environmental law experts such as EDO NSW who have successfully run cutting-edge cases. Rather, there is a growing body of private and government environmental lawyers well-versed in the complexities of environmental law in NSW. In a related sense, the environmental bar in NSW has increased exponentially over the past twenty years,[92] contributing significantly to the development of an environmental jurisprudence before the Court.

Finally, a great deal of environmental litigation requires expert evidence. The Court has dealt with this in part through Court-appointed experts as well as ordering joint experts. At the same time, EDO NSW established a Scientific Advisory Service in 2003 comprising, inter alia, a 150-person strong expert register to provide pro bono or

[84] See *Gloucester Resources Limited v Minister for Planning and Environment (No 2)* (n 70).

[85] In particular, from the Public Purpose Fund and the Law Society and the endorsement of the then Attorney General and Minister for the Environment, the Hon Bob Debus.

[86] *Bulga Milbrodale* (n 52).

[87] *Rocky Hill* (n 52).

[88] *Blue Mountains Conservation Society* (n 48).

[89] *Gray* (n 52).

[90] *Telstra* (n 52).

[91] *Taralga* (n 52).

[92] From an EDO NSW point of view, it has certainly engaged with a much wider variety of barristers during the second period (whereas it once had to rely on a very small clique of barristers willing to assist in public interest matters). This approach has arguably led to an increased sophistication from the bar around environmental issues, principles and solutions, while also being more equitable for overworked barristers acting on pro bono or reduced rates. EDO NSW used 32 barristers in 2007–08; 42 in 2008–09; 35 in 2009–10; 45 in 2010–11; 47 in 2011–12 and 46 apiece in the immediate years before merging into a national EDO (2017–18 and 2018–19): see www.edo.org.au/annual-reports/.

reduced-fee advice to EDO clients.[93] In the *Rocky Hill* case, expert evidence on climate change, energy markets and social impacts were all relied on by the applicant in asking the Court to refuse development consent for the coal mine.[94] Similarly, the *Bulga*[95] merits review case went on for fourteen days with the community calling experts on the social impacts of the mine, the impacts on biodiversity, input–output analysis and benefit–cost analysis. Taking on such cases during the first period of the Court would have been both unthinkable and unworkable in the absence of proper infrastructure and resources.

5. Conclusion

This chapter has traced the development of the Court's jurisprudence over the past forty years through the prism of access to justice. The first period was characterised by a focus on procedural access to justice. It was a time when the Court was determined to make good on the promise of open standing and the importance of the public interest. It was also a time when the Court faced some criticism for being timorous and overly cautious in relation to engaging with ESD. The second period has been characterised by the active development of an environmental jurisprudence on ESD alongside a consolidation of a jurisprudence on the public interest.

The last twenty years has seen the Court become globally influential in the development of an environmental jurisprudence on ESD.[96] The jurisprudential leap that the Court has made in this second period is explicable on a number of bases, including an improved legislative framework; leadership from the Court itself; an engaged and active civil society; and the sustaining power of a public interest jurisprudence that both went before and continues alongside its environmental jurisprudence on ESD.

[93] In 2018/19, EDO NSW engaged 69 experts to provide 87 advices for litigation and other purposes.

[94] See, for example, the evidence from a climate change specialist, Professor Will Steffen, an energy market specialist, Mr Tim Buckley and a social researcher with expertise on the social impacts of the project, Dr Hedda Askland in *Gloucester Resources Limited* (n 52) [309], [436], [438], [441]ff and [547].

[95] *Bulga Milbrodale* (n 52).

[96] As noted in the latest Annual Review, decisions of the Court have been cited over 5,000 times in over 70 courts and tribunals around the world, including every jurisdiction in Australia: see Land and Environment Court of NSW, *Annual Review* (2020), 29, 30.

14

Alternative Dispute Resolution in the Land and Environment Court of New South Wales

MARY WALKER OAM

1. Introduction

This chapter will concentrate on the role of the Land and Environment Court of NSW (the Court) in dispute resolution and will comment on future environmental challenges that may lead to conflicts and the intervention of the Court. A key question in designing and developing any dispute resolution process in this context is: how will these matters of conflict or discontent manifest into disputes and what forms of dispute resolution will be appropriate?

The design of alternative dispute resolution (ADR) processes within the Court are considered and are viewed in the wider context of changes in the ways courts and tribunals resolve disputes beyond traditional adjudication. The development of the concept of a multi-door courthouse and how it has developed for disputes in environmental and planning law is investigated. The cultural shift of managing disputes in the Court via a multi-door courthouse structure has been profound. The nature of disputes before the Court has informed the responses developed over time to create an environmental disputes centre within a state superior court of record.[1] The selection of, and appropriate application of, a dispute resolution process to a particular class of dispute has been fundamental to this transition.

Tillett and French[2] classify three concepts which may have interchangeable meanings in dispute resolution. A 'problem', 'dispute' or 'conflict' can be defined separately and distinctly or interchangeably. The majority of the literature on conflict resolution uses 'conflict' as a generic term and 'conflict resolution' to include problem solving and dispute settlement.[3] In this chapter the terms and their respective meanings

[1] Land and Environment Court Act 1979 (NSW) (LEC Act), s 5.

[2] G Tillett and B French, *Resolving Conflict, A Practical Approach*, 3rd edn (Oxford, Oxford University Press, 2006) 7–8; see also National Alternative Dispute Resolution Advisory Council (NADRC), *Fairness and Justice in Alternative Dispute Resolution* (Discussion Paper, November 1997) 15.

[3] Tillett and French (n 2), 8.

described by Tillett and French will be adopted. 'Conflict' arises when values or needs are incompatible; for example, broad environmental disputes which affect communities and political interests. A 'problem' or 'dispute' arises when a specific action or situation exists where individuals or groups perceive that their interests, needs or goals are incompatible in a particular situation; for example, a planning dispute over the development of a site.

2. Background

ADR is not new. The Hon TF Bathurst AC, Chief Justice of the New South Wales Supreme Court, has noted that negotiated settlements, mediation and arbitration have for centuries been used to resolve disputes. Our system of law recognises that the administration of justice does not prescribe an inflexible or invariable standard of justice so long as a minimum standard of procedural fairness is observed in the processes adopted by the parties.[4]

Over its history the Land and Environment Court has institutionalised primary and hybrid forms of ADR which are best suited to the nature of disputes within the ambit of environmental and planning law and has retained a flexible approach to dispute resolution innovation to adapt to the changing needs of society. As recounted in other chapters, the Court was created as a court that would be able to 'function with the benefits of procedural reform and lack of legal technicalities as the requirements of justice permit'.[5] A focus on public consultation and participation in decision-making to resolve disputes in ADR processes are innovations adopted by the Court which have created an ability, not only to explore the resolution of disputes via different ADR processes, but also to attempt to create durable outcomes acceptable to the parties and host communities.

In most environmental disputes the issues or problems are multifaceted. The emphasis on ADR in this context is not accidental. Justice Preston, Fuller, Jowell and Weiler contend that there are limits to the capacity of adjudication to resolve polycentric problems. Polycentric problems cannot be resolved by identifying issues and working sequentially through them to adjudicate on each issue as the resolution of one issue may have ramifications on other issues.[6]

Polycentricity is not the only factor catalysing the use of ADR. When the Court was established, the focus was on rationalisation and specialisation.[7] The idea of the Court as a 'one-stop shop' has developed to refer to the Court's multiple jurisdictions

[4] TF Bathurst AC, 'The Future of Alternative Dispute Resolution', *Bar News* (Sydney, Autumn 2020) 50.

[5] Cognate Environmental Planning Bills, Second Reading (NSW Legislative Assembly, Hansard, 14 November 1979) 3051.

[6] B Preston, 'Limits of Environmental Dispute Resolution Mechanisms' (1995) 13 *Australian Bar Review*, 148, 166–67; L Fuller, 'The Forms and Limits of Adjudication' (1978) 92 *Harvard Law Review* 353, 395; J Jowell, 'The Legal Control of Administrative Discretion' [1973] *PL* 178, 231; P Weiler, 'Two Models of Judicial Decision-Making' (1968) 46 *Canadian Bar Review* 406, 420–26.

[7] B Preston, 'Conciliation in the Land and Environment Court of NSW: History, Nature and Benefits' (2007) 13 *Local Government Law Journal* 110, 110.

and capacity to deal with a myriad of substantive issues which also incorporates a problem-solving approach to dispute resolution.[8] This approach not only focuses on individual disputes and applicable remedies but on designing dispute resolution mechanisms which create systems for resolving disputes. Inherently, problem solving is not confined to the resolution of each individual dispute but to the development of ADR systems to streamline approaches for the resolution of classes of disputes in the Court. The Court has optimised this approach in developing a multi-door courthouse focusing on dispute resolution in environmental and planning law.

Other influences have also contributed to the philosophy adopted by the Court including the goals, principles and targets noted in United Nations initiatives, which have been integrated into the systems design processes of the Court. The United Nations environmental programmes focus on access to information, justice and public participation in dispute resolution which have been underlying tenets of the work of the Court and innovations in ADR.[9]

3. The Idea of a Multi-door Courthouse

The Court provides a form of multi-door courthouse with a range of dispute resolution options at different stages in proceedings including conciliation, mediation, early neutral evaluation, administrative merits review, litigation and references to an external referee.[10] The precursor to the development of the idea of a multi-door courthouse was a general discourse in common law jurisdictions noting dissatisfaction with the administration of justice and the cost and delay of proceedings in common law jurisdictions. These matters were debated in the United States from the early twentieth century onward and included such legal luminaries as Roscoe Pound, Frank Sander and Chief Justice Warren Burger as well as having the support of the American Bar Association.[11] From these debates, and particularly the work of Sander, came the idea of the 'multi-door courthouse',[12] where disputes can be resolved by a range of different

[8] G Pring and C Pring, *Environmental Courts & Tribunals: A Guide for Policy Makers* (UNEP, 2016) 48–49. The jurisdiction of an ECT is recommended to be comprehensive and to include geographical and general accessibility, jurisdiction over a broad subject matter in environmental law and planning and multiple jurisdictional levels ranging from merits reviews at first instance to trials and appeals at a superior court level.

[9] United Nations General Assembly, 'Transforming Our World: The 2030 Agenda for Sustainable Development' (25 September, 2015); A/RES/70/1 and United Nations Environment Programme, 'Rio Declaration on Environment and Development issued at the United Nations Conference on Environment and Development', Principle 10.

[10] B Preston, 'The Role of Environmental Courts and Tribunals in Promoting the Rule of Law and Ensuring Equal Access to Justice for All', *International Symposium on Environmental Adjudication in the 21st Century* (Auckland, 11 April 2017) 16, fn 108.

[11] R Pound, 'The Causes of Popular Dissatisfaction with the Administration of Justice' (1906) 29 *ABA Reports* 395; a call for the improvement of court administration which has remained a classic statement on the need for efficient and equitable judicial administration; F Sander, 'Varieties of Dispute Processing' (1976) 70 *Federal Rules Decisions* 79, 1; E Johnson, 'The Pound Conference Remembered' (2012) 19(1) *American Bar Association Dispute Resolution Magazine* 6; and S Goldberg, F Sander and N Rogers, *Dispute Resolution, Negotiation, Mediation, and Other Processes*, 2nd edn (Boston, MA, Little, Brown and Co, 1992) 432.

[12] Johnson (n 11); noted: '[Professor Sander's] speech was entitled "Varieties of Dispute Processing" and never mentioned the term "multi-door courthouse"; a magazine editor coined the phrase when he used it for a headline for an article about Sander's speech'.

approaches – adjudication through the courts, as well as mediation, arbitration or other dispute resolution mechanisms.[13]

In Australia, the discourse relating to the development and institutionalisation of ADR commenced with a focus on the early resolution of disputes to reduce the cost of litigation and delay in the finalisation of disputes which was later grounded in the context of 'access to justice'. An Australian Law Reform Commission (ALRC) Issues Paper was disseminated in 1998 entitled 'Review of the Adversarial System of Litigation, ADR – Its Role in Federal Dispute Resolution',[14] which led to an ALRC inquiry into 'Managing Justice: A Review of the Federal Civil Justice System', and represented the culmination of a major four-year inquiry, which commenced with terms of reference directing the Commission to consider 'the need for a simpler, cheaper and more accessible legal system'. The ALRC was asked to focus particular attention on issues relating to the causes of excessive costs and delay, case management, ADR, pleadings, and other court processes, expert evidence and unrepresented litigants.[15] Later, the Australian Attorney-General's Department[16] and the Australian Productivity Commission[17] released several reports referring to similar themes. The Productivity Commission Inquiry Report into 'Access to Justice Arrangements'[18] included within its terms of reference an investigation into alternative mechanisms to improve equity and access to justice with a cost–benefit analysis of elements such as specialist courts, the use of technology, early intervention as well as models of ADR.[19] These studies sought to identify remedies for excessive cost and delay and to remove impediments to access to justice with an investigation of how ADR could serve as a remedy for concerns raised in these reviews. Another influential academic analysis which encouraged the idea of a multi-door courthouse was undertaken by Sander and Goldberg, who outlined criteria for allocating various types of disputes to different dispute resolution processes.[20] Applying this analysis from a public policy perspective rather than simply the procedure preferred by individual disputants, Sander and Goldberg identified the public policy perspective for the choice of ADR process to be one that would be 'the best for all those with an interest in the dispute'.[21]

As is implicit in the above, identifying the characteristics of disputes and dispute resolution processes is essential to understanding the methodologies utilised in any ADR process. There have been attempts by practitioners to define groupings of ADR processes. Some describe a continuum commencing with informal dispute resolution processes moving to formal processes,[22] or a continuum of dispute resolution processes

[13] Sander (n 11) 1; see also F Sander and S Goldberg, 'Fitting the Forum to the Fuss: A User-Friendly Guide to Selecting an ADR Procedure' (1994) 10 *Negotiation Journal* 49.

[14] Australian Law Reform Commission (ALRC), *Review of the Adversarial System of Litigation, ADR – Its Role in Federal Dispute Resolution* (Issues Paper 25, 1998).

[15] ALRC, *Managing Justice: A Review of the Federal Justice System* (Report No 89, 2000) 6, 8.

[16] Report by the Access to Justice Taskforce, Attorney-General's Department, *A Strategic Framework for Access to Justice in the Federal Civil Justice System*, September 2009.

[17] The Productivity Commission is an Australian Government's independent research and policy advisory body.

[18] Productivity Commission, *Access to Justice Arrangements – Inquiry Report* (No 72, 2014).

[19] ibid, Terms of Reference No 8, v.

[20] Sander and Goldberg (n 13) 50; see also Sander (n 11) 1.

[21] Sander and Goldberg (n 13) 50.

[22] Pring and Pring (n 8) 47.

moving from self-determining processes such as those termed 'consensual'[23] in nature to advisory, regulatory or determinative processes.[24] Others refer to groupings of adjudicative and non-adjudicative processes with internal categories[25] or refer to an 'escalation' of processes describing the level of determinative intervention by an independent party commencing with the least directive and moving to the most directive (eg commencing with negotiation and concluding with litigation) or from less adversarial to more adversarial.[26] Policy-makers talk of a differentiation among facilitative, advisory or determinative processes and a distinction between institutionalised ADR found in courts and tribunals as compared to private ADR. These distinctions focus on structured dispute resolution processes available either within courts or societal institutions but do not raise the 'do nothing' option or the outcome of conflict manifesting in social disruption.

There is, however, a critical distinguishing factor in classifying ADR processes. The distinguishing factor is determining whether the ADR practitioner[27] has power to impose a solution, advise or solely to assist the disputants to arrive at their own solution.[28] This analysis is useful in considering the design elements to be adopted within ADR systems. Another design element, although basic, is the need for uniformity of definitions of ADR processes and the timely provision of information to the Court and exchange of information amongst the relevant parties or stakeholders. Consideration of ADR processes within an adversarial system and court paradigm is different to an analysis of ADR processes in a private context. The multi-door courthouse concept involves the amalgamation of ADR options within a dispute system design[29] in a context where procedural fairness and access to justice are paramount.

It is also important to note that the first step in designing ADR processes requires a review of dispute resolution processes available in the relevant judicial system, and the second is understanding local cultural mores about dispute resolution held by policy-makers, judicial officers, lawyers and disputants. Stipanowich argues that in the last quarter of the twentieth century significant changes occurred in the ways lawyers approached conflict with unprecedented efforts to develop strategies aimed at more efficient, less costly and more satisfying methods of resolving disputes.[30] Menkel-Meadow

[23] That is, the parties have a choice to enter a process and a choice of outcomes from a process.

[24] NADRAC, *Terminology: Discussion Paper* (2002) 12.

[25] T Stipanowich and V Fraser, 'The International Task Force on Mixed Mode Dispute Resolution: Exploring The Interplay Between Mediation, Evaluation and Arbitration in Commercial Cases' (2017) 40 *Fordham International Law Journal* 868.

[26] M King, A Freiberg, B Batagol and R Hyams, *Non-adversarial Justice*, 2nd edn (Sydney, The Federation Press, 2014) 109.

[27] Goldberg, Sander and Rogers (n 11) 3. Dispute resolution practitioners are required to be neutral and impartial. The term 'neutral' has become a descriptor of dispute resolution practitioners; Stipanowich and Fraser (n 25).

[28] Goldberg, Sander and Rogers, (n 11) 3; Sander and Goldberg (n 13) 50. See also NADRAC, *Terminology: Discussion Paper* (n 24) 12.

[29] Or 'dispute processing system'; N Rogers, R Bordone, F Sander and C McEwan, *Designing Systems and Processes for Managing Disputes* (Alphen aan den Rijn, Wolters Kluwer, 2013) 4.

[30] T Stipanowich, 'ADR and the "Vanishing Trial": The Growth and Impact of "Alternative Dispute Resolution' (2004) 1 *Journal of Empirical Legal Studies* 843.

opines that the mind-set or behaviour brought to a dispute resolution process such as negotiation has consequences.[31] An orientation either adversarial or problem-solving leads to a mind-set about what can be achieved, which affects the behaviour chosen being either competitive or solution searching which in turn affects dispute resolution outcomes.[32] The philosophy underpinning consensual ADR processes that have negotiation at their core, such as conciliation and mediation, rely upon a focus on interest based-bargaining and creative solutions rather than narrow compromises or narrow remedies. These ideas, which have created an orientation towards problem-solving, rather than position-based or adversarial behaviour, have opened an area of dispute resolution that has capacity to manage polycentric disputes and conflict.

4. Dispute Resolution Processes Available in the Land and Environment Court

The Court is well known for its leadership in the development of the multi-door courthouse concept in environmental dispute resolution and its ability to innovate and respond to changes in the types and character of environmental disputes over time, such as the design of hybrid processes particularly concilio-adjudications and the implementation of online access during the COVID-19 pandemic.[33] The Court has received recognition for its development of, and innovation in, the practice of ADR processes, being awarded the 'Courts and Tribunals ADR Group of the Year' in 2018 and 'ADR Innovation of the Year in 2020' at the Australian Disputes Centre ADR Awards.[34]

Resolving disputes in the Court spans the spectrum of dispute resolution processes. The Court promotes appropriate dispute resolution and, as noted above, provides for matching the appropriate dispute resolution methods with the characteristics of a dispute.[35] Matters before the Court may be resolved by a facilitative, advisory or determinative process or through the use of a combination of these as hybrid ADR processes. When deciding which method of dispute resolution is appropriate for a particular matter, the Court may consider the type of case and whether any dispute resolution methods are compulsory for that type of case. The factors which may be taken into account include the preference of the parties; the nature of the parties and whether or not they have legal representation; the potential cost of the case; the time it might take to reach finalisation; the complexity of the matter; which method of resolution constitutes

[31] C Menkel-Meadow, 'Toward Another View of Legal Negotiation: The Structure of Problem Solving' (1984) 31 *UCLA Law Review* 754, 760.

[32] ibid.

[33] BJ Preston, 'The Land and Environment Court of New South Wales: Moving Towards a Multi-door Courthouse – Part I' (2008) 19 *Australian Dispute Resolution Journal* 72 and BJ Preston, "The Land and Environment Court of New South Wales: Moving Towards a Multi-door Courthouse – Part II (2008) 19 *Australian Dispute Resolution Journal* 144.

[34] Land and Environment Court of NSW, 'ADR Innovation of the Year Award', https://lec.nsw.gov.au/lec/news-and-announcements/adr-innovation-of-the-year-award.html (accessed 2 August 2021).

[35] Land and Environment Court of NSW, 'Resolving Disputes' https://www.lec.nsw.gov.au/lec/dispute-resolution.html (accessed 2 August 2021).

an appropriate and efficient use of a court's time; and the public interest in the outcome of the matter.

One of the crucial elements in the design of a multi-door courthouse is the triage element; 'fitting the forum to the fuss'.[36] This function is undertaken by Judges and the Registrar of the Court through case management. Triage can be undertaken for individual matters and circumstances but also as part of the referral systems designed for use by the Court. The Court undertakes both triage approaches. Triage occurs during the intake process, at the registry counter, at the first return date before the Court and at any subsequent case management or dispute resolution management session. Collectively, these interactions and case assessments constitute intake screening, diagnosis and referral to an appropriate dispute resolution process.[37] The screening and diagnostic processes undertaken by the Court via initial case evaluation are noted in the practice notes and protocols promulgated by the Court.[38] The key elements include an intake or triage process, which can include specific referral criteria for matching disputes to ADR processes and a range of dispute resolution processes undertaken by court officers skilled in ADR.[39] As discussed elsewhere in this collection, disputes are classified into eight classes in the Court.[40]

Goldberg, Sander and Rogers identify three primary dispute resolution processes: negotiation, mediation and adjudication. Hybrid processes are described as primary processes which have been combined.[41] Astor and Chinkin consider hybrid dispute resolution processes in the Australian context and note that the flexibility inherent in various models of primary dispute resolution processes allows for modification and combinations to suit the needs of the parties in the context of a particular dispute.[42] Designing dispute resolution processes requires an ADR practitioner to consider the nature of an individual dispute and to consider the complexities, nuances and features of a dispute to design a procedure which best meets the needs of the parties and issues.[43] The Court offers primary and hybrid dispute resolution processes. The Court also provides a unique hybrid procedure designed for environmental planning disputes; a concilio-adjudication process.

The Court has adopted mediation, neutral evaluation, expert appraisal, conciliation and adjudication and the use of experts as referees in its ADR offerings.[44] Some ADR processes, such as negotiation, are engaged prior to initiating proceedings. Others may run in parallel to the adversarial Court process, such as private mediation, and some have been integrated into the Court case management and dispute resolution processes.

[36] Sander and Goldberg (n 13).

[37] Preston (n 31) part II, 147–48.

[38] Available at www.lec.nsw.gov.au/lec/practice-and-procedure/practice-notes.html and www.lec.nsw.gov.au/lec/practice-and-procedure/directions.html (accessed 2 August 2021).

[39] Preston (n 31) part I, 78; see also ALRC, *Review of the Adversarial System of Litigation* (n 14) ch 5, para 5.62.

[40] Preston, this volume.

[41] Goldberg, Sander and Rogers (n 11) 3.

[42] H Astor and C Chinkin, *Dispute Resolution in Australia*, 2nd edn (London, Butterworths Lexis Nexis, 2002) 91.

[43] ibid.

[44] For an overview, see https://lec.nsw.gov.au/lec/dispute-resolution.html (accessed 2 August 2021).

Figure 1 illustrates the dispute resolution methods available in the Court and how and when they may be accessed during case management.[45]

Figure 1 Dispute resolution methods in the Land and Environment Court of NSW

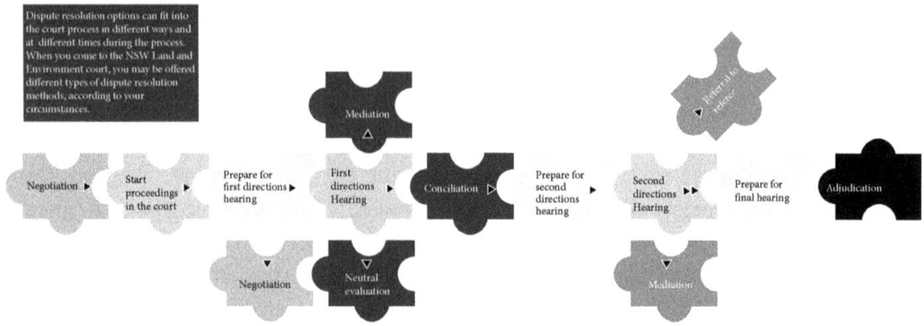

It is important to distinguish each of the processes so that parties to a dispute, stakeholders and legal representatives are able to understand and engage in each step. This provides clarity when engaging in hybrid processes.

4.1. Negotiation

The most common form of dispute resolution is negotiation.[46] Negotiation frequently occurs in private and is not visible to the Court other than the notation of a settlement or a consent judgment when a case is resolved. Although negotiating settlements is regarded as a commonplace event in the adversarial system and part of the ordinary process of litigation, it is regarded as being undertaken as a 'negotiation within the shadow of the court'.[47] The ALRC in its Discussion Paper 62 on the 'Review of the Federal Civil Justice System' referred to settlement in the following terms:

> Settlement is not regarded as an 'alternative' process separate from adjudication, but is intimately and inseparably entwined with it. Both may be thought of as aspects of a single process of strategic manoeuvre and bargaining in the (actual or threatened) presence of courts.[48]

Negotiation is, however, visible as the core activity in processes which fall within the consensual models of dispute resolution such as mediation or versions or portions of facilitation, conciliation and hybrid dispute resolution processes. If one accepts that

[45] Sourced at https://lec.nsw.gov.au/lec/dispute-resolution/diagram-showing-dispute-resolution-methods-and-how-they-fit-into.html (accessed 2 August 2021).

[46] Goldberg, Sander and Rogers (n 11) 3.

[47] *Tresize v National Australia Bank Ltd* (1994) 50 FCR 134, 137 per Black CJ; see also RH Mnookin and L Kronhouser, 'Bargaining in the Shadow of the Law: The Case of Divorce' (1979) 88 *Yale Law Journal* 950.

[48] ALRC, *Review of the Federal Civil Justice System* (Discussion Paper 62, August 1999) 2.14, citing M Galanter, 'The Federal Rules and the Quality of Settlements: A Comment on Rosenberg's, "The Federal Rules of Civil Procedure in Action"' (1989) 137 *University of Pennsylvania Law Review* 2231, 2232–33.

negotiation is the kernel of facilitative processes, the introduction of mediation or conciliation, either in parallel to the litigation process or as part of an integrated court dispute resolution system, assists in the administration of justice and promotes the resolution of disputes via self-determination.[49]

4.2. Adjudication

Adjudication is a process in which the parties present arguments and evidence to a neutral third party, the adjudicator, who makes a determination that is enforceable within the traditional judicial system.[50] Adjudication is available for all proceedings in all classes of the Court's jurisdiction. The hearing may be held in court, or for certain types of matters in Classes 1 and 2 of the Court's jurisdiction, at an on-site hearing. The form and venue of the hearing varies depending upon the type of proceedings, the complexity of the case and the number of issues in dispute. Judges, Commissioners and Registrars of the Court may hear proceedings and make a decision which is stated in orders and documented in a judgment. The decision of a Judge, Commissioner or Registrar is final and binding on the parties.

4.3. Neutral Evaluation

Neutral evaluation, as adopted by the Court, is a process of evaluation of a dispute by an impartial evaluator to identify and reduce the issues of fact and law in dispute. The evaluator's role includes assessing the relative strengths and weaknesses of each party's case and offering an opinion as to the likely outcome of the proceedings, including any likely findings of liability or the award of damages.[51] Neutral evaluation is purely an advisory process.

The Court may order that a matter be referred to neutral evaluation pursuant to Part 6 rule 6.2 of the Land and Environment Court Rules 2007 (the Rules) with or without the consent of the parties, by a Commissioner of the Court (at no cost) or by agreement to a person external to the Court. The parties bear the cost of an external neutral evaluator. Neutral evaluation is available for all proceedings in Classes 1, 2, 3, 4 and 8.[52] Each party to proceedings whose case has been referred for neutral evaluation is under a duty to participate, in good faith, in the neutral evaluation.[53] After consideration of the neutral evaluation, the parties may agree terms through negotiation. If the Court considers the terms to be appropriate, the Court will

[49] Sir Laurence Street, 'The Court System and ADR Procedures: FS Dethridge Memorial Address of 1989' (1990) 7 *Maritime Law Association of Australia and New Zealand Journal* 9.

[50] NADRAC, *Terminology: Discussion Paper* (n 24) 4.

[51] See commentary on the Land and Environment Court website at: https://lec.nsw.gov.au/lec/dispute-resolution/neutral-evaluation.html; see also https://legislation.nsw.gov.au/view/html/inforce/current/sl-2007-0578#sec.6.1https://legislation.nsw.gov.au/view/html/inforce/current/sl-2007-0578#sec.6.2 (accessed 2 August 2021).

[52] Land and Environment Court Rules 2007 (NSW), Pt 6 r 6.

[53] ibid, r 6.2(4).

make orders in accordance with the terms agreed by the parties. If after consideration of the evaluation the parties do not agree to consent orders, the matter is referred to the Court to be listed for hearing before a different Commissioner or Judge.

4.4. Reference to Referee

The Court may refer proceedings, or any question arising in the proceedings, to a person for inquiry and report to the Court, pursuant to Part 20 rule 20.14 of the Uniform Civil Procedure Rules 2005 (NSW) (UCPR) or section 35(1) of the Land and Environment Court Act 1979 (NSW) (the LEC Act). A reference may be made in all proceedings in Classes 1, 2, 3, 4 and 8.[54] The referee, usually an expert in a relevant field, is not bound by the rules of evidence and may inform himself or herself in relation to any matter as the referee thinks fit.[55] The Court may give directions with respect to the conduct of proceedings under the reference[56] and evidence before the referee may be given orally or in writing and, if the referee requires, may be given on oath or by affidavit.[57] The Court, pursuant to Part 20 rule 20.24 may adopt, vary or reject a report prepared by a referee. Court officers are unable to undertake a reference pursuant to UCPR without the concurrence of the Chief Judge (Part 20 rule 20.15(2)). In addition to the jurisdiction conferred by the UCPR, the Court may also, with the consent of the parties, direct an inquiry and report on any issue raised in, or other matter connected with, proceedings in Class 3 which includes matters dealing with land tenure, valuation, rating and compensation matters. References ordered in Class 3 are undertaken by a Commissioner of the Court. A Commissioner in making such an inquiry is disqualified from further participation in the relevant proceedings unless the parties agree.[58]

4.5. Mediation

Mediation in the Court is undertaken pursuant to section 26 of the Civil Procedure Act, 2005 (NSW) (CPA),[59] by a Commissioner or Registrar of the Court who is a trained mediator (at no cost) or by a mediator external to the Court.[60] The parties bear the cost of an external mediator. Mediation is available for all proceedings in

[54] See commentary on the Land and Environment Court website at: https://lec.nsw.gov.au/lec/dispute-resolution/reference-to-referee.html (accessed 2 August 2021).
[55] UCPR, Pt 20 r 20.20(2).
[56] UCPR, Pt 20 r 20(1).
[57] UCPR, Pt 20 r 20(3).
[58] LEC Act, s 35(1).
[59] Civil Procedure Act 2005 (NSW).
[60] For further details. see https://lec.nsw.gov.au/lec/dispute-resolution.html (accessed 2 August 2021). Also, mediations in tree disputes in Class 2 are facilitated by a mediator from the NSW Community Justice Centre. See Land and Environment Court of NSW, *The Land and Environment Court of NSW: Annual Review 2019* (State of NSW 2020) 21.

Classes 1, 2, 3, 4 and 8.[61] Section 26 of the CPA permits the Court to refer matters to mediation with or without the consent of the parties.

Mediation is utilised in a facilitative mode in this jurisdiction.[62] 'Mediation' is defined in section 25 of the CPA as 'a structured negotiation process in which the mediator, as a neutral and independent party assists the parties to a dispute to achieve their own resolution of the dispute'. The role of mediator does not include an advisory or determinative role. Pursuant to section 32 of the CPA, the mediator has power to order or give directions as to the preparation for, and conduct of, the mediation process. The role of the mediator is to facilitate the process and for the parties to exercise self-determination as to any negotiated outcomes. The mediation process is intentionally designed to be flexible and less structured than other ADR processes adopted by the Court.

If the Court refers a matter to mediation, Part 4 of the CPA and Part 20 of the UCPR govern the design of the process and the obligations of the mediator and practitioners. Section 27 of the CPA outlines the duty of the parties to participate in mediation in good faith, and sections 30 and 31 outline the privilege and confidentiality requirements of mediation under Part 4 of the CPA.[63] If the dispute resolves via mediation the Court will only incorporate the agreed outcomes or negotiated solutions in Court orders if, as with conciliation or section 34 outcomes, the Court considers the orders or determination can be a decision of the Court made in the proper exercise of its functions.

As the Court also offers to conciliate disputes, it is important to consider the differences in these processes. The 'conciliation–mediation distinction' is described by the National Alternative Dispute Resolution Advisory Council (NADRAC) in the following terms:

> '[M]ediation' is a purely facilitative process, whereas 'conciliation' may comprise a mixture of different processes including facilitation and advice. The term 'mediation' should be used where the practitioner has no advisory role on the content of the dispute and the term 'conciliation' where the practitioner does have such a role.[64]

4.6. Conciliation

From the inception of the Court, conciliation was required pursuant to section 34 of the Act.[65] Conciliation is described by the Court as a process in which the parties to a dispute, with the assistance of an impartial conciliator, identify the issues in dispute, develop options, consider alternatives and endeavour to reach agreement. The conciliator may have an advisory role on the content of the dispute or the outcome of its resolution but not a determinative role. The conciliator may advise on or determine the process of

[61] See commentary on the Land and Environment Court website at: https://lec.nsw.gov.au/lec/dispute-resolution/mediation.html (accessed 2 August 2021).

[62] NADRAC, *Terminology: Discussion Paper* (n 24) 2; L Riskin, 'Understanding Mediators' Orientations, Strategies, and Techniques: A Grid for the Perplexed' (1996) 1 *Harvard Negotiation Law Review* 8, 26–32.

[63] Civil Procedure Act, 2005 (NSW), Part 4 and UCPR, Part 20.

[64] NADRAC, *Terminology: Discussion Paper* (n 24) 3.

[65] Preston, 'Conciliation in the Land and Environment Court of NSW' (n 7) 111 and generally for a comprehensive examination of the development of conciliation in the Court.

conciliation whereby resolution is attempted, and may make suggestions for terms of settlement, give expert advice on likely terms, and may actively encourage the parties to reach agreement. The conciliator's role includes an advisory element.[66] Conciliation is available for all proceedings in Classes 1, 2 and 3 of the Court's jurisdiction.

Environmental litigation and dispute resolution involve matters of significant scientific and technical complexity that need to be assessed and decided.[67] Due to the extent and nature of the jurisdiction exercisable by the Court, a provision was enacted to allow for the Chief Judge to delegate to one or more conciliation or technical assessors the functions of the Court in proceedings in Classes 1, 2 and 3.[68] Conciliators are appointed from various technical backgrounds who bring a range of substantive knowledge to their role. Specialist knowledge of, and experience in, the administration of local government, town and country or environmental planning, environmental science, environment assessment and management of natural resources, land valuation, architecture, surveying, engineering or building, and construction, urban design and heritage, Aboriginal land rights and mining are some of the areas of expertise of conciliators in the Court.[69]

4.7. A Hybrid Model – Section 34 Conferences

Section 34 Conciliation Conferences[70] are the hallmark of the bespoke ADR processes developed by the Court. Section 34 and section 34AA conferences are a hybrid process and have been designed specifically for matters before the Court, providing an opportunity for the parties to resolve their dispute consensually, and if there is no resolution, then for finalisation by a determination by a Court officer. The hybrid process used in section 34 and 34AA conferences is an exemplar of what can be achieved in an efficient process directed to the resolution of disputes in environment and planning law.[71]

Section 34 conferences are designed as concilio-adjudications, being a hybrid or blended ADR process. This is to be distinguished from advisory, authoritative or evaluative mediation models.[72] Essentially, the process commences as a conciliation

[66] See commentary on the Land and Environment Court website at: https://www.lec.nsw.gov.au/lec/dispute-resolution/conciliation.html (accessed 2 August 2021).

[67] Z Minchun and Z Bao, 'Specialised Environmental Courts in China: Status Quo, Challenges and Responses' (2012) 30 *Journal of Energy and Natural Resources Law* 361, 367–68; G Pring and C Pring, *Greening Justice: Creating and Improving Environmental Courts and Tribunals* (The Access Initiative, 2009) 55; B Preston, 'Characteristics of Successful Environmental Courts and Tribunals' (2014) 26 *Journal of Environmental Law* 365, 379.

[68] LEC Act, ss 30(1) and 36(1) and Cognate Environmental Planning Bills, Second Reading, (NSW Legislative Assembly, Hansard, 14 November 1979) 3345.

[69] LEC Act, s 12(2AB).

[70] ibid, s 34. For a legislative history of s 34, see *Al Maha Pty Ltd v Huajun Investments Pty Ltd* (2018) 233 LGERA 170; [2018] NSWCA 245 at [54]–[79] per Preston CJ of LEC.

[71] Section 34 of the LEC Act was amended to allow for the new concilio-adjudication design of the conciliation conference process; Court Legislation Amendment Act 2007 (NSW) Schedule 6.

[72] A Gabrieli, N Zimerman and M Alberstein, 'Authority-Based Mediation' (2018) 20 *Cardozo Journal of Conflict Resolution* 1; NADRAC, *Terminology: Discussion Paper* (n 24) 4, 7.

where the Commissioner trained in mediation[73] utilises facilitative skills to encourage the parties and stakeholders to reach a negotiated agreement. If no agreement is reached the Commissioner may, with the consent of the parties, determine the matter by way of adjudication. The transition from a consensual process to a determinative process is clearly identified.[74] The model utilised for a section 34 conference is similar to a 'med-arb'[75] and has two distinct phases; a non-determinative phase which focuses on the process of negotiation between the parties; and a determinative phase in which a decision is made on any outstanding matters after the negotiation phase has been concluded. The outcome is a binding determination by the ADR practitioner, in this instance a Commissioner of the Court.

Commissioners, when exercising the powers conferred on them, are to accord procedural fairness.[76] During the facilitative conciliation phase, no private sessions are held to avoid concerns as to what might be divulged to a Commissioner during the conciliation phase but not divulged to an opposing party. This is to accord with procedural fairness if the Commissioner becomes a decision-maker and to avoid breaches of the fair hearing rule and rule against bias.[77] The New South Wales Court of Appeal in *Al Maha Pty Ltd v Huajun Investments Pty Ltd*[78] identified a specific obligation for a Commissioner to give reasons with respect to the jurisdiction of the Court to dispose of the proceedings in accordance with the parties' agreement pursuant to section 34(3) and confirmed that Commissioners are obliged to give reasons in exercising their adjudicative functions pursuant to section 34(5) noting that orders made by Commissioners are taken to be an order of the Court.[79]

If the parties do not consent that the Commissioner who had carriage of the conciliation determine the matter, the matter will be referred to the Registrar for reallocation to another Commissioner or a Judge for determination.[80] Special arrangements for conciliation apply for residential development appeals pursuant to section 34AA. Although a section 34AA conference has the same design elements as a section 34 conference, if the parties do not reach an agreement in a section 34AA conference, the Commissioner assigned to determine the matter must dispose of the proceedings.[81] The procedures for conducting a conciliation conference, including section 34 and 34AA conferences,

[73] The Court and the Australian Commercial Disputes Centre presented the first training course for Commissioners in the concilio-adjudication model and mediation skills, August 2007.

[74] Combined or hybrid dispute resolution processes are processes in which the dispute resolution practitioner plays multiple roles, for example, such as in med-arb, the practitioner first uses one process (mediation) and then another (arbitration); NADRAC, *Terminology: Discussion Paper* (n 24) 5.

[75] 'Med-arb' is a hybrid or blended process: an ADR practitioner commences with the mediation process but if there is no agreement determines the matter via an arbitration process.

[76] *Al Maha Pty Ltd v Huajun Investments Pty Ltd* [2018] NSWCA 245; (2018) 233 LGERA 170, [14] per Basten JA.

[77] ALRC, *Traditional Rights and Freedoms – Encroachments by Commonwealth Laws* (Report 129, 2016) [14.11]–[14.26], ibid [14]; *Kioa v West* (1985) 159 CLR 550, 563 per Gibbs CJ and 585 per Mason J; *Re Minister for Immigration and Multicultural Affairs Ex parte Lam* (2003) 214 CLR 1,37, per Gleeson CJ.

[78] *Al Maha Pty Ltd* (n 76).

[79] ibid, [26] per Basten JA and [199]–[202] per Preston CJ of LEC and LEC Act, s 34(8).

[80] LEC Act, s 34(13).

[81] For an overview, see https://lec.nsw.gov.au/lec/dispute-resolution/conciliation.html (accessed 2 August 2021).

are set out in the Court's 'Conciliation Conference Policy'.[82] The Court may arrange a conciliation conference with or without the consent of the parties.[83]

5. Public Participation and the Public Interest

5.1. Public Participation

Designing ADR processes that can manage the dynamics of polycentric disputes is challenging. We are now emerging from an era of experimentation with basic ADR processes and the institutionalisation of ADR within courts and tribunals and moving towards an era of engaging in dispute resolution with elements of public participation. Professor Lon Fuller analysed the adjudicative process in terms of public participation as a social process of decision-making which assures affected parties a particular form of participation, that of presenting proofs and arguments before a decision-maker such as is available in traditional court adjudication.[84] Justice Preston has stated that a court needs to promote access to justice by removing or lowering barriers to public participation and public interest litigation, to be responsive to the needs of court users and to facilitate access to justice by the court taking a more user-orientated approach.[85] Public participation, as noted above, is a focus of United Nations initiatives in the environmental context. In ADR terms this is generally manifested in ADR processes which incorporate self-determination, being negotiation and facilitative processes such as mediation and conciliation where consensual outcomes can be achieved.

Resolving disputes and overcoming the challenges of the twenty-first century will require the three elements of underlying philosophy – access to information, public participation, and access to justice in environmental matters – to be included in the dispute systems designs of courts and tribunals. These challenges are likely to include increased stakeholder engagement, managing changing community expectations, resolving emerging class actions in the environmental arena, and resolving disputes relating to pollution and climate change. In addition to communities and individuals voicing concerns over development and planning controversies there will be an increased focus on concerns such as environmental degradation, the extinction of species, pollution and ramifications relating to climate change. This trend is unlikely to diminish.

Legislative and government policy responses will frame rights which will frame the character of inevitable disputes. In environmental conflicts it is predictable that values will clash. How does ADR assist in the realignment of values reflected in past events, evaluated in the present and formulated for the future? The character of facilitative models of ADR, the flexibility and focus on interest-based bargaining, needs, goals and expectations and concentrating on consensus-based outcomes rather than defined

[82] Land and Environment Court, *Conciliation Conference Policy* (27 March 2017).
[83] LEC Act, s34(1)(a).
[84] Fuller (n 6) 325.
[85] Preston (n 10) 79–80.

rights provides an avenue for exploration for courts and tribunals for the selection of appropriate dispute resolution processes in the early management of these polycentric conflicts and disputes. ADR skills will need to be harnessed and further developed to respond to these emerging conflicts and disputes. The Court is well-placed as a multi-door courthouse to consider mobilising a response which can be used to engage with contemporary broad ranging conflicts involving environmental concerns. These conflicts require early intervention otherwise exacerbation of conflict is likely and class actions or multiple lawsuits may result.

The Court may be required to facilitate urgent issues, concerns, complaints and matters of conflict broader than disputes initiated in the traditional adversarial manner. The skills utilised to identify, manage and problem-solve disputes that arise in environmental 'hot spots' require a sophisticated understanding of dispute resolution as well as relevant legal principles. Resolving these disputes is likely to fall within the province of environmental courts as part of urgent relief or interlocutory applications. The gateway for seeking ADR assistance is not clear in this arena. The Court has the ability, with the necessary legislative reforms for pre-litigation intervention, to be a repository of all environmental conflicts and disputes at different stages of the development of these disputes. The gateways to entry into the Court need review if the Court is to capture opportunities to assist society in resolving emerging environmental disputes.

Comparative opportunities exist to have, as part of the Court structure, a pathway for early intervention. There are many schemes currently active in NSW which allow for such intervention, for example the Retail Leases Act 1994 (NSW)[86] requires mediation to be attempted and a certificate to be obtained prior to the initiation of court proceedings. A National Cabinet Mandatory Code of Conduct[87] was implemented by the Australian federal government during 2020 in response to the economic turmoil induced by government restrictions due to the COVID-19 pandemic. The Code imposed a set of good-faith leasing principles that set out parameters in which negotiations were to be conducted involving issues relating to commercial and retail leases prior to proceedings being commenced. This example ought not be taken as a suggestion to replicate these schemes as the polycentric nature of environmental disputes has more elements to manage; however, the idea of a dispute resolution centre envisaged by Sander may allow for separate early pathways to operate. The caveat is the need for training highly skilled dispute resolution professionals with the requisite skills to facilitate these conflicts and disputes.

Access to information provides capacity for understanding the conflict or issues in dispute and enhances the capacity for productive dialogue and stability. An example of this has been the adoption of community right-to-know charters which have been developed by the facilitation of community groups, industry and government entities utilising mediation skills that have in some instances arisen out of community

[86] Retail Leases Act 1994 (NSW), s 68, the pre-litigation mediation process is implemented by the Office of the New South Wales Small Business Commission.

[87] National Cabinet Mandatory Code of Conduct, 'SME Commercial Leasing Principles During COVID-19' (2020) www.pm.gov.au/sites/default/files/files/national-cabinet-mandatory-code-ofconduct-sme-commercial-leasing-principles.pdf (accessed 2 August 2021).

concerns or disputes. An illustration is the Australian Nuclear Science and Technology Organisation (ANSTO) and host community, 'Community Right to Know Charter', an outcome document resulting from community participation. Through a facilitation process, community representatives, residents of the host community, environmental groups, representatives of ANSTO and government departments were involved in the identification of issues, drafting the charter and its implementation.[88] Facilitative processes can be effective in moving stakeholders towards resolution. Outcomes may be agreements or protocols for ongoing engagement or for modifying behaviour. The flexibility of facilitative processes that enhance dialogue and reframe conflicts are well adapted to managing public interests and to develop appropriate dispute resolution processes by consensus.

Public participation may have different meanings to different people in different situations. Is public participation merely public consultation or does it involve an element of decision-making? How is public decision-making invoked? The definition of functionally different concepts such as information exchange, consultation, process participation or participation in decision-making need to be clarified. The generic notion of involvement of the public and identifying the public need to be defined. Expectations in respect to the decision-making capacity of the public need to be agreed. Should consideration be made for pre-litigation intervention and pathways not necessarily in the image of a traditional Court? The simple concept of identifying stakeholders even at a basic level can be complicated. If one thinks of concentric circles of engagement, the identification may move from individuals, neighbours, local activist groups, local companies, local government institutions, to state, federal and international entities and institutions with interlinking connections. Problems relating to access to information can include physical access problems, lack of information, culturally inappropriate or ineffective means of information distribution, fear of conflict, intimidation, suspicion of authorities, physical or mental impairment,[89] and perceptions of power imbalances such as the exercise of economic and political power which affect access to relevant information.

Courts with jurisdiction and expertise to deal with conflicts in environmental law are well placed to expand their dispute resolution offerings but crucially must recognise that a different mind-set is required to manage or assist stakeholders to resolve emerging environmental issues than that available in traditional rights-based adjudication. High-level skills in conflict diagnosis and ADR design are required to engage in what are often volatile conflicts. Shallow recognition of the complexity of the issues which are incumbent in these conflicts or a minimum skill base in ADR is not sufficient and is likely to exacerbate the conflict. Another challenge for court-based resolution of these conflicts is that often there is a lack of visibility of these conflicts or a lack of visibility of the layers of the conflicts or disputes. Consideration of a gateway for these disputes to become visible for court intervention and early triage or the implementation of protocols without escalating the conflict is paramount. Locus standi is currently an impediment for many stakeholders, as is the status of interveners for capacity to engage

[88] ANSTO, *Community Right to Know Charter* (November 2003).

[89] NADRAC, *Issues of Fairness and Justice in Alternative Dispute Resolution* (November 1997) 191.

in court-based dispute resolution.[90] Broader interpretation of these concepts needs to be considered at any entry point if courts are to be regarded as the repository of these conflicts. Threshold criteria for entry need to be identified. The concept of ADR triage may also need to be expanded.

It is difficult to assess how these matters will finally manifest in disputes in which the Court will have jurisdiction; however, the philosophy underpinning the idea of a 'one-stop shop' and a user-orientated approach will bring a focus on designing appropriate dispute resolution systems and bespoke responses for use in resolving environmental disputes in the twenty-first century.

5.2. The Public Interest

Closely connected to the idea of public participation is that of the public interest. ADR in the public interest is a complex ideal. Historically, attention on public interest advocacy in Australian courts was directed to access to justice for disadvantaged claimants and groups.[91] Public interest advocacy was levelled on concerns relating to impediments to access to justice by public interest groups seeking to commence claims or intervene if they had standing to do so and later examined in relation to applications against public interest groups in adverse cost order applications.[92] The characterisation of litigation brought in the public interest in this context was explored by Justice Lloyd in *Engadine Area Traffic Action Group Inc v Sutherland Shire Council (No 2)*.[93] Several matters were identified in determining whether the proceedings could be characterised as public interest litigation. Questions[94] were considered such as what is the public interest served by the litigation; whether the interest involves a significant number of members of the public and concern for a wider and significant geographic area; whether the applicant seeks to enforce public law obligations; whether the prime motivation of the litigation is to uphold the public interest and the rule of law; and whether the applicant has any pecuniary interest in the outcome of the proceedings? Recent cases such as *Sharma by her litigation representative Sister Marie Brigid Arthur v Minister for the Environment*[95] and *Gloucester Resources Limited v Minister for Planning*[96] have

[90] ALRC, *Standing in Public Interest Litigation* (Report 27, 1985), ALRC, *Beyond the Doorkeeper – Standing to Sue for Public Remedies* (Report 78, 1996).

[91] Justice R Sackville, 'Access to Justice: Assumptions and Reality Checks' [2002] *Fed J Schol* 12.

[92] Cases such as *Botany Municipal Council v Department of Arts, Sports and Environment* (1992) 34 FCR 412; *Engadine Area Traffic Action Group Inc v Sutherland Shire Council (No 2)* (2004) 136 LGERA 365; [2004] NSWLEC 434 [15]; *Caroona Coal Action Group Inc v Coal Mines Australia Pty Ltd (No 3)* (2010) 173 LGERA 280; [2010] NSWLEC 59, and *Oshlack v Richmond River Council and Muswellbrook Shire Council v Hunter Valley Energy Coal Pty Ltd* (2019) 238 LGERA 295, [2019] NSWCA 216; and focused on outcomes and the application of adverse costs orders.

[93] *Engadine Area Traffic Action Group Inc* (n 92) [15].

[94] *Engadine Area Traffic Action Group Inc* (n 92) [15]; *Darlinghurst Residents' Association v Elarossa Investments Pty Ltd (No 3)* (1992) 75 LGRA 214,215; *Liverpool City Council v Roads and Traffic Authority (No 2)* (1992) LGRA 210; and *Oshlack* (n 92) 80–81.

[95] *Sharma by her litigation representative Sister Marie Brigid Arthur v Minister for the Environment* (2021) 391 ALR 1; [2021] FCA 560 [97]–[103], [117] overturned on appeal, *Minister for the Environment v Sharma* [2022] FCAFC 35.

[96] *Gloucester Resources Limited v Minister for Planning* [2019] NSWLEC 7, (2019) 234 LGERA 257, [688].

considered public interest rights as rights of the public under the public trust doctrine, constitutional rights (particularly the right to life and the right to a quality environment), human rights and a multifactorial assessment including the assessment of the impacts of climate change.

In an ADR context, factors to be considered when managing issues relating to the public interest include the identification of stakeholders, facilitating a basic understanding of relevant information across the various stakeholder categories, encouraging dialogue through mediation skills as well as a public dialogue including, if applicable, communication with the media, engaging stakeholders via facilitative methods in the design of bespoke dispute resolution or conflict resolution processes, and implementing the process. Essential in any ADR process is the identification of cultural matters affecting engagement with the process including language, cultural and religious barriers and practical matters which can also be affected by cultural differences such as expectations as to the length of time or the evolution of outcomes from the process. In these circumstances what does the public interest look like and how is it to be engaged in the various forms of dispute resolution?

Many more questions arise. What are the long-term local community interests? Is it sufficient for local governments and stakeholders to resolve a dispute that may affect many outside of the local region without any oversight of the terms of the resolution or the effect of any agreement outside of the consulted stakeholders? Should consideration be made as to an oversight mechanism of agreements in environmental disputes by courts if the agreement is categorised to be within the concerns of the public interest? What parameters should be set for such an oversight? Is there a place for court intervention? For example, recognising the existence of licencing regimes, should parties and stakeholders resolving a dispute of this nature be required to seek approval of any negotiated agreement from a court with jurisdiction? Should there be certain parameters akin to court approvals in other matters such as in settlement agreements involving a person of legal incapacity? How would a legislative framework be created? Should these approvals only relate to matters to which a court referred a matter to ADR with relevant public interest criteria or generally? What are the interests to be taken into account? Should there be legislative intervention? Who decides?

If an agreement is reached involving public interest issues, how is it to be implemented? For example, if a dispute were to arise locally over the designation of land use to include a coal mine and local interests determine that it is productive for jobs and the local economy and the agreement falls within a licensing regime for land use but there are wider detrimental environmental implications and concerns – if there is no voice or objection would there be any oversight?[97] What oversight is required, if any? Should a court be required to approve agreements reached that involve public interest issues in environmental law? Could interveners engage a court if an oversight mechanism was developed? What are fundamental public interest rights in this context? How are rights-based claims adapted into ADR processes?[98] Are public interest environmental disputes

[97] Contrast ibid.

[98] Council of Europe, *Manual on Human Rights and the Environment*, 2nd edn (Strasbourg, COE Publishing, 2012); B Preston 'The Evolving Role of Environmental Rights in Climate Change Litigation' (2018) 2 *Chinese Journal of Environmental Law* 131, 133.

appropriate disputes for resolution in ADR procedures? If so, what elements are to be taken into account? Is transparency in the negotiations necessary? In relation to the public interest and agreements being reached outside of the court structure without legislative oversight, what protections should be considered? Is any of this necessary? All of these questions are an example of the need to take into account the complexity of environmental disputes in crafting appropriate ADR processes.

6. Conclusion

Courts are both resolvers of individual disputes and managers of a justice delivery system.[99] The civil justice system provides mechanisms for dispute resolution which contribute to the continuing development of a stable democratic society.[100] Many reviews of the justice system in Australia have elucidated common themes as desirable objectives for the civil justice system being accessible, just, fair, efficient and effective whilst upholding the rule of law.[101] In 2017, Chief Justice Bathurst AC described ADR's relationship with the justice system as not merely 'additional or supplementary but complementary and integrative'.[102]

The Court has adapted existing legal frameworks for environmental problems. Many environmental laws and interventions by local government authorities seek to regulate behaviour. Interventions and the need for the provision or exchange of information often occur early in the sequence of change, disruption or dispute resolution. This is a different trajectory to most legal disputes which focus on past events and sunk costs. The litigation path is narrow with identified events in case management. Polycentric disputes require a different mind-set for those interacting in dispute resolution management.

Conflict is inevitable. There is no single formula to resolve conflict.[103] The forms of appropriate dispute resolution which may assist with the environmental challenges of the twenty-first century are bespoke designs which incorporate elements of consensual models of dispute resolution. Early intervention pathways and a multi-door courthouse incorporating flexibility and a capacity to design bespoke dispute resolution processes provides opportunities to minimise the effects of conflict. The Court as a multi-door courthouse offering ADR for environmental and planning law disputes has demonstrated an ability to respond to the changing needs of society and is capable of continuing to develop mechanisms of dispute resolution to respond to the environmental challenges of the twenty-first century.

[99] Australian Federal Attorney-General, *Federal Civil Justice Paper*, (December 2003), 4.
[100] ibid, 4.
[101] ibid, 5; ALRC, *Review of the Adversarial System of Litigation* (Issue Paper 20, 1997) paras 3.9 and following; Lord Woolf, *Access to Justice: Final* Report (1996); K Mason 'The Rule of Law' in P Finn (ed), *Essays on Law and Government*, vol 1: *Principles and Values* (London, Thomson Reuters, 1995) 114.
[102] The Hon TF Bathurst AC, 'Off with the Wig: Issues that Arise for Advocates when Switching from the Courtroom to the Negotiating Table' (speech to the Australian Disputes Centre, 30 March 2017) 3.
[103] Tillett and French (n 2) 2.

15

The Land and Environment Court of New South Wales: Normative Legitimacy and Adjudicative Integrity

CERI WARNOCK*

1. Introduction

What makes an adjudicative body legitimate? In respect of the Land and Environment Court of New South Wales (the Court), this question has proven surprisingly difficult to answer. Within the Australian legal system, formal legitimacy can be bestowed upon institutions by legislation enacted by Parliament. The Court attracts this form of legal legitimacy: it is a creature of statute, having been created by and operating in accordance with the Land and Environment Court Act 1979 (NSW). But whether a community regards an institution as legitimate requires more than legislative formality. Institutions must be also be justified by considerations that lie beyond the rules establishing them – their form and functions must be well-grounded in normative beliefs shared by the relevant community.[1] Those shared beliefs might not have any formal or tangible existence but nevertheless constitute a type of intersubjective understanding.[2] This form of legitimacy is termed *normative legitimacy*.[3] In the context of a court, the institution will be regarded as normatively legitimate if it aligns with people's expectations as to what a court is, does and should be.

As part 2 of this chapter shows, the Land and Environment Court is a novel adjudicative institution and does not align with traditional understandings of courtness. It is a specialist court with tenured judges and expert lay commissioners acting as decision-makers; it has the power to review administrative decisions of elected

* This chapter draws upon C Warnock, *Environmental Courts and Tribunals: Powers, Integrity and the Search for Legitimacy* (Oxford, Hart Publishing, 2020).

[1] D Beetham, *The Legitimation of Power*, 2nd edn (Basingstoke, Palgrave Macmillan, 2013) 17, 35, 70, 74–75.

[2] JS Dryzek, 'Paradigms and Discourses' in D Bodansky, J Brunnée and E Hey (eds), *The Oxford Handbook of International Environmental Law* (Oxford, Oxford University Press, 2007).

[3] Beetham (n 1).

councillors and ministers on the merits, and so approve, amend or decline development permits; and it is not bound by the rules of evidence or traditional adjudicative procedures in hearing contested cases, so enabling it to resolve environmental disputes creatively.[4] As a result, the Court is lauded by some, and criticised by others who claim that the Court's powers are *illegitimate*.[5] Throughout its history, debates about the Court's normative legitimacy have played out in public inquiries, academic and extra-judicial writing, and case law, as I note in part 3 of this chapter.

In an attempt to facilitate productive debates about the worth and the work of the Court, this chapter suggests that we analyse the Court through a unifying model of normative legitimacy: 'the interactional theory'. I discuss the interactional theory in part 4 below (and have explored it in greater depth elsewhere)[6] but it is premised on the following contention: a shared belief of near-universal support is that *integrity* in adjudication is important and adjudicators will act with integrity if they *respond to* rather than *ignore* the legal and factual context in which they work.[7] Employing the interactional theory to analyse the Court helps shift attention from unproductive disputes about normative legitimacy to what matters, that is, the Court's actual work and worth in adjudicating environmental disputes.

The fourth part of this chapter begins the process of analysing the Court through the interactional theory, before looking in detail at one strand of the Court's jurisprudence in the final part to analyse whether the Court actually has used its flexible powers to respond to the context in which it works. I could select any number of jurisprudential strands to trace – charting the Court's approach to, for example, the collective action nature of environmental problems, indigenous issues, or how it has managed the interaction between the social–environmental–economic realms[8] – but this chapter traces the Court's procedural and doctrinal responses to epistemic uncertainty, a characteristic of many environmental disputes that creates a significant challenge for litigation. In focusing upon uncertainty, risk and precaution, I may be accused of cherry-picking. I do so deliberately, to give an example of where the Court *has* used its flexible functions, powers and procedures to develop substantive doctrine that makes sense of the factual and legal context in which it works. No doubt, scholars may point to other jurisprudential developments that run counter to the interactional theory, but this possibility is not a flaw invalidating its use. To the contrary, it demonstrates the analytical power of the interactional theory – shifting the focus onto the Court's integrity and allowing its work to be assessed and rigorously debated within a standard frame. Productive discussions about the Court will help finesse and future-proof environmental adjudication, and enable the Court to respond to future environmental challenges in a way that best serves its subject community.

[4] See section 2 below.
[5] See section 3 below.
[6] C Warnock, *Environmental Courts and Tribunals: Powers, Integrity and the Search for Legitimacy* (Oxford, Hart Publishing, 2020).
[7] ibid, ch 4.
[8] ibid, ch 6.

2. The Court's Legal Nature

While others in this edited collection have discussed certain functions and features of the Court, I want to provide a wide-ranging overview of its legal nature to highlight quite what an unusual adjudicative institution it is. Doing so begins to reveal why normative legitimacy has been so controversial. From the outset, it would appear that the government's intention in creating the Court was for a novel form of dispute resolution that would reap efficiencies from coordination and specialisation.[9] Upon introducing the legislation that created the Land and Environment Court, the Minister for Planning and Environment described the new court as an

> innovative experiment in dispute resolution mechanisms. It attempts to combine judicial and administrative dispute resolving techniques and it will utilize non-legal experts as technical and conciliation assessors.[10]

The Court was to be an important component in an 'emergent environmental justice system', supported by a whole raft of legislative changes geared towards the 'social and economic welfare of the community and a better environment',[11] and its unusual legal nature reflects this aim.

The Court is a superior court of record (with a status equivalent to the Supreme Court in the New South Wales court hierarchy) but also a specialist court with tenured judges and expert lay commissioners determining disputes.[12] The Court has a wide jurisdictional remit, leading the Chief Judge to describe it as a 'one stop shop'.[13] For example, the Court possesses the *inherent jurisdiction* of the Supreme Court to judicially review administrative decisions[14] (although it does not have a general common law jurisdiction and cannot award damages other than those provided by statute) and also has the *statutory* power to judicially review executive action and to determine appeals, including merits appeals, under a wide array of statutes.[15] These statutes address, for example: developmental planning decisions;[16] pollution matters;[17] threatened species protection;[18] minerals claims and the granting, refusal or cancellation

[9] NSW Parliamentary Debates (1979) No 46, 3349–50.

[10] NSW Parliamentary Debates, 21 November 1979, 3345, Second Reading Speech of the Hon Paul Landa MP, Minister for Planning and Environment quoted in Stewart Smith, *A Review of the Land and Environment Court: Briefing Paper No 13/01* (NSW Parliamentary Library Research Service, 2001) 1.

[11] P Ryan, 'Court of Hope and False Expectations: Land and Environment Court 21 Years On' (2002) 14 *Journal of Environmental Law* 301, 301.

[12] Land and Environment Court Act 1979 (NSW) Pt 2. Note that the original intention for mixed panels of judges and commissioners in every dispute did not eventuate due to resourcing issues (see Ryan (n 11) 304); however, commissioners may sit with and assist judges in an advisory capacity on cases concerning complex scientific and technical matters (Land and Environment Court Act 1979 (NSW), s 37 (1),); see eg *Providence Projects Pty Ltd v Gosford City Council* (2006) 147 LGERA 274, [13].

[13] BJ Preston, 'Benefits of Judicial Specialization in Environmental Law: The Land and Environment Court of New South Wales as a Case Study' (2011–12) 29 *Pace Environmental Law Review* 396, 604.

[14] *Longwon Pty Ltd v Warringah Shire Council* (1993) 33 NSWLR 13 (CA).

[15] Land and Environment Court Act 1979 (NSW) ss 20 (2), (3).

[16] Environmental Planning and Assessment Act 1979 (NSW).

[17] Protection of the Environment Operations Act 1997 (NSW) Pt 9.2.

[18] Biodiversity Conservation Act 2016 (NSW).

of petroleum titles;[19] Aboriginal land claims;[20] and compensation for compulsory acquisition.[21]

The form that the adjudication takes before the Court – either judicial review, legality appeal or merits review – depends on the issue at hand and the governing regulatory regime. However, approximately two-thirds of its work constitutes merits review appeals.[22] The Court undertakes merits review of certain classes of cases encompassing local and state development decisions; residential development; tree disputes; objections to the valuation of land; compulsory acquisition compensation claims; Aboriginal land claims; and miscellaneous appeals under a host of statutes such as the National Parks and Wildlife Act 1974 (NSW), the Biodiversity Conservation Act 2016 (NSW), the Water Management Act 2000 (NSW), and the Environmentally Hazardous Chemicals Act 1985 (NSW).[23] Initial administrative decisions may have been made by local authorities, government ministers or other members of the executive. In many of those Acts, decision-makers are required to apply the 'principles of ecologically sustainable development' (ESD).[24] For example, in development appeals the objectives of the governing legislation requires all decision-makers to facilitate ESD 'by integrating relevant economic, environmental and social considerations in decision-making'[25] and considering a list of statutory criteria that includes 'the public interest'.[26]

In its merits review role, the Court undertakes a re-hearing to decide 'the correct or preferable decision' on the material before it,[27] can admit new evidence, and has all the 'functions and discretions' of the original decision-maker.[28] Critically, proceedings are 'conducted with as little formality and technicality' as the Court permits.[29] The Court is 'not bound by the rules of evidence' and 'may inform itself on any matter in such manner as it thinks appropriate',[30] including drawing upon evidence from court-appointed experts.[31] Further, the Court has a wide remit to impose suitable remedies

[19] Mining Act 1992 s 293; Petroleum (Onshore) Act 1991 (NSW) s 112B.

[20] Aboriginal Land Rights Act 1983 (NSW).

[21] Land Acquisition (Just Terms Compensation) Act 1991 (NSW); Roads Act 1993 (NSW); Crown Lands Act 1989 (NSW).

[22] Z Lipman, 'The NSW Land and Environment Court: Reforms to the Merits Review Process' (2004) 21 *Environmental and Planning Law Journal* 415. The Land and Environment Court Annual Review 2019 records that Class 1 merit appeals constituted 68% of the Court's finalised caseload (32) and merits appeals and other civil proceedings finalised in Classes 1, 2 and 3 comprise 83% of the Court's finalised caseload in 2019 (30), available at www.lec.nsw.gov.au.

[23] Land and Environment Court Act 1979 (NSW) ss 17–19.

[24] eg Water Management Act 2000 (NSW) s 3; Biodiversity Conservation Act 2016 (NSW) s 1.3; Protection of the Environmental Operations Act 1997 (NSW) s 3; Pesticides Act 1999 (NSW) s 3; National Parks and Wildlife Act 1974 (NSW) s 2A, etc.

[25] Environmental Planning and Assessment Act 1979 (NSW) s 1.3 (b) (now s 1.1) (NB along with a host of other sustainability measures).

[26] ibid, s 4.15.

[27] *Drake v Minister for Immigration and Ethnic Affairs (No 1)* (1979) 24 ALR 577, 589.

[28] Land and Environment Court Act 1979 (NSW) s 39(2); see also *Ku-ring-gai Council v Bunnings Properties Pty Ltd* (2019) 236 LGERA 35, [150]–[151].

[29] Land and Environment Court Act 1979 (NSW) s 38(1).

[30] ibid, s 38(2).

[31] ibid, s 38(3). See eg *Telstra Corporation v Hornby Shire Council* (2006) 146 LGERA 10. See also BJ Preston, 'Practice and Procedure in the Land and Environment Court of New South Wales' (Planning, Development and Environmental Law Conference, Sydney, 8–9 February 2007).

in its merits review jurisdiction, and can affirm, amend or cancel the decision being appealed against;[32] adjourn and retain control of proceedings;[33] grant injunctions;[34] and employ alternative dispute resolution (ADR) processes.[35] Merits review in effect enables the Court to grant (or to refuse, or to amend) permits, which is more traditionally seen as a function of the executive branch. Although there is a prohibition in the Australian Constitution against a judicial body exercising administrative functions at federal level,[36] this clear separation is not required at state level[37] and there is no constitutional prohibition against the Court exercising both judicial and administrative functions.[38] Nevertheless, the Court's 'hybrid' nature has proven perennially controversial and there has not always been a unified view between politicians, lawyers and members of the public that use the Court, or even the judiciary, as to whether that is an appropriate role for the Court.[39]

3. Debates Surrounding the Court

In the introduction to this chapter I suggested that critics of the Court have questioned its *legitimacy*. Illegitimacy is an odd criticism for a body deliberately set up through parliamentary legislation but closer analysis shows that discord exists because commentators are drawing on different frames of *normative legitimacy* through which to analyse the Court.[40] At its simplest, normative legitimacy is based upon shared beliefs and common understandings about what is important.[41] We use frames of normative legitimacy to make sense of legal institutions – to help construct and limit their powers. Common frames of normative legitimacy used in debates about the Court are premised upon: a pure or functionalist separation of powers;[42] the necessity of adjudicative pluralism within administrative justice;[43] generic instrumentalism;[44] and a frame that regards the judiciary's primary role as protecting individuals' rights.[45] On their own, these frames

[32] eg Environmental Planning and Assessment Act 1979 (NSW) s 8.14.
[33] eg Civil Procedure Act 2005 (NSW) ss 66–67.
[34] eg Land and Environment Court Act 1979 (NSW) ss 20(2), 23.
[35] eg ibid, Civil Procedure Act 2005 (NSW) ss 34, 34AA, 26.
[36] Commonwealth of Australia Constitution Act 1900; *R v Kirkby; ex p Boilermakers' Society of Australia* (1965) 94 CLR 254 (HCA).
[37] New South Wales Constitution Act 1902; *Trust Company of Australia Ltd v (T/A Stockland Property Management) v Skiwing Pty Ltd (T/A Cafe Tiffany's)* (2006) 66 NSWLR 77.
[38] J Cripps et al, *Report of the Land and Environment Court Working Party* (Government of New South Wales, 2001) 45–46.
[39] Smith (n 10).
[40] Warnock (n 6) ch 3.
[41] DBeetham (n 1) 17, 35, 70, 74–75.
[42] See discussion below of *Ku-ring-gai Council* (n 28).
[43] Which reflects the messy realities of a complex state and acknowledges the role for multifunctional institutions. For general discussion, see HW Arthurs, *Without the Law: Administrative Justice and Legal Pluralism in Nineteenth-Century England* (Toronto, University of Toronto Press, 1985).
[44] Which sees law simply as a mechanism for implanting political direction: see eg discussion in B Tamanaha, *On the Rule of Law: History, Politics, Theory* (Cambridge, Cambridge University Press, 2004) 79.
[45] See section 3 below.

are all contestable, incomplete or fail in their purpose of illuminating the Court specifically or specialist environmental adjudication more generally.[46] Critically, employing different frames of normative legitimacy can lead to 'a cacophony as people talk across each other, following different and often mutually unintelligible trajectories'.[47]

I accept this discussion appears rather abstract but considering the way that the Court has been conceived – by the judiciary, politicians, policy-makers, lawyers and the public – helps illustrate the point about normative legitimacy. In terms of the judiciary, some judges welcomed the ministerial view of the Court as an important component in a new environmental justice system and, as Justice Pain reports, readily embraced legal innovation.[48] Preston CJ has written of the *leadership* of the Court in filling in legislative interstices and fleshing out the principles of ecological sustainable development.[49] Twenty years after the creation of the Court, Justice Stein opined that:

> [T]here is the opportunity, if not the obligation, in the absence of clear legislative guidance, to apply the common law and assist in the development and fleshing out of the principles. Our task is to turn soft law into hard law. This is an opportunity to be bold spirits rather than timorous souls and provide a lead for the common law world. It will make a contribution to the ongoing development of environmental law.[50]

In contrast, only a few years later, Pearlman CJ expressed her view that:

> The most obvious function of the Court is … to apply the law, and so in applying the law there is often little scope to achieve the advancements in environmental law that some people may wish to see … the successful application of ESD requires the principles themselves to be made more workable and tangible. It is for the legislature to provide more guidance to the Court as to how it wishes this objective to be achieved, and particularly how it relates to other provisions. The Court has a limited role in that it must act according to law. It cannot be expected to fill gaps in policy, or to stretch the law where it does not go.[51]

Other judges of the Court have also played down its legal innovations and its novel legal nature[52] and the debate continues to this day. In *Ku-ring-gai Council v Bunnings Properties Pty Ltd*,[53] the Council's legal submissions and the minority judgment draw

[46] C Warnock, 'Reconceptualising Specialist Environment Courts and Tribunals' (2017) 37 *Legal Studies* 391.

[47] J Waldron, 'Thoughtfulness and the Rule of Law' (2011) 18 *British Academy Review* 1, 8 citing J Rawls, *Political Liberalism* (New York, Columbia University Press, 1996).

[48] N Pain and S Wright, 'The Rise of Environmental Law in New South Wales and Federally: Perspectives from the Past and Issues for the Future' (National Environmental Law Association Annual Conference, Broken Hill NSW, 24 October 2003).

[49] B Preston, 'Leadership by the Courts in Achieving Sustainability' (2010) 6 *Resource Management Theory and Practice* 17.

[50] P Stein, 'New Directions in the Prevention and Resolution of Environmental Disputes – Specialist Environmental Courts' (South-East Asian Regional Symposium on the Judiciary and the Law of Sustainable Development, Manila, 6 March 1999) [30]. See also *F Hannan Pty Ltd v Electricity Commission of New South Wales [No 3]* (1985) 66 LGRA 306 (NSWCA), 310 per Street CJ.

[51] M Pearlman, 'Managing Environmental Impacts – The Role of the Land and Environment Court of New South Wales' (New Zealand Planning Congress, Wellington, New Zealand, 9 April 2002) 3.

[52] T Sheahan, 'Environmental Law – Present and Future – Lessons Learned and Visions for the Future – the Experience of the Land and Environment Court of New South Wales, Australia' (International Seminar on Environmental Law, Superior Court of Justice Auditorium, Brasilia, 9–11 May 2001).

[53] *Ku-ring-gai Council* (n 28).

on particular models of adjudicatory legitimacy to anchor legal reasoning, conceiving of the Court in its merits review role as a 'judicial' body (with all the formalism associated with that concept) as opposed to one exercising administrative powers.[54] The majority focused squarely on the empowering legislation, without gilding the interpretative exercise with normative conceptions of courtness. *Ku-ring-gai* demonstrates that judges sitting within the same court, hearing the same case, have different views about what that court is and what it should be.

Within the wider community, various criticisms have been levelled against the Court, including that it was constitutionally illegitimate because it did not align with a pure separation-of-powers frame; did not have the institutional competence for the 'policy-making' role it allegedly played; and/or processes should be faster and cheaper.[55] Some believed that the Court should not have merits review jurisdiction at all[56] and should be restricted to procedural judicial review.[57] From time to time, politicians called for the abolition of the Court, arguing its jurisdiction should be incorporated within the 'ordinary' Supreme Court.[58] In 2001, a Working Party chaired by Justice Cripps, a retired Chief Judge of the Court, was established by the NSW Government to review the Court.[59] The Review invited public submissions. Those critical of the Court were concerned that it: should not make or consider matters of policy[60] or determine any 'value judgements';[61] was systematically biased towards developers;[62] had made socially and aesthetically controversial decisions;[63] and was out of touch with local concerns.[64] The President of the Local Government Association was reported as saying: 'It's appalling that you have one character sitting up there thinking they know the area better than nine or 12 elected representatives of the people.'[65] Strong themes emerged in the submissions with opponents drawing on ideas concerning the separation of powers, adjudicatory formalism, parliamentary supremacy and representative democracy. Critics tended to focus on the inappropriateness of judicial method in this context and ignored the specialised, expert nature of the Court.

[54] ibid, [62], [65]. Basten JA in the minority refers to the Court as a 'judicial' body throughout and appears to use a particular conception of 'judicial' to bolster his reasoning; see E Fisher, 'Administrative Tribunals: An Essay about the Legal Imagination of Administrative Law Scholars' in J Goudkamp, L McDonald and M Lunney, (eds) *Taking Law Seriously: Essays in Honour of Peter Cane* (Oxford, Hart Publishing, 2022).

[55] P Lalich and S Neilson, 'Review of the Land & Environment Courts Jurisdiction' (2001) 7 *Local Government Law Journal* 49, 52–56.

[56] eg Local Government Association, quoted in Smith (n 10) 7.

[57] See eg John Cooke, 'Design Merit Appeals and the Test of Reasonableness' (1996) 13 *Environmental and Planning Law Journal* 431 (design quality should be subject to judicial review only given subjective nature of assessment).

[58] P Stein, 'Specialist Environment Courts: The Land and Environment Court of New South Wales Australia' (2002) 4 *Environmental Law Review* 5, 7.

[59] Cripps et al (n 38).

[60] Sydney City Council submission cited in Lalich and Neilson (n 55) 52.

[61] Smith (n 10) 16.

[62] 'Decisions, Decisions: A Score Card on the Decision Makers of the Land and Environment' LEC Review Issue 3 (City of Sydney 2001), quoted in Smith (n 10) 11.

[63] Sydney City Council, *Unwanted Legacies* (2001).

[64] Smith (n 10) 7.

[65] 'Call to Overhaul the Land and Environment Court' *Australian Financial Review* (8 July 1999), quoted in Smith (n 10) 7.

In contrast, supporters of the Court pointed to the enhancement of primary administration afforded by merits review[66] and suggested that it was perverse to assume that the application of natural justice, testing evidence in an adversarial manner and the duty to give reasons led to a less just outcome.[67] Some argued that local authorities operated in a politicised climate where election cycles led to short-term thinking that could prove problematic when the law required decisions to balance economic benefits against, for example, the long-term advantages of preserving biodiversity; in contrast, independent courts were suitably impartial.[68] Supporters saw the advantages of a flexible, creative, problem-solving body but also stressed the importance of independent court-based resolution to protect legal rights and apolitical decision-making about the environment.[69] Supporters tended to focus on the specialist, expert nature of the Court. Many contributors to the debate thought *less* legal formality and a greater use of the inquisitorial process with increased ADR was important for accurately ascertaining the public interest and solving problems creatively.[70]

Fundamentally, however, all groups of submitters to the Review – those opposed to the Court, those supportive, and all in between – were concerned with the legitimacy of adjudicative institutions and, perhaps ultimately, the idea of institutional trust. Trust in institutions can be bolstered by the use of normative frames, particularly those deeply embedded within a community. But without conceptual buttressing, trust can be eroded. At its conclusion, the Cripps Review recommended few substantive changes and the retention of full merits review.[71] Nevertheless, the Review did capture the deep tension between diverse points of view and the use of different conceptual frames to justify the legitimacy or illegitimacy of the Court's novel legal nature – a debate that continues to this day and that can prove unproductive by shifting the focus away from the Court's actual work.

4. Evaluating the Court Through a Unifying Frame

If discussants about the Court are able to draw upon a unifying frame of normative legitimacy, their focus will be directed to whether the Court is effectively promoting the environmental, sociocultural and economic well-being of the communities it serves, rather than continually returning to a conceptual first-base. As explained above, the 'interactional theory' provides a neutral frame for evaluation. It is premised on a shared belief that has near-universal support – that is, that *integrity* in adjudication matters.[72] In this context, integrity means *coherence* between acts, reasoning and essential foundations (such as core principles, values or the immutable nature of context) – that is, it is

[66] Cripps et al (n 38), 90.
[67] Lalich and Neilson (n 55) 51.
[68] ibid.
[69] ibid.
[70] Cripps et al (n 38) 90, 91, 93; Lalich and Neilson (n 55) 58.
[71] Cripps et al (n 38) vi–xiii, ch 6.
[72] Warnock (n 6) ch 4.

the link or the response between the component parts that matters.[73] Environmental courts will have integrity if they have the ability to and *in fact actually do* respond to the legal and factual context in which they work. To respond appropriately in the context of environmental adjudication requires four factors to be considered as integral parts of the whole.

The first factor concerns identifying the immutable, structural characteristics of environmental problems – such as environmental dynamism (ie conditions are constantly changing), inherent interaction (between the ecological, sociocultural and economic spheres), epistemic uncertainty, the collective-action nature of environmental problems, and the prevalence of ethical pluralism, etc. Identifying the structural realities of environmental problems provides the essential foundation, anchoring acts and reasoning. The second factor is acknowledging the impact those characteristics have on primary law and the challenges they create for resolving factual disputes in adjudication.[74] For example, these structural features affect the form and content of environmental statute law and often make comprehensive ex ante rules-based legislation challenging. In response, the government tends to set general goals, principles and standards in legislation, and then relies upon more dynamic instruments (such as plans, policies and guidelines) and disaggregated decision-making institutions to direct action and manage disputes.[75] The third factor is accepting the need for adjudicative bodies to develop procedure, doctrine and remedies that respond to those legal and factual challenges. And the fourth factor is understanding that particular adjudicative forms and functions facilitate this process – that is, courts with flexible powers and specialist expertise will be better able to respond to the nature of environmental problems. Acknowledging and addressing these four component parts enables pragmatic yet principled responses to the challenges of adjudicating over the environment, in turn shoring up adjudicative integrity.

We can employ the interactional theory to analyse the Court and its jurisprudence by considering each of the four component parts in turn. Section 1 of this chapter demonstrated that the Court *has* the specialist constitution and flexible powers, functions and features enabling it to respond to the challenges of adjudicating over environmental disputes, that is, it meets the fourth component of the interactional theory. In relation to the first three components – 'problem–challenge–response' – jurisprudence in the Court identifies the immutable structural characteristics of environmental problems, acknowledges the adjudicative challenges that flow from it and has at times created processes and doctrine to respond to these challenges. For example, case law in the Court explicitly references the dynamic complexity of ecosystems, including natural variability and inherent randomness (which means facts are seldom fixed in environmental disputes),[76] and also notes that environmental problems are found at the

[73] ibid, ch 4.

[74] Elizabeth Fisher, 'Environmental Law as "Hot" Law' (2013) 25 *Journal of Environmental Law* 347.

[75] eg Environmental Planning and Assessment Act 1979 (NSW). See also E Fisher, 'Towards Environmental Constitutionalism: A Different Vision of the Resource Management Act 1991?' (2015) 11 *Resource Management Theory and Practice* 63.

[76] eg *Bentley v BGP Properties Pty Ltd* (2006) 145 LGERA 234, [60]–[63].

intersection of the environmental, sociocultural and economic spheres, meaning that environmental problems present as polycentric problems.[77]

In its merits review jurisdiction, the Court is tasked with predicting effects on the environment and it has acknowledged that eco-systemic dynamism and interaction magnify the importance and challenges of assessing effects, including cumulative effects;[78] local, regional and/or global effects;[79] short- and long-term effects;[80] and the fact that indirect effects can be as damaging as direct impacts.[81]

In *Plumb v Penrith City Council*, the Court observed that determining future effects on the environment 'can never truly be an objective fact – it must always be a matter of opinion'.[82] Accordingly, the Court relies heavily upon scientific opinion evidence, which can be complex and contested due to prevalent epistemic uncertainty (ie lack of knowledge about the state of a system) and linguistic uncertainty (ie arising through the need to translate scientific vocabulary into legally meaningful concepts).[83] As the Court said in *Newcastle & Hunter Speleological Society Inc v Upper Hunter Shire Council*: 'Both forms of uncertainty are inherent in discussion of many environmental issues.'[84]

The Court has also noted the need for interdisciplinarity in environmental problem-solving,[85] while accepting that assessing the probative value of scientific expert evidence can prove challenging due to blurred lines of expertise in environmental science.[86] Contested expert evidence will often require the Court to consider the methodologies behind the opinion, necessitating a particular understanding and expertise on the part of decision-makers.[87] To address the need for expert evidence, the Court has at times instructed court-appointed witnesses[88] and admitted different *forms* of expert opinion evidence. For example, in *Newcastle & Hunter Speleological Society Inc*, '[t]he Court drew the parties' attention to some recent literature on stygofauna and requested that, if considered appropriate, they make submissions' on it.[89]

[77] *Bulga Milbrodale Progress Association Inc v Minister for Planning and Infrastructure and Warkworth Mining Limited* (2013) 194 LGERA 347, [31].

[78] eg *Friends of Tumblebee Inc v ATB Morton Pty Ltd (No 2)* (2016) 215 LGERA 157, [113], [83], [227]: 'The cumulative impact of the development is a relevant matter to consider … as a separate factor given the broad discretion given to a decision-maker under s 78A (8) (b) of the [Environmental Planning and Assessment Act]', [214]. See also *Bulga Milbrodale Progress Association Inc* (n 77); *Newcastle & Hunter Speleological Society Inc v Upper Hunter Shire Council* (2013) 210 LGERA 126, [104]; *BT Goldsmith Planning Services v Blacktown City Council* [2005] NSWLEC 210, [89]–[90]; N Pain, 'Air Pollution – Challenges for Courts' (World Conference on Environment, New Delhi, 25–25 March 2017) 11.

[79] *Telstra* (n 31) [131].

[80] *Friends of Tumblebee Inc* (n 78) [169]–[170], [198].

[81] *Gloucester Resources Ltd v Minister for Planning* (2019) 234 LGERA 257, [494]–[524].

[82] *Plumb v Penrith City Council* [2002] NSWLEC 223, per Pearlman CJ at [16].

[83] eg Brian J Preston, 'Biodiversity Offsets: Adequacy and Efficiency in Theory and Practice' (2016) 33 *Environmental and Planning Law Journal* 93 (a paper presented at the IUCN Academy of Environmental Law 13th Annual Colloquium, Jakarta, 7–12 September 2015) 27.

[84] *Newcastle & Hunter Speleological Society Inc* (n 78) [167].

[85] *Telstra* (n 31) [132].

[86] R Pepper, 'Making Sure That Curiosity Does Not Kill The CAT: The Use of Expert Evidence in Merits Review Fora Where the Rules of Evidence Do Not Apply' (COAT NSW Conference, Sydney, 6 September 2019) [69]: between ecology and planning for example.

[87] See, for example, the Court's analysis of the economic cost and benefits in *Gloucester* (n 81) [557]–[685].

[88] *Telstra* (n 31).

[89] *Newcastle & Hunter Speleological Society Inc* (n 78) [154]. That literature assisted the Court in finding that biota in the limestone caves was a 'possibility', so engaging the precautionary principle, [153]–[177].

To assist in the *evaluation* of contested evidence, the Court has developed novel procedures, such as witness conferences[90] and the giving of evidence concurrently – so called 'hot-tubbing'.[91] Other cases decided by the Court discuss the impact of polycentricism[92] and the requirement to account for ethics, equity and distributive justice when considering the public interest in environmental disputes,[93] leading to a 'management style' of decision-making.[94] But it is the Court's need to assess and manage risk in all its permutations that best illustrates its responsive nature, and where the links between the four component parts of the interactional theory are seen most clearly, as the following part of this chapter demonstrates. In the context of uncertainty, the Court's ability to create procedures that respond to the nature of the problem – admitting different forms of probative evidence, adjusting standards and evidential requirements, and creating novel remedies – has coalesced into substantive doctrine in the form of the precautionary principle.

5. Responsive Process and Doctrine: From *Leatch* to *Telstra* and Case Law in between

Leatch v National Parks and Wildlife Service[95] is a good example of how the institutional features of the Court enabled legal reasoning to respond to the features of environmental problem-solving. *Leatch* concerned an appeal against the decision of the Director General to grant a licence under the National Parks and Wildlife Act 1974 (NPWA) permitting endangered fauna – the yellow-bellied glider and giant burrowing frog – to be taken or killed for the purposes of building a road. Reports before the Director General stated that there was a likelihood of the fauna being killed by the development 'even though precise estimates cannot be given as to current population distribution and abundances'.[96] The appeal to the Court took the form of a merits review, for which the Court received expert evidence and had all the statutory functions and discretions of the Director General to determine the matter.[97] Opponents to the proposal submitted that the Court should apply the precautionary principle in the case and refuse the licence.

The Court allowed the appeal and drew on precautionary reasoning to do so. Stein J accepted that there was no express reference to the precautionary principle (or even to ESD, which was later found to encompass the precautionary principle)[98] in the legislation.[99] However, the Court noted that it must have regard to the Land and Environment Court Act, any other relevant Act or instrument, 'the circumstances of

[90] eg *Brunsdon v The Council of the City of Wagga Wagga* [2003] NSWLEC 168, [47], [75].
[91] R Pepper, '"Hot-Tubbing": The Use of Concurrent Expert Evidence in the Land and Environment Court of New South Wales and Beyond' (Alaska Bar Convention, Fairbanks, Alaska, 14 May 2015).
[92] *Bulga Milbrodale Progress Association Inc* (n 77) [31]–[42].
[93] ibid, [485]–[495]; *Telstra* (n 31) [116]–[117], [123]–[124].
[94] *Bulga Milbrodale Progress Association Inc* (n 77) [31]–[42].
[95] *Leatch v National Parks and Wildlife Service* (1993) 81 LGERA 270 (NSWLEC).
[96] ibid, 277.
[97] Land and Environment Court Act 1979 (NSW), s 39(2).
[98] *Telstra* (n 31) [124]–[127].
[99] *Leatch* (n 95) 281, 282.

the case and the public interest',[100] and the list of criteria in the NPWA including 'any other matter which the Court considers relevant'.[101] The question (one of statutory interpretation) became: 'what was a relevant matter?' While the Court noted the range of international treaties that incorporated the precautionary principle, the legal reasoning in the case does not rely on the incorporation of international law into domestic law with Stein J stating, 'it seems to me unnecessary to enter this debate. In my opinion the precautionary principle is a statement of common sense'[102] and

> consideration of the state of knowledge or uncertainty regarding a species, the potential for serious or irreversible harm to an endangered fauna is clearly consistent with the subject matter, scope and purpose of the Act. … Upon an examination of the available material relevant to the Giant Burrowing Frog (*Heleioporus australiacus*) and the knowledge of the frog in this particular habitat, one is driven to the conclusion that there is a dearth of knowledge.[103]

Stein J's approach *is* 'common sense'[104] as he describes it *but only* in the context of understanding the nature of environmental problems. The legal reasoning in this case (ie to adopt a precautionary approach) is undoubtedly driven by environmental understanding, facilitated by the receipt of expert opinion evidence and the Court's own specialist understanding (ie what the risks of the uncertainty were; the relevance of sustainable population size; the implications of potential geographical reach or habitat restrictions; and why species extinction is problematic). Thus, the Court bolstered the 'scope and purpose of the Act' by taking the features of environmental problems into account. This is subtle, but important because the inherent nature of environmental problems impacted statutory interpretation.[105]

Critically, the particular constitution, powers and functions of the Court enable that environmental understanding, and you see clear evidence of that understanding throughout the case.[106] For example, his Honour suggested that the statutory requirements for Fauna Impact Statements were lacking: they should require information on how the proposed development would impact the wider species population and its chances for survival,[107] and additional evidence was received by the Court on this point.

[100] Land and Environment Court Act 1979 (NSW) s 39(4).

[101] At the time, s 92A(6)(e),National Parks and Wildlife Act 1974 (NSW).

[102] *Leatch* (n 95) 282. Note, however, Stein J later rationalised the decision as one that accords with interpreting statutes in conformity with customary international law (see L Stein, 'A Cautious Application of the Precautionary Principle' (2000) 2 *Environmental Law Review* 1, 3). See also BJ Preston 'Jurisprudence on Ecologically Sustainable Development: Paul Stein's Contribution' (2012) 29 *Environmental and Planning Law Journal* 3.

[103] *Leatch* (n 95) 282.

[104] Reflecting a long-standing acknowledgement that 'a certain amount of common sense must be applied in construing statutes', see *Barnes v Jarvis* [1953] 1 All ER 1061 (HL), 1063. Cf *Friends of Hinchinbrook Soc Inc v Minister for Environment* (1997) 142 ALR 632 (FCA).

[105] In a different jurisdictional context, see *Conservation Council of South Australia v Development Assessment Committee and Tuna Boat Owners Association (No 2)* [1999] SAERDC 86, [22], where the Court relies on scholarly articles that explain the ecological value of precaution, 'the environment could not assimilate all the consequences of activities impacting upon it. Implicit in this recognition is an acknowledgment that science and the scientific method have limitations'.

[106] *Leatch* (n 95) 275: '[I]t is somewhat strange that under State law rare and endangered plants are not accorded similar protection to rare and endangered fauna, especially since flora are important for biological diversity and advances in medical science sometimes involve the application of rare plants.'

[107] ibid, 283–84.

Accordingly, the fact that the Court is a trial court – with a specialist bench determining facts, and with wide powers enabling the receipt of additional evidence – is not insignificant, rather this feature directly impacts legal doctrine and adjudicative integrity.[108] We can clearly see the four components of the interactional theory at work in *Leatch*: the features of environmental problems (here, scientific uncertainty created by the complexity of ecosystems) and the recognition of the challenges they create for adjudication, led to the embryonic development of new doctrine (the precautionary principle), a process that was facilitated by the merging of legal and non-legal expertise.

Following *Leatch*, many other decisions of the Court referred to and employed precautionary thinking in order to respond to uncertainty before the precautionary principle was included in legislation.[109] In these early cases, there was undoubtedly an inconsistent approach to the issue of precaution. However, the important point is that adjudicating in situations of factual uncertainty led to the Court striving to respond, and that development was not catalysed by any express legislative requirement. It came rather from the need to react in a principled but pragmatic way to the adjudicative challenges created by environmental problems.

From the mid-1990s amendments were made to various NSW statutes in order to incorporate reference to ESD[110] (which the Court found encompassed the precautionary principle)[111] and at times, direct reference to the principle itself often in the form of statutory objectives.[112] Nevertheless, very little guidance was given as to how the principle should be *operationalised* within adjudication, leaving the Court to develop legal tests and procedures iteratively.[113] The case of *Telstra Corporation v Hornby Shire Council*[114] is perhaps regarded as the apex of that development.

[108] See also E Fisher, 'Is the Precautionary Principle Justiciable?' (2001) 13 *Journal of Environmental Law* 315, 327; A Edgar, 'Institutions and Sustainability: Merits Review Tribunal and the Precautionary Principle' (2013) 16 *Australasia Journal of Natural Resources Law and Policy* 61, 64, suggesting that 'merits review has institutional characteristics that make it highly suited to operationalising precautionary decision-making'.

[109] eg *Nicholls v Director-General of National Parks and Wildlife Service* (1994) 84 LGERA 397 (NSWLEC); *Simpson v Ballina Shire Council* (1994) 82 LGERA 392; *Greenpeace Australia Ltd v Redbank Power Co Ltd* (1994) 86 LGERA 143 (NSWLEC); *Alumino (Aust) Pty Ltd v Minister Administering the Environmental Planning and Assessment Act 1979* [1995] NSWLEC 177; *K A Cox v Concord Council* [1995] NSWLEC 24; *Northcompass Inc v Hornby Shire Council* (1996) 130 LGERA 248.

[110] eg The Environmental Planning and Assessment Act 1979 (NSW) was amended in 1998 to incorporate the objective of ecological sustainable development in s 5(a)(vii) (now see s 1.3).

[111] eg *Hub Action Group Inc v Minister for Planning* (2008) 161 LGERA 136 [1]; *Carstens v Pittwater Council* (1999) 111 LGERA 1 (NSWLEC); *BGP Properties Pty Limited v Lake Macquarie City Council* (2004) 138 LGERA 237; *Minister for Planning v Walker* (2008) 161 LGERA 423; *Telstra* (n 31); *Friends of Tumblebee* (n 78); and see E Scotford, *Environmental Principles and the Evolution of Environmental Law* (Oxford, Hart Publishing, 2017) for a comprehensive treatment of the issue.

[112] eg Protection of the Environment Administration Act 1991 (NSW) s 6(2).

[113] Stein (n 102) 2; BJ Preston, 'The Role of the Judiciary in Promoting Sustainable Development: The Experience of Asia and the Pacific' (2005–06) 9 *Asia Pacific Journal of Environmental Law* 109; Preston (n 49). For other cases decided prior to *Telstra* and post legislative incorporation, see eg *Providence Projects Pty Ltd* (n 12); *Port Stephens Pearls Pty Limited v Minister for Infrastructure and Planning* [2005] NSWLEC 426; *Murrumbidgee Ground-Water Preservation Association v Minister for Natural Resources* [2004] NSWLEC 122; *Gales Holdings Pty Ltd v Tweed Shire Council* (2006) 146 LGERA 236; *BT Goldsmith Planning Services* (n 78); *BGP Properties Pty Limited* (n 111); *Anderson & Anor v Director-General of the Department of Environment & Conservation & Anor* (2006) 144 LGERA 43 (NSWLEC).

[114] *Telstra* (n 31) approved in *Minister for Planning v Walker* (n 111).

In *Telstra*, which was a merits appeal, the Court referred to evaluating uncertainty as involving 'an assessment of risk in its usual formulation'.[115] Summarising other cases and a wide array of academic scholarship (forms of knowledge that demonstrates the wide problem-solving methods available to the Court),[116] *Telstra* set down procedures to operationalise the principle, which it found would apply where there were threats of serious or irreversible damage and there was a lack of full scientific certainty as to the nature and scope of that threat. The Court addressed: the threshold conditions for the application of the precautionary principle; probative forms of evidence and standards of evidentiary proof; shifting the burden of proof; alternate remedies (including adaptive management); and determining the proportionality of response. In *Telstra*, the Court heard and had to make findings in relation to complex evidence from physics, engineering and epidemiology, and the legally trained judge sat with an expert commissioner. The decision clearly shows the interactional links between the 'problem–challenge–response-institutional form'. However, *Telstra* was an unusual case because it paralleled the interactional theory almost in the abstract: the Court set down a comprehensive guide to the operationalisation of the precautionary principle without necessarily needing to do so in the particular circumstances of the case.[117] To that end, it reveals the Court's view of itself as a problem-solving court, with a role to play in environmental governance and having a wider societal influence.

Tracing other cases makes it possible to see how the Court's flexible processes enabled substantive doctrine to develop iteratively, leading to the fully formed precautionary principle in *Telstra* and its application in later cases. For example, the Court has had to address the required quality and form of scientific information upon which to base a finding of risk or to activate the precautionary principle, and again its particular institutional form and powers to receive 'any evidence' has facilitated a responsive approach. While phantom risks or mere conjecture would not be factored into decision-making,[118] given the inherent features of environmental problems, a credible scientific hypothesis may suffice to establish a real risk of harm. *Newcastle & Hunter Speleological Society Inc v Upper Hunter Shire Council*[119] provides a good example. In that case, the Court was concerned with a merits appeal against the grant of development consent for a limestone quarry. Objections were based on impacts to the land-based endangered ecological community and also karst formations and fauna in the underground caves. Although there was no site-specific evidence of cave-dwelling fauna, there was evidence of biota in caves nearby and the Court accepted generalist studies that established the presence of biota in limestone which 'make it scientifically likely that some form of biota will be found within the limestone on the site'.[120]

[115] ibid, [161].
[116] ibid, [130]–[139].
[117] *Telstra* (n 31) is discussed further in a number of chapters in this book. See also Edgar (n 108) 72–73.
[118] *Bulga Milbrodale Progress Association Inc* (n 77) [63]; *Telstra* (n 31), [193]–[196]. For a critique of this approach, see J Peel, 'When (Scientific) Rationality Rules: (Mis)Application of the Precautionary Principle in Australian Mobile Phone Tower Cases' (2007) 19 *Journal of Environmental Law* 103, noting this approach does not factor in genuine scientific ignorance and can be criticised accordingly. See in response BJ Preston, 'The Judicial Development of the Precautionary Principle' (2018) 35 *Environmental and Planning Law Journal* 123.
[119] *Newcastle & Hunter Speleological Society Inc* (n 78).
[120] ibid, [177].

Accordingly, the Court found that '[w]ithout being able to predict the particular species which would be present, *it is beyond a mere possibility that biota will be present*'.[121] This possibility was sufficient to engage the application of the precautionary principle and, given the circumstances of the case, an adaptive management regime was imposed on the consent.[122] In determining the severity of possible harm, the Court in *Newcastle* and indeed other cases found that ecological context is critical, and a quantitative and qualitative assessment of the impacted environment is required.[123]

The Land and Environment Court, and indeed other Australian courts, have found that the traditional civil law standard of proof does not apply to assessing future effects on the environment, and the statutory test of likelihood (eg 'likely to be a significant effect on threatened species') means 'a real or not remote chance or possibility regardless of whether it is less or more than a fifty per cent chance'.[124] For example, in *Friends of Tumblebee Inc v ATB Morton Pty Ltd*, the Court rejected the evidence of an expert witness that a proposed development was unlikely to impact the regent honeyeater, a threatened species, because they had misunderstood the test of likelihood (amongst other reasons). Pepper J found that: 'In cross-examination [the expert] stated initially that he believed that "likely" (wrongly) meant "more chance than not" … [and] stated, also incorrectly, that the words "more likely than not" were equivalent to a "more than 50% probability"'.[125]

Contextual uncertainty in environmental disputes has also led the Court to reconsider the traditional approach taken with regards to the *burden* of evidentiary proof. Once adequate evidence of a risk of harm has been adduced so that the precautionary principle is activated, the Court has found that the evidential burden shifts to the applicant to disprove the risk or to show that any harm can be adequately mitigated.[126] In *Providence Projects Pty Ltd v Gosford City Council*[127] – a case in which there was scientific uncertainty as to whether a threatened ecological community, the Umina Coastal Sandplain Woodland, was widely distributed over the development site or present in limited areas only – the Court employed the precautionary principle to shift the burden of proof onto the applicant. Bignold J held that the precautionary principle justified a margin of error approach 'which avoids the risk of serious or irreversible environmental damage by assuming the existence of the wide distribution of [Umina Coastal Sandplain Woodland] over the development site'.[128] It was for the applicant to tender expert evidence disproving this assumption.

[121] ibid, [177] (emphasis added).

[122] ibid, [178]–[189].

[123] eg *Friends of Tumblebee Inc* (n 78) [165], [208]; *Newcastle & Hunter Speleological Society Inc* (n 78) [104].

[124] Both in the Land and Environment Court, the higher NSW courts and other jurisdictions, eg *Lend Lease Developments Pty Ltd v Manly Council* [1998] NSWLEC 136, [24] quoting *Matthews v Goulburn Wool Processing Pty Ltd* Smart J, 6 November 1986 (unreported) (NSWSC), 15 that interpreted the meaning of 'likely' in s 16(2)(a) of the Clean Waters Act 1970 (NSW), and applied that interpretation to 'likely' in the context of the Environmental Planning and Assessment Act 1979 (NSW) (EPA Act).

[125] *Friends of Tumblebee Inc* (n 78) [105].

[126] *Telstra* (n 31) [150].

[127] *Providence Projects Pty Ltd* (n 12).

[128] ibid, [77]; see also *SHCAG Pty Ltd v Minister for Planning and Infrastructure and Boral Cement Ltd* [2013] NSWLEC 1032, [90]: 'The burden of proof that the proposal is not harmful falls on the proponent [Colliery].'

Precautionary thinking also influenced the evidential burden and standard of proof in *Simpson v Ballina Shire Council*.[129] The Court rejected an error of law appeal after the initial Assessor refused to permit a development on a deep slope that released effluent to the soil in a sensitive area.[130] The developer said the design enabled the effluent to percolate safely down through the ground, and although there was no scientific risk assessment contesting the developer's evidence (or actually supporting it), the Assessor found that

> the percolation argument for the disposal of effluent seems to involve an 'out of sight out of mind' attitude. In dealing with such a sensitive eco-system, this is not only anthropocentric but unrealistic.[131]

Once the Court has found that there is a risk of environmental harm, or the precautionary principle is activated, it must decide what to do. Contextual uncertainty has impacted the Court's approach to remedies. Some environmental risks are deemed wholly unacceptable and the Court takes a risk-averse approach to them. For example, even a small risk of annihilation of an endangered species or culturally important heritage site may result in a development being refused in its entirety.[132] However, a number of the legislative regimes under which the Court operates are neither 'zero-risk' regimes[133] nor premised solely upon environmental conservation, and the Court is frequently required to weigh development and conservation considerations.

To minimise adverse environmental effects where development was consented to, early cases in the Court tended to impose monitoring and reporting conditions on permits, which increased the possibility for enforcement actions if harm occurred.[134] For example, in *Nicholls v Director General of National Parks and Wildlife Service*, the general need to be 'cautious' in the face of uncertainty led to the Court imposing copious conditions on the order 'to take account of the need for ongoing survey, research and assessment':[135] a response enabled by the Court's wide power to impose remedies. In later cases, the Court adjourned proceedings, requiring additional assessments such as biodiversity assessments to be undertaken to inform decisions,[136] or provided for short 'trial periods' of the activity.[137] With the feed-in of evidence from environmental

[129] *Simpson* (n 109).
[130] ibid. Specifically, Pearlman CJ found that the appellants were really arguing about an error of fact. The Assessor had to consider impacts on the environment and he had done so. As there was no risk analysis that disturbed his findings, the Assessor did not make an error of law.
[131] ibid, 393.
[132] eg *Darkinjung Local Aboriginal Land Council v Minister for Planning and Infrastructure & Anor; Australian Walkabout Wildlife Park Pty Limited (ACN 115 219 791) as Trustee for the Gerald and Catherine Barnard Family Trust v Minister for Planning and Infrastructure & Anor* [2015] NSWLEC 1465 (possible destruction of cultural heritage landscapes; proposed adaptive management inadequate because once harm discovered it would be too late to remedy [461]); *Scott v The Hills Shire Council* [2016] NSWLEC 1359 (threatened destruction of critically endangered ecological community); *Radray Constructions v Hornsby Shire Council* [2014] NSWLEC 1024 (flooding risk of retirement homes); *Shannon Pacific v Minister for Planning* [2007] NSWLEC 669, [41] (caravan park too difficult to scale back once started).
[133] *Telstra* (n 31) [157]–[158].
[134] *Nicholls* (n 109) 398.
[135] ibid, 398; see also *Alumino (Aust) Pty Ltd* (n 109).
[136] *Hamilton v Sutherland Shire Council* [2012] NSWLEC 1015.
[137] *Andre & Anor v Northern Beaches Council* [2016] NSWLEC 1478.

managers and recourse to wider environmental policy – again, made possible because of the institutional features of the Court – the Court developed highly refined remedies such as biodiversity offsetting[138] and adaptive management regimes in order to mitigate risk.[139] The Court developed legal tests as to when these remedies might appropriately be employed – emphasising their use depends upon ecological context[140] – and created frameworks as to the various components of these remedies. For example, the Court set down a detailed legal framework for when and how adaptive management might be appropriate in *Newcastle & Hunter Speleological Society Inc v Upper Hunter Shire Council*.[141] The Court cautioned that 'adaptive management is not a "suck it and see", trial and error approach' to environmental management, rather it is 'an iterative approach involving explicit testing of the achievement of defined goals':

> Through feedback to the management process, the management procedures are changed in steps until monitoring shows that the desired outcome is obtained. The monitoring program has to be designed so that there is statistical confidence in the outcome. In adaptive management the goal to be achieved is set, so there is no uncertainty as to the outcome and conditions requiring adaptive management do not lack certainty, but rather they establish a regime which would permit changes, within defined parameters, to the way the outcome is achieved.[142]

Before imposing adaptive management regimes, the Court requires baseline studies of the existing environment but there may be insufficient knowledge about a particular environment and no way to obtain the necessary data through external channels (eg there may be no interest in or resources available from government or independent researchers). However, the Court has been willing to require applicants to conduct baseline data with the possibility of deferring the substantive activity until this is obtained and ultimately preventing that activity if necessary.[143] This rationale takes environmental dispute resolution far outside the confines of processes and doctrine developed in other contexts.[144]

None of these concepts – offsetting or adaptive management – were included in the relevant statutory regimes. While they have attracted critics and undoubtedly deserve close scrutiny,[145] the Court striving to develop creative remedies makes sense in the factual and legal context in which it operates, that is, where the legislative requirement is for ESD (integrating 'economic and environmental considerations into the decision-making process').[146] Notably, the development of these legal remedies is directly related

[138] E.g. *Sanctuary Investments Pty Ltd v Baulkham Hills Shire Council* (2006) 153 LGERA 355.

[139] eg *Telstra* (n 31); *Newcastle & Hunter Speleological Society Inc* (n 78); *Ulan Coal Mines Ltd v Minister for Planning* (2008) 160 LGERA 20; *Rivers SOS Inc v Minister for Planning* (2009) 178 LGERA 347.

[140] eg *Telstra* (n 31) [131].

[141] *Newcastle & Hunter Speleological Society Inc* (n 78).

[142] ibid, [184]. Applied in *Sustain Our Sounds Inc v The New Zealand King Salmon Co Ltd* [2014] 1 NZLR 673, 708 [125] (NZSC).

[143] ibid.

[144] cf property law where the substantive grant or right has to exist in fact and law, in order for conditions to be imposed on the holder; for discussion (albeit in another jurisdiction), see *Director-General of Conservation v Marlborough District Council* [2004] 3 NZLR 127 (HC).

[145] eg P England, 'Trends in the Evolution of Floodplain Management in Australia: Risk Assessment, Precaution and Robust Decision-Making' (2019) 31 *Journal of Environmental Law* 315.

[146] *Telstra* (n 31) [110].

to the institutional form of the Court – scientific expertise fed information from environmental management to the courts, which responded by transforming scientific practice into legal doctrine through the adjudicative process.[147] Empowering the Court to adopt its own procedures facilitated legal reasoning that responded to rather than ignored context and, in turn, this responsive adjudication can help to shore up normative legitimacy because the Court is seen as adjudicating with integrity.

6. Conclusion

The Court has proven to be a controversial institution during its forty-year existence. Debates about the Court tend to have arisen because participants employ different conceptual frames of normative legitimacy through which to assess the Court.[148] Some criticise the Court for not aligning with a pure separation-of-powers frame; others point to the need for adjudicative pluralism and innovative adjudicative institutions to address the challenges of modernity. Alternate frames, such as instrumentalist conceptions of adjudication, can pull the debate in different directions still. However, employing competing frames of legitimacy can prove unproductive, with discussants talking past each other and constantly returning to conceptual bickering. Using the interactional theory for normative legitimacy as a unifying frame allows the discussion about the Court to move past conceptual roadblocks.

This chapter has assessed the Court's jurisprudence on risk, uncertainty and precaution against the interactional theory. In the cases discussed above, the Court demonstrated an awareness of the adjudicative challenges presented by the nature of environmental problems, developed new adjudicative processes and substantive legal doctrine to respond to those challenges, and its particular form and functions facilitated this creative legal reasoning. These doctrinal developments often took place in the absence of clear legislative direction[149] but were necessary to resolve disputes in a way that made sense of rather than ignoring the legal and factual context in which the Court works. The interactional theory may be used to test other doctrinal developments by the Court, and in that way scholars will be able to build a clearer picture of the Court's commitment to adjudicative integrity or relative shortcomings. Accordingly, the use of the interactional frame is not to suppress debate, far from it. Rather, it helps to refocus the debate onto issues that matter – critiquing the worth and the work of the Court and its contribution to ecological sustainable development, differentiating between good and bad practice in specialist environmental adjudication, and reinforcing the importance of adjudicative integrity.

[147] eg *Port Stephens Pearls Pty Limited* (n 113); Edgar (n 108).
[148] Beetham (n 1) 17.
[149] Stein (n 58).

Conclusion

16

Afterword: Law in ~~Un~~expected Places

ELIZABETH FISHER*

I

Although not an appellation that rolls off the tongue, the Land and Environment Court of New South Wales (the Court) is often name-dropped in environmental law discussions as a desirable environmental law destination. As one of the oldest environmental courts in the world, it is perceived to be a site where environmental law realises its possibilities.[1] With that said, like many things wished for, what the Court is, and what it *actually* does, has remained obscure to the wider law community.[2] After forty years of energetic existence, this is the first major scholarly collection on the Court.

The chapters collected here illuminate the multifaceted nature of the Court.[3] Although there can be no attempt to capture all that they have revealed, what they expose is how inherently 'legal' the Court is. This might sound a statement of the obvious. But it is significant for two reasons. First, analysis of environmental courts often places greater emphasis on their 'environmental' function, rather than on their 'court' status.[4] Discussion tends to understand environmental courts and environmental law as 'tools' for achieving particular outcomes. Seeing the legal nature of the Court makes clear that understanding environmental courts requires understanding their complex legal practices.

Second, it also must be recognised that the Court does not fit into classic legal pigeonholes.[5] Its structure combines judicial power with powers conventionally vested

* Thanks to Mitchell Cleaver, Navya Jannu, Brian Preston, Eloise Scotford and Ceri Warnock for astute comments on an earlier draft. Any errors or omissions remain my own.

[1] G Pring and K Pring, *Environmental Courts and Tribunals: A Guide for Policy Makers* (United Nations Environment Programme, 2016) v; United Nations Environment Programme, *Environmental Rule of Law: First Global Report* (2019) 206; and M Grant, *Environmental Court Project: Final Report* (London, Department of Environment 1999) ch 5.

[2] Although this is changing – see the important work of Warnock: C Warnock, *Environmental Courts and Tribunals: Powers, Integrity and the Search for Legitimacy* (Oxford, Hart Publishing, 2020).

[3] That multifaceted nature is explored in Preston, this volume.

[4] A point made in a different way by Warnock (n 2).

[5] ibid.

in tribunals.[6] In doing so, the legally conventional is interrelated with the legally novel. To describe the Court as a 'legal' or 'judicial' institution begs the question of what these terms mean.[7] A study of the Court thus not only draws attention to the importance of law in environmental law, but the importance of reflecting on the nature of 'law' and how legal scholars imagine it.

It is easy to read those two last paragraphs as an example of how academics tend to make things more complicated by engaging in theorising. Given that the Court is playing a role in adjudicating on matters of upmost importance and urgency, requiring readers to take a 'thicker' approach[8] to studying environmental courts and to reflect on the nature of law might appear acts of self-indulgence. But while I would never pretend to be anything other than an academic, my arguing the need for such an approach and such reflection is not navel-gazing. It emerges from my own experiences with the Court and as a scholar. Let me explain.

II

The mid-1980s. I am a teenager living in the low-density fringes of Sydney in a dormitory suburb built blithely out along a hilly ridge with steep bushy valleys all around. Our neighbours apply for development consent to turn three properties into a retirement village. A new state environmental planning policy makes the building of speculative medium-density housing for the over-55s possible, and potentially financially lucrative.[9] *The higher density of the development gives rise to local protest. There are petitions, demonstrations, council meetings, and articles in the local paper. The Council rejects the application. The developers appeal, as is their right, to the Land and Environment Court for a review on the merits of the decision.*[10] *The Assessor upholds the Council's decision – the steep nature of the site as well as the lack of proper onsite servicing means that the development does not meet the criteria of the policy.*[11]

Environmental and planning decisions give rise to conflict. The story of the opposition to our neighbours' planning application reflects the inevitability of disputes over what the nature of the built environment should look like.[12] This dispute was one among tens of thousands the Court has resolved over its forty years of existence. These are real disputes in real places.

[6] See Preston, this volume.

[7] Warnock (n 2) 76–90.

[8] E Fisher, 'Through "Thick" and "Thin": Comparison in Administrative Law and Regulatory Studies Scholarship' in P Cane et al (eds), *The Oxford Handbook of Comparative Administrative Law* (Oxford, Oxford University Press, 2020) and Preston, this volume.

[9] State Environmental Planning Policy No 5 – Housing for Aged or Disabled Persons (NSW) made in 1982, but repealed and replaced in 2004.

[10] *B D Wholohan & Associates v Ku-ring-gai Municipal Council* (1987) 26 Australian Planning Appeal Decisions 295 (Assessor BM O'Neile).

[11] ibid.

[12] For discussion of the inevitability of disputes, see S Roberts, *Order and Dispute: An Introduction to Legal Anthropology*, 2nd edn (New Orleans, LA, Quid Pro Books, 2013) ch 4.

Dispute resolution is a fundamental function of the Court. As often quoted, the NSW Government in creating the Land and Environment Court described it as 'a somewhat innovative experiment in dispute resolution'.[13] The 'somewhat' signifies that the Court did not appear out of nowhere; it was grounded on long-established tribunal structures.[14] It, and the tribunals and inferior courts that preceded it, were initiatives in state-sponsored legal pluralism.[15] Governments through legislative reform created tailored adjudicative dispute resolution processes that did not sit easily in traditional separation-of-powers structures.[16]

The dispute resolution function of the Court is not surprising. Environment and planning law are areas fraught with conflicts between developers, local communities, local government, state government, environmental groups, primary industries, business, and much else besides.[17] These disputes embody what Hanoch Dagan, discussing law more generally, has called a set of 'constitutive tensions'.[18] These are tensions between: power and reason; science and craft; and tradition and progress.[19] Places are not static, and they do not change with an even uniformity. The polycentric forces of change are also many – economic, social and political.

Much of the dispute resolution work of the Court, as in the case of that neighbour's development, has happened through merits review.[20] The Court has also in the last two decades actively evolved a robust architecture for alternative dispute resolution.[21] The Court in 1980 is a world away from the Court in 2021.[22] The ability to effectively resolve disputes has been a continual aspiration in the Court's history. Thus, for example, one of the criticisms that led to the Working Party on the Court in 2000 was that some parties perceived it did not do this job well.[23]

This emphasis on dispute resolution and merits review may suggest little role for law. Approximately two-thirds of what the Court does is in its Class 1 merits review jurisdiction, and approximately two-thirds of disputes are resolved by different forms of alternative resolution or negotiated settlement.[24] But law is ever present. The law

[13] NSW Parliamentary Debates, 21 November 1979, 3345, Second Reading Speech of the Hon Paul Landa MP, Minister for Planning and Environment. On a discussion of this quote in these chapters, see Smith and Higginson, this volume; Warnock, this volume.

[14] Stein, this volume. See also Warnock (n 2) 65–73, discussing the history of adjudicatory pluralism.

[15] Which also has a long pedigree. See HW Arthurs, *'Without the Law': Administrative Justice and Legal Pluralism in Nineteenth-Century England* (Toronto, University of Toronto Press, 1985). On the court as state-sponsored legal pluralism, see E Fisher, 'Administrative Law, Pluralism and the Legal Construction of Merits Review in Australian Environmental Courts and Tribunals' in L Pearson, C Harlow and M Taggart (eds), *Administrative Law in a Changing State: Essays in Honour of Mark Aronson* (Oxford, Hart Publishing, 2008).

[16] Warnock (n 2) and P Cane, 'Merits Review and Judicial Review – The AAT as Trojan Horse' (2000) 28 *Federal Law Review* 213.

[17] Stein, this volume; Bonyhady, this volume.

[18] Hanoch Dagan, *Reconstructing American Legal Realism and Rethinking Private Law* (Oxford, OUP 2013) 3.

[19] ibid, 3.

[20] For a discussion of the first third party merits appeal see Bonyhady, this volume.

[21] Walker, this volume.

[22] Compare Bonyhady with Peel, this volume. See also White, this volume.

[23] The Hon J S Cripps QC et al, *Report of the Land and Environment Court Working Party* (September 2001) 11–16.

[24] Land and Environment Court of New South Wales, *Annual Review 2020* (State of New South Wales, 2021) 34–35.

'provides the mandate and the context'[25] for what the Court does. The regulatory frameworks for public and private actors are primarily created through law.[26] So too are the powers of the Court.[27] This means that in resolving these disputes many legal issues and questions may arise.[28]

III

The early 1990s – a time before the internet. I am a summer clerk in a Sydney law firm. I spend much time sitting in my office reading Land and Environment Court judgments published in the Local Government Reports of Australia. I am chastised by a partner of the firm. Not for reading the cases – that is relevant to the work I am doing. The problem is my hoarding of the volumes. The reports, and the judgments of the Court published in them, are a heavily used legal resource in the firm. Squirrelling them away in my office is not acceptable.

The importance of law is not just in how it frames what the Court does. The Court's decisions quickly became a *legal* resource. As Patricia Ryan has noted, an early perceived problem with the court was the 'decision not to have a set of authorised law reports of its decisions'.[29] Legal publishers stepped into the vacuum. The Local Government Reports of Australia (now the Local Government and Environmental Reports of Australia) and the discontinued Australian Planning Appeal Decisions included Court decisions in what they published. While a fraction of what the Court decided, what was published often became heavily used precedents. Hence my sitting in that office reading those reports.

All decisions of the Court are now published online.[30] 'Planning principles' have emerged out of merits review decisions.[31] Conciliation conferences are required to provide reasons setting out the jurisdiction of the Commissioner.[32] All this means that the 'active' legal work[33] of the Court is accessible to lawyers and non-lawyers. Publicising the Court's jurisprudence has stabilised understanding of its legal frameworks, legal doctrine, how these apply to facts, and what is relevant in resolving disputes. That in turn has made the law of the Court more 'calculable'.[34] The Court's judgments are not

[25] K Hawkins, *Environment and Enforcement: Regulation and the Social Definition of Pollution* (Oxford, Clarendon Press, 1984) 191.

[26] eg Environmental Planning and Assessment Act 1979.

[27] eg *Al Maha Pty Ltd v Huajun Investments Pty Ltd* [2018] NSWCA 245, 233 LGERA 170 and Fisher (n 14).

[28] eg *Planners North v Ballina Shire Council* [2021] NSWLEC 120 and Fisher (n 14).

[29] P Ryan, 'Court of Hope and False Expectations: Land and Environment Court 21 Years On' (2002) 14 *Journal of Environmental Law* 301, 304. See also the problems of access to decisions discussed in Bonyhady, this volume.

[30] The Court's website contains a link to judgments on the free to use Austlii and New South Wales Case Law databases. They are also available on Jade.io.

[31] www.lec.nsw.gov.au/lec/practice-and-procedure/principles/planning-principals.html (accessed 26 September 2021).

[32] *Al Maha Pty Ltd* (n 27) [200]–[202].

[33] Elizabeth Fisher, this volume.

[34] J Waldron, *The Rule of Law and the Measure of Property* (Cambridge, Cambridge University Press, 2012) 53.

only important to parties operating in NSW but have also become a legal resource for legal communities across the world.[35]

The fact that the decisions of the Court have become valuable legal resources is not surprising. The Court's judgments are examples of what Karl Llewellyn described as 'concrete instances' without which 'the general proposition is baggage, impediments, stuff about the feet'.[36] Environmental and planning law is full of general propositions – in statute,[37] in policy[38] and in principle.[39] The Court, in adjudicating on, and resolving, myriad disputes has created a 'mine-run'[40] of judgments that make those propositions 'concrete'. In some situations, these relate to the interpretation of a specific legislative provision.[41] In other cases, judgments have set out more general legal concepts or approaches.[42]

Overall, the adjudicative work of the Court has created stable ways to reason. The judgments of the Court, depending on the class of jurisdiction it is exercising,[43] create either informal or formal precedents. Those precedents provide a foundation for how as a society we do, and should, live together in the environment. Given that environmental and planning law are riven with win/lose situations among diverse parties, the Court's judgments are particularly important in establishing transparent, trusted, and reasoned resolutions to such conflicts.

IV

1994. I leave Australia to study for my doctorate in administrative law in Oxford. I begin my studies by spending long days in the Bodleian Law Library reading every single case that had been reported in the Local Government Reports of Australia from the Land and Environment Court. The result is a folder full of notes and a paper for my supervisor. The paper is lost a few years later in between computer upgrades. I go on to write a doctorate on United States administrative law. I still have the folder full of notes though.

The legal work of the Court and those writing about it[44] sparked my scholarly imagination. To those schooled to focus on the work of apex courts, the legal substance of the Court's work can be hard to see. The Court can be easily characterised as legally marginal – inhabiting legal borderlands that are not deemed worth an analytical visit.[45]

[35] Peel, this volume; Boer, this volume.

[36] K Llewellyn, *The Bramble Bush: The Classic Lectures on the Law and the Law School* (Oxford, Oxford University Press, 2008) 4.

[37] DE Fisher, this volume.

[38] Elizabeth Fisher, this volume.

[39] Scotford, this volume.

[40] K Llewellyn, *The Common Law Tradition: Deciding Appeals* (Boston, MA, Little, Brown, 1960) ch 1.

[41] eg s 9(1) Protection of the Environment Administration Act 1991 as examined in *Bushfire Survivors for Climate Action Incorporated v Environment Protection Authority* (2021) 250 LGERA 1; [2021] NSWLEC 92.

[42] *Palm Beach Protection Group Incorporated v Northern Beaches Council* (2020) 250 LGERA 212; [2020] NSWLEC 156 discussing the nature of environmental impact assessment obligations.

[43] See Preston, this volume.

[44] B Preston, *Environmental Litigation* (Sydney, Law Book, 1989) and DE Fisher, *Environmental Law: Text and Materials* (Sydney, Law Book, 1993).

[45] Environmental courts are not the only institutions in these borderlands. See Arthurs (n 15).

It is not an apex court akin to the High Court of Australia. It is a superior court of record, but it is a specialist court in one state of Australia, a country with a relatively small population.

But as the chapters in this collection show, the Court is a very legal place. It is created by law.[46] It is working with law.[47] It creates law.[48] It is a multifaceted legal institution.[49] It has a complex legal architecture.[50] It is producing doctrine.[51] Its work is not legally peripheral.[52] It is interrelated with environmental law work in other places.[53]

Moreover, and this was what so captivated me, the work of the Court is very 'active' legal work.[54] I do not mean activist.[55] What I mean is that the Court has had to develop a robust body of legal reasoning in relation to a dynamic legislative and policy landscape. In doing so, judges have built on mainstream legal doctrines, but also needed to evolve those doctrines in light of environmental problems and the legal frameworks they are adjudicating in relation to.[56] Warnock, for example, has shown how important it is for the Court to interact with the nature of environmental problems in adjudication.[57]

Much of this has produced a distinctive set of doctrines concerning environmental and planning law. The Court's case law concerning environmental principles is one high-profile example.[58] But it is only one of many ways the Court has carried out active legal work. As seen in chapters throughout the book, the Court has developed legal doctrine in relation to environmental offences,[59] Indigenous legal thought,[60] statutory interpretation,[61] administrative law,[62] biodiversity law,[63] access to justice[64] and climate change.[65] It has not done this work in isolation. It has operated within a wider common law system and an important feature of the Court over its existence has been its interrelationship with the New South Wales Court of Appeal. This is both in terms of appeals to that Court, and that judges of the Land and Environment Court can, and do, sit on the Court of Appeal.

[46] Land and Environment Court Act 1979 (NSW).
[47] See DE Fisher, this volume in particular.
[48] eg Scotford, this volume; White, this volume.
[49] Preston, this volume.
[50] Walker, this volume; Smith and Higginson, this volume.
[51] See the chapters in Part Two, this volume.
[52] Peel, this volume.
[53] ibid; Gill, this volume; Boer, this volume.
[54] Elizabeth Fisher, this volume.
[55] A term that suffers from a lack of serious of analytical precision. See T Josev, *The Campaign Against the Courts: A History of the Judicial Activism Debate* (Alexandria, Federation Press 2017).
[56] See Elizabeth Fisher, this volume.
[57] Warnock, this volume.
[58] Scotford, this volume.
[59] White, this volume.
[60] Davis, this volume.
[61] DE Fisher, this volume.
[62] Elizabeth Fisher, this volume.
[63] Adam, this volume.
[64] Smith and Higginson, this volume.
[65] Peel, this volume.

To put the matter a different way, a study of the work of the Court makes clear that the Court is not just a specialist in environmental problems but a specialist in *certain types of legal problems*. Its contributory expertise is in many ways more significant than its interactional expertise, albeit these are interrelated.[66] The doctorate I went on to write explored how generalist courts adjudicated on similar type problems in US administrative law.[67] But I didn't leave the work of the Land and Environment Court behind. Not only did I keep writing about it, but my work on the Court served as an important foundation for the conceptual ideas I was developing about environmental and administrative law.[68]

V

The early 2010s. I am sitting at a dinner with an academic colleague. We are discussing his theory of an area of private law. He describes a subject that has coherence – it is neat, it is ordered, it has clarity. I know one thing. This is not a description of environmental and planning law. These areas have no graceful and overarching logic. There are multiple legal interests, fragmented legal regimes, numerous norms in operation, facts are uncertain, and it is constantly under revision. I sit there pondering. Finally, I say: 'Your legal world is not my legal world.'

There was one simple reason why the Land and Environment Court animated my legal thinking, and still does. Here was a legal world I hadn't been taught about in law school and I couldn't easily find in books. It was not how law typically figured in the legal imagination of legal scholars. It could not be adequately described in neat flow diagrams setting out relevant parties, their interests and rights. The facts often required engagement with science, and more importantly scientific uncertainty. Law was less a clearly framed doctrine and more a crowded miscellany of statutory provisions and evolving administrative law doctrines – each with their own normative and legal logics. Existing legal doctrine was relevant to factual and legal scenarios, but those scenarios were often novel.

I was, and am, fascinated in how courts as legal institutions could, and should, adjudicate in such circumstances. Making an inquiry into this is an intertwined descriptive and normative exercise. It also requires making legal sense of courts and of environmental law.

Regarding courts, as Ceri Warnock has noted, when it comes to debating the virtues (and vices) of environmental courts, 'many contributors appear to hold pre-formed, homogenised views about adjudication, what it is and how it should be undertaken.'[69]

[66] On these types of expertises, see Preston, this volume and E Fisher, 'The Rise of Transnational Environmental Law and the Expertise of Environmental Lawyers' (2012) 1 *Transnational Environmental Law* 43.

[67] E Fisher, 'Risk, Expertise and Judicial Review: Scope of Review and Decision-Making Under Scientific Uncertainty' (DPhil thesis, Faculty of Law, Oxford University, 1998).

[68] E Fisher, *Risk Regulation and Administrative Constitutionalism* (Oxford, Hart Publishing, 2007) ch 4.

[69] Warnock (n 2) 59.

The Land and Environment Court is a Court. It adjudicates. But as Warnock has also pointed out, it has evolved to interact with the problems it is adjudicating on. It does not fit a narrow vision of what a Court is.[70] But then that is the case with many courts and tribunals.[71] Moreover, the Land and Environment Court and these other 'atypical' institutions are often active legal subjects in law – shaping not just their specialist areas of law, but also law more generally.[72] Scotford, for example, has shown how much the Court's case law on environmental principles is shaped by the nature of the Court and its legal context.[73]

A study of the Court thus shows the need to think about the substance of doctrinal environmental law and what makes it distinctive.[74] As noted above, the structural features of environmental problems – polycentricity, scientific uncertainty, and socio-political controversy – do make environmental law distinct. This leads to an expansion in legal imagination – that is, an evolution in the mental constructs that both constrain and empower legal reasoning.[75] But in many ways the legal work of the Court is not distinctive. As Preston has noted: 'Judges must adjudicate in accordance with principle and reason, technique and logic, to ensure consistency and predictability, and public confidence, in the administration of justice.'[76] The decisions of the Court are examples of this. The nature of reasoning will vary from context to context – but there is no doubt that principle and reason are on display.[77]

VI

2016. I am at a comparative planning law conference at a US law school. I am talking about the doctrines of third-party objector rights in Australian and UK law – an issue that encompasses the Land and Environment Court. I am explaining Australian legal culture. 'Australians', I say, 'take law and legal reasoning very seriously.' This generalisation results in laughter and the shaking of heads. The US scholars in the room see this as naivety on the part of Australians (or at least how I am representing them) in failing to understand the implications of legal realism.

To talk of reason 'on display' begs the question of what is 'reason'. Australian legal thought, particularly public law thought, has been understood as legally formalist.[78] Hence my comment at that conference. But, as Julius Stone states, while logic is an

[70] Warnock, this volume.

[71] Arthurs (n 15).

[72] E Fisher, 'Administrative Tribunals: An Essay about the Legal Imagination of Administrative Law Scholars' in J Goudkamp, L McDonald and M Lunney (eds), *Taking Law Seriously: Essays in Honour of Peter Cane* (Oxford, Hart Publishing, 2022).

[73] Scotford, this volume and E Scotford, *Environmental Principles and the Evolution of Environmental Law* (Oxford, Hart Publishing, 2017) ch 5.

[74] E Fisher, 'Environmental Law as "Hot" Law' (2013) 25 *Journal of Environmental Law* 347.

[75] E Fisher, 'Legal Imagination and European Union Environmental Law' in P Craig and G de Búrca (eds), *The Evolution of European Union Law*, 3rd edn (Oxford, Oxford University Press, 2021).

[76] B Preston, 'The Art of Judging Environmental Disputes' (2008) 12 *Southern Cross Law Review* 103, 128.

[77] Even in the context of dispute resolution, see *Al Maha Pty Ltd* (n 26) [201].

[78] M Taggart, '"Australian Exceptionalism" in Judicial Review' (2008) 36 *Federal Law Review* 1.

'indispensable ingredient' of legal processes, it is not the means 'of creating law'.[79] As he notes:

> To treat the results of logical deduction from existing premisses as a substitute for the assessment of all aspects of the given situation and notably for its ethical and sociological aspects is essentially an abuse of logic, leading to legal anomalies and distortions.[80]

What is distinctive about the work of the Court is not just that it deals with environmental problems but that in doing so there is a commitment to robust doctrinal reasoning that incorporates mainstream legal doctrine in dealing in a responsive way with environmental problems and environmental law.[81]

The legal reasoning of the Court is, however, often overlooked. In part this is to do with the atypical nature of the Court as discussed above – attention of scholars is on apex courts. It is, however, also to do with the fact that, as noted in the introduction, discussions about environmental courts tend to treat them as instruments for achieving environmental protection.[82] That reflects a broader purposive vision of environmental law.[83]

There are many problems with this way of understanding the subject. 'Environmental protection' – like the 'public interest' – has many different meanings. Legal disputes are about those meanings and the implications of those meanings. Likewise, even if the environmental protection goal is clear, there are legal disputes over how it must be achieved. A study of the legal work of the Court shows that the Court's work is often not directly about protecting the environment.[84] Many of the legal disputes it resolves are about the basic legal elements of planning and environmental law.[85] The legitimacy of the Court comes from the rigour of its legal and dispute resolution work. It comes from its ability to 'adjudicate well' on complex environmental problems. It comes from the quality of its precedents.

What, then, is striking is how much a study of the Court also shows how environmental law academic discourse and legal realities have got 'out of joint' with each other.[86] The work of the Court shows that environmental law is more legal, more doctrinal and 'thicker' than often presumed by environmental law scholars.[87] Likewise, as Hanoch Dagan puts it, 'law is neither brute power nor pure reason'.[88] But it is definitely something very legal.

With all that said, there are reasons why environmental law is often understood in instrumental terms. Much of current environmental law discourse reflects what is

[79] J Stone, *The Province and Function of Law* (Sydney, Associated General Publications, 1946) 145–46.
[80] ibid, 146.
[81] See also Preston (n 76) and Preston, this volume.
[82] Warnock (n 2).
[83] E Fisher, B Lange and E Scotford, *Environmental Law: Text, Cases and Materials*, 2nd edn (Oxford, Oxford University Press, 2019) 10–12.
[84] Elizabeth Fisher, this volume.
[85] *The Owners Strata Plan 83556 trading as Aspect Apartments v Dehsabzi* [2020] NSWLEC 175.
[86] Paraphrasing Llewellyn in K Llewellyn, 'Some Realism About Realism – Responding to Dean Pound' (1931) 44 *Harvard Law Review* 1222.
[87] See Preston, this volume.
[88] Dagan (n 18) 3.

perceived to be the legacy of mid-twentieth-century legal realism.[89] As legal scholars told me at that conference, 'we are all legal realists now'. They saw paying attention to doctrine as naive because they saw law driven by ideology. What mattered was outcomes not reasoning. The approach to take to the study of law was external not internal.[90] From this perspective, environmental law was about environmental protection and if it didn't achieve that, then it was not fit for purpose.

As many scholars have pointed out, legal realism is all too easy to misunderstand.[91] Legal realism was a product of an era in which legal scholarship was disconnected with what was going on in the legal world of the New Deal. Legislation created new laws and new institutions and courts were dealing with new questions. While some scholars did understand this as an ideological story, in which legal reasoning was perceived to reflect preferences and outcomes,[92] there were those such as Karl Llewelyn who emphasised the importance of legal reasoning but also stressed the importance of not seeing law as autonomous.[93]

The chapters in this collection are thus not only significant in drawing attention to the legal complexity of what the Land and Environment Court does. They also invite a re-engagement with debates over legal realism. Peter Cane, an assiduous scholar of tribunals, has reflected on the need for a more 'realistic-inspired' and 'contextualised' law.[94] He states: 'In my view, there can be no law in context, no realism *about law*, without law *in itself* to be realistic and contextual about.'[95] He also states:

> [L]aw is a set of rules and principles ('doctrines', 'norms'), institutions, structures, personnel, processes, practices and so on that publicly manage tensions between, and disagreements about, the irreducibly plural values that characterise the human condition.[96]

In much of Cane's recent work, he has explored a 'non essentialist' approach to theorising about law which maps 'pervasive, common (even if not commonly known or appreciated) features of actual legal systems that are plausibly considered to be significant'.[97] As someone who has spent decades working with Land and Environment Court and environmental law doctrine, Cane's discussion of law resonates with me.

VII

In 2017, I published a short book on environmental law for a generalist audience.[98] The last photograph in the book was of litigants celebrating a win outside the Land and

[89] For an overview of legal realism, see D Priel, 'The Return of Legal Realism' in M Dubbers and C Tomlins (eds), *Oxford Handbook of Legal History* (Oxford, Oxford University Press, 2018).
[90] Fisher (n 8) 617–18.
[91] ibid and Dagan (n 18).
[92] eg Jerome Frank: see Jerome Frank, 'Experimentalist Jurisprudence and the New Deal' (address before the Association of American Law Schools, 30 December 1933).
[93] Llewellyn (n 40).
[94] P Cane, 'Context, Context, Everywhere' (2020) 16 *International Journal of Law in Context* 459.
[95] ibid, 463 (original emphasis).
[96] ibid, 461.
[97] P Cane, 'Public Law in *The Concept of Law*' (2013) 33 *OJLS* 649, 651–52.
[98] E Fisher, *Environmental Law: A Very Short Introduction* (Oxford, Oxford University Press, 2017) 123.

Environment Court.[99] My choice was a deliberate one. The litigants, who were ordinary residents, came from an area close to where I grew up. The photograph thus evoked how environmental law (and the Court) first came into my life.

But I also picked the photograph to make a deeper point. My wonderful editor had encouraged me to include in the book a photograph of litigants standing outside a court after winning an environmental law case. I suspect she had in mind the type of court that has grand judicial architecture and the type of case that makes newspaper headlines across the world. That type of picture gives no feeling for either the legal realities or legal possibilities of environmental law.

The picture I included in the book was of a very different type. The Land and Environment Court, being in an office building, was not visible. There were no lawyers in the photograph, but litigants carried bundles of legal files and in the background was a shop sign for the 'Legal Grounds Cafe'. Most importantly, the case was not of global legal significance. It was a case concerning the legality of local consultation processes for a plan that would promote higher-density building in certain suburban areas. In winning, the litigants did not save the world. The success of the judgment was in holding decision-makers to account and the maintenance of the rule of law.

As these chapters attest, a study of the Land and Environment Court illustrates that the work of environmental law is complex legal work. What these chapters also show is that not only is the Court a desirable environmental law destination but also a very real one. As such, the idea of environmental law realising its possibilities is not just wishful thinking. It lies within the province of legal imagination.[100]

[99] *Friends of Turramurra Inc v Minister for Planning* [2011] NSWLEC 128.

[100] On the difference between wishful thinking and legal imagination, see E Fisher, 'Legal Imagination and Teaching International Environmental Law' in J Peel and L Rajamani (eds) *Oxford Handbook of International Environmental Law*, 2nd edn (Oxford, Oxford University Press, 2021).

INDEX

www.ingramcontent.com/pod-product-compliance
Ingram Content Group UK Ltd.
Pitfield, Milton Keynes, MK11 3LW, UK
UKHW020236290926
15470UKWH00002B/570

9 781509 941032